Get the eBooks FREE!

(PDF, ePub, Kindle, and liveBook all included)

We believe that once you buy a book from us, you should be able to read it in any format we have available. To get electronic versions of this book at no additional cost to you, purchase and then register this book at the Manning website.

Go to https://www.manning.com/freebook and follow the instructions to complete your pBook registration.

That's it!
Thanks from Manning!

Deep Reinforcement Learning in Action

Deep Reinforcement Learning in Action

BRANDON BROWN
AND ALEXANDER ZAI

MANNING

SHELTER ISLAND

Manning Publications Co.
20 Baldwin Road
PO Box 761
Shelter Island, NY 11964

Development editor:	Karen Miller
Technical development editor:	Marc-Philippe Huget
Review editor:	Ivan Martinović
Production editor:	Deirdre Hiam
Copy editor:	Andy Carroll
Proofreader:	Jason Everett
Technical proofreader:	Al Krinker
Typesetter:	Dennis Dalinnik
Cover designer:	Marija Tudor

ISBN: 9781617295430
Printed in the United States of America

brief contents

contents

11   **In conclusion: A review and roadmap   329**

preface

Deep reinforcement learning was launched into the spotlight in 2015, when Deep-Mind produced an algorithm capable of playing a suite of Atari 2600 games at super-human performance. Artificial intelligence seemed to be finally making some real progress, and we wanted to be a part of it.

Both of us have software engineering backgrounds and an interest in neuroscience, and we've been interested in the broader field of artificial intelligence for a long time (in fact, one of us actually wrote his first neural network before high school in C#). These early experiences did not lead to any sustained interest, since this was before the deep learning revolution circa 2012, when the superlative performance of deep learning was clear. But after seeing the amazing successes of deep learning around this time, we became recommitted to being a part of the exciting and bur-geoning fields of deep learning and then deep reinforcement learning, and both of us have incorporated machine learning more broadly into our careers in one way or another. Alex transitioned into a career as a machine learning engineer, making his mark at little-known places like Amazon, and Brandon began using machine learning in academic neuroscience research. As we delved into deep reinforcement learning, we had to struggle through dozens of textbooks and primary research articles, parsing advanced mathematics and machine learning theory. Yet we found that the funda-mentals of deep reinforcement learning are actually quite approachable from a soft-ware engineering background. All of the math can be easily translated into a language that any programmer would find quite readable.

We began blogging about the things we were learning in the machine learning world and projects that we were using in our work. We ended up getting a fair amount of positive feedback, which led us to the idea of collaborating on this book. We believe that most of the resources out there for learning hard things are either too simple and leave out the most compelling aspects of the topic or are inaccessible to people without sophisticated mathematics backgrounds. This book is our effort at translating a body of work written for experts into a course for those with nothing more than a programming background and some basic knowledge of neural networks. We employ some novel teaching methods that we think set our book apart and lead to much faster understanding. We start from the basics, and by the end you will be implementing cutting-edge algorithms invented by industry-based research groups like DeepMind and OpenAI, as well as from high-powered academic labs like the Berkeley Artificial Intelligence Research (BAIR) Lab and University College London.

acknowledgments

This book took way longer than we anticipated, and we owe a lot to our editors Candace West and Susanna Kline for helping us at every stage of the process and keeping us on track. There are a lot of details to keep track of when writing a book, and without the professional and supportive editorial staff we would have floundered.

We'd also like to thank our technical editors Marc-Philippe Huget and Al Krinker and all of the reviewers who took the time to read our manuscript and provide us with crucial feedback. In particular, we thank the reviewers: Al Rahimi, Ariel Gamiño, Claudio Bernardo Rodriguez, David Krief, Dr. Brett Pennington, Ezra Joel Schroeder, George L. Gaines, Godfred Asamoah, Helmut Hauschild, Ike Okonkwo, Jonathan Wood, Kalyan Reddy, M. Edward (Ed) Borasky, Michael Haller, Nadia Noori, Satyajit Sarangi, and Tobias Kaatz. We would also like to thank everyone at Manning who worked on this project: Karen Miller, the developmental editor; Ivan Martinović, the review editor; Deirdre Hiam, the project editor; Andy Carroll, the copy editor; and Jason Everett, the proofreader.

In this age, many books are self-published using various online services, and we were initially tempted by this option; however, after having been through this whole process, we can see the tremendous value in professional editing staff. In particular, we thank copy editor Andy Carroll for his insightful feedback that dramatically improved the clarity of the text.

Alex thanks his PI Jamie who introduced him to machine learning early in his undergraduate career.

Brandon thanks his wife Xinzhu for putting up with his late nights of writing and time away from the family and for giving him two wonderful children, Isla and Avin.

about this book

Who should read this book

Deep Reinforcement Learning in Action is a course designed to take you from the very foundational concepts in reinforcement learning all the way to implementing the latest algorithms. As a course, each chapter centers around one major project meant to illustrate the topic or concept of that chapter. We've designed each project to be something that can be efficiently run on a modern laptop; we don't expect you to have access to expensive GPUs or cloud computing resources (though access to these resources does make things run faster).

This book is for individuals with a programming background, in particular, a working knowledge of Python, and for people who have at least a basic understanding of neural networks (a.k.a. deep learning). By "basic understanding," we mean that you have at least tried implementing a simple neural network in Python even if you didn't fully understand what was going on under the hood. Although this book is focused on using neural networks for the purposes of reinforcement learning, you will also probably learn a lot of new things about deep learning in general that can be applied to other problems outside of reinforcement learning, so you do not need to be an expert at deep learning before jumping into deep reinforcement learning.

How this book is organized: A roadmap

The book has two sections with 11 chapters.

Part 1 explains the fundamentals of deep reinforcement learning.

- Chapter 1 gives a high-level introduction to deep learning, reinforcement learning, and the marriage of the two into deep reinforcement learning.
- Chapter 2 introduces the fundamental concepts of reinforcement learning that will reappear through the rest of the book. We also implement our first practical reinforcement learning algorithm.
- Chapter 3 introduces deep Q-learning, one of the two broad classes of deep reinforcement algorithms. This is the algorithm that DeepMind used to outperform humans at many Atari 2600 games in 2015.
- Chapter 4 describes the other major class of deep reinforcement learning algorithms, policy-gradient methods. We use this to train an algorithm to play a simple game.
- Chapter 5 shows how we can combine deep Q-learning from chapter 3 and policy-gradient methods from chapter 4 into a combined class of algorithms called actor-critic algorithms.

Part 2 builds on the foundations we built in part 1 to cover the biggest advances in deep reinforcement learning in recent years.

- Chapter 6 shows how to implement evolutionary algorithms, which use principles of biological evolution, to train neural networks.
- Chapter 7 describes a method to significantly improve the performance of deep Q-learning by incorporating probabilistic concepts.
- Chapter 8 introduces a way to give reinforcement learning algorithms a sense of curiosity to explore their environments without any external cues.
- Chapter 9 shows how to extend what we have learned in training single agent reinforcement learning algorithms into systems that have multiple interacting agents.
- Chapter 10 describes how to make deep reinforcement learning algorithms more interpretable and efficient by using attention mechanisms.
- Chapter 11 concludes the book by discussing all the exciting areas in deep reinforcement learning we didn't have the space to cover but that you may be interested in.

The chapters in part 1 should be read in order, as each chapter builds on the concepts in the previous chapter. The chapters in part 2 can more or less be approached in any order, although we still recommend reading them in order.

About the code

As we noted, this book is a course, so we have included all of the code necessary to run the projects within the main text of the book. In general, we include shorter code blocks as inline code which is formatted in `this font` as well as code in separate numbered code listings that represented larger code blocks.

At press time we are confident all the in-text code is working, but we cannot guarantee that the code will continue to be bug free (especially for those of you reading this in print) in the long term, as the deep learning field and consequently its libraries are evolving quickly. The in-text code has also been pared down to the minimum necessary to get the projects working, so we highly recommend you follow the projects in the book using the code in this book's GitHub repository: http://mng.bz/JzKp. We intend to keep the code on GitHub up to date for the foreseeable future, and it also includes additional comments and code that we used to generate many of the figures in the book. Hence, it is best if you read the book alongside the corresponding code in the Jupyter Notebooks found on the GitHub repository.

We are confident that this book will teach you the concepts of deep reinforcement learning and not just how to narrowly code things in Python. If Python were to somehow disappear after you finish this book, you would still be able to implement all of these algorithms in some other language or framework, since you will understand the fundamentals.

liveBook discussion forum

Purchase of *Deep Reinforcement Learning in Action* includes free access to a private web forum run by Manning Publications where you can make comments about the book, ask technical questions, and receive help from the authors and from other users. To access the forum, go to https://livebook.manning.com/#!/book/deep-reinforcement-learning-in-action/discussion. You can also learn more about Manning's forums and the rules of conduct at https://livebook.manning.com/#!/discussion.

Manning's commitment to our readers is to provide a venue where a meaningful dialogue between individual readers and between readers and the authors can take place. It is not a commitment to any specific amount of participation on the part of the authors, whose contribution to the forum remains voluntary (and unpaid). We suggest you try asking the authors some challenging questions lest their interest stray! The forum and the archives of previous discussions will be accessible from the publisher's website as long as the book is in print.

about the authors

ALEX ZAI has worked as Chief Technology Officer at Codesmith, an immersive coding bootcamp where he remains a Technical Advisor, as a software engineer at Uber, and as a machine learning engineer at Banjo and Amazon and he is a contributor to the open source deep learning framework Apache MXNet. He is also an entrepreneur who has co-founded two companies, one of which was a Y-combinator entrant.

BRANDON BROWN grew up programming and worked as a part-time software engineer through college but ended up pursuing a career in medicine; he worked as a software engineer in the healthcare technology space along the way. He is now a physician and is pursuing his research interests in computational psychiatry inspired by deep reinforcement learning.

about the cover illustration

The figure on the cover of *Deep Reinforcement Learning in Action* is captioned "Femme de l'Istria," or woman from Istria. The illustration is taken from a collection of dress costumes from various countries by Jacques Grasset de Saint-Sauveur (1757-1810), titled *Costumes de Différents Pays*, published in France in 1797. Each illustration is finely drawn and colored by hand. The rich variety of Grasset de Saint-Sauveur's collection reminds us vividly of how culturally apart the world's towns and regions were just 200 years ago. Isolated from each other, people spoke different dialects and languages. In the streets or in the countryside, it was easy to identify where they lived and what their trade or station in life was just by their dress.

The way we dress has changed since then and the diversity by region, so rich at the time, has faded away. It is now hard to tell apart the inhabitants of different continents, let alone different towns, regions, or countries. Perhaps we have traded cultural diversity for a more varied personal life—certainly for a more varied and fast-paced technological life.

At a time when it is hard to tell one computer book from another, Manning celebrates the inventiveness and initiative of the computer business with book covers based on the rich diversity of regional life of two centuries ago, brought back to life by Grasset de Saint-Sauveur's pictures.

Part 1

Foundations

Part 1 consists of five chapters that teach the most fundamental aspects of deep reinforcement learning. After reading part 1, you'll be able to understand the chapters in part 2 in any order.

Chapter 1 begins with a high-level introduction to deep reinforcement learning, explaining its main concepts and its utility. In chapter 2 we'll start building practical projects that illustrate the basic ideas of reinforcement learning. In chapter 3 we'll implement a deep Q-network—the same kind of algorithm that DeepMind famously used to play Atari games at superhuman levels.

Chapters 4 and 5 round out the most common reinforcement learning algorithms, namely policy gradient methods and actor-critic methods. We'll look at the pros and cons of these approaches compared to deep Q-networks.

What is reinforcement learning?

This chapter covers

- A brief review of machine learning
- Introducing reinforcement learning as a subfield
- The basic framework of reinforcement learning

Computer languages of the future will be more concerned with goals and less with procedures specified by the programmer.

—Marvin Minksy, 1970 ACM Turing Lecture

If you're reading this book, you are probably familiar with how deep neural networks are used for things like image classification or prediction (and if not, just keep reading; we also have a crash course in deep learning in the appendix). *Deep reinforcement learning* (DRL) is a subfield of machine learning that utilizes deep learning models (i.e., neural networks) in reinforcement learning (RL) tasks (to be defined in section 1.2). In image classification we have a bunch of images that correspond to a set of discrete categories, such as images of different kinds of animals, and we want a machine learning model to interpret an image and classify the kind of animal in the image, as in figure 1.1.

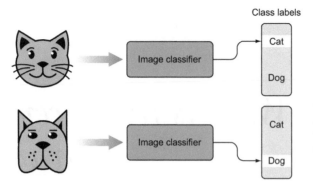

Figure 1.1 An image classifier is a function or learning algorithm that takes in an image and returns a class label, classifying the image into one of a finite number of possible categories or classes.

1.1 The "deep" in deep reinforcement learning

Deep learning models are just one of many kinds of machine learning models we can use to classify images. In general, we just need some sort of function that takes in an image and returns a class label (in this case, the label identifying which kind of animal is depicted in the image), and usually this function has a fixed set of adjustable *parameters*—we call these kinds of models *parametric* models. We start with a parametric model whose parameters are initialized to random values—this will produce random class labels for the input images. Then we use a *training* procedure to adjust the parameters so the function iteratively gets better and better at correctly classifying the images. At some point, the parameters will be at an optimal set of values, meaning that the model cannot get any better at the classification task. Parametric models can also be used for *regression,* where we try to fit a model to a set of data so we can make predictions for unseen data (figure 1.2). A more sophisticated approach might perform even better if it had more parameters or a better internal architecture.

Deep neural networks are popular because they are in many cases the most accurate parametric machine learning models for a given task, like image classification. This is largely due to the way they represent data. Deep neural networks have many layers (hence the "deep"), which induces the model to learn layered representations of input data. This layered representation is a form of *compositionality*, meaning that a complex piece of data is represented as the combination of more elementary components, and those components can be further broken down into even simpler components, and so on, until you get to atomic units.

Human language is compositional (figure 1.3). For example, a book is composed of chapters, chapters are composed of paragraphs, paragraphs are composed of sentences, and so on, until you get to individual words, which are the smallest units of meaning. Yet each individual level conveys meaning—an entire book is meant to convey meaning, and its individual paragraphs are meant to convey smaller points. Deep neural networks can likewise learn a compositional representation of data—for example, they can represent an image as the composition of primitive contours and textures,

Untrained parametric function

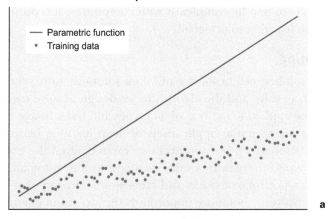

Trained parametric function

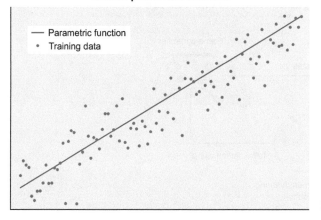

Figure 1.2 Perhaps the simplest machine learning model is a simple linear function of the form $f(x) = mx + b$, with parameters m (the slope) and b (the intercept). Since it has adjustable parameters, we call it a *parametric* function or model. If we have some 2-dimensional data, we can start with a randomly initialized set of parameters, such as [m = 3.4, b = 0.3], and then use a training algorithm to optimize the parameters to fit the training data, in which case the optimal set of parameters is close to [m = 2, b = 1].

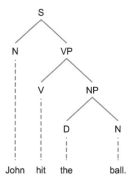

Figure 1.3 A sentence like "John hit the ball" can be decomposed into simpler and simpler parts until we get the individual words. In this case, we can decompose the sentence (denoted S) into a subject noun (N) and a verb phrase (VP). The VP can be further decomposed into a verb, "hit," and a noun phrase (NP). The NP can then be decomposed into the individual words "the" and "ball."

which are composed into elementary shapes, and so on, until you get the complete, complex image. This ability to handle complexity with compositional representations is largely what makes deep learning so powerful.

1.2   Reinforcement learning

It is important to distinguish between problems and their solutions, or in other words, between the tasks we wish to solve and the algorithms we design to solve them. Deep learning algorithms can be applied to many problem types and tasks. Image classification and prediction tasks are common applications of deep learning because automated image processing before deep learning was very limited, given the complexity of images. But there are many other kinds of tasks we might wish to automate, such as driving a car or balancing a portfolio of stocks and other assets. Driving a car includes some amount of image processing, but more importantly the algorithm needs to learn how to *act*, not merely to classify or predict. These kinds of problems, where decisions must be made or some behavior must be enacted, are collectively called *control tasks.*

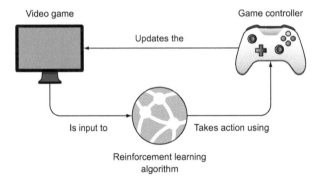

Figure 1.4   As opposed to an image classifier, a reinforcement learning algorithm dynamically interacts with data. It continually consumes data and decides what actions to take—actions that will change the subsequent data presented to it. A video game screen might be input data for an RL algorithm, which then decides which action to take using the game controller, and this causes the game to update (e.g. the player moves or fires a weapon).

Reinforcement learning is a generic framework for representing and solving control tasks, but within this framework we are free to choose which algorithms we want to apply to a particular control task (figure 1.4). Deep learning algorithms are a natural choice as they are able to process complex data efficiently, and this is why we'll focus on *deep* reinforcement learning, but much of what you'll learn in this book is the general reinforcement framework for control tasks (see figure 1.5). Then we'll look at how you can design an appropriate deep learning model to fit the framework and solve a task. This means you will learn a lot about reinforcement learning, and you'll probably will learn some things about deep learning that you didn't know as well.

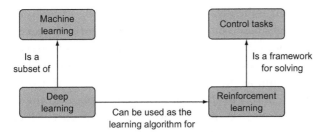

Figure 1.5 Deep learning is a subfield of machine learning. Deep learning algorithms can be used to power RL approaches to solving control tasks.

One added complexity of moving from image processing to the domain of control tasks is the additional element of time. With image processing, we usually train a deep learning algorithm on a fixed data set of images. After a sufficient amount of training, we typically get a high-performance algorithm that we can deploy to some new, unseen images. We can think of the data set as a "space" of data, where similar images are closer together in this abstract space and distinct images are farther apart (figure 1.6).

In control tasks, we similarly have a space of data to process, but each piece of data also has a time dimension—the data exists in both time and space. This means that what the algorithm decides at one time is influenced by what happened at a previous time. This isn't the case for ordinary image classification and similar problems. Time

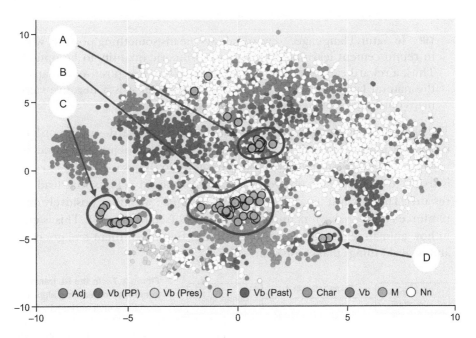

Figure 1.6 This graphical depiction of words in a 2D space shows each word as a colored point. Similar words cluster together, and dissimilar words are farther apart. Data naturally lives in some kind of "space" with similar data living closer together. The labels A, B, C, and D point to particular clusters of words that share some semantics.

makes the training task dynamic—the data set upon which the algorithm is training is not necessarily fixed but changes based on the decisions the algorithm makes.

Ordinary image classification-like tasks fall under the category of *supervised learning*, because the algorithm is trained on how to properly classify images by giving it the right answers. The algorithm at first takes random guesses, and it is iteratively corrected until it learns the features in the image that correspond to the appropriate label. This requires us to already know what the right answers are, which can be cumbersome. If you want to train a deep learning algorithm to correctly classify images of various species of plants, you would have to painstakingly acquire thousands of such images and manually associate class labels with each one and prepare the data in a format that a machine learning algorithm can operate on, generally some type of matrix.

In contrast, in RL we don't know exactly what the right thing to do is at every step. We just need to know what the ultimate goal is and what things to avoid doing. How do you teach a dog a trick? You have to give it tasty treats. Similarly, as the name suggests, we train an RL algorithm by incentivizing it to accomplish some high-level goal and possibly disincentivize it from doing things we don't want it to do. In the case of a self-driving car, the high-level goal might be "get to point B from starting point A without crashing." If it accomplishes the task, we reward it, and if it crashes, we penalize it. We would do this all in a simulator, rather than out on the real roads, so we could let it repeatedly try and fail at the task until it learns and gets rewarded.

> **TIP** In natural language, "reward" always means something positive, whereas in reinforcement learning jargon, it is a numeric quantity to be optimized. Thus, a reward can be positive or negative. When it is positive, it maps onto the natural language usage of the term, but when it is a negative value, it maps onto the natural language word "penalty."

The algorithm has a single objective—maximizing its reward—and in order to do this it must learn more elementary skills to achieve the main objective. We can also supply negative rewards when the algorithm chooses to do things we do not like, and since it is trying to maximize its reward, it will learn to avoid actions that lead to negative rewards. This is why it is called *reinforcement learning*: we either positively or negatively reinforce certain behaviors using reward signals (see figure 1.7). This is quite similar to how animals learn: they learn to do things that make them feel good or satisfied and to avoid things that cause pain.

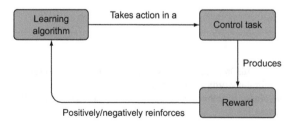

Figure 1.7 In the RL framework, some kind of learning algorithm decides which actions to take for a control task (e.g., driving a robot vacuum), and the action results in a positive or negative reward, which will positively or negatively reinforce that action and hence train the learning algorithm.

1.3   *Dynamic programming versus Monte Carlo*

You now know that you can train an algorithm to accomplish some high-level task by assigning the completion of the task a high reward (i.e., positive reinforcement) and negatively reinforce things we don't want it to do. Let's make this concrete. Say the high-level goal is to train a robot vacuum to move from one room in a house to its dock, which is in the kitchen. It has four actions: go left, go right, go forward, and go reverse. At each point in time, the robot needs to decide which of these four actions to take. If it reaches the dock, it gets a reward of +100, and if it hits anything along the way, it gets a negative reward of –10. Let's say the robot has a complete 3D map of the house and has the precise location of the dock, but it still doesn't know exactly what sequence of primitive actions to take to get to the dock.

One approach to solving this is called *dynamic programming* (DP), first articulated by Richard Bellman in 1957. Dynamic programming might better be called *goal decomposition* as it solves complex high-level problems by decomposing them into smaller and smaller subproblems until it gets to a simple subproblem that can be solved without further information.

Rather than the robot trying to come up with a long sequence of primitive actions that will get it to the dock, it can first break the problem down into "stay in this room" versus "exit this room." Since it has a complete map of the house, it knows it needs to exit the room, because the dock is in the kitchen. Yet it still doesn't know what sequence of actions will allow it to exit the room, so it breaks the problem down further to "move toward the door" or "move away from the door." Since the door is closer to the dock, and there is a path from the door to the dock, the robot knows it needs to move toward the door, but again it doesn't know what sequence of primitive actions will get it toward the door. Lastly, it needs to decide whether to move left, right, forward, or reverse. It can see the door is in front of it, so it moves forward. It keeps this process up until it exits the room, when it must do some more goal decomposition until it gets to the dock.

This is the essence of dynamic programming. It is a generic approach for solving certain kinds of problems that can be broken down into subproblems and sub-subproblems, and it has applications across many fields including bioinformatics, economics, and computer science.

In order to apply Bellman's dynamic programming, we have to be able to break our problem into subproblems that we know how to solve. But even this seemingly innocuous assumption is difficult to realize in the real world. How do you break the high-level goal for a self-driving car of "get to point B from point A without crashing" into small non-crashing subproblems? Does a child learn to walk by first solving easier sub-walking problems? In RL, where we often have nuanced situations that may include some element of randomness, we can't apply dynamic programming exactly as Bellman laid it out. In fact, DP can be considered one extreme of a continuum of problem-solving techniques, where the other end would be random trial and error.

Another way to view this learning continuum is that in some situations we have maximal knowledge of the environment and in others we have minimal knowledge of the environment, and we need to employ different strategies in each case. If you need to use the bathroom in your own house, you know exactly (well, unconsciously at least) what sequence of muscle movements will get you to the bathroom from any starting position (i.e., dynamic programming-ish). This is because you know your house extremely well—you have a more or less perfect *model* of your house in your mind. If you go to a party at a house that you've never been to before, you might have to look around until you find the bathroom on your own (i.e., trial and error), because you don't have a good model of that person's house.

The trial and error strategy generally falls under the umbrella of *Monte Carlo methods*. A Monte Carlo method is essentially a random sampling from the environment. In many real-world problems, we have at least some knowledge of how the environment works, so we end up employing a mixed strategy of some amount of trial and error and some amount of exploiting what we already know about the environment to directly solve the easy sub-objectives.

A silly example of a mixed strategy would be if you were blindfolded, placed in an unknown location in your house, and told to find the bathroom by throwing pebbles and listening for the noise. You might start by decomposing the high-level goal (find the bathroom) into a more accessible sub-goal: figure out which room you're currently in. To solve this sub-goal, you might throw a few pebbles in random directions and assess the size of the room, which might give you enough information to infer which room you're in—say the bedroom. Then you'd need to pivot to another sub-goal: navigating to the door so you can enter the hallway. You'd then start throwing pebbles again, but since you remember the results of your last random pebble throwing, you could target your throwing to areas of less certainty. Iterating over this process, you might eventually find your bathroom. In this case, you would be applying both the goal decomposition of dynamic programming and the random sampling of Monte Carlo methods.

1.4   *The reinforcement learning framework*

Richard Bellman introduced dynamic programming as a general method of solving certain kinds of control or decision problems, but it occupies an extreme end of the RL continuum. Arguably, Bellman's more important contribution was helping develop the standard framework for RL problems. The RL framework is essentially the core set of terms and concepts that every RL problem can be phrased in. This not only provides a standardized language for communicating with other engineers and researchers, it also forces us to formulate our problems in a way that is amenable to dynamic programming-like problem decomposition, such that we can iteratively optimize over local sub-problems and make progress toward achieving the global high-level objective. Fortunately, it's pretty simple too.

To concretely illustrate the framework, let's consider the task of building an RL algorithm that can learn to minimize the energy usage at a big data center. Computers need to be kept cool to function well, so large data centers can incur significant costs from cooling systems. The naive approach to keeping a data center cool would be to keep the air conditioning on all the time at a level that results in no servers ever running too hot; this would not require any fancy machine learning. But this is inefficient, and you could do better, since it's unlikely that all servers in the center are running hot at the same times and that the data center usage is always at the same level. If you targeted the cooling to where and when it mattered most, you could achieve the same result for less money.

Step one in the framework is to define your overall objective. In this case, our overall objective is to minimize money spent on cooling, with the constraint that no server in our center can surpass some threshold temperature. Although this appears to be two objectives, we can bundle them together into a new composite *objective function*. This function returns an error value that indicates how off-target we are at meeting the two objectives, given the current costs and the temperature data for the servers. The actual number that our objective function returns is not important; we just want to make it as low as possible. Hence, we need our RL algorithm to minimize this objective (error) function's return value with respect to some input data, which will definitely include the running costs and temperature data, but may also include other useful contextual information that can help the algorithm predict the data center usage.

The input data is generated by the *environment*. In general, the environment of a RL (or control) task is any dynamic process that produces data that is relevant to achieving our objective. Although we use "environment" as a technical term, it's not too far abstracted from its everyday usage. As an instance of a very advanced RL algorithm yourself, you are always in some environment, and your eyes and ears are constantly consuming information produced by your environment so you can achieve your daily objectives. Since the environment is a *dynamic process* (a function of time), it may be producing a continuous stream of data of varied size and type. To make things algorithm-friendly, we need to take this environment data and bundle it into discrete packets that we call the *state* (of the environment) and then deliver it to our algorithm at each of its discrete time steps. The state reflects our knowledge of the environment at some particular time, just as a digital camera captures a discrete snapshot of a scene at some time (and produces a consistently formatted image).

To summarize so far, we defined an objective function (minimize costs by optimizing temperature) that is a function of the state (current costs, current temperature data) of the environment (the data center and any related processes). The last part of our model is the RL algorithm itself. This could be *any* parametric algorithm that can learn from data to minimize or maximize some objective function by modifying its parameters. It does *not* need to be a deep learning algorithm; RL is a field of its own, separate from the concerns of any particular learning algorithm.

As we noted before, one of the key differences between RL (or control tasks generally) and ordinary supervised learning is that in a control task the algorithm needs to make decisions and take actions. These actions will have a causal effect on what happens in the future. Taking an action is a keyword in the framework, and it means more or less what you'd expect it to mean. However, every action taken is the result of analyzing the current state of the environment and attempting to make the best decision based on that information.

The last concept in the RL framework is that after each action is taken, the algorithm is given a *reward*. The reward is a (local) signal of how well the learning algorithm is performing at achieving the global objective. The reward can be a positive signal (i.e., doing well, keep it up) or a negative signal (i.e., don't do that) even though we call both situations a "reward."

The reward signal is the only cue the learning algorithm has to go by as it updates itself in hopes of performing better in the next state of the environment. In our data center example, we might grant the algorithm a reward of +10 (an arbitrary value) whenever its action reduces the error value. Or more reasonably, we might grant a reward proportional to how much it decreases the error. If it increases the error, we would give it a negative reward.

Lastly, let's give our learning algorithm a fancier name, calling it the *agent*. The agent is the action-taking or decision-making learning algorithm in any RL problem. We can put this all together as shown in figure 1.8.

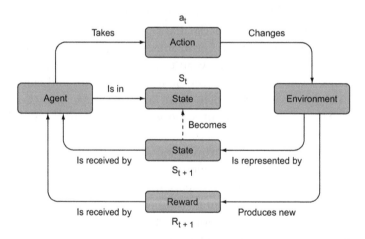

Figure 1.8   The standard framework for RL algorithms. The agent takes an action in the environment, such as moving a chess piece, which then updates the state of the environment. For every action it takes, it receives a reward (e.g., +1 for winning the game, –1 for losing the game, 0 otherwise). The RL algorithm repeats this process with the objective of maximizing rewards in the long term, and it eventually learns how the environment works.

In our data center example, we hope that our agent will learn how to decrease our cooling costs. Unless we're able to supply it with complete knowledge of the environment, it will have to employ some degree of trial and error. If we're lucky, the agent might learn so well that it can be used in different environments than the one it was originally trained in. Since the agent is the learner, it is implemented as some sort of learning algorithm. And since this is a book about *deep* reinforcement learning, our agents will be implemented using *deep learning* algorithms (also known as *deep neural networks*, see figure 1.9). But remember, RL is more about the type of problem and solution than about any particular learning algorithm, and you could certainly use alternatives to deep neural networks. In fact, in chapter 3 we'll begin by using a very simple non-neural network algorithm, and we'll replace it with a neural network by the end of the chapter.

Agent

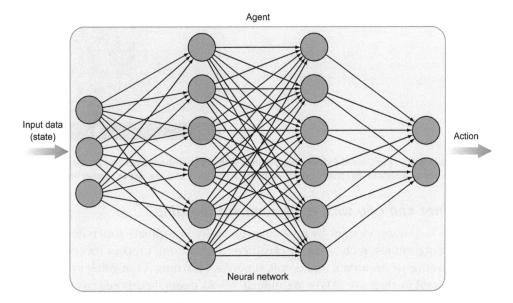

Neural network

Figure 1.9 The input data (which is the state of the environment at some point in time) is fed into the agent (implemented as a deep neural network in this book), which then evaluates that data in order to take an action. The process is a little more involved than shown here, but this captures the essence.

The agent's only objective is to maximize its expected rewards in the long term. It just repeats this cycle: process the state information, decide what action to take, see if it gets a reward, observe the new state, take another action, and so on. If we set all this up correctly, the agent will eventually learn to understand its environment and make reliably good decisions at every step. This general mechanism can be applied to autonomous vehicles, chatbots, robotics, automated stock trading, healthcare, and much more. We'll explore some of these applications in the next section and throughout this book.

Most of your time in this book will be spent learning how to structure problems in our standard model and how to implement sufficiently powerful learning algorithms (agents) to solve difficult problems. For these examples, you won't need to construct environments—you'll be plugging into existing environments (such as game engines or other APIs). For example, OpenAI has released a Python Gym library that provides us with a number of environments and a straightforward interface for our learning algorithm to interact with. The code on the left of figure 1.10 shows how simple it is to set up and use one of these environments—a car racing game requires only five lines of code.

```
import gym
env = gym.make('CarRacing-v0')
env.reset()
env.step(action)
env.render()
```

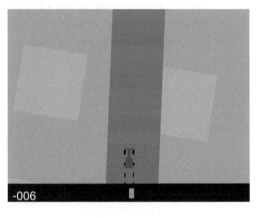

Figure 1.10 The OpenAI Python library comes with many environments and an easy-to-use interface for a learning algorithm to interact with. With just a few lines of code, we've loaded up a car racing game.

1.5   *What can I do with reinforcement learning?*

We began this chapter by reviewing the basics of ordinary supervised machine learning algorithms, such as image classifiers, and although recent successes in supervised learning are important and useful, supervised learning is not going to get us to artificial general intelligence (AGI). We ultimately seek general-purpose learning machines that can be applied to multiple problems with minimal to no supervision and whose repertoire of skills can be transferred across domains. Large data-rich companies can gainfully benefit from supervised approaches, but smaller companies and organizations may not have the resources to exploit the power of machine learning. General-purpose learning algorithms would level the playing field for everyone, and reinforcement learning is currently the most promising approach toward such algorithms.

RL research and applications are still maturing, but there have been many exciting developments in recent years. Google's DeepMind research group has showcased some impressive results and garnered international attention. The first was in 2013 with an algorithm that could play a spectrum of Atari games at superhuman levels. Previous attempts at creating agents to solve these games involved fine-tuning the underlying algorithms to understand the specific rules of the game, often called *feature engineering*. These feature engineering approaches can work well for a particular game, but they are unable to transfer any knowledge or skills to a new game or domain. DeepMind's deep Q-network (DQN) algorithm was robust enough to work on seven games without any game-specific tweaks (see figure 1.11). It had nothing more than the raw pixels from the screen as input and was merely told to maximize the score, yet the algorithm learned how to play beyond an expert human level.

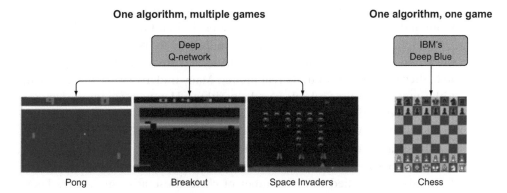

Figure 1.11   DeepMind's DQN algorithm successfully learned how to play seven Atari games with only the raw pixels as input and the player's score as the objective to maximize. Previous algorithms, such as IBM's Deep Blue, needed to be fine-tuned to play a specific game.

More recently, DeepMind's AlphaGo and AlphaZero algorithms beat the world's best players at the ancient Chinese game Go. Experts believed artificial intelligence would not be able to play Go competitively for at least another decade because the game has characteristics that algorithms typically don't handle well. Players do not know the best move to make at any given turn and only receive feedback for their actions at the end of the game. Many high-level players saw themselves as artists rather than calculating strategists and described winning moves as being beautiful or elegant. With over 10^{170} legal board positions, brute force algorithms (which IBM's Deep Blue used to win at chess) were not feasible. AlphaGo managed this feat largely by playing simulated games of Go millions of times and learning which actions maximized the rewards of playing the game well. Similar to the Atari case, AlphaGo only had access to the same information a human player would: where the pieces were on the board.

While algorithms that can play games better than humans are remarkable, the promise and potential of RL goes far beyond making better game bots. DeepMind was able to create a model to decrease Google's data center cooling costs by 40%, something we explored earlier in this chapter as an example. Autonomous vehicles use RL to learn which series of actions (accelerating, turning, breaking, signaling) leads to passengers reaching their destinations on time and to learn how to avoid accidents. And researchers are training robots to complete tasks, such as learning to run, without explicitly programming complex motor skills.

Many of these examples are high stakes, like driving a car. You cannot just let a learning machine learn how to drive a car by trial and error. Fortunately, there are an increasing number of successful examples of letting learning machines loose in harmless simulators, and once they have mastered the simulator, letting them try real hardware in the real world. One instance that we will explore in this book is algorithmic trading. A substantial fraction of all stock trading is executed by computers with little to no input from human operators. Most of these algorithmic traders are wielded by huge hedge funds managing billions of dollars. In the last few years, however, we've seen more and more interest by individual traders in building trading algorithms. Indeed, Quantopian provides a platform where individual users can write trading algorithms in Python and test them in a safe, simulated environment. If the algorithms perform well, they can be used to trade real money. Many traders have achieved relative success with simple heuristics and rule-based algorithms. However, equity markets are dynamic and unpredictable, so a continuously learning RL algorithm has the advantage of being able to adapt to changing market conditions in real time.

One practical problem we'll tackle early in this book is advertisement placement. Many web businesses derive significant revenue from advertisements, and the revenue from ads is often tied to the number of clicks those ads can garner. There is a big incentive to place advertisements where they can maximize clicks. The only way to do this, however, is to use knowledge about the users to display the most appropriate ads. We generally don't know what characteristics of the user are related to the right ad choices, but we can employ RL techniques to make some headway. If we give an RL algorithm some potentially useful information about the user (what we would call the environment, or state of the environment) and tell it to maximize ad clicks, it will learn how to associate its input data to its objective, and it will eventually learn which ads will produce the most clicks from a particular user.

1.6   *Why deep reinforcement learning?*

We've made a case for reinforcement learning, but why *deep* reinforcement learning? RL existed long before the popular rise of deep learning. In fact, some of the earliest methods (which we will look at for learning purposes) involved nothing more than storing experiences in a lookup table (e.g., a Python dictionary) and updating that table on each iteration of the algorithm. The idea was to let the agent play around in the environment and see what happened, and to store its experiences of what happened in some sort of database. After a while, you could look back on this database of knowledge and observe what worked and what didn't. No neural networks or other fancy algorithms.

For very simple environments this actually works fairly well. For example, in Tic-Tac-Toe there are 255,168 valid board positions. The *lookup table* (also called a *memory table*) would have that many entries, which mapped from each state to a specific action (as shown in figure 1.12) and the reward observed (not depicted). During training, the algorithm could learn which move led toward more favorable positions and update that entry in the memory table.

Once the environment gets more complicated, using a memory table becomes intractable. For example, every screen configuration of a video game could be considered a

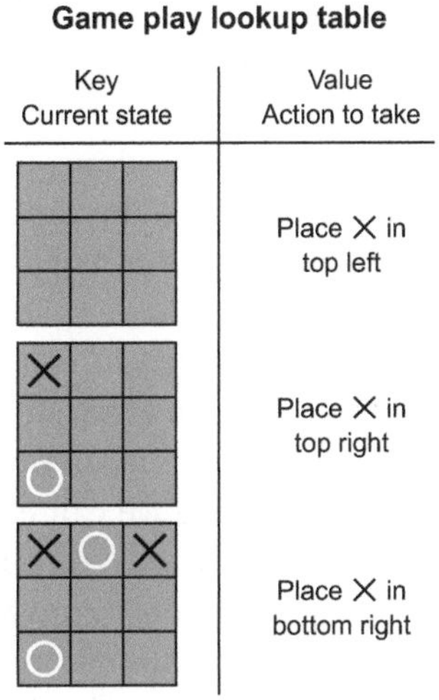

Game play lookup table

Key Current state	Value Action to take
	Place X in top left
	Place X in top right
	Place X in bottom right

Figure 1.12 An action lookup table for Tic-Tac-Toe with only three entries, where the "player" (an algorithm) plays X. When the player is given a board position, the lookup table dictates the move that they should make next. There will be an entry for every possible state in the game.

different state (figure 1.13). Imagine trying to store every possible combination of valid pixel values shown on screen in a video game! DeepMind's DQN algorithm, which played Atari, was fed four 84 × 84 grayscale images at each step, which would lead to 256^{28228} unique game states (256 different shades of grey per pixel, and 4*84*84=28228 pixels). This number is much larger than the number of atoms in the observable universe and would definitely not fit in computer memory. And this was after the images were scaled down to reduce their size from the original 210 × 160 pixel color images.

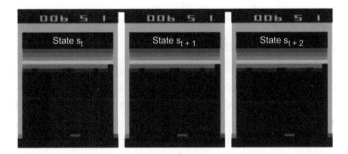

Figure 1.13 A series of three frames of Breakout. The placement of the ball is slightly different in each frame. If you were using a lookup table, this would equate to storing three unique entries in the table. A lookup table would be impractical as there are far too many game states to store.

Storing every possible state isn't possible, but we could try to limit the possibilities. In the game Breakout, you control a paddle at the bottom of the screen that can move right or left; the objective of the game is to deflect the ball and break as many blocks at the top of the screen. In that case, we could define constraints—only look at the states when the ball is returning to the paddle, since our actions are not important while we are waiting for the ball at the top of the screen. Or we could provide our own features—instead of providing the raw image, just provide the position of the ball, paddle, and the remaining blocks. However, these methods require the programmer to understand the underlying strategies of the game, and they would not generalize to other environments.

That's where deep learning comes in. A deep learning algorithm can learn to abstract away the details of specific arrangements of pixels and can learn the important features of a state. Since a deep learning algorithm has a finite number of parameters, we can use it to compress any possible state into something we can efficiently process, and then use that new representation to make our decisions. As a result of using neural networks, the Atari DQN only had 1792 parameters (convolutional neural network with 16 8×8 filters, 32 4×4 filters, and a 256-node fully connected hidden layer) as opposed to the 256^{28228} key/value pairs that would be needed to store the entire state space.

In the case of the Breakout game, a deep neural network might learn on its own to recognize the same high-level features a programmer would have to hand-engineer in a lookup table approach. That is, it might learn how to "see" the ball, the paddle, the blocks, and to recognize the direction of the ball. That's pretty amazing given that it's only being given raw pixel data. And even more interesting is that the learned high-level features may be transferable to other games or environments.

Deep learning is the secret sauce that makes all the recent successes in RL possible. No other class of algorithms has demonstrated the representational power, efficiency, and flexibility of deep neural networks. Moreover, neural networks are actually fairly simple!

1.7   *Our didactic tool: String diagrams*

The fundamental concepts of RL have been well-established for decades, but the field is moving very quickly, so any particular new result could soon be out of date. That's why this book focuses on teaching skills, not details with short half-lives. We do cover some recent advances in the field that will surely be supplanted in the not too distant future, but we do so only to build new skills, not because the particular topic we're covering is necessarily a time-tested technique. We're confident that even if some of our examples become dated, the skills you learn will not, and you'll be prepared to tackle RL problems for a long time to come.

Moreover, RL is a huge field with a lot to learn. We can't possibly hope to cover all of it in this book. Rather than be an exhaustive RL reference or comprehensive course, our goal is to teach you the foundations of RL and to sample a few of the most exciting recent developments in the field. We expect that you will be able to take what you've learned here and easily get up to speed in the many other areas of RL. Plus, we have a section in chapter 11 that gives you a roadmap of areas you might want to check out after finishing this book.

This book is focused on teaching well, but also rigorously. Reinforcement learning and deep learning are both fundamentally mathematical. If you read any primary research articles in these fields, you will encounter potentially unfamiliar mathematical notations and equations. Mathematics allows us to make precise statements about what's true and how things are related, and it offers rigorous explanations for how and why things work. We could teach RL without any math and just use Python, but that approach would handicap you in understanding future advances.

So we think the math is important, but as our editor noted, there's a common saying in the publishing world: "for every equation in the book, the readership is halved," which probably has some truth to it. There's an unavoidable cognitive overhead in deciphering complex math equations, unless you're a professional mathematician who reads and writes math all day. Faced with wanting to present a rigorous exposition of DRL to give readers a top-rate understanding, and yet wanting to reach as many people as possible, we came up with what we think is a very distinguishing feature of this book. As it turns out, even professional mathematicians are becoming tired of traditional math notation with its huge array of symbols, and within a particular branch of advanced mathematics called *category theory*, mathematicians have developed a purely graphical language called *string diagrams*. String diagrams look very similar to flowcharts and circuit diagrams, and they have a fairly intuitive meaning, but they are just as rigorous and precise as traditional mathematical notations largely based on Greek and Latin symbols.

Figure 1.14 shows a simple example of one type of string diagram that depicts, at a high level, a neural network with two layers. Machine learning (especially deep learning) involves a lot of matrix and vector operations, and string diagrams are particularly well-suited to describing these kinds of operations graphically. String diagrams are also great for describing complex processes because we can describe the process at varying levels of abstraction. The top panel of figure 1.14 shows two rectangles representing the two layers of the neural network, but then we can "zoom in" (look inside the box) on layer 1 to see what it does in more detail, which is shown in the bottom panel of figure 1.14.

We will frequently use string diagrams throughout the book to communicate everything from complex mathematical equations to the architectures of deep neural networks. We will describe this graphical syntax in the next chapter, and we'll continue to refine and build it up throughout the rest of the book. In some cases, this graphical notation is overkill for what we're trying to explain, so we'll use a combination of clear prose and Python or pseudocode. We will also include traditional math notation in most cases, so you will be able to learn the underlying mathematical concepts one way or another, whether diagrams, code, or normal mathematical notation most connect with you.

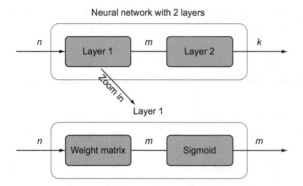

Figure 1.14   A string diagram for a two-layer neural network. Reading from left to right, the top string diagram represents a neural network that accepts an input vector of dimension *n*, multiplies it by a matrix of dimensions *n* x *m*, returning a vector of dimension *m*. Then the non-linear sigmoid activation function is applied to each element in the *m*-dimensional vector. This new vector is then fed through the same sequence of steps in layer 2, which produces the final output of the neural network, which is a *k*-dimensional vector.

1.8   What's next?

In the next chapter, we will dive right into the real meat of RL, covering many of the core concepts, such as the tradeoff between exploration and exploitation, Markov decision processes, value functions, and policies (these terms will make sense soon). But first, at the beginning of the next chapter we'll introduce some of the teaching methods we'll employ throughout the book.

The rest of the book will cover core DRL algorithms that much of the latest research is built upon, starting with deep Q-networks, followed by policy gradient approaches, and then model-based algorithms. We will primarily be utilizing OpenAI's Gym (mentioned earlier) to train our algorithms to understand nonlinear dynamics, control robots and play games (figure 1.15).

In each chapter, we will open with a major problem or project that we will use to illustrate the important concepts and skills for that chapter. As each chapter progresses, we may add complexity or nuances to the starting problem to go deeper into some of the principles. For example, in chapter 2 we will start with the problem of maximizing rewards at a casino slot machine, and by solving that problem we'll cover most of the foundations of RL. Later we'll add some complexity to that problem and change the setting from a casino to a business that needs to maximize advertising clicks, which will allow us to round out a few more core concepts.

Although this book is for those who already have experience with the basics of deep learning, we expect to not only teach you fun and useful RL techniques but also to hone your deep learning skills. In order to solve some of the more challenging projects, we'll need to employ some of the latest advances in deep learning, such as

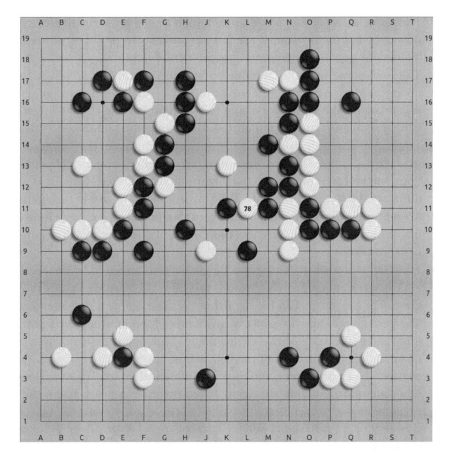

Figure 1.15 A depiction of a Go board, an ancient Chinese game that Google DeepMind used as a testbed for its AlphaGo reinforcement learning algorithm. Professional Go player Lee Sedol only won one game out of five, marking a turning point for reinforcement learning, as Go was long thought to be impervious to the kind of algorithmic reasoning that chess is subject to. Source: http://mng.bz/DNX0.

generative adversarial networks, evolutionary methods, meta-learning, and transfer learning. Again, this is all in line with our skills-focused mode of teaching, so the particulars of these advances is not what's important.

Summary

- Reinforcement learning is a subclass of machine learning. RL algorithms learn by maximizing rewards in some environment, and they're useful when a problem involves making decisions or taking actions. RL algorithms can, in principle, employ any statistical learning model, but it has become increasingly popular and effective to use deep neural networks.

- The agent is the focus of any RL problem. It is the part of the RL algorithm that processes input to determine which action to take. In this book we are primarily focused on agents implemented as deep neural networks.

- The environment is the potentially dynamic conditions in which the agent operates. More generally, the environment is whatever process generates the input data for the agent. For example, we might have an agent flying a plane in a flight simulator, so the simulator would be the environment.

- The state is a snapshot of the environment that the agent has access to and uses to make decisions. The environment is often a set of constantly changing conditions, but we can sample from the environment, and these samples at particular times are the state information of the environment we give to the agent.

- An action is a decision made by an agent that produces a change in its environment. Moving a particular chess piece is an action, and so is pressing the gas pedal in a car.

- A reward is a positive or negative signal given to an agent by the environment after it takes an action. The rewards are the only learning signals the agent is given. The objective of an RL algorithm (i.e., the agent) is to maximize rewards.

- The general pipeline for an RL algorithm is a loop in which the agent receives input data (the state of the environment), the agent evaluates that data and takes an action from a set of possible actions given its current state, the action changes the environment, and the environment then sends a reward signal and new state information to the agent. Then the cycle repeats. When the agent is implemented as a deep neural network, each iteration evaluates a loss function based on the reward signal and backpropagates to improve the performance of the agent.

Modeling reinforcement learning problems: Markov decision processes

This chapter covers

- String diagrams and our teaching methods
- The PyTorch deep learning framework
- Solving *n*-armed bandit problems
- Balancing exploration versus exploitation
- Modeling a problem as a Markov decision process (MDP)
- Implementing a neural network to solve an advertisement selection problem

This chapter covers some of the most fundamental concepts in all of reinforcement learning, and it will be the basis for the rest of the book. But before we get into that, we want to first go over some of the recurring teaching methods we'll employ in this book—most notably, the string diagrams we mentioned last chapter.

2.1 String diagrams and our teaching methods

In our experience, when most people try to teach something complicated, they tend to teach it in the reverse order in which the topic itself was developed. They'll give you a bunch of definitions, terms, descriptions, and perhaps theorems, and then they'll say, "great, now that we've covered all the theory, let's go over some practice problems." In our opinion, that's exactly the opposite order in which things should be presented. Most good ideas arise as solutions to real-world problems, or at least imagined problems. The problem-solver stumbles across a potential solution, tests it, improves it, and then eventually formalizes and possibly mathematizes it. The terms and definitions come *after* the solution to the problem was developed.

We think learning is most motivating and effective when you take the place of that original idea-maker, who was thinking of how to solve a particular problem. Only once the solution crystalizes does it warrant formalization, which is indeed necessary to establish its correctness and to faithfully communicate it to others in the field.

There is a powerful urge to engage in this reverse chronological mode of teaching, but we will do our best to resist it and develop the topic as we go. In that spirit, we will introduce new terms, definitions, and mathematical notations as we need them. For example, we will use "callouts" like this:

> **DEFINITION**   A *neural network* is a kind of machine learning model composed of multiple "layers" that perform a matrix-vector multiplication followed by the application of a nonlinear "activation" function. The matrices of the neural network are the model's learnable parameters and are often called the "weights" of the neural network.

You will only see these callouts once per term, but we will often repeat the definition in different ways in the text to make sure you really understand and remember it. This is a course on reinforcement learning, not a textbook or reference, so we won't shy away from repeating ourselves when we think something is important to remember.

Whenever we need to introduce some math, we will typically use a box showing the math and a pseudo-Python version of the same underlying concept. Sometimes it's easier to think in terms of code or of math, and we think it's good to get familiar with both. As a super simple example, if we were introducing the equation of a line, we would do it like this:

Table 2.1   Example of the side-by-side mathematics and pseudocode we use in this book

Math	Pseudocode
$y = mx + b$	```def line(x,m,b):``` ``` return m*x + b```

We will also include plenty of inline code (short snippets) and code listings (longer code examples) as well as the code for complete projects. All of the code in the book is provided in Jupyter Notebooks categorized by chapter on the book's GitHub repository (http://mng.bz/JzKp). If you're actively following the text and building the projects in this book, we strongly recommend following the code in this associated

GitHub repository rather than copying the code in the text—we will keep the GitHub code updated and bug-free, whereas the code in the book may get a bit out of date as the Python libraries we use are updated. The GitHub code is also more complete (e.g., showing you how to generate the visualizations that we include), whereas the code in the text has been kept as minimal as possible to focus on the underlying concepts.

Since reinforcement learning involves a lot of interconnecting concepts that can become confusing when just using words, we will include a lot of diagrams and figures of varying sorts. The most important kind of figure we'll use is the *string diagram*. It's perhaps an odd name, but it's a really simple idea and is adapted from category theory, a branch of math we mentioned in the first chapter where they tend to use a lot of diagrams to supplement or replace traditional symbolic notation.

You already saw the string diagram in figure 2.1 when we introduced the general framework for reinforcement learning in chapter 1. The idea is that the boxes contain nouns or noun phrases, whereas the arrows are labeled with verbs or verb phrases. It's slightly different from typical flow diagrams, but this makes it easy to translate the string diagram into English prose and vice versa. It's also very clear what the arrows are *doing* functionally. This particular kind of string diagram is also called an *ontological log,* or *olog* ("oh-log"). You can look them up if you're curious about learning more.

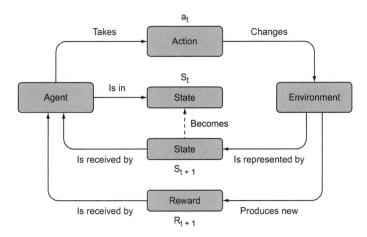

Figure 2.1   The standard reinforcement learning model in which an agent takes actions in an evolving environment that produces rewards to reinforce the actions of the agent.

More generally, string diagrams (sometimes referred to as *wiring diagrams* in other sources) are flow-like diagrams that represent the flow of typed data along strings (i.e., directed or undirected arrows) into processes (computations, functions, transformations, processes, etc.), which are represented as boxes. The important difference between string diagrams and other similar-looking flow diagrams you may have seen is that all the data on the strings is explicitly typed (e.g., a numpy array with shape [10, 10], or maybe a floating-point number), and the diagrams are fully compositional. By compositional, we mean that we can zoom in or out on the diagram to see the bigger more abstract picture or to drill down to the computational details.

If we're showing a higher-level depiction, the process boxes may just be labeled with a word or short phrase indicating the kind of process that happens, but we could also show a zoomed-in view of that process box that reveals all its internal details, composed of its own set of substrings and subprocesses. The compositional nature of these diagrams also means that we can plug parts of one diagram into another diagram, forming more complex diagrams, as long as all the strings' types are compatible. For example, here's a single layer of a neural network as a string diagram:

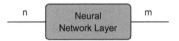

Reading from left to right, we see that some data of type n flows into a process box called Neural Network Layer and produces output of type m. Since neural networks typically take vectors as inputs and produce vectors as outputs, these types refer to the dimensions of the input and output vectors respectively. That is, this neural network layer accepts a vector of length or dimension n and produces a vector of dimension m. It's possible that $n = m$ for some neural network layers.

This manner of *typing* the strings is simplified, and we do it only when it's clear what the types mean from the context. In other cases, we may employ mathematical notation such as $\mathbb{R}$ for the set of all real numbers, which in programming languages basically translates to floating-point numbers. So for a vector of floating-point numbers with dimension n, we could type the strings like this:

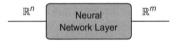

Now that the typing is richer, we not only know the dimensions of the input and output vectors, we know that they're real/floating-point numbers. While this is almost always the case, sometimes we may be dealing with integers or binary numbers. In any case, our Neural Network Layer process box is left as a black box; we don't know exactly what's going on in there other than the fact that it transforms a vector into another vector of possibly different dimensions. We can decide to zoom in on this process to see what specifically is happening:

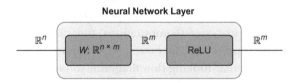

Now we can see the inside the original process box, and it is composed of its own set of subprocesses. We can see that our n-dimensional vector gets multiplied by a matrix of dimensions $n \times m$, which produces an m-dimensional vector product. This vector then passes through some process called "ReLU," which you may recognize as a standard neural network activation function, the rectified linear unit. We could continue to zoom in on the ReLU sub-subprocess if we wanted. Anything that deserves the name *string diagram* must be able to be scrutinized at any level of abstraction and remain *well typed* at any level (meaning the types of the data entering and exiting the processes must be compatible and make sense—a process that is supposed to produce sorted lists should not be hooked up to another process that expects integers).

As long as the strings are well typed, we can string together a bunch of processes into a complex system. This allows us to build components once and re-use them wherever they're type-matched. At a somewhat high level, we might depict a simple two-layer recurrent neural network (RNN) like this:

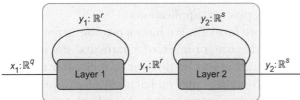

This RNN takes in a q vector and produces an s vector. However, we can see the inside processes. There are two layers, and each one looks identical in its function. They each take in a vector and produce a vector, except that the output vector is copied and fed back into the layer process as part of the input, hence the recurrence.

String diagrams are a very general type of diagram; in addition to diagramming neural networks, we could use them to diagram how to bake a cake. A *computational graph* is a special kind of string diagram where all the processes represent concrete computations that a computer can perform, or that can be described in some programming language like Python. If you've ever visualized a computational graph in TensorFlow's TensorBoard, you'll know what we mean. The goal of a good string diagram is that we can view an algorithm or machine learning model at a high level to get the big picture, and then gradually zoom in until our string diagram is detailed enough for us to actually implement the algorithm based almost solely on our knowledge of the diagram.

Between the mathematics, simple Python code, and string diagrams that we'll present in this book, you should have no problem understanding how to implement some pretty advanced machine learning models.

2.2   *Solving the multi-arm bandit*

We're now ready to get started with a real reinforcement learning problem and look at the relevant concepts and skills needed to solve this problem as we go. But before we get too fancy, building something like AlphaGo, let's first consider a simple problem. Let's say you're at a casino, and in front of you are 10 slot machines with a flashy sign that says "Play for free! Max payout is $10!" Wow, not bad! Intrigued, you ask one of the employees what's going on, because it seems too good to be true, and she says, "It's really true, play as much as you want, it's free. Each slot machine is guaranteed to give you a reward between $0 and $10. Oh, by the way, keep this to yourself, but those 10 slot machines each have a different average payout, so try to figure out which one gives the most rewards on average, and you'll be making tons of cash!"

What kind of casino is this? Who cares, let's just figure out how to make the most money! Oh by the way, here's a joke: What's another name for a slot machine? A one-armed bandit! Get it? It has one arm (a lever) and it generally steals your money. We could call our situation a 10-armed bandit problem, or an *n*-armed bandit problem more generally, where *n* is the number of slot machines. While this problem sounds pretty fanciful so far, you'll see later that these *n*-armed bandit (or multi-armed bandit) problems do have some very practical applications.

Let's restate our problem more formally. We have *n* possible actions (here *n* = 10) where an action means pulling the arm, or lever, of a particular slot machine, and at each play (*k*) of this game we can choose a single lever to pull. After taking an action (*a*) we will receive a reward, R_k (reward at play *k*). Each lever has a unique probability distribution of payouts (rewards). For example, if we have 10 slot machines and play many games, slot machine #3 may give out an average reward of $9 whereas slot machine #1 only gives out an average reward of $4. Of course, since the reward at each play is probabilistic, it is possible that lever #1 will by chance give us a reward of $9 on a single play. But if we play many games, we expect on average that slot machine #1 will be associated with a lower reward than #3.

Our strategy should be to play a few times, choosing different levers and observing our rewards for each action. Then we want to only choose the lever with the largest observed average reward. Thus, we need a concept of expected reward for taking an action (*a*) based on our previous plays. We'll call this expected reward $Q_k(a)$ mathematically: you give the function an action (given we're at play *k*), and it returns the expected reward for taking that action. This is shown formally here:

Table 2.2   The expected reward calculation in math and pseudocode

Math	Pseudocode

$$Q_k(a) = \frac{R_1 + R_2 + \ldots + R_k}{k_a}$$	```def exp_reward(action, history):```
	``` rewards_for_action = history[action]```
	``` return sum(rewards_for_action) /```
	``` len(rewards_for_action)```

That is, the expected reward at play k for action a is the arithmetic mean of all the previous rewards we've received for taking action a. Thus, our previous actions and observations influence our future actions. We might even say some of our previous actions *reinforce* our current and future actions, but we'll come back to this later. The function $Q_k(a)$ is called a *value function* because it tells us the value of something. In particular, it is an *action-value function* because it tells us the value of taking a particular action. Since we typically denote this function with the symbol Q, it's also often called a Q *function*. We'll come back to value functions later and give a more sophisticated definition, but this will suffice for now.

2.2.1 Exploration and exploitation

When we first start playing, we need to play the game and observe the rewards we get for the various machines. We can call this strategy *exploration*, since we're essentially randomly exploring the results of our actions. This is in contrast to a different strategy we could employ called *exploitation*, which means that we use our current knowledge about which machine seems to produce the most rewards, and keep playing that machine. Our overall strategy needs to include some amount of exploitation (choosing the best lever based on what we know so far) and some amount of exploration (choosing random levers so we can learn more). The proper balance of exploitation and exploration will be important to maximizing our rewards.

How can we come up with an algorithm to figure out which slot machine has the largest average payout? Well, the simplest algorithm would be to just select the action associated with the highest Q value:

Table 2.3 Computing the best action, given the expected rewards

Math	Pseudocode

$\forall a_i \in A_k$	```def get_best_action(actions, history):```
	``` exp_rewards = [exp_reward(action, history) for action in```
	``` actions]```

$a^* = \text{argmax}_a Q_k(a_i)$	``` return argmax(exp_rewards)```

The following listing shows it as legitimate Python 3 code.

Listing 2.1 Finding the best actions given the expected rewards in Python 3

```
def get_best_action(actions):
    best_action = 0
    max_action_value = 0
    for i in range(len(actions)):          ← Loops through all possible actions
        cur_action_value = get_action_value(actions[i])   ← Gets the value of the current action
        if cur_action_value > max_action_value:
            best_action = i
            max_action_value = cur_action_value
    return best_action
```

We use our above function $Q_k(a)$ on all the possible actions, and select the action that returns the maximum average reward. Since $Q_k(a)$ depends on a record of our previous actions and their associated rewards, this method will not evaluate actions that we haven't already explored. Thus, we might have previously tried levers #1 and #3 and noticed that lever #3 gives us a higher reward, but with this method we'll never think to try another lever, say #6, which, unbeknownst to us, actually gives out the highest average reward. This method of simply choosing the best lever that we know of so far is called a *greedy* (or exploitation) method.

2.2.2 *Epsilon-greedy strategy*

We need some exploration of other levers (other slot machines) to discover the true best action. One simple modification to our previous algorithm is to change it to an ε (epsilon)-greedy algorithm, such that with a probability, ε, we will choose an action, a, at random, and the rest of the time (probability $1 - \varepsilon$) we will choose the best lever based on what we currently know from past plays. Most of the time we will play greedy, but sometimes we will take a risk and choose a random lever to see what happens. The result will, of course, influence our future greedy actions. Let's see if we can solve this in code with Python.

Listing 2.2 Epsilon-greedy strategy for action selection

```
import numpy as np
from scipy import stats
import random                              Number of arms
import matplotlib.pyplot as plt            (number of slot machines)

n = 10                              ◁──┘    ┃  Hidden probabilities
probs = np.random.rand(n)          ◁───────┘  associated with each arm
eps = 0.2                      ◁──┐  Epsilon for epsilon-greedy
                                  ┃  action selection
```

In this casino example, we will be solving a 10-armed bandit problem, so $n = 10$. We've also defined a numpy array of length n filled with random floats that can be understood as probabilities. Each position in the probs array corresponds to an arm, which is a possible action. For example, the first element has index position 0, so action 0 is arm 0. Each arm has an associated probability that weights how much reward it pays out.

The way we've chosen to implement our reward probability distributions for each arm is this: Each arm will have a probability, e.g., 0.7, and the maximum reward is $10. We will set up a for loop going to 10, and at each step it will add 1 to the reward if a random float is less than the arm's probability. Thus, on the first loop it makes up a random float (e.g., 0.4). 0.4 is less than 0.7, so reward += 1. On the next iteration, it makes up another random float (e.g., 0.6) which is also less than 0.7, so reward += 1. This continues until we complete 10 iterations, and then we return the final total reward, which could be anything between 0 and 10. With an arm probability of 0.7, the *average* reward of doing this to infinity would be 7, but on any single play it could be more or less.

Listing 2.3 Defining the reward function

```
def get_reward(prob, n=10):
    reward = 0
    for i in range(n):
        if random.random() < prob:
            reward += 1
    return reward
```

You can check this by running it:

```
>>> np.mean([get_reward(0.7) for _ in range(2000)])
7.001
```

This output shows that running this code 2,000 times with a probability of 0.7 indeed gives us a mean reward of close to 7 (see the histogram in figure 2.2).

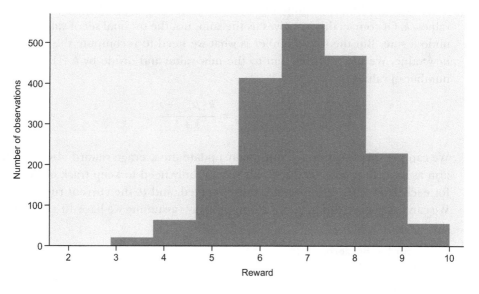

Figure 2.2   The distribution of rewards for a simulated *n*-armed bandit with a 0.7 probability of payout.

The next function we'll define is our greedy strategy of choosing the best arm so far. We need a way to keep track of which arms were pulled and what the resulting reward was. Naively, we could just have a list and append observations such as (arm, reward), e.g., (2, 9), indicating we chose arm 2 and received reward 9. This list would grow longer as we played the game.

There's a much simpler approach, however, since we really only need to keep track of the average reward for each arm—we don't need to store each observation. Recall that to calculate the mean of a list of numbers, x_i (indexed by i), we simply need sum up all the x_i values and then divide by the number of x_i, which we will denote k. The mean is often denoted with the Greek letter μ (mu).

$$\mu = \frac{1}{k}\sum_i x_i$$

The Greek uppercase symbol Σ (sigma) is used to denote a summation operation. The i notation underneath means we sum each element, x_i. It's basically the math equivalent of a for loop like:

```
sum = 0
x = [4,5,6,7]
for j in range(len(x)):
    sum = sum + x[j]
```

If we already have an average reward μ for a particular arm, we can update this average when we get a new reward by recomputing the average. We basically need to undo the average and then recompute it. To undo it, we multiply μ by the total number of values, k. Of course, this just gives us the sum, not the original set of values—you can't undo a sum. But the total number is what we need to recompute the average with a new value. We just add this sum to the new value and divide by $k + 1$, the new total number of values.

$$\mu_{new} = \frac{k \cdot \mu_{old} + x}{k + 1}$$

We can use this equation to continually update the average reward observed for each arm as we collect new data, and this way we only need to keep track of two numbers for each arm: k, the number of values observed, and μ, the current running average. We can easily store this in a 10×2 numpy array (assuming we have 10 arms). We'll call this array the record.

```
>>> record = np.zeros((n,2))
array([[0., 0.],
       [0., 0.],
       [0., 0.],
       [0., 0.],
       [0., 0.],
       [0., 0.],
       [0., 0.],
       [0., 0.],
       [0., 0.],
       [0., 0.]])
```

The first column of this array will store the number of times each arm has been pulled, and the second column will store the running average reward. Let's write a function for updating the record, given a new action and reward.

Listing 2.4 Updating the reward record

```
def update_record(record,action,r):
    new_r = (record[action,0] * record[action,1] + r) / (record[action,0] +
    1)
    record[action,0] += 1
    record[action,1] = new_r
    return record
```

This function takes the record array, an action (which is the index value of the arm), and a new reward observation. To update the average reward, it simply implements the mathematical function we described previously, and then increments the counter recording how many times that arm has been pulled.

Next we need a function that will select which arm to pull. We want it to choose the arm associated with the highest average reward, so all we need to do is find the row in the record array with biggest value in column 1. We can easily do this using numpy's built-in argmax function, which takes in an array, finds the largest value in the array, and returns its index position.

Listing 2.5 Computing the best action

```
def get_best_arm(record):
    arm_index = np.argmax(record[:,1],axis=0)      ◁——  Uses numpy argmax
    return arm_index                                      on column 1 of the
                                                          record array
```

Now we can get into the main loop for playing the *n*-armed bandit game. If a random number is greater than the epsilon parameter, we just calculate the best action using the get_best_arm function and take that action. Otherwise we take a random action to ensure some amount of exploration. After choosing the arm, we use the get_reward function and observe the reward value. We then update the record array with this new observation. We repeat this process a bunch of times, and it will continually update the *record* array. The arm with the highest reward probability should eventually get chosen most often, since it will give out the highest average reward.

We've set it to play 500 times in the following listing, and to display a matplotlib scatter plot of the mean reward against plays. Hopefully we'll see that the mean reward increases as we play more times.

Listing 2.6 Solving the *n*-armed bandit

```
fig, ax = plt.subplots(1,1)           Initializes the record
ax.set_xlabel("Plays")                array to all zeros
ax.set_ylabel("Avg Reward")
record = np.zeros((n,2))       ◁──┘
probs = np.random.rand(n)      ◁───── Randomly initializes the probabilities
eps = 0.2                             of rewards for each arm
rewards = [0]
for i in range(500):                  Chooses the best action with 0.8
    if random.random() > eps:  ◁──┘   probability, or randomly otherwise
        choice = get_best_arm(record)
```

```
else:
    choice = np.random.randint(10)
    r = get_reward(probs[choice])
    record = update_record(record,choice,r)
    mean_reward = ((i+1) * rewards[-1] + r)/(i+2)
    rewards.append(mean_reward)
ax.scatter(np.arange(len(rewards)),rewards)
```

Computes the reward for choosing the arm

Updates the record array with the new count and reward observation for this arm

Keeps track of the running average of rewards to assess overall performance

As you can see in figure 2.3, the average reward does indeed improve after many plays. Our algorithm is *learning*; it is getting reinforced by previous good plays! And yet it is such a simple algorithm.

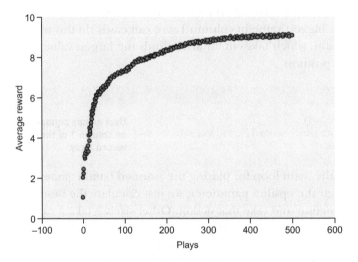

Figure 2.3   This plot shows that the average reward for each slot machine play increases over time, indicating we are successfully learning how to solve the *n*-armed bandit problem.

The problem we've considered here is a *stationary* problem because the underlying reward probability distributions for the arms does not change over time. We certainly could consider a variant of this problem where this is not true—a nonstationary problem. In this case, a simple modification would be to allow new reward observations to update the average reward value stored in the record in a skewed way, so that it would be a weighted average, weighted toward the newest observation. This way, if things change over time, we would be able to track them to some degree. We won't implement this slightly more complex variant here, but we will encounter nonstationary problems later in the book.

2.2.3 *Softmax selection policy*

Imagine another type of bandit problem: A newly minted doctor specializes in treating patients with heart attacks. She has 10 treatment options, of which she can choose only 1 to treat each patient she sees. For some reason, all she knows is that these 10 treatments have different efficacies and risk profiles for treating heart attacks—she doesn't know which one is the best yet. We could use the *n*-armed bandit algorithm from the previous solution, but we might want to reconsider our *ε*-greedy policy of randomly choosing a treatment once in a while. In this new problem, randomly choosing a treatment could result in patient death, not just losing some money. We really want to make sure we don't choose the worst treatment, but we still want some ability to explore our options to find the best one.

This is where a *softmax* selection might be most appropriate. Instead of just choosing an action at random during exploration, softmax gives us a probability distribution across our options. The option with the largest probability would be equivalent to the best arm action in the previous solution, but it will also give us some idea about which are the second and third best actions, for example. This way we can randomly choose to explore other options while avoiding the very worst options, since they will be assigned tiny probabilities or even 0. Here's the softmax equation:

Table 2.4　The softmax equation

Math	Pseudocode

$\Pr(A) = \dfrac{e^{Q_k(A)/\tau}}{\sum_{i=1}^{n} e^{Q_k(i)/\tau}}$	`def softmax(vals, tau):`
	　　`softm = pow(e, vals / tau) / sum( pow(e, vals / tau))`
	　　`return softm`

$\Pr(A)$ is a function that accepts an action-value vector (array) and returns a probability distribution over the actions, such that higher value actions have higher probabilities. For example, if your action-value array has four possible actions and they all currently have the same value, say A = [10, 10, 10, 10], then Pr(A) = [0.25, 0.25, 0.25, 0.25]. In other words, all the probabilities are the same and must sum to 1.

The numerator of the fraction exponentiates the action-value array divided by a parameter, τ, yielding a vector of the same size (i.e., length) as the input. The denominator sums over the exponentiation of each individual action value divided by τ, yielding a single number.

τ is a parameter called *temperature* that scales the probability distribution of actions. A high temperature will cause the probabilities to be very similar, whereas a low temperature will exaggerate differences in probabilities between actions. Selecting a value for this parameter requires an educated guess and some trial and error. The mathematical exponential e^x is a function call to np.exp(...) in numpy. It will apply the function element-wise across the input vector. Here's how we actually write the softmax function in Python.

Listing 2.7 The softmax function

```
def softmax(av, tau=1.12):
    softm = np.exp(av / tau) / np.sum( np.exp(av / tau) )
    return softm
```

When we implement the previous 10-armed bandit problem using `softmax`, we don't need the `get_best_arm` function anymore. Since `softmax` produces a weighted probability distribution across our possible actions, we can randomly select actions according to their relative probabilities. That is, our best action will get chosen more often because it will have the highest `softmax` probability, but other actions will be chosen at lower frequencies.

To implement this, all we need to do is apply the `softmax` function over the second column (column index 1) of the `record` array, since that's the column that stores the current mean reward (the action values) for each action. It will transform these action values into probabilities. Then we use the `np.random.choice` function, which accepts an arbitrary input array, *x*, and a parameter, *p*, that is an array of probabilities that correspond to each element in *x*. Since our record is initialized to all zeros, `softmax` at first will return a uniform distribution over all the arms, but this distribution will quickly skew toward whatever action is associated with the highest reward. Here's an example of using `softmax` and the random choice function:

```
>>> x = np.arange(10)
>>> x
array([0, 1, 2, 3, 4, 5, 6, 7, 8, 9])
>>> av = np.zeros(10)
>>> p = softmax(av)
>>> p
array([0.1, 0.1, 0.1, 0.1, 0.1, 0.1, 0.1, 0.1, 0.1, 0.1])
>>> np.random.choice(x,p=p)
3
```

We used the numpy `arange` function to create an array from 0 to 9, corresponding to the indices of each arm, so the random choice function will return an arm index according to the supplied probability vector. We can use the same training loop as we did previously; we just need to change the arm selection part so it uses `softmax` instead of `get_best_arm`, and we need to get rid of the random action selection that's part of the epsilon-greedy strategy.

Listing 2.8 Softmax action-selection for the *n*-armed bandit

```
n = 10
probs = np.random.rand(n)
record = np.zeros((n,2))
```

```
fig,ax = plt.subplots(1,1)
ax.set_xlabel("Plays")
ax.set_ylabel("Avg Reward")
fig.set_size_inches(9,5)
rewards = [0]
for i in range(500):
    p = softmax(record[:,1])
    choice = np.random.choice(np.arange(n),p=p)
    r = get_reward(probs[choice])
    record = update_record(record,choice,r)
    mean_reward = ((i+1) * rewards[-1] + r)/(i+2)
    rewards.append(mean_reward)
ax.scatter(np.arange(len(rewards)),rewards)
```

Computes softmax probabilities for each arm with respect to their current action values

Chooses an arm randomly but weighted by the softmax probabilities

Softmax action selection seems to do better than the epsilon-greedy method for this problem as you can tell from figure 2.4; it looks like it converges on an optimal policy faster. The downside to softmax is having to manually select the τ parameter. Softmax here was pretty sensitive to τ, and it takes some time playing with it to find a good value. Obviously with epsilon-greedy we had to set the epsilon parameter, but choosing that parameter was much more intuitive.

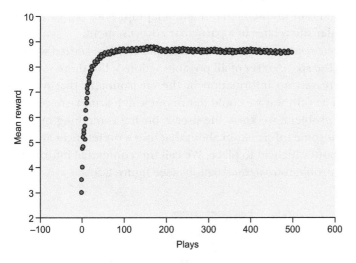

Figure 2.4 With the softmax policy, the *n*-armed bandit algorithm tends to converge faster on the maximal mean reward.

2.3 *Applying bandits to optimize ad placements*

The slot machine example may not seem to be a particularly real-world problem, but if we add one element, it does become a practical business problem, with one big example being advertisement placement. Whenever you visit a website with ads, the company placing the ads wants to maximize the probability that you will click them.

Let's say we manage 10 e-commerce websites, each focusing on selling a different broad category of retail items such as computers, shoes, jewelry, etc. We want to increase sales by referring customers who shop on one of our sites to another site that they might be interested in. When a customer checks out on a particular site in our network, we will display an advertisement to one of our other sites in hopes they'll go there and buy something else. Alternatively, we could place an ad for another product on the same site. Our problem is that we don't know which sites we should refer users to. We could try placing random ads, but we suspect a more targeted approach is possible.

2.3.1 *Contextual bandits*

Perhaps you can see how this just adds a new layer of complexity to the *n*-armed bandit problem we considered at the beginning of the chapter. At each play of the game (each time a customer checks out on a particular website) we have *n* = 10 possible actions we can take, corresponding to the 10 different types of advertisements we could place. The twist is that the best ad to place may depend on which site in the network the current customer is on. For example, a customer checking out on our jewelry site may be more in the mood to buy a new pair of shoes to go with their new diamond necklace than they would be to buy a new laptop. Thus our problem is to figure out how a particular site relates to a particular advertisement.

This leads us to *state spaces*. The *n*-armed bandit problem we started with had an *n*-element *action space* (the space or set of all possible actions), but there was no concept of state. That is, there was no information in the environment that would help us choose a good arm. The only way we could figure out which arms were good is by trial and error. In the ad problem, we know the user is buying something on a particular site, which may give us some information about that user's preferences and could help guide our decision about which ad to place. We call this contextual information a *state* and this new class of problems *contextual* bandits (see figure 2.5).

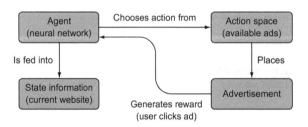

Figure 2.5   Overview of a contextual bandit for advertisement placement. The agent (which is a neural network algorithm) receives state information (in this case, the current website the user is on), which it uses to choose which of several advertisements it should place at the checkout step. Users will click on the advertisement or not, resulting in reward signals that get relayed back to the agent for learning.

DEFINITION   A *state* in a game (or in a reinforcement learning problem more generally) is the set of information available in the environment that can be used to make decisions.

2.3.2   States, actions, rewards

Before we move on, let's consolidate some of the terms and concepts we've introduced so far. Reinforcement learning algorithms attempt to model the world in a way that computers can understand and calculate. In particular, RL algorithms model the world as if it merely involved a set of *states, S* (state space), which are a set of features about the environment, a set of *actions, A* (action space), that can be taken in a given state, and *rewards, r,* that are given for taking an action in a specific state. When we speak of taking a particular action in a particular state, we often call it a *state-action pair* (*s, a*).

NOTE   The objective of any RL algorithm is to maximize the rewards over the course of an entire episode.

Since our original *n*-armed bandit problem did not have a state space, only an action space, we just needed to learn the relationship between actions and rewards. We learned the relationship by using a lookup table to store our experience of receiving rewards for particular actions. We stored action-reward pairs (a_k, r_k) where the reward at play k was an average over all past plays associated with taking action a_k.

In our *n*-armed bandit problem, we only had 10 actions, so a lookup table of 10 rows was very reasonable. But when we introduce a state space with contextual bandits, we start to get a combinatorial explosion of possible state-action-reward tuples. For example, if we have a state space of 100 states, and each state is associated with 10 actions, we have 1,000 different pieces of data we need to store and recompute. In most of the problems we'll consider in this book, the state space is intractably large, so a simple lookup table is not feasible.

That's where deep learning comes in. When they're properly trained, neural networks are great at learning abstractions that get rid of the details of little value. They can learn composable patterns and regularities in data such that they can effectively compress a large amount of data while retaining the important information. Hence, neural networks can be used to learn complex relationships between state-action pairs and rewards without us having to store all such experiences as raw memories. We often call the part of an RL algorithm that makes the decisions based on some information the *agent*. In order to solve the contextual bandit we've been discussing, we'll employ a neural network as our agent.

First, though, we will take a moment to introduce PyTorch, the deep learning framework we will be using throughout this book to build neural networks.

2.4   *Building networks with PyTorch*

There are many deep learning frameworks available today, with TensorFlow, MXNet, and PyTorch probably being the most popular. We chose to use PyTorch for this book because of its simplicity. It allows you to write native-looking Python code and still get all the goodies of a good framework like automatic differentiation and built-in optimization. We'll give you a quick introduction to PyTorch here, but we'll explain more as we go along. If you need to brush up on basic deep learning, see the appendix where we have a fairly detailed review of deep learning and more thorough coverage of PyTorch.

If you're comfortable with the numpy multidimensional array, you can replace almost everything you do with numpy with PyTorch. For example, here we instantiate a 2×3 matrix in numpy:

```
>>> import numpy

>>> numpy.array([[1, 2, 3], [4, 5, 6]])
array([[1, 2, 3],
       [4, 5, 6]])
```

And here is how you instantiate the same matrix with PyTorch:

```
>>> import torch

>>> torch.Tensor([[1, 2, 3], [4, 5, 6]])
1  2  3
4  5  6
[torch.FloatTensor of size 2x3]
```

The PyTorch code is basically the same as the numpy version, except in PyTorch we call multidimensional arrays *tensors*. Unsurprisingly, this is also the term used in TensorFlow and other frameworks, so get used to seeing multidimensional arrays referred to as tensors. We can and do refer to the *tensor order*, which is basically how many indexed dimensions the tensor has. This gets a little confusing because sometimes we speak of the dimension of a vector, in which case we're referring to the length of the vector. But when we speak of the order of a tensor, we mean how many indices it has. A vector has one index, meaning every element can be "addressed" by a single index value, so it's an order 1 tensor or 1-tensor for short. A matrix has two indices, one for each dimension, so it's a 2-tensor. Higher order tensors can be referred to as a k-tensor, where k is the order, a non-negative integer. On the other end, a single number is a 0-tensor, also called a *scalar*, since it has no indices.

2.4.1   *Automatic differentiation*

The most important features of PyTorch that we need and that numpy doesn't offer are automatic differentiation and optimization. Let's say we want to set up a simple linear model to predict some data of interest. We can easily define the model using ordinary numpy-like syntax:

```
>>> x = torch.Tensor([2,4]) #input data
>>> m = torch.randn(2, requires_grad=True) #parameter 1
>>> b = torch.randn(1, requires_grad=True) #parameter 2
>>> y = m*x+b #linear model
>>> loss = (torch.sum(y_known - y))**2 #loss function
>>> loss.backward() #calculate gradients
>>> m.grad
tensor([  0.7734, -90.4993])
```

You simply supply the `requires_grad=True` argument to PyTorch tensors that you want to compute gradients for, and then call the `backward()` method on the last node in your computational graph, which will backpropagate gradients through all the nodes with `requires_grad=True`. You can then do gradient descent with the automatically computed gradients.

2.4.2 Building Models

For most of this book, we won't bother dealing directly with automatically computed gradients. Instead we'll use PyTorch's nn module to easily set up a feedforward neural network model and then use the built-in optimization algorithms to automatically train the neural network without having to manually specify the mechanics of back-propagation and gradient descent. Here's a simple two-layer neural network with an optimizer set up:

```
model = torch.nn.Sequential(
    torch.nn.Linear(10, 150),
    torch.nn.ReLU(),
    torch.nn.Linear(150, 4),
    torch.nn.ReLU(),
)

loss_fn = torch.nn.MSELoss()
optimizer = torch.optim.Adam(model.parameters(), lr=0.01)
```

We've set up a two-layer model with `ReLU` (rectified linear units) activation functions, defined a mean-squared error loss function, and set up an optimizer. All we have to do to train this model, given that we have some labeled training data, is start a training loop:

```
for step in range(100):
    y_pred = model(x)
    loss = loss_fn(y_pred, y_correct)
        optimizer.zero_grad()
        loss.backward()
        optimizer.step()
```

The x variable is the input data to the model. The y_correct variable is a tensor representing the labeled, correct output. We make the prediction using the model, calculate the loss, and then compute the gradients using the `backward()` method on the last node in the computational graph (which is almost always the `loss` function).

Then we just run the `step()` method on the optimizer, and it will run a single step of gradient descent. If we need to build more complex neural network architectures than the sequential model, we can write our own Python class, inhereit from PyTorch's module class, and use that instead:

```python
from torch.nn import Module, Linear

class MyNet(Module):
    def __init__(self):
        super(MyNet, self).__init__()
        self.fc1 = Linear(784, 50)
        self.fc2 = Linear(50, 10)

    def forward(self, x):
        x = F.relu(self.fc1(x))
        x = F.relu(self.fc2(x))
        return x

model = MyNet()
```

That's all you need to know about PyTorch for now to be productive with it. We will discuss a few other bells and whistles as we progress through the book.

2.5   *Solving contextual bandits*

We've built a simulated environment for a contextual bandit. The simulator includes the state (a number from 0 to 9 representing 1 of the 10 websites in the network), reward generation (ad clicks), and a method that chooses an action (which of 10 ads to serve). The following listing shows the code for the contextual bandit environment, but don't spend much time thinking about it as we want to demonstrate how to use it, not how to code it.

Listing 2.9   **Contextual bandit environment**

```python
class ContextBandit:
    def __init__(self, arms=10):
        self.arms = arms
        self.init_distribution(arms)
        self.update_state()

    def init_distribution(self, arms):
        self.bandit_matrix = np.random.rand(arms,arms)

    def reward(self, prob):
        reward = 0
        for i in range(self.arms):
            if random.random() < prob:
                reward += 1
        return reward

    def get_state(self):
        return self.state
```

Number of states = number of arms, to keep things simple. Each row represents a state and each column an arm.

```
def update_state(self):
    self.state = np.random.randint(0,self.arms)

def get_reward(self,arm):
    return self.reward(self.bandit_matrix[self.get_state()][arm])

def choose_arm(self, arm):
    reward = self.get_reward(arm)
    self.update_state()
    return reward
```

◁─┐ **Choosing an arm
returns a reward and
updates the state.**

The following code snippet demonstrates how to use the environment. The only part we need to build is the agent, which is generally the crux of any RL problem, since building an environment usually just involves setting up input/output with some data source or plugging into an existing API.

```
env = ContextBandit(arms=10)
state = env.get_state()
reward = env.choose_arm(1)
print(state)
>>> 2
print(reward)
>>> 8
```

The simulator consists of a simple Python class called ContextBandit that can be initialized to a specific number of arms. For simplicity, the number of states equals the number of arms, but in general the state space is often much larger than the action space. The class has two methods: One is get_state(), which is called with no arguments and will return a state sampled randomly from a uniform distribution. In most problems your state will come from a much more complex distribution. Calling the other method, choose_arm(...), will simulate placing an advertisement, and it returns a reward (e.g., proportional to the number of ad clicks). We need to always call get_state and then choose_arm, in that order, to continually get new data to learn from.

The ContextBandit module also includes a few helper functions, such as the softmax function and a *one-hot encoder.* A one-hot encoded vector is a vector where all but 1 element is set to 0. The only nonzero element is set to 1 and indicates a particular state in the state space.

Rather than using a single static reward probability distribution over n actions, like our original bandit problem, the contextual bandit simulator sets up a different reward distribution over the actions for each state. That is, we will have n different softmax reward distributions over actions for each of n states. Hence, we need to learn the relationship between the states and their respective reward distributions, and then learn which action has the highest probability for a given state.

As with all of our projects in this book, we'll be using PyTorch to build the neural network. In this case, we're going to build a two-layer feedforward neural network that uses rectified linear units (ReLU) as the activation function. The first layer accepts a

10-element one-hot (also known as 1-of-K, where all elements but one are 0) encoded vector of the state, and the final layer returns a 10-element vector representing the predicted reward for each action given the state.

Figure 2.6 shows the forward pass of the algorithm we've described. Unlike the lookup table approach, our neural network agent will learn to predict the rewards that each action will result in for a given state. Then we use the softmax function to give us a probability distribution over the actions and sample from this distribution to choose an arm (advertisement). Choosing an arm will give us a reward, which we will use to train our neural network.

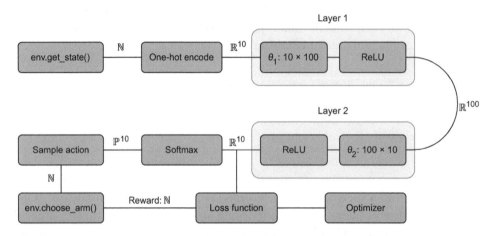

Figure 2.6   A computational graph for a simple 10-armed contextual bandit. The `get_state()` function returns a state value, which is transformed into a one-hot vector that becomes the input data for a two-layer neural network. The output of the neural network is the predicted reward for each possible action, which is a dense vector that is run through a softmax to sample an action from the resulting probability distribution over the actions. The chosen action will return a reward and updates the state of the environment. θ_1 and θ_2 represent the weight parameters for each layer. The $\mathbb{N}$, $\mathbb{R}$, and $\mathbb{P}$ symbols denote the natural numbers (0, 1, 2, 3, ...), the real numbers (a floating-point number, for our purposes), and a probability, respectively. The superscript indicates the length of the vector, so $\mathbb{P}^{10}$ represents a 10-element vector where each element is a probability (such that all the elements sum to 1).

Initially our neural network will produce a random vector such as `[1.4, 50, 4.3, 0.31, 0.43, 11, 121, 90, 8.9, 1.1]` when in state 0. We will run softmax over this vector and sample an action, most likely action 6 (from actions 0 through 9), since that is the biggest number in the example vector. Choosing action 6 will generate a reward of say 8. Then we train our neural network to produce the vector `[1.4, 50, 4.3, 0.31, 0.43, 11, 8, 90, 8.9, 1.1]`, since that is the true reward we received for action 6, leaving the rest of the values unchanged. The next time when the neural network sees state 0, it will produce a reward prediction for action 6 closer to 8. As we continually do this over many states and actions, the neural network will eventually learn to predict accurate rewards for each action given a state. Thus, our algorithm will be able to choose the best action each time, maximizing our rewards.

The following code imports the necessary libraries and sets up some *hyperparameters* (parameters to specify model structure):

```
import numpy as np
import torch

arms = 10
N, D_in, H, D_out = 1, arms, 100, arms
```

In the preceding code, `N` is the batch size, `D_in` is the input dimension, `H` is the hidden dimension, and `D_out` is the output dimension.

Now we need to set up our neural network model. It is a simple sequential (feed-forward) neural network with two layers as we described earlier.

```
model = torch.nn.Sequential(
    torch.nn.Linear(D_in, H),
    torch.nn.ReLU(),
    torch.nn.Linear(H, D_out),
    torch.nn.ReLU(),
)
```

We'll use the mean squared error loss function here, but others could work too.

```
loss_fn = torch.nn.MSELoss()
```

Now we set up a new environment by instantiating the `ContextBandit` class, supplying the number of arms to its constructor. Remember, we've set up the environment such that the number of arms will be equal to the number of states.

```
env = ContextBandit(arms)
```

The main `for` loop of the algorithm will be very similar to our original *n*-armed bandit algorithm, but we have added the step of running a neural network and using the output to select an action. We'll define a function called `train` (shown in listing 2.10) that accepts the environment instance we created previously, the number of epochs we want to train for, and the learning rate.

In the function, we'll set a PyTorch variable for the current state, which we'll need to one-hot encode using the `one_hot(...)` encoding function:

```
def one_hot(N, pos, val=1):
    one_hot_vec = np.zeros(N)
    one_hot_vec[pos] = val
    return one_hot_vec
```

Once we enter the main training `for` loop, we'll run our neural network model with the randomly initialized current state vector. It will return a vector that represents its guess for the values of each of the possible actions. At first, the model will output a bunch of random values since it is not trained.

We'll run the softmax function over the model's output to generate a probability distribution over the actions. We'll then select an action using the environment's choose_arm(...) function, which will return the reward generated for taking that action; it will also update the environment's current state. We'll turn the reward (which is a non-negative integer) into a one-hot vector that we can use as our training data. We'll then run one step of backpropagation with this reward vector, given the state we gave the model. Since we're using a neural network model as our action-value function, we no longer have any sort of action-value array storing "memories;" everything is being encoded in the neural network's weight parameters. The whole train function is shown in the following listing.

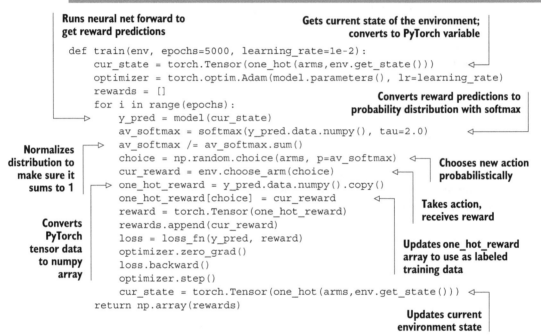

Listing 2.10 The main training loop

Runs neural net forward to get reward predictions

Gets current state of the environment; converts to PyTorch variable

Converts reward predictions to probability distribution with softmax

Normalizes distribution to make sure it sums to 1

Chooses new action probabilistically

Converts PyTorch tensor data to numpy array

Takes action, receives reward

Updates one_hot_reward array to use as labeled training data

Updates current environment state

```
def train(env, epochs=5000, learning_rate=1e-2):
    cur_state = torch.Tensor(one_hot(arms,env.get_state()))
    optimizer = torch.optim.Adam(model.parameters(), lr=learning_rate)
    rewards = []
    for i in range(epochs):
        y_pred = model(cur_state)
        av_softmax = softmax(y_pred.data.numpy(), tau=2.0)
        av_softmax /= av_softmax.sum()
        choice = np.random.choice(arms, p=av_softmax)
        cur_reward = env.choose_arm(choice)
        one_hot_reward = y_pred.data.numpy().copy()
        one_hot_reward[choice] = cur_reward
        reward = torch.Tensor(one_hot_reward)
        rewards.append(cur_reward)
        loss = loss_fn(y_pred, reward)
        optimizer.zero_grad()
        loss.backward()
        optimizer.step()
        cur_state = torch.Tensor(one_hot(arms,env.get_state()))
    return np.array(rewards)
```

Go ahead and run this function. When we train this network for 5,000 epochs, we can plot the moving average of rewards earned over the training time (see figure 2.7; we omitted the code to produce such a graph). Our neural network indeed learns a fairly good understanding of the relationship between states, actions and rewards for this contextual bandit. The maximum reward payout for any play is 10, and our average is topping off around 8.5, which is close to the mathematical optimum for this particular bandit. Our first deep reinforcement learning algorithm works! Okay, it's not a very deep network, but still!

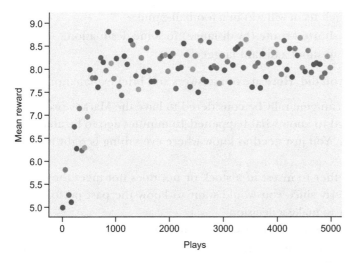

Figure 2.7 A training graph showing the average rewards for playing the contextual bandit simulator using a two-layer neural network as the action-value function. We can see the average reward rapidly increases during training time, demonstrating our neural network is successfully learning.

2.6 *The Markov property*

In our contextual bandit problem, our neural network led us to choose the best action given a state without reference to any other prior states. We just gave it the current state, and it produced the expected rewards for each possible action. This is an important property in reinforcement learning called the *Markov property*. A game (or any other control task) that exhibits the Markov property is said to be a *Markov decision process* (MDP). With an MDP, the current state alone contains enough information to choose optimal actions to maximize future rewards. Modeling a control task as an MDP is a key concept in reinforcement learning.

The MDP model simplifies an RL problem dramatically, as we do not need to take into account all previous states or actions—we don't need to have memory, we just need to analyze the present situation. Hence, we always attempt to model a problem as (at least approximately) a Markov decision processes. The card game Blackjack (also known as 21) is an MDP because we can play the game successfully just by knowing our current state (what cards we have, and the dealer's one face-up card).

To test your understanding of the Markov property, consider each control problem or decision task in the following list and see if it has the Markov property or not:

- Driving a car
- Deciding whether to invest in a stock or not
- Choosing a medical treatment for a patient
- Diagnosing a patient's illness

- Predicting which team will win in a football game
- Choosing the shortest route (by distance) to some destination
- Aiming a gun to shoot a distant target

Okay, let's see how you did. Here are our answers and brief explanations:

- Driving a car can generally be considered to have the Markov property because you don't need to know what happened 10 minutes ago to be able to optimally drive your car. You just need to know where everything is right now and where you want to go.
- Deciding whether to invest in a stock or not does not meet the criteria of the Markov property since you would want to know the past performance of the stock in order to make a decision.
- Choosing a medical treatment seems to have the Markov property because you don't need to know the biography of a person to choose a good treatment for what ails them right now.
- In contrast, *diagnosing* (rather than treating) would definitely require knowledge of past states. It is often very important to know the historical course of a patient's symptoms in order to make a diagnosis.
- Predicting which football team will win does not have the Markov property, since, like the stock example, you need to know the past performance of the football teams to make a good prediction.
- Choosing the shortest route to a destination has the Markov property because you just need to know the distance to the destination for various routes, which doesn't depend on what happened yesterday.
- Aiming a gun to shoot a distant target also has the Markov property since all you need to know is where the target is, and perhaps current conditions like wind velocity and the particulars of your gun. You don't need to know the wind velocity of yesterday.

We hope you can appreciate that for some of those examples you could make arguments for or against it having the Markov property. For example, in diagnosing a patient, you may need to know the recent history of their symptoms, but if that is documented in their medical record and we consider the full medical record as our current state, then we've effectively induced the Markov property. This is an important thing to keep in mind: many problems may not *naturally* have the Markov property, but often we can induce it by jamming more information into the state.

DeepMind's deep Q-learning (or deep Q-network) algorithm learned to play Atari games from just raw pixel data and the current score. Do Atari games have the Markov property? Not exactly. In the game Pacman, if our state is the raw pixel data from our current frame, we have no idea if the enemy a few tiles away is approaching us or moving away from us, and that would strongly influence our choice of actions to take. This is why DeepMind's implementation actually feeds in the last four frames of gameplay, effectively changing a non-MDP into an MDP. With the last four frames, the agent has access to the direction and speed of all players.

Figure 2.8 gives a lighthearted example of a Markov decision process using all the concepts we've discussed so far. You can see there is a three-element state space S = {crying baby, sleeping baby, smiling baby}, and a two-element action space A = {feed, don't feed}. In addition, we have transition probabilities noted, which are maps from an action to the probability of an outcome state (we'll go over this again in the next section). Of course, in real life, you as the *agent* have no idea what the transition probabilities are. If you did, you would have a *model* of the environment. As you'll learn later, sometimes an agent does have access to a model of the environment, and sometimes not. In the cases where the agent does not have access to the model, we may want our agent to learn a model of the environment (which may just approximate the true, underlying model).

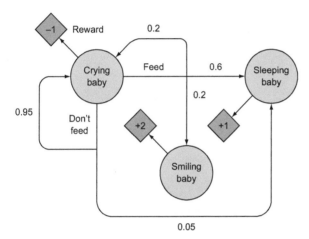

Figure 2.8 A simplified MDP diagram with three states and two actions. Here we model the parenting decision process for taking care of an infant. If the baby is crying, we can either administer food or not, and with some probability the baby will transition into a new state, and we'll receive a reward of -1, +1, or +2 (based on the baby's satisfaction).

2.7 *Predicting future rewards: Value and policy functions*

Believe it or not, we actually smuggled a lot of knowledge into the previous sections. The way we set up our solutions to the *n*-armed bandit and contextual bandit are standard reinforcement learning methods, and as such, there is a whole bunch of established terminology and mathematics behind what we did. We introduced a few terms already, such as state and action spaces, but we mostly just described things in natural language. In order for you to understand the latest RL research papers and for us to make future chapters less verbose, it's important to become acquainted with the jargon and the mathematics.

Let's review and formalize what you've learned so far (summarized in figure 2.9). A reinforcement learning algorithm essentially constructs an *agent,* which acts in some *environment.* The environment is often a game, but is more generally whatever process produces states, actions, and rewards. The agent has access to the current state of the environment, which is all the data about the environment at a particular time point, $s_t \in S$. Using this state information, the agent takes an action, $a_t \in A$, which may deterministically or probabilistically change the environment to be in a new state, s_{t+1}.

The probability associated with mapping a state to a new state by taking an action is called the *transition probability*. The agent receives a reward, r_t, for having taken action a_t in state s_t leading to a new state, s_{t+1}. And we know that the ultimate goal of the agent (our reinforcement learning algorithm) is to maximize its rewards. It's really the state transition, $s_t \rightarrow s_{t+1}$, that produces the reward, not the action per se, since the action may probabilistically lead to a bad state. If you're in an action movie (no pun intended) and you jump off a roof onto another roof, you may land gracefully on the other roof or miss it completely and fall—your peril is what's important (the two possible resulting states), not the fact that you jumped (the action).

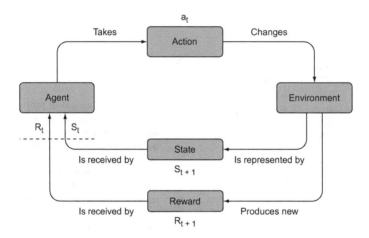

Figure 2.9 **The general process of a reinforcement learning algorithm. The environment produces states and rewards. The agent takes an action, a_t, given a state, s_t, at time t and receives a reward, r_t. The agent's goal is to maximize rewards by learning to take the best actions in a given state.**

2.7.1   *Policy functions*

How exactly do we use our current state information to decide what action to take? This is where the key concepts of *value functions* and *policy functions* come into play, which we already have a bit of experience with. Let's first tackle policies.

In words, a policy, π, is the strategy of an agent in some environment. For example, the strategy of the dealer in Blackjack is to always hit until they reach a card value of 17 or greater. It's a simple fixed strategy. In our *n*-armed bandit problem, our policy was an epsilon-greedy strategy. In general, a policy is a function that maps a state to a probability distribution over the set of possible actions in that state.

Table 2.5 The policy function

Math	English
$\pi, s \rightarrow Pr(A\,|\,s)$, where $s \in S$	A policy, π, is a mapping from states to the (probabilistically) best actions for those states.

In the mathematical notation, s is a state and $Pr(A\,|\,s)$ is a probability distribution over the set of actions A, given state s. The probability of each action in the distribution is the probability that the action will produce the greatest reward.

2.7.2 *Optimal policy*

The policy is the part of our reinforcement learning algorithm that chooses actions given its current state. We can then formulate the *optimal policy*—it's the strategy that maximizes rewards.

Table 2.6 The optimal policy

Math	English
$\pi* = \text{argmax } E(R\,|\,\pi)$,	If we know the expected rewards for following any possible policy, π, the optimal policy, $\pi*$, is a policy that, when followed, produces the maximum possible rewards.

Remember, a particular policy is a map or function, so we have some sort of set of possible policies; the optimal policy is just an `argmax` (which selects the maximum) over this set of possible policies as a function of their expected rewards.

Again, the whole goal of a reinforcement learning algorithm (our agent) is to choose the actions that lead to the maximal expected rewards. But there are two ways we can train our agent to do this:

- *Directly*—We can teach the agent to learn what actions are best, given what state it is in.
- *Indirectly*—We can teach the agent to learn which states are most valuable, and then to take actions that lead to the most valuable states.

This indirect method leads us to the idea of value functions.

2.7.3 *Value functions*

Value functions are functions that map a state or a state-action pair to the *expected value* (the expected reward) of being in some state or taking some action in some state. You may recall from statistics that the expected reward is just the long-term average of rewards received after being in some state or taking some action. When we speak of *the* value function, we usually mean a state-value function.

Table 2.7 The state-value function

Math	English
$V_\pi : s \rightarrow E(R\|s,\pi)$,	A value function, V_π, is a function that maps a state, s, to the expected rewards, given that we start in state s and follow some policy, π.

This is a function that accepts a state, *s*, and returns the expected reward of starting in that state and taking actions according to our policy, π. It may not be immediately obvious why the value function depends on the policy. Consider that in our contextual bandit problem, if our policy was to choose entirely random actions (i.e., sample actions from a uniform distribution), the value (expected reward) of a state would probably be pretty low, since we're definitely not choosing the best possible actions. Instead, we want to use a policy that is not a uniform distribution over the actions, but is the probability distribution that would produce the maximum rewards when sampled. That is, the policy is what determines observed rewards, and the value function is a reflection of observed rewards.

In our first *n*-armed bandit problem, you were introduced to state-action-value functions. These functions often go by the name *Q function* or *Q value*, which is where deep Q-learning comes from, since, as you'll see in the next chapter, deep learning algorithms can be used as Q functions.

Table 2.8 The action-value (Q) function

Math	English
$Q_\pi : (s\|a) \rightarrow E(R\|a,s,\pi)$,	Q_π is a function that maps a pair, (s, a), of a state, s, and an action, a, to the expected reward of taking action *a* in state s, given that we're using the policy (or "strategy") π.

In fact, we sort of implemented a deep Q-network to solve our contextual bandit problem (although it was a pretty shallow neural network), since it was essentially acting as a Q function. We trained it to produce accurate estimates of the expected reward for taking an action given a state. Our policy function was the softmax function over the output of the neural network.

We've covered many of the foundational concepts in reinforcement learning just by using *n*-armed and contextual bandits as examples. We also got our feet wet with deep reinforcement learning in this chapter. In the next chapter we'll implement a full-blown deep Q-network similar to the algorithm that DeepMind used to play Atari games at superhuman levels. It will be a natural extension of what we've covered here.

Summary

- State spaces are the set of all possible states a system can be in. In Chess, this would be the set of all valid board configurations. An action is a function that maps a state, s, to a new state, s'. An action may be stochastic, such that it maps a state, s, probabilistically to a new state, s'. There may be some probability distribution over the set of possible new states from which one is selected. The action-space is the set of all possible actions for a particular state.

- The environment is the source of states, actions, and rewards. If we're building an RL algorithm to play a game, then the game is the environment. A model of an environment is an approximation of the state space, action space, and transition probabilities.

- Rewards are signals produced by the environment that indicate the relative success of taking an action in a given state. An expected reward is a statistical concept that informally refers to the long-term average value of some random variable X (in our case, the reward), denoted $E[X]$. For example, in the n-armed bandit case, $E[R|a]$ (the expected reward given action a) is the long-term average reward of taking each of the n-actions. If we knew the probability distribution over the actions, a, then we could calculate the precise value of the expected reward for a game of N plays as $E[R|a_i] = \Sigma_{i=1}^{N} a_i p_i \cdot r$, where N is the number of plays of the game, p_i refers to the probability of action a_i, and r refers to the maximum possible reward.

- An agent is an RL algorithm that learns to behave optimally in a given environment. Agents are often implemented as a deep neural network. The goal of the agent is to maximize expected rewards, or equivalently, to navigate to the highest value state.

- A policy is a particular strategy. Formally, it's a function that either accepts a state and produces an action to take or produces a probability distribution over the action space, given the state. A common policy is the epsilon-greedy strategy, where with probability ε we take a random action in the action space, and with probability $\varepsilon - 1$ we choose the best action we know of so far.

- In general, a value function is any function that returns expected rewards given some relevant data. Without additional context, it typically refers to a state-value function, which is a function that accepts a state and returns the expected reward of starting in that state and acting according to some policy. The Q value is the expected reward given a state-action pair, and the Q function is a function that produces Q values when given a state-action pair.

- The Markov decision process is a decision-making process by which it is possible to make the best decisions without reference to a history of prior states.

Predicting the best states and actions: Deep Q-networks

This chapter covers

- Implementing the Q function as a neural network
- Building a deep Q-network using PyTorch to play Gridworld
- Counteracting catastrophic forgetting with experience replay
- Improving learning stability with target networks

In this chapter we'll start off where the deep reinforcement learning revolution began: DeepMind's deep Q-networks, which learned to play Atari games. We won't be using Atari games as our testbed quite yet, but we will be building virtually the same system DeepMind did. We'll use a simple console-based game called Gridworld as our game environment.

Gridworld is actually a family of similar games, but they all generally involve a grid board with a player (or agent), an objective tile (the "goal"), and possibly one or more special tiles that may be barriers or may grant negative or positive rewards. The player can move up, down, left, or right, and the point of the game is to get the player to the goal tile where the player will receive a positive reward. The player must not only reach the goal tile but must do so following the shortest path, and they may need to navigate through various obstacles.

3.1 The Q function

We will use a very simple Gridworld engine that's included in the GitHub repository for this book. You can download it at http://mng.bz/JzKp in the Chapter 3 folder.

The Gridworld game depicted in figure 3.1 shows the simple version of Gridworld we'll start with; we'll progressively tackle more difficult variants of the game. Our initial goal is to train a DRL agent to navigate the Gridworld board to the goal, following the most efficient route every time. But before we get too far into that, let's review the key terms and concepts from the previous chapter, which we will continue to use here.

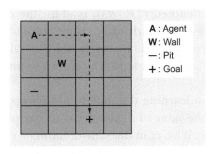

A : Agent
W : Wall
— : Pit
+ : Goal

Figure 3.1 This is a simple Gridworld game setup. The agent (A) must navigate along the shortest path to the goal tile (+) and avoid falling into the pit (–).

The *state* is the information that our agent receives and uses to make a decision about what action to take. It could be the raw pixels of a video game, sensor data from an autonomous vehicle, or, in the case of Gridworld, a tensor representing the positions of all the objects on the grid.

The *policy*, denoted π, is the strategy our agent follows when provided a state. For example, a policy in Blackjack might be to look at our hand (the state) and hit or stay randomly. Although this would be a terrible policy, the important point to stress is that the policy confers which actions we take. A better policy would be to always hit until we have 19.

The *reward* is the feedback our agent gets after taking an action, leading us to a new state. For a game of chess, we could reward our agent +1 when it performs an action that leads to a checkmate of the other player and –1 for an action that leads our agent to be checkmated. Every other state could be rewarded 0, since we do not know if the agent is winning or not.

Our agent makes a series of actions based upon its policy π, and repeats this process until the episode ends, thereby we get a succession of states, actions and the resulting rewards.

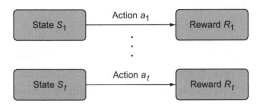

We call the weighted sum of the rewards while following a policy from the starting state S_1 the *value* of that state, or a state value. We can denote this by the *value function* $V_\pi(s)$, which accepts an initial state and returns the expected total reward.

$$V_\pi(s) = \sum_{i=1}^{t} w_i R_i = w_1 R_1 + w_2 R_2 + \ldots + w_t R_t$$

The coefficients w_1, w_2, etc., are the weights we apply to the rewards before summing them. For example, we often want to weight more recent rewards greater than distant future rewards. This weighted sum is an expected value, a common statistic in many quantitative fields, and it's often concisely denoted $E[R \mid \pi,s]$, read as "the expected rewards given a policy π and a starting state s." Similarly, there is an *action-value function*, $Q_\pi(s,a)$, that accepts a state S and an action A and returns the value of taking that action given that state; in other words, $E[R \mid \pi,s,a]$. Some RL algorithms or implementations will use one or the other.

Importantly, if we base our algorithm on learning the state values (as opposed to action values), we must keep in mind that the value of a state depends completely on our policy, π. Using Blackjack as an example, if we're in the state of having a card total of 20, and we have two possible actions, hit or stay, the value of this state is only high if our policy says to stay when we have 20. If our policy said to hit when we have 20, we would probably bust and lose the game, so the value of that state would be low. In other words, the value of a state is equivalent to the value of the highest action taken in that state.

3.2   *Navigating with Q-learning*

In 2013, DeepMind published a paper entitled "Playing Atari with Deep Reinforcement Learning" that outlined their new approach to an old algorithm, which gave them enough performance to play six of seven Atari 2600 games at record levels. Crucially, the algorithm they used only relied on analyzing the raw pixel data from the games, just like a human would. This paper really set off the field of deep reinforcement learning.

The old algorithm they modified is called *Q-learning*, and it has been around for decades. Why did it take so long to make such significant progress? A large part is due to the general boost that artificial neural networks (deep learning) got a few years prior with the use of GPUs that allowed the training of much larger networks. But a significant amount is due to the specific novel features DeepMind implemented to address some of the other issues that reinforcement learning algorithms struggled with. We'll be covering it all in this chapter.

3.2.1   *What is Q-learning?*

What is Q-learning, you ask? If you guessed it has something to do with the action-value function $Q_\pi(s,a)$ that we previously described, you are right, but that's only a small part of the story. Q-learning is a particular method of learning optimal action values, but there are other methods. That is to say, value functions and action-value functions are general concepts in RL that appear in many places; Q-learning is a particular algorithm that uses those concepts.

Believe it or not, we sort of implemented a Q-learning algorithm in the last chapter when we built a neural network to optimize the ad placement problem. The main idea of Q-learning is that your algorithm predicts the value of a state-action pair, and then you compare this prediction to the observed accumulated rewards at some later time and update the parameters of your algorithm, so that next time it will make better predictions. That's essentially what we did in the last chapter when our neural network predicted the expected reward (value) of each action given a state, observed the actual reward, and updated the network accordingly. That was a particular and simple implementation of a broader class of Q-learning algorithms that is described by the following update rule:

Table 3.1 Q-learning update rule

Math

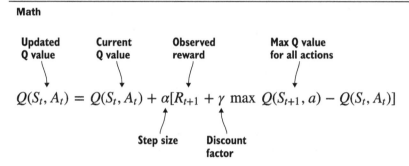

$$Q(S_t, A_t) = Q(S_t, A_t) + \alpha[R_{t+1} + \gamma \max_a Q(S_{t+1}, a) - Q(S_t, A_t)]$$

Pseudocode

```
def get_updated_q_value(old_q_value, reward, state, step_size, discount):
    term2 = (reward + discount * max([Q(state, action) for action in
        actions]))
    term2 = term2 - old_q_value
    term2 = step_size * term2
    return (old_q_value + term2)
```

English

The Q value at time *t* is updated to be the current predicted Q value plus the amount of value we expect in the future, given that we play optimally from our current state.

3.2.2 Tackling Gridworld

You've now seen the formula for Q-learning. Let's take a step back and apply this formula to our Gridworld problem. Our goal in this chapter is to train a neural network to play a simple Gridworld game from scratch. All the agent will have access to is what the board looks like, just as a human player would; the algorithm has no informational advantage. Moreover, we're starting with an untrained algorithm, so it literally knows nothing at all about the world. It has no prior information about how games work. The only thing we'll provide is the reward for reaching the goal. The fact that we will be able to teach the algorithm to learn to play, starting from nothing, is actually quite impressive.

Unlike us humans who live in what appears to be a continuous flow of time, the algorithm lives in a discrete world, so something needs to happen at each discrete time step. At time step 1 the algorithm will "look" at the game board and make a decision about what action to take. Then the game board will be updated, and so on.

Let's sketch out the details of this process now. Here's the sequence of events for a game of Gridworld.

1   We start the game in some state that we'll call S_t. The state includes all the information about the game that we have. For our Gridworld example, the game state is represented as a $4 \times 4 \times 4$ tensor. We will go into more detail about the specifics of the board when we implement the algorithm.

2   We feed the S_t data and a candidate action into a deep neural network (or some other fancy machine-learning algorithm) and it produces a prediction of how valuable taking that action in that state is (see figure 3.2).

Figure 3.2   The Q function could be any function that accepts a state and action and returns the value (expected rewards) of taking that action given that state.

Remember, the algorithm is not predicting the reward we will get after taking a particular action; it's predicting the expected value (the expected rewards), which is the long-term average reward we will get from taking an action in a state and then continuing to behave according to our policy π. We do this for several (perhaps all) possible actions we could take in this state.

3   We take an action, perhaps because our neural network predicted it is the highest value action or perhaps we take a random action. We'll label the action A_t. We are now in a new state of the game, which we'll call S_{t+1}, and we receive or observe a reward, labelled R_{t+1}. We want to update our learning algorithm to reflect the actual reward we received, after taking the action it predicted was the best. Perhaps we got a negative reward or a really big reward, and we want to improve the accuracy of the algorithm's predictions (see figure 3.3).

4   Now we run the algorithm using S_{t+1} as input and figure out which action our algorithm predicts has the highest value. We'll call this value $Q(S_{t+1},a)$. To be clear, this is a single value that reflects the highest predicted Q value, given our new state and all possible actions.

5 Now we have all the pieces we need to update the algorithm's parameters. We'll perform one iteration of training using some loss function, such as mean-squared error, to minimize the difference between the predicted value from our algorithm and the target prediction of $Q(S_t,A_t) + \alpha*[R_{t+1} + \gamma*\max Q(S_{t+1},A) - Q(S_t,A_t)]$.

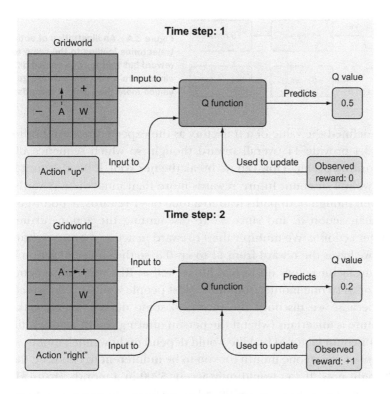

Figure 3.3 Schematic of Q-learning with Gridworld. The Q function accepts a state and an action, and returns the predicted reward (value) of that state-action pair. After taking the action, we observe the reward, and using the update formula, we use this observation to update the Q function so it makes better predictions.

3.2.3 *Hyperparameters*

The parameters γ and α are called *hyperparameters* because they're parameters that influence how the algorithm learns but they're not involved in the actual learning. The parameter α is the *learning rate* and it's the same hyperparameter used to train many machine-learning algorithms. It controls how quickly we want the algorithm to learn from each move: a small value means it will only make small updates at each step, whereas a large value means the algorithm will potentially make large updates.

3.2.4 *Discount factor*

The parameter γ, the *discount factor*, is a variable between 0 and 1 that controls how much our agent discounts future rewards when making a decision. Let's take a simple example. Our agent has a decision between picking an action that leads to 0 reward then +1 reward, or an action that leads to +1 and then 0 reward (see figure 3.4).

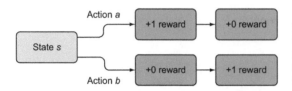

Figure 3.4 **An illustration of action trajectories leading to the same total reward but that may be valued differently since more recent rewards are generally valued more than distant rewards.**

Previously, we defined the value of a trajectory as the expected reward. Both trajectories in figure 3.4 provide +1 overall reward though, so which sequence of actions should the algorithm prefer? How can we break the tie? Well, if the discount factor, γ, is less than 1, we will discount future rewards more than immediate rewards. In this simple case, even though both paths lead to a total of +1 rewards, action *b* gets the +1 reward later than action *a*, and since we're discounting the action further in the future, we prefer action *a*. We multiply the +1 reward in action *b* by a weighting factor less than 1, so we lower the reward from +1 to say 0.8, so the choice of action is clear.

The discount factor comes up in real life as well as RL. Suppose someone offers you $100 now or $110 one month from now. Most people would prefer to receive the money now, because we discount the future to some degree, which makes sense because the future is uncertain (what if the person offering you the money dies in two weeks?). Your discount factor in real life would depend on how much money someone would have to offer you in one month for you to be indifferent to choosing that versus getting $100 right now. If you would only accept $200 in a month versus $100 right now, your discount factor would be $100/$200 = 0.5 (per month). This would mean that someone would have to offer you $400 in two months for you to choose that option over getting $100 now, since we'd discount 0.5 for 1 month, and 0.5 again for the next month, which is $0.5 \times 0.5 = 0.25$, and $100 = 0.25x$, so $x = 400$. Perhaps you might see the pattern that discounting is exponential in time. The value of something at time t with a discount factor of $\gamma:[0,1)$ is γ^t.

The discount factor needs to be between 0 and 1, and we shouldn't set it exactly equal to 1, because if we don't discount at all, we would have to consider the future rewards infinitely far into the future, which is impossible in practice. Even if we discount at 0.99999, there will eventually come a time beyond which we no longer consider any data, since it will be discounted to 0.

In Q-learning, we face the same decision: how much do we consider future observed rewards when learning to predict Q values? Unfortunately, there's no definitive answer to this, or to setting pretty much any of the hyperparameters we have control over. We just have to play around with these knobs and see what works best empirically.

It's worth pointing out that most games are *episodic*, meaning that there are multiple chances to take actions before the game is over, and many games like chess don't naturally assign points to anything other than winning or losing the game. Hence, the reward signal in these games is sparse, making it difficult for trial-and-error based learning to reliably learn anything, as it requires seeing a reward fairly frequently.

In Gridworld, we've designed the game so that any move that doesn't win the game receives a reward of –1, the winning move gets a reward of +10, and a losing move rewards –10. It's really only the final move of the game where the algorithm can say "Aha! Now I get it!" Since each episode of a Gridworld game can be won in a fairly small number of moves, the sparse reward problem isn't too bad, but in other games it is such a significant problem that even the most advanced reinforcement learning algorithms have yet to reach human-level performance. One proposed method of dealing with this is to stop relying on the objective of maximizing expected rewards and instead instruct the algorithm to seek novelty, through which it will learn about its environment, which is something we'll cover in chapter 8.

3.2.5 Building the network

Let's dig into how we will build our deep learning algorithm for this game. Recall that a neural network has a particular kind of architecture or network topology. When you build a neural network, you have to decide how many layers it should have, how many parameters each layer has (the "width" of the layer), and how the layers are connected. Gridworld is simple enough that we don't need to build anything fancy. We can get away with a fairly straightforward feedforward neural network with only a few layers, using the typical rectified linear activation unit (ReLU). The only parts that require some more careful thought are how we will represent our input data, and how we will represent the output layer.

We'll cover the output layer first. In our discussion of Q-learning, we said that the Q function is a function that takes some state and some action and computes the value of that state-action pair, $Q(s,a)$. This is how the Q function was originally defined (figure 3.5). As we noted in the previous chapter, there is also a state-value function, usually denoted $V_\pi(s)$, that computes the value of some state, given that you're following a particular policy, π.

Generally, we want to use the Q function because it can tell us the value of taking an action in some state, so we can take the action that has the highest predicted value. But it would be rather wasteful to separately compute the Q values for every possible action given the state, even though the Q function was originally defined that way. A much more efficient procedure, and the one that DeepMind employed in its implementation of deep Q-learning, is to instead recast the Q function as a vector-valued function, meaning that instead of computing and returning a single Q value for a single state-action pair, it will compute the Q values for all actions, given some state, and return the vector of all those Q values. So we might represent this new version of the Q function as $Q_A(s)$, where the subscript A denotes the set of all possible actions (figure 3.5).

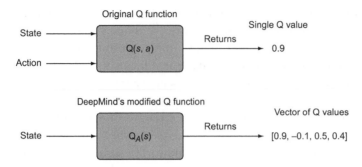

Figure 3.5   The original Q function accepts a state-action pair and returns the value of that state-action pair—a single number. DeepMind used a modified vector-valued Q function that accepts a state and returns a vector of state-action values, one for each possible action given the input state. The vector-valued Q function is more efficient, since you only need to compute the function once for all the actions.

Now it's easy to employ a neural network as our $Q_A(s)$ version of the Q function; the last layer will simply produce an output vector of Q values—one for each possible action. In the case of Gridworld, there are only four possible actions (up, down, left, right) so the output layer will produce 4-dimensional vectors. We can then directly use the output of the neural network to decide what action to take using some action selection procedure, such as a simple epsilon-greedy approach or a softmax selection policy. In this chapter we'll use the epsilon-greedy approach (figure 3.6) as DeepMind did, and instead of using a static ε value like we did in the last chapter, we will initialize it to a large value (i.e., 1, so we'll start with a completely random selection of actions) and we will slowly decrement it so that after a certain number of iterations, the ε value will rest at some small value. In this way, we will allow the algorithm to explore and learn a lot in the beginning, but then it will settle into maximizing rewards by exploiting what it has learned. Hopefully we will set the decrementing process so that it will not underexplore or overexplore, but that will have to be tested empirically.

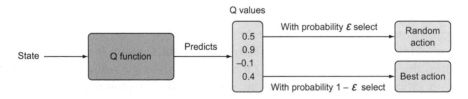

Figure 3.6   In an epsilon-greedy action selection method, we set the epsilon parameter to some value, e.g., 0.1, and with that probability we will randomly select an action (completely ignoring the predicted Q values) or with probability 1 – epsilon = 0.9, we will select the action associated with the highest predicted Q value. An additional helpful technique is to start with a high epsilon value, such as 1, and then slowly decrement it over the training iterations.

We have the output layer figured out—now to tackle the rest. In this chapter, we will construct a network of just three layers with widths of 164 (input layer), 150 (hidden layer), 4 (the output layer you already saw). You are welcome and encouraged to add more hidden layers or to play with the size of the hidden layer—you will likely be able to achieve better results with a deeper network. We chose to implement a fairly shallow network here so that you can train the model with your own CPU (it takes our MacBook Air 1.7 GHz Intel Core i7, with 8 GB of RAM, only a few minutes to train).

We already discussed why the output layer is of width 4, but we haven't talked about the input layer yet. Before we do that, though, we need to introduce the Gridworld game engine we will be using. We developed a Gridworld game for this book, and it is included in the GitHub repository for this chapter.

3.2.6 *Introducing the Gridworld game engine*

In the GitHub repository for this chapter, you'll find a file called Gridworld.py. Copy and paste this file into whatever folder you'll be working out of. You can include it in your Python session by running `from Gridworld import *`. The Gridworld module contains some classes and helper functions to run a Gridworld game instance. To create a Gridworld game instance, run the code in the following listing.

> Listing 3.1 Creating a Gridworld game

```
from Gridworld import Gridworld
game = Gridworld(size=4, mode='static')
```

The Gridworld board is always square, so the size refers to one side's dimension—in this case a 4 × 4 grid will be created. There are three ways to initialize the board. The first is to initialize it statically, as in listing 3.1, so that the objects on the board are initialized at the same predetermined locations. Second, you can set `mode='player'` so that just the player is initialized at a random position on the board. Last, you can initialize it so that all the objects are placed randomly (which is harder for the algorithm to learn) using `mode='random'`. We'll use all three options eventually.

Now that we've created the game, let's play it. Call the `display` method to display the board and the `makeMove` method to make a move. Moves are encoded with a single letter: *u* for up, *l* for left, and so on. After each move, you should display the board to see the effect. Additionally, after each move you'll want to observe the reward/outcome of the move by calling the `reward` method. In Gridworld, every nonwinning move receives a −1 reward. The winning move (reaching the goal) receives a +10 reward, and there's a −10 reward for the losing move (landing on the pit).

```
>>> game.display()
array([['+', '-', ' ', 'P'],
       [' ', 'W', ' ', ' '],
       [' ', ' ', ' ', ' '],
       [' ', ' ', ' ', ' ']], dtype='<U2')
```

```
>>> game.makeMove('d')
>>> game.makeMove('d')
>>> game.makeMove('l')
>>> game.display()
array([['+', '-', ' ', ' '],
       [' ', 'W', ' ', ' '],
       [' ', ' ', 'P', ' '],
       [' ', ' ', ' ', ' ']], dtype='<U2')
>>> game.reward()
-1
```

Now let's look at how the game state is actually represented, since we will need to feed this into our neural network. Run the following command:

```
>>> game.board.render_np()
array([[[0, 0, 0, 0],
        [0, 0, 0, 0],
        [0, 0, 1, 0],
        [0, 0, 0, 0]],

       [[1, 0, 0, 0],
        [0, 0, 0, 0],
        [0, 0, 0, 0],
        [0, 0, 0, 0]],

       [[0, 1, 0, 0],
        [0, 0, 0, 0],
        [0, 0, 0, 0],
        [0, 0, 0, 0]],

       [[0, 0, 0, 0],
        [0, 1, 0, 0],
        [0, 0, 0, 0],
        [0, 0, 0, 0]]], dtype=uint8)

>>> game.board.render_np().shape
(4, 4, 4)
```

The state is represented as a $4 \times 4 \times 4$ tensor where the first dimension indexes a set of four matrices of size 4×4. You can interpret this as having the dimensions *frames* by *height* by *width*. Each matrix is a 4×4 grid of zeros and a single 1, where a 1 indicates the position of a particular object. Each matrix encodes the position of one of the four objects: the player, the goal, the pit, and the wall. If you compare the result from display with the game state, you can see that the first matrix encodes the position of the player, the second matrix encodes the position of the goal, the third matrix encodes the position of the pit, and the last matrix encodes the position of the wall.

In other words, the first dimension of this 3-tensor is divided into four separate grid planes, where each plane represents the position of each element. Figure 3.7 shows an example where the player is at grid position (2,2), the goal is at (0,0), the pit is at (0,1), and the wall is at (1,1), where the planes are (row, column). All other elements are 0s.

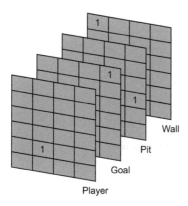

Figure 3.7 This is how the Gridworld board is represented as a numpy array. It is a 4 x 4 x 4 tensor, composed of 4 "slices" of a 4 x 4 grid. Each grid slice represents the position of an individual object on the board and contains a single 1, with all other elements being 0s. The position of the 1 indicates the position of that slice's object.

While we could, in principle, build a neural network that can operate on a $4 \times 4 \times 4$ tensor, it is easier to just flatten it into a 1-tensor (a vector). A $4 \times 4 \times 4$ tensor has $4^3 = 64$ total elements, so the input layer of our neural network must be accordingly shaped. The neural network will have to learn what this data means and how it relates to maximizing rewards. Remember, the algorithm will know absolutely nothing to begin with.

3.2.7 A neural network as the Q function

Let's build the neural network that will serve as our Q function. As you know, in this book we're using PyTorch for all our deep learning models, but if you're more comfortable with another framework such as TensorFlow or MXNet, it should be fairly straightforward to port the models.

Figure 3.8 shows the general architecture for the model we will build. Figure 3.9 shows it in string diagram form with typed strings.

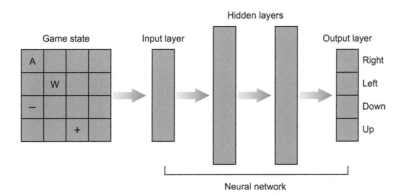

Figure 3.8 The neural network model we will use to play Gridworld. The model has an input layer that can accept a 64-length game state vector, some hidden layers (we use one, but two are depicted for generality), and an output layer that produces a 4-length vector of Q values for each action, given the state.

Deep Q-network

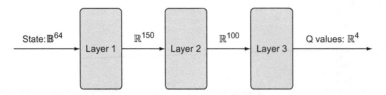

Figure 3.9   String diagram for our DQN. The input is a 64-length Boolean vector, and the output is a 4-length real vector of Q values.

To implement this with PyTorch, we'll use the nn module, which is the higher-level interface for PyTorch, similar to Keras for TensorFlow.

Listing 3.2   Neural network Q function

```python
import numpy as np
import torch
from Gridworld import Gridworld
import random
from matplotlib import pylab as plt

l1 = 64
l2 = 150
l3 = 100
l4 = 4

model = torch.nn.Sequential(
    torch.nn.Linear(l1, l2),
    torch.nn.ReLU(),
    torch.nn.Linear(l2, l3),
    torch.nn.ReLU(),
    torch.nn.Linear(l3,l4)
)
loss_fn = torch.nn.MSELoss()
learning_rate = 1e-3
optimizer = torch.optim.Adam(model.parameters(), lr=learning_rate)

gamma = 0.9
epsilon = 1.0
```

So far, all we've done is set up the neural network model, define a loss function and learning rate, set up an optimizer, and define a couple of parameters. If this were a simple classification neural network, we'd almost be done. We'd just need to set up a `for` loop to iteratively run the optimizer to minimize the model error with respect to the data. It's more complicated with reinforcement learning, which is probably why you're reading this book. We covered the main steps well earlier, but let's zoom in a little.

Listing 3.3 implements the main loop of the algorithm. In broad strokes, this is what it does:

1 We set up a `for` loop for the number of epochs.
2 In the loop, we set up a `while` loop (while the game is in progress).
3 We run the Q-network forward.
4 We're using an epsilon-greedy implementation, so at time t with probability ε we will choose a random action. With probability $1 - \varepsilon$, we will choose the action associated with the highest Q value from our neural network.
5 Take action a as determined in the preceding step, and observe the new state s′ and reward r_{t+1}.
6 Run the network forward using s′. Store the highest Q value, which we'll call max Q.
7 Our target value for training the network is $r_{t+1} + \gamma*\max Q_A(S_{t+1})$, where γ (gamma) is a parameter between 0 and 1. If after taking action a_t the game is over, there is no legitimate s_{t+1}, so $\gamma*\max Q_A(S_{t+1})$ is not valid and we can set it to 0. The target becomes just r_{t+1}.
8 Given that we have four outputs and we only want to update (i.e., train) the output associated with the action we just took, our target output vector is the same as the output vector from the first run, except we change the one output associated with our action to the result we computed using the Q-learning formula.
9 Train the model on this one sample. Then repeat steps 2–9.

To be clear, when we first run our neural network and get an output of action values like this,

```
array([[-0.02812552, -0.04649779, -0.08819015, -0.00723661]])
```

our target vector for one iteration may look like this:

```
array([[-0.02812552, -0.04649779, 1, -0.00723661]])
```

Here we just changed a single entry to the value we wanted to update.

There's one other detail we need to include in the code before we move on. The Gridworld game engine's `makeMove` method expects a character such as u to make a move, but our Q-learning algorithm only knows how to generate numbers, so we need a simple map from numeric keys to action characters:

```
action_set = {
    0: 'u',
    1: 'd',
    2: 'l',
    3: 'r',
}
```

Okay, let's get to coding the main training loop.

Listing 3.3   Q-learning: Main training loop

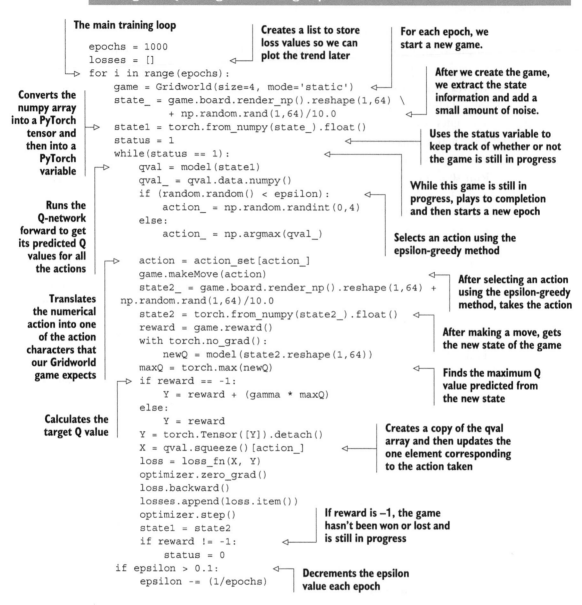

The main training loop

Creates a list to store loss values so we can plot the trend later

For each epoch, we start a new game.

```
epochs = 1000
losses = []
for i in range(epochs):
    game = Gridworld(size=4, mode='static')
    state_ = game.board.render_np().reshape(1,64) \
             + np.random.rand(1,64)/10.0
    state1 = torch.from_numpy(state_).float()
    status = 1
    while(status == 1):
        qval = model(state1)
        qval_ = qval.data.numpy()
        if (random.random() < epsilon):
            action_ = np.random.randint(0,4)
        else:
            action_ = np.argmax(qval_)

        action = action_set[action_]
        game.makeMove(action)
        state2_ = game.board.render_np().reshape(1,64) +
np.random.rand(1,64)/10.0
        state2 = torch.from_numpy(state2_).float()
        reward = game.reward()
        with torch.no_grad():
            newQ = model(state2.reshape(1,64))
        maxQ = torch.max(newQ)
        if reward == -1:
            Y = reward + (gamma * maxQ)
        else:
            Y = reward
        Y = torch.Tensor([Y]).detach()
        X = qval.squeeze()[action_]
        loss = loss_fn(X, Y)
        optimizer.zero_grad()
        loss.backward()
        losses.append(loss.item())
        optimizer.step()
        state1 = state2
        if reward != -1:
            status = 0
    if epsilon > 0.1:
        epsilon -= (1/epochs)
```

Converts the numpy array into a PyTorch tensor and then into a PyTorch variable

Runs the Q-network forward to get its predicted Q values for all the actions

Translates the numerical action into one of the action characters that our Gridworld game expects

Calculates the target Q value

After we create the game, we extract the state information and add a small amount of noise.

Uses the status variable to keep track of whether or not the game is still in progress

While this game is still in progress, plays to completion and then starts a new epoch

Selects an action using the epsilon-greedy method

After selecting an action using the epsilon-greedy method, takes the action

After making a move, gets the new state of the game

Finds the maximum Q value predicted from the new state

Creates a copy of the qval array and then updates the one element corresponding to the action taken

If reward is –1, the game hasn't been won or lost and is still in progress

Decrements the epsilon value each epoch

NOTE   Why did we add noise to the game state? It helps prevent "dead neurons," which can happen with the use of rectified linear units (ReLU) as our activation function. Basically, because most of the elements in our game state array are 0s, they won't play nice with ReLU, which is technically non-differentiable at 0. Hence, we add a tiny bit of noise so that none of the values in the state array are exactly 0. This might also help with *overfitting*, which is when a model learns by memorizing spurious details in the data without learning the abstract features of the data, ultimately preventing it from generalizing to new data.

There are a couple of things to point out that you may not have seen before. The first new thing is the use of the context torch.no_grad() when computing the next state Q value. Whenever we run a PyTorch model with some input, it will implicitly create a computational graph. Each PyTorch tensor is not only a store of tensor data, it also keeps track of which computations were performed to produce it. By using the torch.no_grad() context, we tell PyTorch to *not* create a computational graph for the code within the context; this will save memory when we don't need the computational graph. When we compute the Q values for state2, we're just using them as a target for training. We're not going to backpropagate through the computational graph that would have been created if we hadn't used torch.no_grad. We only want to backpropagate through the computational graph that is created when we call model(state1), because we want to train the parameters with respect to state1, not state2.

Here's a simple example with a linear model:

```
>>> m = torch.Tensor([2.0])
>>> m.requires_grad=True
>>> b = torch.Tensor([1.0])
>>> b.requires_grad=True
>>> def linear_model(x,m,b):
>>>     y = m @ x + b
>>>     return y
>>> y = linear_model(torch.Tensor([4.]), m,b)
>>> y
tensor([9.], grad_fn=<AddBackward0>)
>>> y.grad_fn
<AddBackward0 at 0x128dfb828>
>>> with torch.no_grad():
>>>     y = linear_model(torch.Tensor([4]),m,b)
>>> y
tensor([9.])
>>> y.grad_fn
None
```

We create two trainable parameters, m and b, by setting their requires_grad attribute to True, which means PyTorch will consider these parameters as nodes in a computational graph and will store their history of computations. Any new tensors that are created using m and b, such as y in this case, will also have requires_grad set to True and thus will also keep a memory of their computation history. You can see that the first time we call the linear model and print y, it gives us a tensor with the numeric result and also shows an attribute, grad_fn=<AddBackward0>. We can also see this attribute directly by printing y.grad_fn. This shows that this tensor was created by the addition operation. It is called AddBackward because it actually stores the derivative of the addition function.

If you call this function given one input, it returns two outputs, like the opposite of addition, which takes two inputs and returns one output. Since our addition function is a function of two variables, there is a partial derivative with respect to the first input and a partial derivative with respect to the second input. The partial derivative of $y = a + b$ with respect to m is $\frac{\partial y}{\partial a} = 1$ and $\frac{\partial y}{\partial b} = 1$. Or if $y = a \cdot b$ then $\frac{\partial y}{\partial a} = b$ and $\frac{\partial y}{\partial b} = a$. These are just the basic rules of taking derivatives. When we backpropagate from a given node, we need it to return all the partial derivatives, so that is why the AddBackward0 gradient function returns two outputs.

We can verify that PyTorch is indeed computing gradients as expected by calling the backward method on y:

```
>>> y = linear_model(torch.Tensor([4.]), m,b)
>>> y.backward()
>>> m.grad
tensor([4.])
>>> b.grad
tensor([1.])
```

This is exactly what we would get from computing these simple partial derivatives in our head or on paper. In order to backpropagate efficiently, PyTorch keeps track of all forward computations and stores their derivatives so that eventually when we call the backward() method on the output node of our computational graph, it will backpropagate through these gradient functions node by node until the input node. That's how we get the gradients for all the parameters in the model.

Notice that we also called the detach() method on the Y tensor. This was actually unnecessary, since we used torch.no_grad() when we computed newQ, but we included it because detaching nodes from the computational graph will become ubiquitous throughout the rest of the book, and not properly detaching nodes is a common source of bugs when training a model. If we call loss.backward(X,Y), and Y was associated with its own computational graph with trainable parameters, we would backpropagate into Y *and* X, and the training procedure would learn to minimize the loss by updating the trainable parameters in the X graph and the Y graph, whereas we only want to update the X graph. We *detach* the Y node from the graph so that it is just used as data and not as a computational graph node. You don't need to think too hard about the details, but you do need to pay attention to which parts of the graph you're actually backpropagating into and make sure you're not backpropagating into the wrong nodes.

You can go ahead and run the training loop—1,000 epochs will be more than enough. Once it's done, you can plot the losses to see if the training is successful and the model converges. The loss should more or less decrease and plateau over the training time. Our plot is shown in figure 3.10.

The loss plot is pretty noisy, but the moving average of the plot is significantly trending toward zero. This gives us some confidence the training worked, but we'll never know until we test it. We've written up a simple function in listing 3.4 that allows us to test the model on a single game.

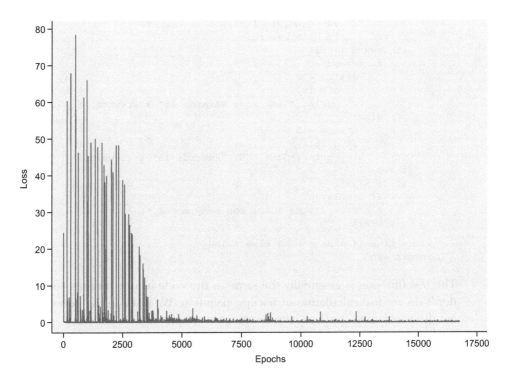

Figure 3.10 The loss plot for our first Q-learning algorithm, which is clearly down-trending over the training epochs.

Listing 3.4 Testing the Q-network

```
def test_model(model, mode='static', display=True):
    i = 0
    test_game = Gridworld(mode=mode)
    state_ = test_game.board.render_np().reshape(1,64) +
     np.random.rand(1,64)/10.0
    state = torch.from_numpy(state_).float()
    if display:
        print("Initial State:")
        print(test_game.display())
    status = 1                              ◁─┐ While the game is
    while(status == 1):                        │ still in progress
        qval = model(state)
        qval_ = qval.data.numpy()            ─┐ Takes the action with
        action_ = np.argmax(qval_)        ◁──┘ the highest Q value
        action = action_set[action_]
        if display:
            print('Move #: %s; Taking action: %s' % (i, action))
        test_game.makeMove(action)
        state_ = test_game.board.render_np().reshape(1,64) +
    np.random.rand(1,64)/10.0
        state = torch.from_numpy(state_).float()
        if display:
```

```
        print(test_game.display())
    reward = test_game.reward()
    if reward != -1:
        if reward > 0:
            status = 2
            if display:
                print("Game won! Reward: %s" % (reward,))
        else:
            status = 0
            if display:
                print("Game LOST. Reward: %s" % (reward,))
    i += 1
    if (i > 15):
        if display:
            print("Game lost; too many moves.")
        break

win = True if status == 2 else False
return win
```

The test function is essentially the same as the code in our training loop, except we don't do any loss calculation or backpropagation. We just run the network forward to get the predictions. Let's see if it learned how to play Gridworld!

```
>>> test_model(model, 'static')

Initial State:
[['+' '-' ' ' 'P']
 [' ' 'W' ' ' ' ']
 [' ' ' ' ' ' ' ']
 [' ' ' ' ' ' ' ' ']]
Move #: 0; Taking action: d
[['+' '-' ' ' ' ']
 [' ' 'W' ' ' 'P']
 [' ' ' ' ' ' ' ']
 [' ' ' ' ' ' ' ' ']]
Move #: 1; Taking action: d
[['+' '-' ' ' ' ']
 [' ' 'W' ' ' ' ']
 [' ' ' ' ' ' 'P']
 [' ' ' ' ' ' ' ' ']]
Move #: 2; Taking action: l
[['+' '-' ' ' ' ']
 [' ' 'W' ' ' ' ']
 [' ' ' ' 'P' ' ']
 [' ' ' ' ' ' ' ' ']]
Move #: 3; Taking action: l
[['+' '-' ' ' ' ']
 [' ' 'W' ' ' ' ']
 [' ' 'P' ' ' ' ']
 [' ' ' ' ' ' ' ' ']]
Move #: 4; Taking action: l
[['+' '-' ' ' ' ']
 [' ' 'W' ' ' ' ']
 ['P' ' ' ' ' ' ']
 [' ' ' ' ' ' ' ' ']]
```

```
Move #: 5; Taking action: u
[['+' '-' ' ' ' ' ' ']
 ['P' 'W' ' ' ' ' ' ']
 [' ' ' ' ' ' ' ' ' ']
 [' ' ' ' ' ' ' ' ' ']]
Move #: 6; Taking action: u
[['+' '-' ' ' ' ' ' ']
 [' ' 'W' ' ' ' ' ' ']
 [' ' ' ' ' ' ' ' ' ']
 [' ' ' ' ' ' ' ' ' ']]
Reward: 10
```

Can we get a round of applause for our Gridworld player here? Clearly it knows what it's doing; it went straight for the goal!

But let's not get too excited; that was the static version of the game, which is really easy. If you use our test function with mode='random', you'll find some disappointment:

```
>>> testModel(model, 'random')

Initial State:
[[' ' '+' ' ' ' ' 'P']
 [' ' ' ' 'W' ' ' ' ' ' ']
 [' ' ' ' ' ' ' ' ' ' ' ']
 [' ' ' ' ' ' '-' ' ' ' ']]
Move #: 0; Taking action: d
[[' ' ' ' '+' ' ' ' ' ' ']
 [' ' ' ' 'W' ' ' ' ' 'P']
 [' ' ' ' ' ' ' ' ' ' ' ']
 [' ' ' ' ' ' '-' ' ' ' ']]
Move #: 1; Taking action: d
[[' ' ' ' '+' ' ' ' ' ' ']
 [' ' ' ' 'W' ' ' ' ' ' ']
 [' ' ' ' ' ' ' ' ' ' 'P']
 [' ' ' ' ' ' '-' ' ' ' ']]
Move #: 2; Taking action: l
[[' ' ' ' '+' ' ' ' ' ' ']
 [' ' ' ' 'W' ' ' ' ' ' ']
 [' ' ' ' ' ' 'P' ' ' ' ']
 [' ' ' ' ' ' '-' ' ' ' ']]
Move #: 3; Taking action: l
[[' ' ' ' '+' ' ' ' ' ' ']
 [' ' ' ' 'W' ' ' ' ' ' ']
 [' ' ' ' 'P' ' ' ' ' ' ']
 [' ' ' ' ' ' '-' ' ' ' ']]
Move #: 4; Taking action: l
[[' ' ' ' '+' ' ' ' ' ' ']
 [' ' ' ' 'W' ' ' ' ' ' ']
 ['P' ' ' ' ' ' ' ' ' ' ']
 [' ' ' ' ' ' '-' ' ' ' ']]
Move #: 5; Taking action: u
[[' ' ' ' '+' ' ' ' ' ' ']
 ['P' 'W' ' ' ' ' ' ' ' ']
 [' ' ' ' ' ' ' ' ' ' ' ']
 [' ' ' ' ' ' '-' ' ' ' ']]
```

```
Move #: 6; Taking action: u
[['P' '+' ' ' ' ' ' ']
 [' ' 'W' ' ' ' ' ' ']
 [' ' ' ' ' ' ' ' ' ']
 [' ' ' ' ' ' '-' ' ' ' ']]
Move #: 7; Taking action: d
[[' ' '+' ' ' ' ' ' ']
 ['P' 'W' ' ' ' ' ' ']
 [' ' ' ' ' ' ' ' ' ']
 [' ' ' ' ' ' '-' ' ' ' ']]

# we omitted the last several moves to save space

Game lost; too many moves.
```

This is really interesting. Look carefully at the moves the network is making. The player starts off the game only two tiles to the right of the goal. If it *really* knew how to play the game, it would take the shortest path to the goal. Instead, it starts moving down and to the left, just like it would in the static game mode. It seems like the model just memorized the particular board it was trained on and didn't generalize at all.

Maybe we just need to train it with the game mode set to random, and then it would really learn? Try it. Retrain it with random mode. Maybe you'll be luckier than us, but figure 3.11 shows our loss plot with random mode and 1,000 epochs. That

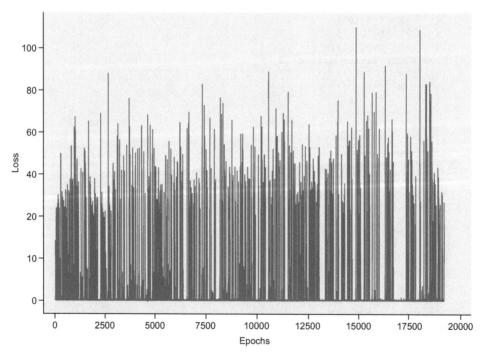

Figure 3.11 The loss plot for Q-learning in random mode, which doesn't show any signs of convergence.

doesn't look pretty. There's no sign that any significant learning is happening with random mode. (We won't show these results, but the model *did* seem to learn how to play with "player" mode, where only the player is randomly placed on the grid.)

This is a big problem. Reinforcement learning won't be worth anything if all it can do is learn how to memorize or weakly learn. But this is a problem that the DeepMind team faced, and one they solved.

3.3 Preventing catastrophic forgetting: Experience replay

We're slowly building up our skills, and we want our algorithm to train on the harder variant of the game where all the board pieces are randomly placed on the grid for each new game. The algorithm can't just memorize a sequence of steps to take, as before. It needs to be able to take the shortest path to the goal (without stepping into the pit) regardless of what the initial board configuration is. It needs to develop a more sophisticated representation of its environment.

3.3.1 Catastrophic forgetting

The main problem we encountered in the previous section when we tried to train our model on random mode has a name: *catastrophic forgetting*. It's actually a very important issue associated with gradient descent-based training methods in *online* training. Online training is what we've been doing: we backpropagate after each move as we play the game.

Imagine that our algorithm is training on (learning Q values for) game 1 of figure 3.12. The player is placed between the pit and the goal such that the goal is on the right and the pit is on the left. Using an epsilon-greedy strategy, the player takes a random move and by chance steps to the right and hits the goal. Great! The algorithm will try to learn that this state-action pair is associated with a high value by updating its weights in such a way that the output will more closely match the target value (i.e. via backpropagation).

Now game 2 is initialized and the player is again between the goal and pit, but this time the goal is on the *left* and the pit is on the right. Perhaps to our naive algorithm, the state *seems* very similar to the last game. Since last time moving right gave a nice positive reward, the player chooses to make one step to the right again, but this time it ends up in the pit and gets –1 reward. The player is thinking, "What is going on? I thought going to the right was the best decision based on my previous experience." It may do backpropagation again to update its state-action value, but because this state-action is very similar to the last learned state-action, it may override its previously learned weights.

This is the essence of catastrophic forgetting. There's a push-pull between very similar state-actions (but with divergent targets) that results in this inability to properly learn anything. We generally don't have this problem in the supervised learning realm, because we do randomized batch learning where we don't update our weights until we've iterated through some random subset of training data and computed the sum or average gradient for the batch. This averages over the targets and stabilizes the learning.

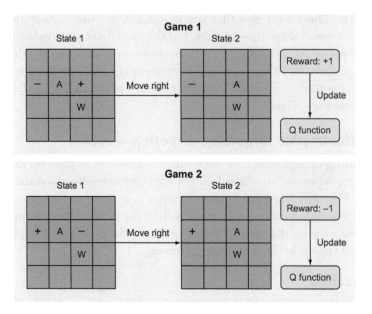

Figure 3.12 The idea of catastrophic forgetting is that when two game states are very similar and yet lead to very different outcomes, the Q function will get "confused" and won't be able to learn what to do. In this example, the catastrophic forgetting happens because the Q function learns from game 1 that moving right leads to a +1 reward, but in game 2, which looks very similar, it gets a reward of –1 after moving right. As a result, the algorithm forgets what it previously learned about game 1, resulting in essentially no significant learning at all.

3.3.2   *Experience replay*

Catastrophic forgetting is probably not something we have to worry about with the first variant of our game because the targets are always stationary, and indeed the model successfully learned how to play it. But with the random mode, it's something we need to consider, and that is why we need to implement something called *experience replay*. Experience replay basically gives us batch updating in an online learning scheme. It's not a big deal to implement

Here's how experience replay works (figure 3.13):

1 In state s, take action a, and observe the new state s_{t+1} and reward r_{t+1}.
2 Store this as a tuple (s, a, s_{t+1}, r_{t+1}) in a list.
3 Continue to store each experience in this list until you have filled the list to a specific length (this is up to you to define).
4 Once the experience replay memory is filled, randomly select a subset (again, you need to define the subset size).
5 Iterate through this subset and calculate value updates for each subset; store these in a target array (such as Y) and store the state, s, of each memory in X.

6 Use *X* and *Y* as a mini-batch for batch training. For subsequent epochs where the array is full, just overwrite old values in your experience replay memory array.

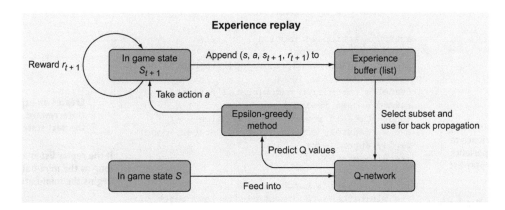

Figure 3.13 This is the general overview of experience replay, a method for mitigating a major problem with online training algorithms: catastrophic forgetting. The idea is to employ mini-batching by storing past experiences and then using a random subset of these experiences to update the Q-network, rather than using just the single most recent experience.

Thus, in addition to learning the action value for the action you just took, you're also going to use a random sample of past experiences to train on, to prevent catastrophic forgetting.

Listing 3.5 shows the same training algorithm from listing 3.4, except with experience replay added. Remember, this time we're training it on the harder variant of the game, where all the board pieces are randomly placed on the grid.

Listing 3.5 DQN with experience replay

```
from collections import deque          Sets the total size of the
epochs = 5000                          experience replay memory
losses = []
mem_size = 1000                              Sets the mini-batch size
batch_size = 200
                                             Creates the memory replay
replay = deque(maxlen=mem_size)              as a deque list
max_moves = 50                         Sets the maximum number of
h = 0                                  moves before game is over
for i in range(epochs):
    game = Gridworld(size=4, mode='random')
    state1_ = game.board.render_np().reshape(1,64) +
     np.random.rand(1,64)/100.0
    state1 = torch.from_numpy(state1_).float()
    status = 1
    mov = 0
    while(status == 1):                Computes Q values from
        mov += 1                       the input state in order
        qval = model(state1)           to select an action
```

```
qval_ = qval.data.numpy()
if (random.random() < epsilon):          ◁── Selects an action using the
    action_ = np.random.randint(0,4)         epsilon-greedy strategy
else:
    action_ = np.argmax(qval_)

action = action_set[action_]
game.makeMove(action)
state2_ = game.board.render_np().reshape(1,64) +
np.random.rand(1,64)/100.0
state2 = torch.from_numpy(state2_).float()         Creates an experience of
reward = game.reward()                             state, reward, action, and
done = True if reward > 0 else False                the next state as a tuple
exp = (state1, action_, reward, state2, done)   ◁──
replay.append(exp)
state1 = state2                                      If the replay list is at least as
                                                    long as the mini-batch size,
if len(replay) > batch_size:               ◁──     begins the mini-batch training
    minibatch = random.sample(replay, batch_size)
    state1_batch = torch.cat([s1 for (s1,a,r,s2,d) in minibatch])
    action_batch = torch.Tensor([a for (s1,a,r,s2,d) in minibatch])
    reward_batch = torch.Tensor([r for (s1,a,r,s2,d) in minibatch])
    state2_batch = torch.cat([s2 for (s1,a,r,s2,d) in minibatch])
    done_batch = torch.Tensor([d for (s1,a,r,s2,d) in minibatch])

    Q1 = model(state1_batch)               ◁── Recomputes Q values for the mini-
    with torch.no_grad():                      batch of states to get gradients
        Q2 = model(state2_batch)           ◁──
                                              Computes Q values for the
    Y = reward_batch + gamma * ((1 - done_batch) *   mini-batch of next states,
torch.max(Q2,dim=1)[0])                         but doesn't compute
    X = \                                       gradients
    Q1.gather(dim=1,index=action_batch.long().unsqueeze(dim=1)).squeeze()
    loss = loss_fn(X, Y.detach())
    optimizer.zero_grad()
    loss.backward()
    losses.append(loss.item())
    optimizer.step()                          If the game is over,
                                              resets status and
if reward != -1 or mov > max_moves:      ◁── mov number
    status = 0
    mov = 0
losses = np.array(losses)
```

Annotations (left margin, top to bottom):

Adds the experience to the experience replay list

Randomly samples a subset of the replay list

Separates out the components of each experience into separate mini-batch tensors

Computes the target Q values we want the DQN to learn

In order to store the agent's experiences, we used a data structure called a *deque* in Python's built-in collections library. It's basically a list that you can set a maximum size on, so that if you try to append to the list and it is already full, it will remove the first item in the list and add the new item to the end of the list. This means new experiences replace the oldest experiences. The experiences themselves are tuples of (state1, reward, action, state2, done) that we append to the replay deque.

The major difference with experience replay training is that we train with mini-batches of data when our replay list is full. We randomly select a subset of experiences from the replay, and we separate out the individual experience components into `state1_batch`, `reward_batch`, `action_batch`, and `state2_batch`. For example, `state1_batch` is of dimensions `batch_size` × 64, or 100 × 64 in this case. And `reward_batch` is just a 100-length vector of integers. We follow the same training formula as we did earlier with fully online training, but now we're dealing with mini-batches. We use the tensor `gather` method to subset the `Q1` tensor (a 100 × 4 tensor) by the action indices so that we only select the Q values associated with actions that were actually chosen, resulting in a 100-length vector.

Notice that the target Q value, `Y = reward_batch + gamma * ((1 - done_batch) * torch.max(Q2,dim=1)[0])`, uses `done_batch` to set the right side to 0 if the game is done. Remember, if the game is over after taking an action, which we call a *terminal state*, there is no next state to take the maximum Q value on, so the target just becomes the reward, r_{t+1}. The `done` variable is a Boolean, but we can do arithmetic on it as if it were a 0 or 1 integer, so we just take 1 - done so that if done = True, 1 - done = 0, and it sets the right-side term to 0.

We trained for 5,000 epochs this time, since it's a more difficult game, but otherwise the Q-network model is the same as before. When we test the algorithm, it seems to play most of the games correctly. We wrote an additional testing script to see what percentage of games it wins out of 1,000 plays.

Listing 3.6   Testing the performance with experience replay

```
max_games = 1000
wins = 0
for i in range(max_games):
    win = test_model(model, mode='random', display=False)
    if win:
        wins += 1
win_perc = float(wins) / float(max_games)
print("Games played: {0}, # of wins: {1}".format(max_games,wins))
print("Win percentage: {}".format(win_perc))
```

When we run listing 3.6 on our trained model (trained for 5,000 epochs), we get about 90% accuracy. Your accuracy may be slightly better or worse. This certainly suggests it has learned *something* about how to play the game, but it's not exactly what we would expect if the algorithm really knew what it was doing (although you could probably improve the accuracy with a much longer training time). Once you actually know how to play, you should be able to win every single game.

There's a small caveat that some of the initialized games may actually be impossible to win, so the win percentage may never reach 100%; there is no logic preventing the goal from being in the corner, stuck behind a wall and pit, making the game unwinnable. The Gridworld game engine does prevent most of the impossible board configurations, but a small number can still get through. Not only does this mean we can't win every game, but it also means the learning will be mildly corrupted, since it will attempt to follow a strategy that normally would work but fails for an unwinnable game. We wanted to keep the game logic simple to focus on illustrating the concepts so we did not program in the sophisticated logic needed to ensure 100% winnable games.

There's also another reason we're being held back from getting into the 95% + accuracy territory. Let's look at our loss plot, shown in figure 3.14 showing our running average loss (yours may vary significantly).

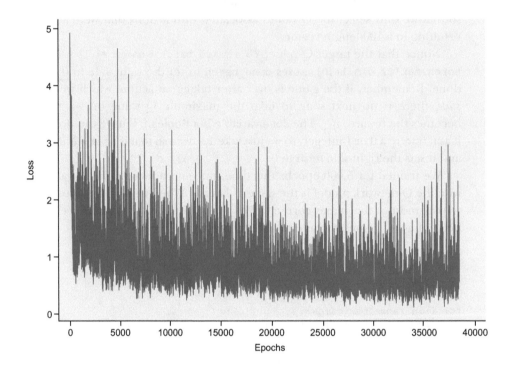

Figure 3.14   The DQN loss plot after implementing experience replay, which shows a clearly down-trending loss, but it's still very noisy.

In the loss in figure 3.14, you can see it's definitely trending downward, but it looks pretty unstable. This is the type of plot you'd be a bit surprised to see in a supervised learning problem, but it's quite common in bare DRL. The experience replay mechanism helps with training stabilization by reducing catastrophic forgetting, but there are other related sources of instability.

3.4   *Improving stability with a target network*

So far, we've been able to successfully train a deep reinforcement learning algorithm to learn and play Gridworld with both a deterministic static initialization and a slightly harder version where the player is placed randomly on the board each game. Unfortunately, even though the algorithm appears to learn how to play, it is quite possible it is just memorizing all the possible board configurations, since there aren't that many on a 4×4 board. The hardest variant of the game is where the player, goal, pit, and wall are all initialized randomly each game, making it much more difficult for the algorithm to memorize. This ought to enforce some amount of actual learning, but as you saw, we're still experiencing difficulty with learning this variant; we're getting very noisy loss plots. To help address this, we'll add another dimension to the updating rule that will smooth out the value updates.

3.4.1 Learning instability

One potential problem that DeepMind identified when they published their deep Q-network paper was that if you keep updating the Q-network's parameters after each move, you might cause instabilities to arise. The idea is that since the rewards may be sparse (we only give a significant reward upon winning or losing the game), updating on every single step, where most steps don't get any significant reward, may cause the algorithm to start behaving erratically.

For example, the Q-network might predict a high value for the "up" action in some state; if it moves up and by chance lands on the goal and wins, we update the Q-network to reflect the fact that it was rewarded +10. The next game, however, it thinks "up" is a really fantastic move and predicts a high Q value, but then it moves up and gets a –10 reward, so we update and now it thinks "up" is not so great after all. Then, a few games later moving up leads to winning again. You can see how this might lead to a kind of oscillatory behavior, where the predicted Q value never settles on a reasonable value but just keeps getting jerked around. This is very similar to the catastrophic forgetting problem.

This is not just a theoretical issue—it's something that DeepMind observed in their own training. The solution they devised is to duplicate the Q-network into two copies, each with its own model parameters: the "regular" Q-network and a copy called the *target network* (symbolically denoted $\hat{Q}$-network, read "Q hat"). The target network is identical to the Q-network at the beginning, before any training, but its own parameters lag behind the regular Q-network in terms of how they're updated.

Let's run through the sequence of events again, with the target network in play (we'll leave out the details of experience replay):

1. Initialize the Q-network with parameters (weights) θ_Q (read "theta Q").
2. Initialize the target network as a copy of the Q-network, but with separate parameters θ_T (read "theta T"), and set $\theta_T = \theta_Q$.
3. Use the epsilon-greedy strategy with the Q-network's Q values to select action a.
4. Observe the reward and new state r_{t+1}, s_{t+1}.
5. The target network's Q value will be set to r_{t+1} if the episode has just been terminated (i.e., the game was won or lost) or to $r_{t+1} + \gamma \max Q_{\theta_T}(S_{t+1})$ otherwise (notice the use of the target network here).
6. Backpropagate the target network's Q value through the Q-network (not the target network).
7. Every C number of iterations, set $\theta_T = \theta_Q$ (i.e., set the target network's parameters equal to the Q-network's parameters).

Notice from figure 3.15 that the only time we use the target network, $\hat{Q}$, is to calculate the target Q value for backpropagation through the Q-network. The idea is that we update the main Q-network's parameters on each training iteration, but we decrease the effect that recent updates have on the action selection, hopefully improving stability.

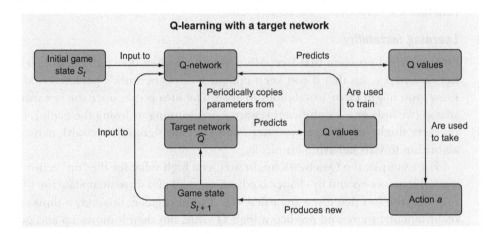

Figure 3.15   This is the general overview for Q-learning with a target network. It's a fairly straightforward extension of the normal Q-learning algorithm, except that you have a second Q-network called the target network whose predicted Q values are used to backpropagate through and train the main Q-network. The target network's parameters are not trained, but they are periodically synchronized with the Q-network's parameters. The idea is that using the target network's Q values to train the Q-network will improve the stability of the training.

The code is getting a bit long now, with both experience replay and a target network, so we'll just look at a portion of the full code here in the book. We'll leave it to you to check out the book's GitHub repository where you'll find all the code for this chapter.

The following code is identical to listing 3.5 except for a few lines that add in the target network capability.

Listing 3.7   Target network

```
import copy

model = torch.nn.Sequential(
    torch.nn.Linear(11, 12),
    torch.nn.ReLU(),
    torch.nn.Linear(12, 13),
    torch.nn.ReLU(),
    torch.nn.Linear(13,14)
)

model2 = model2 = copy.deepcopy(model)
model2.load_state_dict(model.state_dict())
```

Creates a second model by making an identical copy of the original Q-network model

Copies the parameters of the original model

```
sync_freq = 50

loss_fn = torch.nn.MSELoss()
learning_rate = 1e-3
optimizer = torch.optim.Adam(model.parameters(), lr=learning_rate)
```

> **Synchronizes the frequency parameter; every 50 steps we will copy the parameters of model into model2**

> **(Code omitted) Uses the same other settings as in listing 3.5**

The target network is simply a lagged copy of the main DQN. Each PyTorch model has a state_dict() method that returns all of its parameters organized in a dictionary. We use Python's built-in copy module to duplicate the PyTorch model data structure, and then we use the load_state_dict method on model2 to ensure that it has copied the parameters of the main DQN.

Next we include the full training loop, which is mostly the same as listing 3.5 except that we use model2 when computing the maximum Q value for the next state. We also include a couple of lines of code to copy the parameters from the main model to model2 every 50 iterations.

Listing 3.8   DQN with experience replay and target network

```
from collections import deque
epochs = 5000
losses = []
mem_size = 1000
batch_size = 200
replay = deque(maxlen=mem_size)
max_moves = 50
h = 0
sync_freq = 500
j=0
for i in range(epochs):
    game = Gridworld(size=4, mode='random')
    state1_ = game.board.render_np().reshape(1,64) +
     np.random.rand(1,64)/100.0
    state1 = torch.from_numpy(state1_).float()
    status = 1
    mov = 0
    while(status == 1):
        j+=1
        mov += 1
        qval = model(state1)
        qval_ = qval.data.numpy()
        if (random.random() < epsilon):
            action_ = np.random.randint(0,4)
        else:
            action_ = np.argmax(qval_)

        action = action_set[action_]
        game.makeMove(action)
        state2_ = game.board.render_np().reshape(1,64) +
    np.random.rand(1,64)/100.0
```

> **Sets the update frequency for synchronizing the target model parameters to the main DQN**

```
        state2 = torch.from_numpy(state2_).float()
        reward = game.reward()
        done = True if reward > 0 else False
        exp = (state1, action_, reward, state2, done)
        replay.append(exp)
        state1 = state2

        if len(replay) > batch_size:
            minibatch = random.sample(replay, batch_size)
            state1_batch = torch.cat([s1 for (s1,a,r,s2,d) in minibatch])
            action_batch = torch.Tensor([a for (s1,a,r,s2,d) in minibatch])
            reward_batch = torch.Tensor([r for (s1,a,r,s2,d) in minibatch])
            state2_batch = torch.cat([s2 for (s1,a,r,s2,d) in minibatch])
            done_batch = torch.Tensor([d for (s1,a,r,s2,d) in minibatch])
            Q1 = model(state1_batch)
            with torch.no_grad():
                Q2 = model2(state2_batch)          ⟵——  Uses the target network
                                                         to get the maximum Q
                                                         value for the next state

            Y = reward_batch + gamma * ((1-done_batch) * \
            torch.max(Q2,dim=1)[0])
            X = Q1.gather(dim=1,index=action_batch.long() \
            .unsqueeze(dim=1)).squeeze()
            loss = loss_fn(X, Y.detach())
            print(i, loss.item())
            clear_output(wait=True)
            optimizer.zero_grad()
            loss.backward()
            losses.append(loss.item())          ⟵——  Copies the main
            optimizer.step()                           model parameters to
                                                       the target network

            if j % sync_freq == 0:          ⟵——┘
                model2.load_state_dict(model.state_dict())
        if reward != -1 or mov > max_moves:
            status = 0
            mov = 0

losses = np.array(losses)
```

When we plot the loss for a target network approach with experience replay (figure 3.16), we still get a noisy loss plot, but it is significantly less noisy and clearly downtrending. You should try to experiment with the hyperparameters, such as the experience replay buffer size, the batch size, the target network update frequency, and the learning rate. The performance can be quite sensitive to these hyperparameters.

When we test the trained model on 1,000 games, we get about a 3% improvement in win percentage compared to training without a target network. We're getting a top accuracy of around 95%, which we think is probably the maximal accuracy given the limitations of this environment (i.e., the possibility of unwinnable states). We're only training up to 5,000 epochs, where each epoch is a single game. The number of possible game configurations (the size of the state-space) is approximately $16 \cdot 15 \cdot 14 \cdot 13 = 43,680$ (since there are 16 possible positions the agent can be in on a 4×4 grid, and

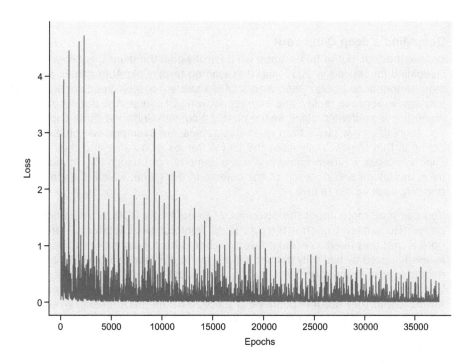

Figure 3.16 **The DQN loss plot after including a target network to stabilize training. This shows a much faster training convergence than without the target network, but it has noticeable spikes of error when the target network synchronizes with the main DQN.**

then 15 possible configurations for the wall, since the agent and wall can't be overlapping in space, etc.), so we're only sampling about $\frac{5,000}{43,680} = 0.11 = 11\%$ of the total number of possible starting game states. If the model can successfully play games it has never seen before, then we have some confidence it has generalized. If you're getting good results with the 4×4 board, you should try training an agent to play on a 5×5 board or larger by changing the size parameter when creating the Gridworld game instance:

```
>>> game = Gridworld(size=6, mode='random')
>>> game.display()

array([[' ', '+', ' ', ' ', ' ', ' '],
       [' ', ' ', ' ', ' ', ' ', ' '],
       [' ', ' ', 'W', ' ', ' ', ' '],
       [' ', '-', ' ', ' ', ' ', ' '],
       [' ', ' ', ' ', ' ', 'P', ' '],
       [' ', ' ', ' ', ' ', ' ', ' ']], dtype='<U2')
```

DeepMind's deep Q-network

Believe it or not, but in this chapter we basically built the deep Q-network (DQN) that DeepMind introduced in 2015 and that learned to play old Atari games at superhuman performance levels. DeepMind's DQN used an epsilon-greedy action-selection strategy, experience replay, and a target network. Of course, the details of our implementation are different, since we are playing a custom Gridworld game and DeepMind was training on raw pixels from real video games. For example, one difference worth noting is that they actually input the last 4 frames of a game into their Q-network. That's because a single frame in a video game is not enough information to determine the speed and direction of the objects in the game, which is important when deciding what action to take.

You can read more about the specifics of DeepMind's DQN by searching for their paper "Human-level control through deep reinforcement learning." One thing to note is that they used a neural network architecture consisting of two convolutional layers followed by two fully connected layers. In our case we used three fully connected layers. It would be a worthwhile experiment to build a model with a convolutional layer, and try training it with Gridworld. One huge advantage of convolutional layers is that they are independent of the size of the input tensor. When we used a fully connected layer, for example, we had to make the first dimension 64—we used a 64×164 parameter matrix for the first layer. A convolutional layer, however, can be applied to input data of any length. This would allow you to train a model on a 4×4 grid and see if it generalizes enough to be able to play on a 5×5 or bigger grid. Go ahead, try it!

3.5   Review

We've covered a lot in this chapter, and once again we've smuggled in a lot of fundamental reinforcement learning concepts. We could have pushed a bunch of academic definitions in your face to start, but we resisted the temptation and decided to get to coding as quickly as possible. Let's review what we've accomplished and fill in a few terminological gaps.

In this chapter we covered a particular RL algorithm called Q-learning. Q-learning has nothing to do with deep learning or neural networks on its own; it is an abstract mathematical construct. Q-learning refers to solving a control task by learning a function called a Q function. You give the Q function a state (e.g., a game state) and it predicts how valuable all the possible actions are that you could take given the input state, and we call these value predictions Q values. You decide what to do with these Q values. You might decide to take the action that corresponds to the highest Q value (a greedy approach), or you might opt for a more sophisticated selection process. As you learned in chapter 2, you have to balance exploration (trying new things) versus exploitation (taking the best action you know of). In this chapter we used the standard epsilon-greedy approach to select actions, where we initially take random actions to explore, and then progressively switch our strategy to taking the highest value actions.

The Q function must be learned from data. The Q function has to learn how to make accurate Q value predictions of states. The Q function could be anything really—anything from an unintelligent database to a complex deep learning algorithm. Since deep learning is the best class of learning algorithms we have at the moment, we employed neural networks as our Q functions. This means that "learning the Q function" is the same as training a neural network with backpropagation.

One important concept about Q-learning that we held back until now is that it is an *off-policy* algorithm, in contrast to an *on-policy* algorithm. You already know what a policy is from the last chapter: it's the strategy an algorithm uses to maximize rewards over time. If a human is learning to play Gridworld, they might employ a policy that first scouts all possible paths toward the goal and then selects the one that is shortest. Another policy might be to randomly take actions until you land on the goal.

An off-policy reinforcement learning algorithm like Q-learning means that the choice of policy does not affect the ability to learn accurate Q values. Indeed, our Q-network could learn accurate Q values if we selected actions at random; eventually it would experience a number of winning and losing games and infer the values of states and actions. Of course, this is terribly inefficient, but the policy matters only insofar as it helps us learn with the least amount of data. In contrast, an on-policy algorithm will explicitly depend on the choice of policy or will directly aim at learning a policy from the data. In other words, in order to train our DQN, we need to collect data (experiences) from the environment, and we could do this using any policy, so DQN is off-policy. In contrast, an on-policy algorithm learns a policy while simultaneously using the same policy to collect experiences for training itself.

Another key concept we've saved until now is the notion of *model-based* versus *model-free* algorithms. To make sense of this, we first need to understand what a model is. We use this term informally to refer to a neural network, and it's often used to refer to any kind of statistical model, others being a linear model or a Bayesian graphical model. In another context, we might say a model is a mental or mathematical representation of how something works in "the real world." If we understand exactly how something works (i.e., what it's composed of and how those components interact) then we can not only explain data we've already seen, but we can predict data we haven't yet seen.

For example, weather forecasters build very sophisticated models of the climate that take into account many relevant variables, and they're constantly measuring real-world data. They can use their models to predict the weather to some degree of accuracy. There's an almost cliché statistics mantra that "all models are wrong, but some are useful," meaning that it is impossible to build a model that 100% corresponds to reality; there will always be data or relationships that we're missing. Nonetheless, many models capture enough truth about a system we're interested in that they're useful for explanation and prediction.

If we could build an algorithm that could figure out how Gridworld works, it would have inferred a model of Gridworld, and it would be able to play it perfectly. In Q-learning, all we gave the Q-network was a numpy tensor. It had no *a priori* model of Gridworld, but it still learned to play by trial and error. We did not task the Q-network with figuring out how Gridworld works; its only job was to predict expected rewards. Hence, Q-learning is a model-free algorithm.

As the human architects of algorithms, we may be able to engineer in some of our own domain knowledge about a problem as a model to optimize our problem. We could then supply this model to a learning algorithm and let it figure out the details. This would be a model-based algorithm. For example, most chess-playing algorithms are model-based; they know the rules of how chess works and what the result of taking certain moves will be. The only part that isn't known (and that we'd want the algorithm to figure out) is what sequence of moves will win the game. With a model in hand, the algorithm can make long-term plans in order to achieve its aim.

In many cases, we want to employ algorithms that can progress from being model-free to planning with a model. For example, a robot learning how to walk may start to learn by trial and error (model-free), but once it has figured out the basics of walking, it can start to infer a model of its environment and then plan a sequence of steps to get from point A to B (model-based). We'll continue to explore on-policy, off-policy, model-based, and model-free algorithms in the rest of the book. In the next chapter we'll look at an algorithm that will help us build a network that can approximate the policy function.

Summary

- A *state-space* is the set of all possible states that the environment can be in. Usually the states are encoded as tensors, so the state space may be a vector of type $\mathbb{R}^n$ or a matrix in $\mathbb{R}^{n \times m}$.
- An *action-space* is the set of all possible actions given a state; for example, the action space for the game chess would be the set of all legal moves given some state of the game.
- A *state-value* is the expected sum of discounted rewards for a state given we follow some policy. If a state has a high state-value, that means that starting from this state will likely lead to high rewards.
- An *action-value* is the expected rewards for taking an action in a particular state. It is the value of a state-action pair. If you know the action-values for all possible actions for a state, you can decide to take the action with the highest action-value, and you would expect to receive the highest reward as a result.
- A *policy function* is a function that maps states to actions. It is the function that "decides" which actions to take given some input state.
- *Q function* is a function that takes a state-action pair and returns the action-value.
- *Q-learning* is a form of reinforcement learning where we attempt to model the Q function; in other words, we attempt to learn how to predict the expected rewards for each action given a state.
- A *deep Q-network (DQN)* is simply where we use a deep learning algorithm as the model in Q-learning.

- *Off-policy learning* is when we learn a policy while collecting data using a different policy.
- *On-policy learning* is when we learn a policy while also simultaneously using it to collect data for learning.
- *Catastrophic forgetting* is a big problem that machine learning algorithms face when training with small batches of data at a time, where the new data being learned erases or corrupts the old information already learned.
- *Experience replay* is a mechanism to allow batch training of reinforcement learning algorithms in order to mitigate catastrophic forgetting and allow stable training.
- A *target network* is a copy of the main DQN that we use to stabilize the update rule for training the main DQN.

Learning to pick the best policy: Policy gradient methods

4

This chapter covers

- Implementing the policy function as a neural network
- Introducing the OpenAI Gym API
- Applying the REINFORCE algorithm on the OpenAI CartPole problem

In the previous chapter we discussed deep Q-networks, an off-policy algorithm that approximates the Q function with a neural network. The output of the Q-network was Q values corresponding to each action for a given state (figure 4.1); recall that the Q value is the expected (weighted average) of rewards.

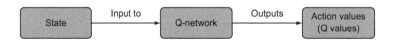

Figure 4.1   A Q-network takes a state and returns Q values (action values) for each action. We can use those action values to decide which actions to take.

Given these predicted Q values from the Q-network, we can use some strategy to select actions to perform. The strategy we employed in the last chapter was the epsilon-greedy approach, where we selected an action at random with probability ε, and with probability $1 - \varepsilon$ we selected the action associated with the highest Q value (the action the Q-network predicts is the best, given its experience so far). There are any number of other policies we could have followed, such as using a softmax layer on the Q values.

What if we skip selecting a policy on top of the DQN and instead train a neural network to output an action directly? If we do that, our neural network ends up being a *policy function*, or a *policy network*. Remember from chapter 3 that a policy function, $\pi.State \rightarrow P(Action \mid State)$, accepts a state and returns the best action. More precisely, it will return a probability distribution over the actions, and we can sample from this distribution to select actions. If a probability distribution is an unfamiliar concept to you, don't worry. We'll discuss it more in this chapter and throughout the book.

4.1 Policy function using neural networks

In this chapter we'll introduce a class of algorithms that allow us to approximate the policy function, $\pi(s)$, instead of the value function, V_π or Q. That is, instead of training a network that outputs action values, we will train a network to output (the probability of) actions.

4.1.1 Neural network as the policy function

In contrast to a Q-network, a policy network tells us exactly what to do given the state we're in. No further decisions are necessary. All we need to do is randomly sample from the probability distribution $P(A \mid S)$, and we get an action to take (figure 4.2). The actions that are most likely to be beneficial will have the highest chance of being selected from random sampling, since they are assigned the highest probability.

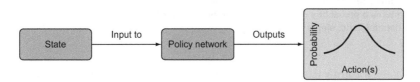

Figure 4.2 A policy network is a function that takes a state and returns a probability distribution over the possible actions.

Imagine the probability distribution $P(A \mid S)$ as a jar filled with little notes with an action written on each. In a game with four possible actions, there will be notes with labels 1–4 (or 0–3 if they're indices in Python). If our policy network predicts that action 2 is the most likely to result in the highest reward, it will fill this jar with a lot of little notes labeled 2, and fewer notes labeled 1, 3, and 4. In order to select an action then, all we do is close our eyes and grab a random note from the jar. We're most likely to choose action 2, but sometimes we'll grab another action, and that gives us the opportunity to explore. Using this analogy, every time the state of the environment changes, we give the state to our policy network, and it uses that to fill the jar with a new set of labeled notes representing the actions in different proportions. Then we randomly pick from the jar.

This class of algorithms is called *policy gradient methods,* and it has a few important differences from the DQN algorithm; we'll explore these differences in this chapter. Policy gradient methods offer a few advantages over value prediction methods like DQN. One is that, as we already discussed, we no longer have to worry about devising an action-selection strategy like epsilon-greedy; instead, we directly sample actions from the policy. Remember, we spent a lot of time cooking up methods to improve the stability of training our DQN—we had to use experience replay and target networks, and there are a number of other methods in the academic literature that we could have used. A policy network tends to simplify some of that complexity.

4.1.2   *Stochastic policy gradient*

There are many different flavors of policy gradient methods. We will start with the *stochastic policy gradient* method (figure 4.3), which is what we just described. With a stochastic policy gradient, the output of our neural network is an action vector that represents a probability distribution.

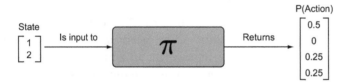

Figure 4.3   A stochastic policy function. A policy function accepts a state and returns a probability distribution over actions. It is *stochastic* because it returns a probability distribution over actions rather than returning a deterministic, single action.

The policy we'll follow is selecting an action from this probability distribution. This means that if our agent ends up in the same state twice, we may not end up taking the same action every time. In figure 4.3 we feed our function the state, which is (1,2), and the output is a vector of probabilities corresponding to each action. If this was a Gridworld agent, for example, the agent would have a 0.50 probability of going up, no chance of going down, a 0.25 probability of going left, and a 0.25 probability of going right.

If the environment is stationary, which is when the distribution of states and rewards is constant, and we use a deterministic strategy, we'd expect the probability distribution to eventually converge to a *degenerate probability distribution,* as shown in figure 4.4. A degenerate probability distribution is a distribution in which all the probability mass is assigned to a single potential outcome. When dealing with discrete probability distributions as we do in this book, all the probabilities must sum to 1, so a

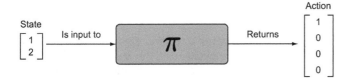

Figure 4.4   A deterministic policy function, often represented by the Greek character pi, takes a state and returns a specific action to take, unlike a stochastic policy, which returns a probability distribution over actions.

degenerate distribution is one where all outcomes are assigned 0 probability except for one, which is assigned 1.

Early in training we want the distribution to be fairly uniform so that we can maximize exploration, but over the course of training we want the distribution to converge on the optimal actions, given a state. If there is only one optimal action for a state, we'd expect to converge toward a degenerate distribution, but if there are two equally good actions, then we would expect the distribution to have two *modes*. A mode of a probability distribution is just another word for a "peak."

I forget … What's a probability distribution?

In Gridworld, we had four possible actions: up, down, left, and right. We call this our action set or actions-space, since we can describe it mathematically as a set, e.g., $A = \{up, down, left, right\}$ where the curly braces indicate a set. (A set in mathematics is just an abstract unordered collection of things with certain operations defined.) So what does it mean to apply a probability distribution over this set of actions?

Probability is actually a very rich and even controversial topic in its own right. There are varying philosophical opinions on exactly what *probability* means. To some people, the probability means that, if you were to flip a coin a very large number of times (ideally an infinite number of times, mathematically speaking) the probability of a fair coin turning up heads is equal to the proportion of heads in that infinitely long sequence of flips. That is, if we flip a fair coin 1,000,000 times, we would expect about half of the flips to be heads and the other half tails, so the probability is equal to that proportion. This is a frequentist interpretation of probability, since probability is interpreted as the long-term frequency of some event repeated many times.

Another school of thought interprets probability only as a degree of belief, a subjective assessment of how much someone can predict an event given the knowledge they currently possess. This degree of belief is often called a *credence*. The probability of a fair coin turning up heads is 0.5 or 50% because, given what we know about the coin, we don't have any reason to predict heads more than tails, or tails more than heads, so we split our belief evenly across the two possible outcomes. Hence, anything that we can't predict deterministically (i.e., with probability 0 or 1, and nothing in between) results from a lack of knowledge.

You're free to interpret probabilities however you want, since it won't affect our calculations, but in this book we tend to implicitly use the credence interpretation of probability. For our purposes, applying a probability distribution over the set of actions in Gridworld, $A = \{up,down,left,right\}$ means we're assigning a degree of belief (a real number between 0 and 1) to each action in the set such that all the probabilities sum to 1. We interpret these probabilities as the probability that an action is the best action to maximize the expected rewards, given that we're in a certain state.

Concretely, a probability distribution over our action set A is denoted $P(A): A_i \rightarrow [0,1]$, meaning that $P(A)$ is a map from a set A to a set of real numbers between 0 and 1. In particular, each element $a_i \in A$ is mapped to a single number between 0 and 1 such that the sum of all these numbers for each action is equal to 1. We might represent this map for our Gridworld action set as just a vector, where we identify each position in the vector with an element in the action set, e.g., [up, down, left, right] $\rightarrow$ [0.25, 0.25, 0.10, 0.4]. This map is called a *probability mass function* (PMF).

What we just described is actually a *discrete* probability distribution, since our action set was discrete (a finite number of elements). If our action set was infinite, i.e., a continuous variable like velocity, we would call this a *continuous* probability distribution and instead we would need to define a *probability density function* (PDF).

The most common example of a PDF is the normal (also known as Gaussian, or just bell-curve) distribution. If we have a probability with a continuous action, say a car game where we need to control the velocity of the car from 0 to some maximum value, which is a continuous variable, how might we do this with a policy network? Well, we could drop the idea of probability distribution and just train the network to produce the single value of velocity that it predicts is best, but then we'd risk not exploring enough (and it is difficult to train such a network). A lot of power comes from a little bit of randomness. The kind of neural networks we employ in this book only produce vectors (or tensors more generally) as output, so they can't produce a continuous probability distribution—we have to be more clever. A PDF like a normal distribution is defined by two parameters, the mean and variance. Once we have those, we have a normal distribution that we can sample from. So we can just train a neural network to produce mean and standard deviation values that we can then plug into the normal distribution equation and sample from that.

Don't worry if this isn't all making sense now. We will continue to go over it again and again because these concepts are ubiquitous in reinforcement learning and machine learning more broadly.

4.1.3 Exploration

Recall from the previous chapter that we needed our policy to include some randomness, which would allow us to visit new states during training. For DQNs we followed the epsilon-greedy policy, where there was a chance we would not follow the action that led to the greatest predicted reward. If we always selected the action that led to the maximum predicted reward, we'd never discover the even better actions and states available to us. For the stochastic policy gradient method, because our output is a probability distribution, there should be a small chance that we explore all spaces; only after sufficient exploration will the action distribution converge to producing the single best action, a degenerate distribution. Or if the environment itself has some randomness, the probability distribution will retain some probability mass to each action. When we initialize our model in the beginning, the probability of our agent picking each action should be approximately equal or uniform, since the model has zero information about which action is better.

There is a variant of policy gradient called *deterministic policy gradient* (DPG) where there is a single output that the agent will always follow (as illustrated in figure 4.4). In the case of Gridworld, for example, it would produce a 4-dimensional binary vector with a 1 for the action to be taken and 0s for the other actions. The agent won't explore properly if it always follows the output because there's no randomness in the action selection. Since the output of a deterministic policy function for a discrete action set would be discrete values, it is also difficult to get this working in the fully differentiable manner that we are accustomed to with deep learning, so we'll focus on stochastic policy gradients. Building a notion of uncertainty into the models (e.g., using probability distributions) is generally a good thing.

4.2 Reinforcing good actions: The policy gradient algorithm

From the previous section, you understand that there is a class of algorithms that attempts to create a function that outputs a probability distribution over actions, and that this policy function $\pi(s)$ can be implemented with a neural network. In this section we'll delve into how to actually implement these algorithms and train (i.e., optimize) them.

4.2.1 Defining an objective

Recall that neural networks need an objective function that is differentiable with respect to the network weights (parameters). In the last chapter we trained the deep Q-network with a minimizing mean squared error (MSE) loss function with respect to its predicted Q values and the target Q value. We had a nice formula for calculating the target Q value based on the observed reward, since Q values are just averaged rewards (i.e., expectations), so this was not much different from how we would normally train a supervised deep learning algorithm.

How do we train a policy network that gives us a probability distribution over actions given a state, $P(A|S)$? There's no obvious way to map our observed rewards after taking an action to updating $P(A|S)$. Training the DQN was not much different from solving a supervised learning problem because our Q-network generated a vector of predicted Q values, and by using a formula we were able to generate the target Q value vector. Then we just minimized the error between the Q-network's output vector and our target vector.

With a policy network, we're predicting actions directly, and there is no way to come up with a target vector of actions we should have taken instead, given the rewards. All we know is whether the action led to positive or negative rewards. In fact, what the best action is secretly depends on a value function, but with a policy network we're trying to avoid computing these action values directly.

Let's go through an example to see how we might optimize our policy network. We'll start with some notation. Our policy network is denoted π and is parameterized by a vector θ, which represents all of the parameters (weights) of the neural network. As you know, neural networks have parameters in the form of multiple weight matrices, but for the purposes of easy notation and discussion, it is standard to consider all the network parameters together as a single long vector that we denote θ (theta).

Whenever we run the policy network forward, the parameter vector θ is fixed; the variable is the data that gets fed into the policy network (i.e., the state). Hence, we denote the parameterized policy as π_θ. Whenever we want to indicate that some input to a function is fixed, we will include it as a subscript rather than as an explicit input like $\pi(x,\theta)$ where x is some input data (i.e., the state of the game). Notations like $\pi(x,\theta)$ suggest θ is a variable that changes along with x, whereas π_θ indicates that θ is a fixed parameter of the function.

Let's say we give our initially untrained policy network π_θ some initial game state for Gridworld, denoted s, and run it forward by computing $\pi_\theta(s)$. It returns a probability distribution over the four possible actions, such as [0.25, 0.25, 0.25, 0.25]. We sample from this distribution, and since it's a uniform distribution, we end up taking a random action (figure 4.5). We continue to take actions by sampling from the produced action distribution until we reach the end of the episode.

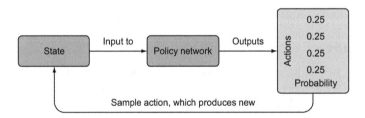

Figure 4.5   The general overview of policy gradients for an environment with four possible discrete actions. First we input the state to the policy network, which produces a probability distribution over the actions, and then we sample from this distribution to take an action, which produces a new state.

Remember, some games like Gridworld are episodic, meaning that there is a well-defined start and end point to an episode of the game. In Gridworld, we start the game in some initial state and play until we either hit the pit, land on the goal, or take too many moves. So an episode is a sequence of states, actions, and rewards from an initial state to the terminal state where we win or lose the game. We denote this episode as

$$\varepsilon = (S_0, A_0, R_1), (S_1, A_1, R_2) \ldots (S_{t-1}, A_{t-1}, R_t)$$

Each tuple is one time-step of the Gridworld game (or a Markov decision process, more generally). After we've reached the end of the episode at time t, we've collected a bunch of historical data on what just happened. Let's say that by chance we hit the goal after just three moves determined by our policy network. Here's what our episode looks like:

$$\varepsilon = (S_0, 3, -1), (S_1, 1, -1), (S_2, 3, +10)$$

We've encoded the actions as integers from 0 to 3 (referring to array indices of the action vector) and we've left the states denoted symbolically since they're actually 64-length vectors. What is there to learn from in this episode? Well, we won the game, indicated by the +10 reward in the last tuple, so our actions must have been "good" to some degree. Given the states we were in, we should encourage our policy network to make those actions more likely next time. We want to reinforce those actions that led to a nice positive reward. We will address what happens when our agent loses (receives a terminal reward of –10) later in this section, but in the meantime we will focus on positive reinforcement.

4.2.2 Action reinforcement

We want to make small, smooth updates to our gradients to encourage the network to assign more probability to these winning actions in the future. Let's focus on the last experience in the episode, with state S_2. Remember, we're assuming our policy network produced the action probability distribution [0.25, 0.25, 0.25, 0.25], since it was untrained, and in the last time step we took action 3 (corresponding to element 4 in the action probability array), which resulted in us winning the game with a +10 reward. We want to positively reinforce this action, given state S_2, such that whenever the policy network encounters S_2 or a very similar state, it will be more confident in predicting action 3 as the highest probability action to take.

A naive approach might be to make a target action distribution, [0, 0, 0, 1], so that our gradient descent will move the probabilities from [0.25, 0.25, 0.25, 0.25] close to [0, 0, 0, 1], maybe ending up as [0.167, 0.167, 0.167, 0.5] (see figure 4.6). This is something we often do in the supervised learning realm, when we are training a softmax-based image classifier. But in that case, there is a single correct classification for an image, and there is no temporal association between each prediction. In our RL case, we want more control over how we make these updates. First, we want to make small, smooth updates because we want to maintain some stochasticity in our action sampling to adequately explore the environment. Second, we want to be able to weight how much we assign credit to each action for earlier actions. Let's review some more notation before diving into these two problems.

Recall that our policy network is typically denoted π_θ when we are running it forward (i.e., using it to produce action probabilities), because we think of the network parameters, θ, as being fixed and the input state is what varies. Hence, calling $\pi_\theta(s)$ for some state s will return a probability distribution over the possible actions, given a

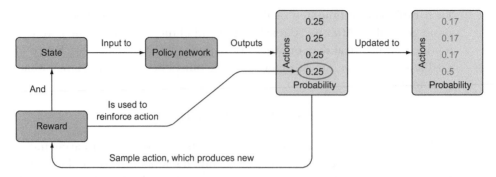

Figure 4.6   Once an action is sampled from the policy network's probability distribution, it produces a new state and reward. The reward signal is used to reinforce the action that was taken, that is, it increases the probability of that action given the state if the reward is positive, or it decreases the probability if the reward is negative. Notice that we only received information about action 3 (element 4), but since the probabilities must sum to 1, we have to lower the probabilities of the other actions.

fixed set of parameters. When we are training the policy network, we need to vary the parameters with respect to a fixed input to find a set of parameters that optimizes our objective (i.e., minimizes a loss or maximizes a utility function), which is the function $\pi_s(\theta)$.

> **DEFINITION** The probability of an action, given the parameters of the policy network, is denoted $\pi_s(a|\theta)$. This makes it clear that the probability of an action, a, explicitly depends on the parameterization of the policy network. In general, we denote a *conditional probability* as $P(x|y)$, read "the probability distribution over x given y." This means we have some function that takes a parameter y and returns a probability distribution over some other parameter x.

In order to reinforce action 3, we want to modify our policy network parameters θ such that we increase $\pi_s(a_3|\theta)$. Our objective function merely needs to maximize $\pi_s(a_3|\theta)$ where a_3 is action 3 in our example. Before training, $\pi_s(a_3|\theta) = 0.25$, but we want to modify θ such that $\pi_s(a_3|\theta) > 0.25$. Because all of our probabilities must sum to 1, maximizing $\pi_s(a_3|\theta)$ will minimize the other action probabilities. And remember, we prefer to set things up so that we're minimizing an objective function instead of maximizing, since it plays nicely with PyTorch's built-in optimizers—we should instead tell PyTorch to minimize $1 - \pi_s(a|\theta)$. This loss function approaches 0 as $\pi_s(a|\theta)$ nears 1, so we are encouraging the gradients to maximize $\pi_s(a|\theta)$ for the action we took. We will subsequently drop the subscript a_3, as it should be clear from the context which action we're referring to.

4.2.3   Log probability

Mathematically, what we've described is correct. But due to computation imprecisions we need to make adjustments to this formula to stabilize the training. One problem is that probabilities are bounded by 0 and 1 by definition, so the range of values that the optimizer can operate over is limited and small. Sometimes probabilities may be extremely tiny or very close to 1, and this runs into numerical issues when optimizing on a computer with limited numerical precision. If we instead use a surrogate objective, namely $-\log\pi_s(a|\theta)$ (where log is the natural logarithm), we have an objective that has a larger "dynamic range" than raw probability space, since the log of probability space ranges from $(-\infty, 0)$, and this makes the log probability easier to compute. Moreover, logarithms have the nice property that $\log(a \cdot b) = \log(a) + \log(b)$, which means when we multiply log probabilities, we can turn this multiplication into a sum, which is also more numerically stable than multiplication. If we set our objective as $-\log\pi_s(a|\theta)$ instead of $1 - \pi_s(a|\theta)$, our loss still abides by the intuition that the loss function approaches 0 as $\pi_s(a|\theta)$ approaches 1. Our gradients will be tuned to try to increase $\pi_s(a|\theta)$ to 1, where a = action 3, for our running example.

4.2.4　*Credit assignment*

Our objective function is $-\log\pi_s(a|\theta)$, but this assigns equal weight to every action in our episode. The weights in the network that produced the last action will be updated to the same degree as the first action. Why shouldn't that be the case? Well, it makes sense that the last action right before the reward deserves more credit for winning the game than does the first action in the episode. For all we know, the first action was actually sub-optimal, but then we later made a comeback and hit the goal. In other words, our confidence in how "good" each action is diminishes the further we are from the point of reward. In a game of chess, we attribute more credit to the last move made than the first one. We're very confident that the move that directly led to us to winning was a good move, but we become less confident the further back we go. How much did the move five time steps ago contribute to winning? We're not so sure. This is the problem of *credit assignment.*

We express this uncertainty by multiplying the magnitude of the update by the discount factor, which you learned in chapter 3 ranges from 0 to 1. The action right before the episode ends will have a discount factor of 1, meaning it will receive the full gradient update, while earlier moves will be discounted by a fraction such as 0.5 so the gradient steps will be smaller.

Let's add those into our objective (loss) function. The final objective function that we will tell PyTorch to minimize is $-\gamma_t * G_t * \log\pi_s(a|\theta)$. Remember, γ_t is the discount factor, and the subscript t tells us its value will depend on the time step t, since we want to discount more distant actions more than more recent ones. The parameter G_t is called the *total return*, or *future return*, at time step t. It is the return we expect to collect from time step t until the end of the episode, and it can be approximated by adding the rewards from some state in the episode until the end of the episode.

$$G_t = r_t + r_{t+1} \dots + r_{T-1} + r_T$$

Actions temporally more distant from the received reward should be weighted less than actions closer. If we win a game of Gridworld, the sequence of discounted rewards from the start to the terminal state might look something like [0.970, 0.980, 0.99, 1.0]. The last action led to the winning state of +1, and it is not discounted at all. The previous action is assigned a scaled reward by multiplying the terminal reward with the γ_{t-1} discount factor, which we've set to 0.99.

The discount is exponentially decayed from 1, $\gamma_t = \gamma_0^{(T-t)}$, meaning that the discount at time t is calculated as the starting discount (here 0.99) exponentiated to the integer time distance from the reward. The length of the episode (the total number of time steps) is denoted T, and the local time step for a particular action is t. For $T - t = 0$, $\gamma_{T-0} = 0.99^0 = 1$. For $T - t = 2$, the $\gamma_{T-2} = 0.99^2 = 0.9801$, and so on. Each time step back, the discount factor is exponentiated to the distance from the terminal step, which results in an exponential decay of the discount factor the more distant (and irrelevant) the action was to the reward outcome.

For example, if the agent is in state S_0 (i.e., time step $t = 0$) and it takes action a_1 and receives reward $t_{t+1} = -1$, the target update will be $-\gamma^0(-1)\log \pi(a_1 \mid \theta, S_0) = \log \pi(a_1 \mid \theta, S_0)$, which is the log-probability output from the policy network (see figure 4.7).

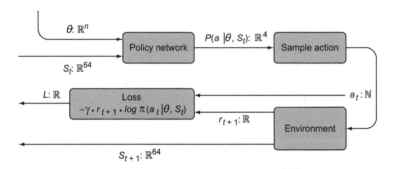

Figure 4.7   A string diagram for training a policy network for Gridworld. The policy network is a neural network parameterized by θ (the weights) that accepts a 64-dimensional vector for an input state. It produces a discrete 4-dimensional probability distribution over the actions. The sample action box samples an action from the distribution and produces an integer as the action, which is given to the environment (to produce a new state and reward) and to the loss function so we can reinforce that action. The reward signal is also fed into the loss function, which we attempt to minimize with respect to the policy network parameters.

4.3   *Working with OpenAI Gym*

To illustrate how policy gradients work, we've been using Gridworld as an example, since it is already familiar to you from last chapter. However, we should use a different problem to actually implement the policy gradient algorithm, both for variety and also to introduce the OpenAI Gym.

The OpenAI Gym is an open source suite of environments with a common API that is perfect for testing reinforcement learning algorithms. If you come up with

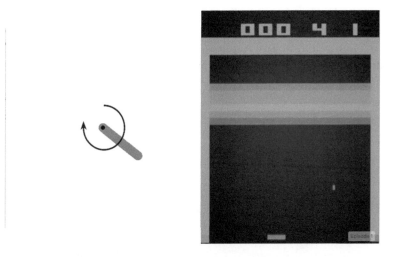

Figure 4.8 Two example environments provided by OpenAI's Gym environment. The OpenAI Gym provides hundreds of environments to test your reinforcement learning algorithms on.

some new DRL algorithm, testing it on a few of the environments in the Gym is a great way to get some idea of how well it performs. The Gym contains a variety of environments from easy ones can be "solved" by simple linear regression all the way through to ones that all but require a sophisticated DRL approach (see figure 4.8). There are games, robotic control, and other types of environments. There's probably something in there you'll be interested in.

OpenAI lists all of its currently supported environments on its website: https://gym .openai.com/envs/. At the time of writing, they are broken down into seven categories:

- Algorithms
- Atari
- Box2D
- Classic control
- MuJoCo
- Robotics
- Toy text

You can also view the entire list of environments from the OpenAI registry in your Python shell with the following code.

Listing 4.1 Listing the OpenAI Gym environments

```
from gym import envs
envs.registry.all()
```

There are hundreds of environments to choose from (797 in v0.9.6). Unfortunately, some of these environments require licenses (MuJoCo) or external dependencies (Box2D, Atari) and will therefore require a bit of setup time. We will be starting with a simple example, CartPole (figure 4.9), to avoid any unnecessary complications and to get us coding right away.

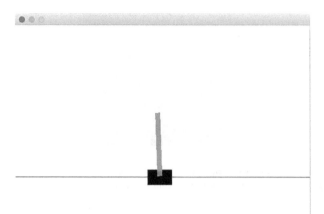

Figure 4.9   A screenshot from the CartPole game environment in OpenAI Gym. There is a cart that can roll left or right, and on top of it is a pole on a pivot. The goal is to balance the pole upright on the cart by carefully moving the cart left or right.

4.3.1   CartPole

The CartPole environment falls under OpenAI's Classic Control section, and it has a very simple objective—don't let the pole fall over. It's the game equivalent of trying to balance a pencil on the tip of your finger. In order to balance the pole successfully, you have to apply just the right amount of small left and right movements to the cart. In this environment, there are only two actions that correspond to making a small push left or right.

In the OpenAI Gym API, environments with discrete action spaces all have actions represented as integers from 0 to the total number of actions for the particular environment, so in CartPole the possible actions are 0 and 1, which denote a push to the left or to the right. The state is represented as a vector of length 4 that indicates the cart position, cart velocity, pole angle, and pole velocity. We receive a reward of +1 for every step the pole has not fallen over, which happens when the pole angle is more than 12° from the center or when the cart position is outside the window. Hence, the goal of CartPole is to maximize the length of the episode, since each step returns a positive +1 reward. More information can be found on the OpenAI Gym GitHub page (https://github.com/openai/gym/wiki/CartPole-v0). Note that not every subsequent problem has a nice specification page like CartPole does, but we will define the scope of the problem beforehand in all subsequent chapters.

4.3.2 *The OpenAI Gym API*

The OpenAI Gym has been built to be incredibly easy to use, and there are less than half a dozen methods that you'll routinely use. You already saw one in listing 4.1 where we listed all the available environments. Another important method is creating an environment.

> **Listing 4.2   Creating an environment in OpenAI Gym**

```
import gym
env = gym.make('CartPole-v0')
```

From now on, we will be interacting solely with this `env` variable. We need a way to observe the current state of the environment and then to interact with it. There are only two methods you need to do this.

> **Listing 4.3   Taking an action in CartPole**

```
state1 = env.reset()
action = env.action_space.sample()
state, reward, done, info = env.step(action)
```

The `reset` method initializes the environment and returns the first state. For this example, we used the `sample` method of the `env.action_space` object to sample a random action. Soon enough, we'll sample actions from a trained policy network that will act as our reinforcement learning agent.

Once we initialize the environment, we are free to interact with it via the `step` method. The `step` method returns four important variables that our training loop needs access to in order to run. The first parameter, `state`, represents the next state after we take the action. The second parameter, `reward`, is the reward at that time step, which for our CartPole problem is 1 unless the pole has fallen down. The third parameter, `done`, is a Boolean that indicates whether or not a terminal state has been reached. For our CartPole problem, this would always return `false` until the pole has fallen or the cart has moved outside the window. The last parameter, `info`, is a dictionary with diagnostic information that may be useful for debugging, but we will not use it. That's all you need to know to get most environments up and running in OpenAI Gym.

4.4   *The REINFORCE algorithm*

Now that you how to create an OpenAI Gym environment and have hopefully developed an intuition for the policy gradient algorithm, let's dive in to getting a working implementation. Our discussion of policy gradients in the previous section focused on a particular algorithm that has been around for decades (like most of deep learning and reinforcement learning) called REINFORCE (yes, it's always fully capitalized). We're going to consolidate what we discussed previously, formalize it, and then turn it into Python code. Let's implement the REINFORCE algorithm for the CartPole example.

4.4.1   Creating the policy network

We will build and initialize a neural network that serves as a policy network. The policy network will accept state vectors as inputs, and it will produce a (discrete) probability distribution over the possible actions. You can think of the agent as a thin wrapper around the policy network that samples from the probability distribution to take an action. Remember, an agent in reinforcement learning is whatever function or algorithm takes a state and returns a concrete action that will be executed in the environment.

Let's express this in code.

Listing 4.4   Setting up the policy network

```
import gym
import numpy as np          The input data is length 4
import torch                ("l1" is short for layer 1)

l1 = 4                      The middle layer produces
l2 = 150                    a vector of length 150
l3 = 2                      The output is a 2-length
                            vector for the left and
model = torch.nn.Sequential(    right actions
    torch.nn.Linear(l1, l2),
    torch.nn.LeakyReLU(),
    torch.nn.Linear(l2, l3),    The output is a softmax
    torch.nn.Softmax()          probability distribution
)                               over actions

learning_rate = 0.0009
optimizer = torch.optim.Adam(model.parameters(), lr=learning_rate)
```

That should all look fairly familiar to you at this point. The model is only two layers: a leaky ReLU activation function for the first layer, and the `Softmax` function for the last layer. We chose the leaky ReLU because it performed better empirically. You saw the `Softmax` function back in chapter 2; it just takes an array of numbers and squishes them into the range of 0 to 1 and makes sure they all sum to 1, basically creating a discrete probability distribution out of any list of numbers that are not probabilities to start with. For example, `softmax([-1,2,3]) = [0.0132, 0.2654, 0.7214]`. Unsurprisingly, the `Softmax` function will turn the bigger numbers into larger probabilities.

4.4.2   Having the agent interact with the environment

The agent consumes the state and takes an action, a, probabilistically. More specifically, the state is input to the policy network, which then produces the probability distribution over the actions $P(A \mid \theta, S_t)$ given its current parameters and the state. Note, the capital A refers to the set of all possible actions given the state, whereas the lowercase a generally refers to a particular action.

The policy network might return a discrete probability distribution in the form of a vector, such as [0.25, 0.75] for our two possible actions in CartPole. This means the policy network predicts that action 0 is the best with 25% probability, and action 1 is the best with 75% probability (or confidence). We call this array `pred`.

Listing 4.5 Using the policy network to sample an action

Calls the policy network model to produce predicted action probabilities

Samples an action from the probability distribution produced by the policy network

```
pred = model(torch.from_numpy(state1).float())
action = np.random.choice(np.array([0,1]), p=pred.data.numpy())
state2, reward, done, info = env.step(action)
```

Takes the action and receives the new state and reward. The info variable is produced by the environment but is irrelevant.

The environment responds to the action by producing a new state, s_2, and a reward, r_2. We store those into two arrays (a states array and an actions array) for when we need to update our model after the episode ends. We then plug the new state into our model, get a new state and reward, store those, and repeat until the episode ends (the pole falls over and the game is finished).

4.4.3 Training the model

We train the policy network by updating the parameters to minimize the objective (i.e., loss) function. This involves three steps:

1 Calculate the probability of the action actually taken at each time step.
2 Multiply the probability by the discounted return (the sum of rewards).
3 Use this probability-weighted return to backpropagate and minimize the loss.

We'll look at these in turn.

CALCULATING THE PROBABILITY OF THE ACTION

Calculating the probability of the action taken is easy enough. We can use the stored past transitions to recompute the probability distributions using the policy network, but this time we extract just the predicted probability for the action that was actually taken. We'll denote this quantity $P(a_t | \theta, s_t)$; this is a single probability value, like 0.75.

To be concrete, let's say the current state is S_5 (the state at time step 5). We input that into the policy network and it returns $P_\theta(A | s_5) = [0.25, 0.75]$. We sample from this distribution and take action $a = 1$ (the second element in the action array), and after this the pole falls over and the episode has ended. The total duration of the episode was $T = 5$. For each of these 5 time steps, we took an action according to $P_\theta(A | s_t)$ and we stored the specific probabilities of the actions that were actually taken, $P_\theta(a | s_t)$, in an array, which might look like [0.5, 0.3, 0.25, 0.5, 0.75]. We simply multiply these probabilities by the discounted rewards (explained in the next section), take the sum, multiply it by –1, and call that our overall loss for this episode. Unlike Gridworld, in CartPole the last action is the one that loses the episode; we discount it the most since we want to penalize the worst move the most. In Gridworld we would do the opposite and discount the first action in the episode most, since it would be the least responsible for winning or losing.

Minimizing this objective function will tend to increase those probabilities $P_\theta(a \mid s_t)$ weighted by the discounted rewards. So every episode we're tending to increase $P_\theta(a \mid s_t)$, but for a particularly long episode (if we're doing well in the game and get a large end-of-episode return) we will increase the $P_\theta(a \mid s_t)$ to a greater degree. Hence, on average over many episodes we will reinforce the actions that are good, and the bad actions will get left behind. Since probabilities must sum to 1, if we increase the probability of a good action, that will automatically steal probability mass from the other presumably less good actions. Without this redistributive nature of probabilities, this scheme wouldn't work (i.e., everything both good and bad would tend to increase).

CALCULATING FUTURE REWARDS

We multiply $P(a_t \mid \theta, s_t)$ by the total reward (a.k.a. return) we received after this state. As mentioned earlier in the section, we can get the total reward by just summing the rewards (which is equal to the number of time steps the episode lasted in CartPole) and create a return array that starts with the episode duration and decrements by 1 until 1. If the episode lasted 5 time steps, the return array would be [5,4,3,2,1]. This makes sense because our first action should be rewarded the most, since it is the least responsible for the pole falling and losing the episode. In contrast, the action right before the pole fell is the worst action, and it should have the smallest reward. But this is a linear decrement—we want to discount the rewards exponentially.

To compute the discounted rewards, we make an array of γ_t by taking our γ parameter, which may be set to 0.99 for example, and exponentiating it according to the distance from the end of the episode. For example, we start with gamma_t = [0.99, 0.99, 0.99, 0.99, 0.99], then create another array of exponents exp = [1,2,3,4,5] and compute torch.power(gamma_t, exp), which will give us [1.0, 0.99, 0.98, 0.97, 0.96].

THE LOSS FUNCTION

Now that we have discounted returns, we can use these to compute the loss function to train the policy network. As we discussed previously, we make our loss function the negative log-probability of the action given the state, scaled by the reward returns. In PyTorch, this is defined as -1 * torch.sum(r * torch.log(preds)). We compute the loss with the data we've collected for the episode, and run the torch optimizer to minimize the loss. Let's run through some actual code.

Listing 4.6 Computing the discounted rewards

```
def discount_rewards(rewards, gamma=0.99):
    lenr = len(rewards)
    disc_return = torch.pow(gamma,torch.arange(lenr).float()) * rewards     ◁─┐
    disc_return /= disc_return.max()     ◁─┐
    return disc_return
```

Computes exponentially decaying rewards

Normalizes the rewards to be within the [0,1] interval to improve numerical stability

Here we define a special function to compute the discounted rewards given an array of rewards that would look like [50,49,48,47,...] if the episode lasted 50 time steps. It essentially turns this linear sequence of rewards into an exponentially decaying sequence of rewards (e.g., [50.0000, 48.5100, 47.0448, 45.6041, ...]), and then it divides by the maximum value to bound the values in the interval [0,1].

The reason for this normalization step is to improve the learning efficiency and stability, since it keeps the return values within the same range no matter how big the raw return is. If the raw return is 50 in the beginning of training but then reaches 200 by the end of training, the gradients are going to change by almost an order of magnitude, which hampers stability. It will still work without normalization, but not as reliably.

BACKPROPAGATING

Now that we have all the variables in our objective function, we can calculate the loss and backpropagate to adjust the parameters. The following listing shows the loss function, which is just a Python translation of the math we described earlier.

> **Listing 4.7 Defining the loss function**

The loss function expects an array of action probabilities for the actions that were taken and the discounted rewards.

```
def loss_fn(preds, r):     <──
    return -1 * torch.sum(r * torch.log(preds))     <──
```

It computes the log of the probabilities, multiplies by the discounted rewards, sums them all, and flips the sign.

4.4.4 The full training loop

Initialize, collect experiences, calculate the loss from those experiences, backpropagate, and repeat. The following listing defines the full training loop of our REINFORCE agent.

> **Listing 4.8 The REINFORCE training loop**

```
MAX_DUR = 200
MAX_EPISODES = 500
gamma = 0.99
score = []                          <──
for episode in range(MAX_EPISODES):
        curr_state = env.reset()
        done = False
        transitions = []            <──

        for t in range(MAX_DUR):    <──
        act_prob = model(torch.from_numpy(curr_state).float())
        action = np.random.choice(np.array([0,1]), p=act_prob.data.numpy())
        prev_state = curr_state
        curr_state, _, done, info = env.step(action)     <──
        transitions.append((prev_state, action, t+1))    <──
```

A list to keep track of the episode length over training time

A list of state, action, rewards (but we ignore the reward)

While in the episode

Gets the action probabilities

Selects an action stochastically

Stores this transition

Takes the action in the environment

Collects all the rewards in the episode in a single tensor

Collects the states in the episode in a single tensor

Collects the actions in the episode in a single tensor

```
    if done:          ◄─┐  If the game is lost,
        break            │  breaks out of the loop

    ep_len = len(transitions)     ◄─  Stores the episode length
    score.append(ep_len)
    reward_batch = torch.Tensor([r for (s,a,r) in
    transitions]).flip(dims=(0,))
    disc_rewards = discount_rewards(reward_batch)   ◄─┐
    state_batch = torch.Tensor([s for (s,a,r) in transitions])
    action_batch = torch.Tensor([a for (s,a,r) in transitions])
    pred_batch = model(state_batch)               ◄─
    prob_batch = pred_batch.gather(dim=1,index=action_
    batch.long().view(-1,1)).squeeze()          ◄─┐
    loss = loss_fn(prob_batch, disc_rewards)
    optimizer.zero_grad()
    loss.backward()
    optimizer.step()
```

Computes the discounted version of the rewards

Recomputes the action probabilities for all the states in the episode

Subsets the action-probabilities associated with the actions that were actually taken

We start an episode, use the policy network to take actions, and record the states and actions we observe. Then, once we break out of an episode, we have to recompute the predicted probabilities to use in our loss function. Since we record all the transitions in each episode as a list of tuples, once we're out of the episode we can separate each component of each transition (the state, action, and reward) into separate tensors to train on a batch of data at a time. If you run this code, you should be able to plot the episode duration against the episode number, and you will hopefully see a nicely increasing trend, as in figure 4.10.

The agent learns how to play CartPole! The nice thing about this example is that it should be able to train in under a minute on your laptop with just the CPU. The state of CartPole is just a 4-dimensional vector, and our policy network is only two small layers, so it's much faster to train than the DQN we created to play Gridworld. OpenAI's documentation says that the game is considered "solved" if the agent can play an episode beyond 200 time steps. Although the plot looks like it tops off at around 190, that's because it's a moving average plot. There are many episodes that reach 200 but a few times where it randomly fails early on, bringing the average down a bit. Also, we capped the episode duration at 200, so if you increase the cap it will be able to play even longer.

4.4.5   *Chapter conclusion*

REINFORCE is an effective and very simple way of training a policy function, but it's a little too simple. For CartPole it works very well, since the state space is very small and there are only two actions. If we're dealing with an environment with many more possible actions, reinforcing all of them each episode and hoping that on average it will only reinforce the good actions becomes less and less reliable. In the next two chapters we'll explore more sophisticated ways of training the agent.

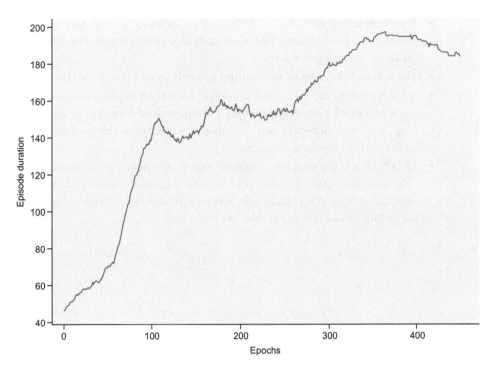

Figure 4.10 After training the policy network to 500 epochs, we get a plot that demonstrates the agent really is learning how to play CartPole. Note that this is a moving average plot with a window of 50 to smooth the plot.

Summary

- *Probability* is a way of assigning degrees of belief about different possible outcomes in an unpredictable process. Each possible outcome is assigned a probability in the interval [0,1] such that all probabilities for all outcomes sum to 1. If we believe a particular outcome is more likely than another, we assign it a higher probability. If we receive new information, we can change our assignments of probabilities.

- *Probability distribution* is the full characterization of assigned probabilities to possible outcomes. A probability distribution can be thought of as a function $P{:}O \rightarrow$ [0,1] that maps all possible outcomes to a real number in the interval [0,1] such that the sum of this function over all outcomes is 1.

- A *degenerate probability distribution* is a probability distribution in which only 1 outcome is possible (i.e., it has probability of 1, and all other outcomes have a probability of 0).

- *Conditional probability* is the probability assigned to an outcome, assuming you have some additional information (the information that is conditioned).

- A *policy* is a function, $\pi{:}S \rightarrow A$, that maps states to actions and is usually implemented as a probabilistic function, $\pi{:}P(A|S)$, that creates a probability distribution over actions given a state.
- The *return* is the sum of discounted rewards in an episode of the environment.
- A *policy gradient method* is a reinforcement learning approach that tries to directly learn a policy by generally using a parameterized function as a policy function (e.g., a neural network) and training it to increase the probability of actions based on the observed rewards.
- *REINFORCE* is the simplest implementation of a policy gradient method; it essentially maximizes the probability of an action times the observed reward after taking that action, such that each action's probability (given a state) is adjusted according to the size of the observed reward.

Tackling more complex problems with actor-critic methods

This chapter covers

- The limitations of the REINFORCE algorithm
- Introducing a *critic* to improve sample efficiency and decrease variance
- Using the advantage function to speed up convergence
- Speeding up the model by parallelizing training

In the previous chapter we introduced a vanilla version of a policy gradient method called REINFORCE. This algorithm worked fine for the simple CartPole example, but we want to be able to apply reinforcement learning to more complex environments. You already saw that deep Q-networks can be quite effective when the action space is discrete, but it has the drawback of needing a separate policy function such as epsilon-greedy. In this chapter you'll learn how to combine the advantages of REINFORCE and those of DQN to create a class of algorithms called actor-critic models. These have proven to yield state-of-the-art results in many domains.

The REINFORCE algorithm is generally implemented as an *episodic algorithm*, meaning that we only apply it to update our model parameters after the agent has completed an entire episode (and collected rewards along the way). Recall that the policy is a function, $\pi: S \rightarrow P(a)$. That is, it's a function that takes a state and returns a probability distribution over actions (figure 5.1).

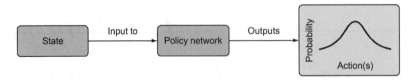

Figure 5.1   A policy function takes a state and returns a probability distribution over actions, where a higher probability indicates an action that is more likely to result in the highest reward.

Then we sample from this distribution to get an action, such that the most probable action (the "best" action) is most likely to be sampled. At the end of the episode, we compute the *return* of the episode, which is essentially the sum of the discounted rewards in the episode. The return is calculated as

$$R = \sum_t \gamma_t \cdot r_t$$

After the game is over, the return for that episode is the sum of all the rewards acquired, multiplied by their respective discount rate, where γ_t exponentially decays as a function of time. For example, if action 1 was taken in state A and resulted in a return of +10, the probability of action 1 given state A will be increased a little, whereas if action 2 was taken in state A and resulted in a return of –20, the probability of action 2 given state A will decrease. Essentially, we minimize this loss function:

$$\text{Loss} = -log(P(a \mid S)) \cdot R$$

This says "minimize the logarithm of the probability of the action a given state S times the return R." If the reward is a big positive number, and $P(a_1 \mid S_A) = 0.5$ for example, minimizing this loss will involve increasing this probability. So with REINFORCE we just keep sampling episodes (or trajectories more generally) from the agent and environment, and periodically update the policy parameters by minimizing this loss.

NOTE   Remember, we only apply the logarithm to the probability because a probability is bounded by 0 and 1, whereas the log probability is bounded by $-\infty$ (negative infinity) and 0. Given that numbers are represented by a finite number of bits, we can represent very small (close to 0) or very large (close to 1) probabilities without underflowing or overflowing the computer's numerical precision. Logarithms also have nicer mathematical properties that we won't cover, but that is why you'll almost always see log probabilities used in algorithms and machine learning papers, even though we are conceptually interested in the raw probabilities themselves.

By sampling a full episode, we get a pretty good idea of the true value of an action because we can see its downstream effects rather than just its immediate effect (which may be misleading due to randomness in the environment); this full episode sampling is under the umbrella of Monte Carlo approaches. But not all environments are episodic, and sometimes we want to be able to make updates in an incremental or *online* fashion, i.e., make updates at regular intervals irrespective of what is going on in the environment. Our deep Q-network did well in the non-episodic setting and it could be considered an online-learning algorithm, but it required an experience replay buffer in order to effectively learn.

The replay buffer was necessary because true online learning where parameter updates are made after each action is unstable due to the inherent variance in the environment. An action taken once may by chance result in a big negative reward, but in expectation (the average long-term rewards) it may be a good action—updating after a single action may result in erroneous parameter updates that will ultimately prevent adequate learning.

In this chapter, we will introduce a new kind of policy gradient method called *distributed advantage actor-critic* (DA2C) that will have the online-learning advantages of DQN without a replay buffer. It will also have the advantages of policy methods where we can directly sample actions from the probability distribution over actions, thereby eliminating the need for choosing a policy (such as the epsilon-greedy policy) that we needed with DQN.

5.1 Combining the value and policy function

The great thing about Q-learning is that it learns directly from the available information in the environment, which are the rewards. It basically learns to predict rewards, which we call values. If we use a DQN to play pinball, it will learn to predict the values for the two main actions—operating the left and right paddles. We're then free to use these values to decide which action to take, generally opting for the action associated with the highest value.

A policy gradient function is more directly connected to the concept of *reinforcement*, since we positively reinforce actions that result in a positive reward and negatively reinforce actions that lead to a negative reward. Hence, the policy function learns which actions are best in a more hidden way. In pinball, if we hit the left paddle and score a bunch of points, that action will get positively reinforced and will be more likely to be selected the next time the game is in a similar state.

In other words, Q-learning (such as DQN) uses a trainable function to directly model the value (the expected reward) of an action, given a state. This is a very intuitive way of solving a Markov decision process (MDP) since we only observe states and rewards—it makes sense to predict the rewards and then just take actions that have high predicted rewards. On the other hand, we saw the advantage of direct policy learning (such as policy gradients). Namely, we get a true conditional probability distribution over actions, $P(a|S)$, that we can directly sample from to take an action.

Naturally, someone decided it might be a good idea to combine these two approaches to get the advantages of both.

In building such a combined value-policy learning algorithm, we will start with the policy learner as the foundation. There are two challenges we want to overcome to increase the robustness of the policy learner:

- We want to improve the sample efficiency by updating more frequently.
- We want to decrease the variance of the reward we used to update our model.

These problems are related, since the reward variance depends on how many samples we collect (more samples yields less variance). The idea behind a combined value-policy algorithm is to use the value learner to reduce the variance in the rewards that are used to train the policy. That is, instead of minimizing the REINFORCE loss that included direct reference to the observed return, R, from an episode, we instead add a baseline value such that the loss is now:

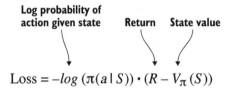

$$\text{Loss} = -log\,(\pi(a\,|\,S)) \cdot (R - V_{\pi}(S))$$

Here, $V(S)$ is the value of state S, which is the state-value function (a function of the state) rather than an action-value function (a function of both state and action), although an action-value function could be used as well. This quantity, $V(S) - R$, is termed the *advantage*. Intuitively, the advantage quantity tells you how much better an action is, relative to what you expected.

> **NOTE**   Remember that the value function (state value or action value) implicitly depends on the choice of policy, so we ought to write $V_{\pi}(S)$ to make it explicit; however, we drop the π subscript for notational simplicity. The policy's influence on the value is crucial, since a policy of taking random actions all the time would result in all states being of more or less equally low value.

Imagine that we're training a policy on a Gridworld game with discrete actions and a small discrete state-space, such that we can use a vector where each position in the vector represents a distinct state, and the element is the average rewards observed after that state is visited. This look-up table would be the $V(S)$. We might sample action 1 from the policy and observe reward +10, but then we'd use our value look-up table and see that on average we get +4 after visiting this state, so the advantage of action 1 given this state is $10 - 4 = +6$. This means that when we took action 1, we got a reward that was significantly better than what we expected based on past rewards from that state, which suggests that it was a good action. Compare this to the case where we take action 1 and receive reward +10 but our value look-up table says we expected to see

+15, so the advantage is 10 − 15 = −5. That suggests this was a relatively bad action despite the fact that we received a reasonably large positive reward.

Rather than using a look-up table, we will use some sort of parameterized model, such as a neural network that can be trained to predict expected rewards for a given state. So we want to simultaneously train a policy neural network and a state-value or action-value neural network.

Algorithms of this sort are called *actor-critic* methods, where "actor" refers to the policy, because that's where the actions are generated, and "critic" refers to the value function, because that's what (in part) tells the actor how good its actions are. Since we're using $R − V(S)$ to train the policy rather than just $V(S)$, this is called *advantage actor-critic* (figure 5.2).

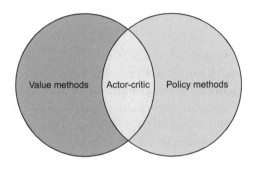

Figure 5.2   **Q-learning falls under the category of value methods, since we attempt to learn action values, whereas policy gradient methods like REINFORCE directly attempt to learn the best actions to take. We can combine these two techniques into what's called an actor-critic architecture.**

NOTE   What we have described so far would not be considered a true actor-critic method by some, because we're only using the value function as a baseline and not using it to "bootstrap" by making a prediction about a future state based on the current state. You will see how bootstrapping comes into play soon.

The policy network has a sensitive loss function that depends on the rewards collected at the end of the episode. If we naively tried to make online updates with the wrong type of environment, we might never learn anything because the rewards might be too sparse.

In Gridworld, which we introduced in chapter 3, the reward is −1 on every move except for the end of the episode. The vanilla policy gradient method wouldn't know what action to reinforce, since most actions result in the same reward of −1. In contrast, a Q-network can learn decent Q values even when the rewards are sparse, because it *bootstraps*. When we say an algorithm bootstraps, we mean it can make a prediction from a prediction.

If we ask you what the temperature will be like two days from now, you might first predict what the temperature will be tomorrow, and then base your 2-day prediction on that (figure 5.3). You're bootstrapping. If your first prediction is bad, your second may be even worse, so bootstrapping introduces a source of *bias*. Bias is a systematic deviation from the true value of something, in this case from the true Q values. On the other hand, making predictions from predictions introduces a kind of self-consistency that results in lower *variance.* Variance is exactly what it sounds like: a lack of precision in the predictions, which means predictions that vary a lot. In the temperature example, if we make our day 2 temperature prediction based on our day 1 prediction, it will likely not be too far from our day 1 prediction.

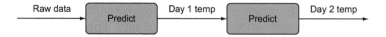

Figure 5.3   Read from left to right, raw data is fed into a predict temperature model that predicts the next day's temperature. That prediction is then used in another prediction model that predicts day 2's temperature. We can keep doing this, but initial errors will compound and our predictions will become inaccurate for distant predictions.

Bias and variance are key concepts relevant to all of machine learning, not just deep learning or deep reinforcement learning (figure 5.4). Generally, if you reduce bias you will increase variance, and vice versa (figure 5.5). For example, if we ask you to predict the temperature for tomorrow and the next day, you could give us a specific temperature: "The 2-day temperature forecast is 20.1 C and 20.5 C." This is a high-precision prediction—you've given us a temperature prediction to a tenth of a degree! But you don't have a crystal ball, so your prediction is almost surely going to be systematically off, biased toward whatever your prediction procedure involved. Or you could have told us,

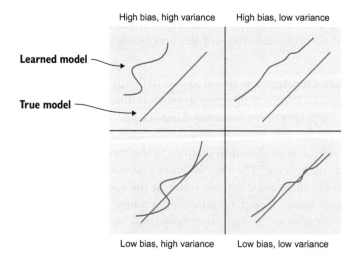

Figure 5.4   The bias-variance tradeoff is a fundamental machine learning concept that says any machine learning model will have some degree of systematic deviation from the true data distribution and some degree of variance. You can try to reduce the variance of your model, but it will always come at the cost of increased bias.

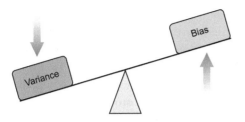

Figure 5.5 The bias-variance tradeoff. Increasing model complexity can reduce bias, but it will increase variance. Reducing variance will increase bias.

"The 2-day temperature forecast is 15–25 C and 18–27 C." In this case, your prediction has a lot of spread, or variance, since you're giving fairly wide ranges, but it has low bias, meaning that you have a good chance of the real temperatures falling in your intervals. This spread might be because your prediction algorithm didn't give undue weight to any of the variables used for prediction, so it's not particularly biased in any direction. Indeed, machine learning models are often *regularized* by imposing a penalty on the magnitude of the parameters during training; i.e., parameters that are significantly bigger or smaller than 0 are penalized. Regularization essentially means modifying your machine learning procedure in a way to mitigate overfitting.

We want to combine the potentially high-bias, low-variance value prediction with the potentially low-bias, high-variance policy prediction to get something with moderate bias and variance—something that will work well in the online setting. The role of the critic is hopefully starting to become clear. The actor (the policy network) will take a move, but the critic (the state-value network) will tell the actor how good or bad the action was, rather than only using the potentially sparse raw reward signals from the environment. Thus the critic will be a term in the actor's loss function. The critic, just like with Q-learning, will learn directly from the reward signals coming from the environment, but the sequence of rewards will depend on the actions taken by the actor, so the actor affects the critic too, albeit more indirectly (figure 5.6).

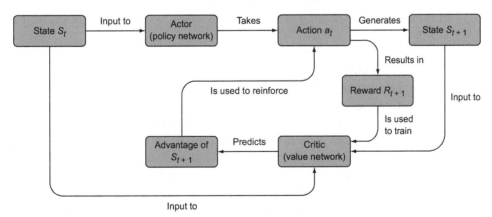

Figure 5.6 The general overview of actor-critic models. First, the actor predicts the best action and chooses the action to take, which generates a new state. The critic network computes the value of the old state and the new state. The relative value of S_{t+1} is called its advantage, and this is the signal used to reinforce the action that was taken by the actor.

The actor is trained in part by using signals coming from the critic, but how exactly do we train a state-value function as opposed to the action value (Q) functions we're more accustomed to? With action values, we computed the expected return (the sum of future discounted rewards) for a given state-action pair. Hence, we could predict whether a state-action pair would result in a nice positive reward, a bad negative reward, or something in between. But recall that with our DQN, our Q-network returned separate action values for each possible discrete action, so if we employ a reasonable policy like epsilon-greedy, the state value will essentially be the highest action value. Thus, the state-value function just computes this highest action value rather than separately computing action values for each action.

5.2   *Distributed training*

As we mentioned in the introduction, our goal in this chapter is to implement a model called distributed advantage actor-critic (DA2C), and we've discussed the "advantage actor-critic" part of the name at a conceptual level. Let's do the same for the "distributed" part now.

For virtually all deep learning models we do *batch training*, where a random subset of our training data is batched together and we compute the loss for this entire batch before we backpropagate and do gradient descent. This is necessary because the gradients, if we trained with single pieces of data at a time, would have too much variance, and the parameters would never converge on their optimal values. We need to average out the noise in a batch of data to get the real signal before updating the model parameters.

For example, if you're training an image classifier to recognize hand-drawn digits, and you train it with one image at a time, the algorithm would think that the background pixels are just as important as the digits in the foreground; it can only see the signal when averaged together with other images. The same concept applies in reinforcement learning, which is why we had to use an experience replay buffer with DQN.

Having a sufficiently large replay buffer requires a lot of memory, and in some cases a replay buffer is impractical. A replay buffer is possible when your reinforcement learning environment and agent algorithm follow the strict criteria of a Markov decision process, and in particular, the Markov property. Recall the Markov property says that the optimal action for a state S_t can be computed without reference to any prior states S_{t-1}; there is no need to keep a history of previously visited states. For simple games, this is the case, but for more complex environments, it may be necessary to remember the past in order to select the best option now.

Indeed, in many complex games it is common to use recurrent neural networks (RNNs) like a long short-term memory (LSTM) network or a gated recurrent unit (GRU). These RNNs can keep an internal state that can store traces of the past (figure 5.7). They are particularly useful for natural language processing (NLP) tasks where keeping track of preceding words or characters is critical to being able to

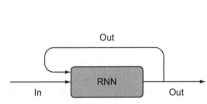

Figure 5.7 A generic recurrent neural network (RNN) layer processes a sequence of data by incorporating its previous output with the new input. The input on the left, along with a previous output is fed into an RNN module, which then produces an output. The output is fed back into the RNN on the next time step, and a copy may be fed into another layer. An RNN will not work properly with single experiences in an experience replay buffer since it needs to work on sequences of experiences.

encode or decode a sentence. Experience replay doesn't work with an RNN unless the replay buffer stores entire trajectories or full episodes, because the RNN is designed to process sequential data.

One way to use RNNs without an experience replay is to run multiple copies of the agent in parallel, each with separate instantiations of the environment. By distributing multiple independent agents across different CPU processes (figure 5.8), we can collect a varied set of experiences and therefore get a sample of gradients that we can average together to get a lower variance mean gradient. This eliminates the need for experience replay and allows us to train an algorithm in a completely online fashion, visiting each state only once as it appears in the environment.

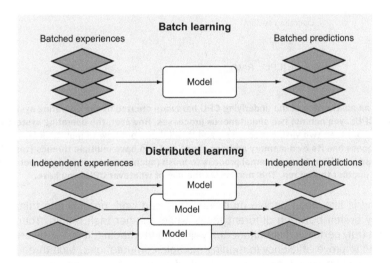

Figure 5.8 The most common form of training a deep learning model is to feed a batch of data together into the model to return a batch of predictions. Then we compute the loss for each prediction and average or sum all the losses before backpropagating and updating the model parameters. This averages out the variability present across all the experiences. Alternatively, we can run multiple models with each taking a single experience and making a single prediction, backpropagate through each model to get the gradients, and then sum or average the gradients before making any parameter updates.

Multiprocessing versus multithreading

Modern desktop and laptop computers have central processing units (CPUs) with multiple cores, which are independent processing units capable of running computations simultaneously. Therefore, if you can split a computation into pieces that can be computed separately and combined later, you can get dramatic speed increases. The operating system software abstracts the physical CPU processors into virtual processes and threads. A process contains its own memory space, and threads run within a single process. There are two forms of parallel computations, *multithreading* and *multiprocessing*, and only in the latter form are computations performed truly simultaneously. In multiprocessing, computations are performed simultaneously on multiple, physically distinct processing units such as CPU or GPU cores.

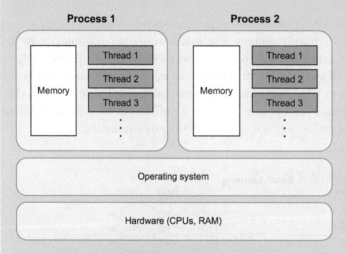

Processes are an abstraction of the underlying CPU hardware created by the operating system. If you have two CPUs, you can run two simultaneous processes. However, the operating system will let you spawn more than two virtual processes, and it will figure out how to multitask between them. Each process has its own memory address space and can have multiple threads (tasks). While one thread is waiting for an external process to finish (such as an input/output operation), the OS can let another thread run. This maximizes the use of whatever CPUs you have.

Multithreading is like when people multitask: they can work on only one thing at a time but they switch between different tasks while another task is idle. Therefore, tasks are not truly performed simultaneously with multithreading; it is a software-level mechanism to improve efficiency in running multiple computations. Multithreading is really effective when your task requires a lot of input/output operations, such as reading and writing data to the hard disk. When data is being read into RAM from the hard disk, computation on the CPU is idle as it waits for the required data, and the operating system can use that idle CPU time to work on a different task and then switch back when the I/O operation is done.

Machine learning models generally do not require I/O operations; machine learning is limited by computation speed, so it benefits from true simultaneous computation with multiprocessing.

Large machine learning models all but require graphics processing units (GPUs) to perform efficiently, but distributed models on multiple CPUs can be competitive in some cases. Python provides a library called "multiprocessing" that makes multiprocessing very easy. Additionally, PyTorch wraps this library and has a method for allowing a model's parameters to be shared across multiple processes. Let's look at a simple example of multiprocessing.

As a contrived simple example, suppose we have an array with the numbers 0, 1, 2, 3 … 64 and we want to square each number. Since squaring a number does not depend on any other numbers in the array, we can easily parallelize this across multiple processors.

Listing 5.1   Introduction to multiprocessing

```
import multiprocessing as mp        │ This function takes an array
import numpy as np                  │ and squares each element.
def square(x):
return np.square(x)            ◁┘
x = np.arange(64)          ◁─┐ Sets up an array with a
>>> print(x)                 │ sequence of numbers
array([ 0,  1,  2,  3,  4,  5,  6,  7,  8,  9, 10, 11, 12, 13, 14, 15, 16,
       17, 18, 19, 20, 21, 22, 23, 24, 25, 26, 27, 28, 29, 30, 31, 32, 33,
       34, 35, 36, 37, 38, 39, 40, 41, 42, 43, 44, 45, 46, 47, 48, 49, 50,
       51, 52, 53, 54, 55, 56, 57, 58, 59, 60, 61, 62, 63])
>>> mp.cpu_count()
    8                        │ Sets up a multiprocessing
pool = mp.Pool(8)         ◁─┘ processor pool with 8 processes
squared = pool.map(square, [x[8*i:8*i+8] for i in range(8)])  ◁─┐ Uses the pool's
>>> squared                                                      │ map function to
[array([ 0,  1,  4,  9, 16, 25, 36, 49]),                        │ apply the square
 array([ 64,  81, 100, 121, 144, 169, 196, 225]),                │ function to each
 array([256, 289, 324, 361, 400, 441, 484, 529]),                │ array in the list
 array([576, 625, 676, 729, 784, 841, 900, 961]),                │ and returns the
 array([1024, 1089, 1156, 1225, 1296, 1369, 1444, 1521]),        │ results in a list
 array([1600, 1681, 1764, 1849, 1936, 2025, 2116, 2209]),
 array([2304, 2401, 2500, 2601, 2704, 2809, 2916, 3025]),
 array([3136, 3249, 3364, 3481, 3600, 3721, 3844, 3969])]
```

Here we define a function, `square`, that takes an array and squares it. This is the function that will get distributed across multiple processes. We create some sample data that is simply the list of numbers from 0 to 63, and rather than sequentially squaring them in a single process, we chop up the array into 8 pieces and compute the squares for each piece independently on a different processor (figure 5.9).

You can see how many hardware processors your computer has by using the `mp.cpu_count()` function. You can see in listing 5.1 that we have 8. Many modern computers may have 4 independent hardware processors, but they will have twice as many "virtual" processors via something called *hyperthreading*. Hyperthreading is a performance trick some processors use that can allow two processes to run essentially simultaneously on one physical processor. It is important not to create more processes

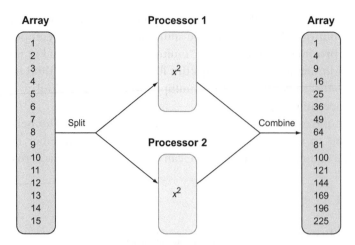

Figure 5.9   A simple multiprocessing example. We want to more efficiently square all the numbers in an array. Rather than squaring each element one by one, we can split the array into two pieces and send each piece to a different processor that will square them simultaneously. Then we can recombine the pieces back into a single array.

than there are CPUs on your machine, as the additional processes will essentially function as threads, and the CPU will have to rapidly switch between processes.

In listing 5.1 we set up a processor pool of 8 processes with `mp.Pool(8)`, and then we used `pool.map` to distribute the square function across the 8 pieces of data. You can see we get a list of 8 arrays with all their elements squared, just as we wanted. Processes will return as soon as they're complete, so the order of the elements in the returned list may not always be in the order they were mapped.

We're going to need a bit more control over our processes than a processor pool allows, so we will create and start a bunch of processes manually.

Listing 5.2   Manually starting individual processes

```
def square(i, x, queue):
    print("In process {}".format(i,))
queue.put(np.square(x))
processes = []
queue = mp.Queue()
x = np.arange(64)
for i in range(8):
    start_index = 8*i
    proc = mp.Process(target=square,args=(i,x[start_index:start_index+8],
                      queue))
    proc.start()
    processes.append(proc)

for proc in processes:
    proc.join()
```

Sets up a list to store a reference to each process

Sets up a multiprocessing queue, a data structure that can be shared across processes

Sets up some sample data, a sequence of numbers

Starts 8 processes with the square function as the target and an individual piece of data to process

Waits for each process to finish before returning to the main thread

```
for proc in processes:          ⟵┐  Terminates each
proc.terminate()                 │  process
results = []
while not queue.empty():        ⟵┐  Converts the multiprocessing
    results.append(queue.get())  │  queue into a list
>>> results
[array([ 0,   1,   4,    9,   16,   25,   36,   49]),
 array([256, 289, 324,  361,  400,  441,  484,  529]),
 array([ 64,  81, 100,  121,  144,  169,  196,  225]),
 array([1600, 1681, 1764, 1849, 1936, 2025, 2116, 2209]),
 array([576, 625, 676,  729,  784,  841,  900,  961]),
 array([1024, 1089, 1156, 1225, 1296, 1369, 1444, 1521]),
 array([2304, 2401, 2500, 2601, 2704, 2809, 2916, 3025]),
 array([3136, 3249, 3364, 3481, 3600, 3721, 3844, 3969])]
```

This is more code, but functionally it's the same as what we did before with the Pool. Now, though, it's easy to share data between processes using special shareable data structures in the multiprocessing library, and we have more control over the processes.

We modified our square function a little to accept an integer representing the process ID, the array to square, and a shared global data structure called a queue that we can put data into and extract data from using the .get() method.

To run through the code, we first set up a list to hold the instances of our processes, we created the shared queue object, and we created our sample data as before. We then define a loop to create (in our case) 8 processes and start them using the .start() method. We add them to our processes list so we can access them later. Next we run through the processes list and call each process's .join() method; this lets us wait to return anything until all the processes have finished. Then we call each process's .terminate() method to ensure it is killed. Lastly, we collect all the elements of the queue into a list and print it out.

The results look the same as with the process pool, except they were in a random order. That's really all there is to distributing a function across multiple CPU processors.

5.3 Advantage actor-critic

Now that we know how to distribute computation across processes, we can get back to the real reinforcement learning. In this section we'll put together the pieces of the full distributed advantage actor-critic model. To allow fast training and to compare the results to the previous chapter, we will again use the CartPole game as our test environment. If you choose, though, you can easily adapt the algorithm to a more difficult game such as Pong in OpenAI Gym; you can find such an implementation on this chapter's GitHub page: http://mng.bz/JzKp.

So far we've presented the actor and critic as two separate functions, but we can combine them into a single neural network with two output "heads." That's what we'll do in the following code. Instead of a normal neural network that returns a single vector, it can return two different vectors: one for the policy and one for the value. This allows for some parameter sharing between the policy and value that can make things more efficient, since some of the information needed to compute values is also useful for predicting the best action for the policy. But if a two-headed neural network seems too exotic right now, you can go ahead and write two separate neural networks—it will work just fine. Let's look at some pseudocode for the algorithm. Then we'll translate it to Python.

Listing 5.3   Pseudocode for online advantage actor-critic

Predicts the value of the state

Predicts the probability distribution over actions given the state

```
gamma = 0.9
for i in epochs:                                     Iterates over epochs
    state = environment.get_state()                  Gets the current state
    value = critic(state)                            of the environment
    policy = actor(state)
    action = policy.sample()
    next_state, reward = environment.take_action(action)
    value_next = critic(next_state)                  Predicts the value
    advantage = reward + (gamma * value_next - value)   of the next state
    loss = -1 * policy.logprob(action) * advantage
    minimize(loss)
```

Samples an action from the policy's action distribution

Reinforces the action that was just taken based on the advantage

Calculates the advantage as the reward plus the difference between the next state value and the current state value

---

This is very simplified pseudocode, but it gets the main idea across. The important part to point out is the advantage calculation. Consider the case where we take an action, we receive reward +10, the value prediction is +5, and the value prediction for the next state is +7. Since future predictions are always less valuable than the currently observed reward, we discount the value of the next state by the gamma discount factor. Our advantage = 10 + 0.9*7 − 5 = 10 + (6.3 − 5) = 10 + 1.3 = +11.3. Since the difference between the next state value and the current state value is positive, it increases the overall value of the action we just took, so we will reinforce it more. Notice that the advantage function *bootstraps* because it computes a value for the current state and action based on predictions for a future state.

In this chapter we're going to use our DA2C model on CartPole again, which is episodic, so if we do a full Monte Carlo update where we update after the full episode is complete, value_next will always be 0 for the last move since there is no next state when the episode is over. In this case, the advantage term actually reduces to advantage = reward − value, which is the value baseline we discussed at the beginning of the chapter. The full advantage expression, $A = r_{t+1} + \gamma * v(s_{t+1}) - v(s_t)$, is used when we do online or *N-step learning*.

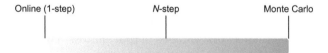

N-step learning is what's in between fully online learning and waiting for a full episode before updating (i.e., Monte Carlo). As the name suggests, we accumulate rewards over *N* steps and then compute our loss and backpropagate. The number of steps can be anywhere from 1, which reduces to fully online learning, to the maximum number of steps in the episode, which is Monte Carlo. Usually we pick something in between to get the advantages of both. We will first show the episodic actor-critic algorithm, and then we will adapt it to *N*-step with *N* set to 10.

Figure 5.10 shows the broad overview of an actor-critic algorithm. An actor-critic model needs to produce both a state value and action probabilities. We use the action probabilities to select an action and receive a reward, which we compare with the state value to compute an advantage. The advantage is ultimately what we use to reinforce the action and train the model.

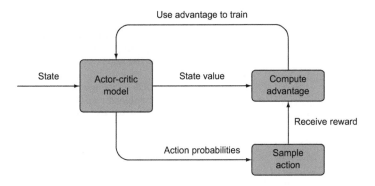

Figure 5.10   An actor-critic model produces a state value and action probabilities, which are used to compute an advantage value and this is the quantity that is used to train the model rather than raw rewards as with just Q-learning.

With that in mind, let's get to coding an actor-critic model to play CartPole. Here's the sequence of steps.

1. Set up our actor-critic model, a two-headed model (or you can set up two independent actor and critic networks). The model accepts a CartPole state as input, which is a vector of 4 real numbers. The actor head is just like the policy network (actor) from the previous chapter, so it outputs a 2-dimensional vector representing a discrete probability distribution over the 2 possible actions. The critic outputs a single number representing the state value. The critic is denoted $v(s)$ and the actor is denoted $\pi(s)$. Remember that $\pi(s)$ returns the log probabilities for each possible action, which in our case is 2 actions.

2. While we're in the current episode
   a. Define the hyperparameter: γ (gamma, discount factor).
   b. Start a new episode, in initial state s_t.
   c. Compute the value $v(s_t)$ and store it in the list.

   d Compute $\pi(s_t)$, store it in the list, sample, and take action a_t. Receive the new state s_{t+1} and the reward r_{t+1}. Store the reward in the list.

3 Train

   a Initialize $R = 0$. Loop through the rewards in reverse order to generate returns: $R = r_i + \gamma * R$.

   b Minimize the actor loss: $-1 * \gamma_t * (R - v(s_t)) * \pi(a|s)$.

   c Minimize the critic loss: $(R - v)^2$.

4 Repeat for a new episode.

The following listing implements these steps in Python.

Listing 5.4   CartPole actor-critic model

```
import torch
from torch import nn
from torch import optim
import numpy as np
from torch.nn import functional as F
import gym
import torch.multiprocessing as mp
class ActorCritic(nn.Module):
    def __init__(self):
        super(ActorCritic, self).__init__()
        self.l1 = nn.Linear(4,25)
        self.l2 = nn.Linear(25,50)
        self.actor_lin1 = nn.Linear(50,2)
        self.l3 = nn.Linear(50,25)
        self.critic_lin1 = nn.Linear(25,1)
    def forward(self,x):
        x = F.normalize(x,dim=0)
        y = F.relu(self.l1(x))
        y = F.relu(self.l2(y))
        actor = F.log_softmax(self.actor_lin1(y),dim=0)
        c = F.relu(self.l3(y.detach()))
        critic = torch.tanh(self.critic_lin1(c))
        return actor, critic
```

PyTorch wraps Python's built-in multiprocessing library, and the API is the same.

Defines a single combined model for the actor and critic

The actor head returns the log probabilities over the 2 actions.

Returns the actor and critic results as a tuple

The critic returns a single number bounded by –1 and +1.

For CartPole, we have a fairly simple neural network, apart from having two output heads. In listing 5.4 we first normalize the input so that the state values are all within the same range; then the normalized input is fed through the first two layers, which are ordinary linear layers with the ReLU activation functions. Then we fork the model into two paths.

The first path is the actor head that takes the output of layer 2 and applies another linear layer and then the log_softmax function. The log_softmax is logically equivalent to doing log(softmax(...))), but the combined function is more numerically stable because if you compute the functions separately you might end up with overflowed or underflowed probabilities after the softmax.

The second path is the critic head, which applies a linear layer and ReLU to the output of layer 2, but notice that we call `y.detach()`, which detaches the y node from the graph so the critic's loss won't backpropagate and modify the weights in layers 1 and 2 (figure 5.11). Only the actor will cause these weights to be modified. This prevents conflict between what the actor and critic want when the actor and critic are trying to make opposing updates to the earlier layers. With two-headed models, it often makes sense to make one head dominant and allow it to control most of the parameters by detaching the other head from the first several layers. Lastly, the critic applies another linear layer with the tanh activation function that bounds the output to the interval (–1,1), which is perfect for CartPole since the rewards are +1 and –1.

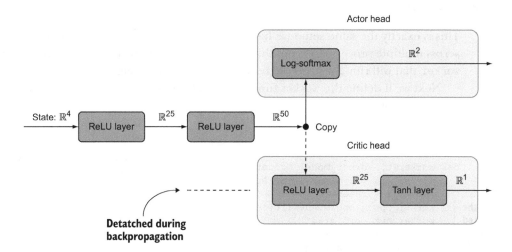

Figure 5.11 This is an overview of the architecture for our two-headed actor-critic model. It has two shared linear layers and a branching point where the output of the first two layers is sent to a log-softmax layer of the actor head and also to a ReLU layer of the critic head before finally passing through a tanh layer, which is an activation function that restricts output between –1 and 1. This model returns a 2-tuple of tensors rather than a single tensor. Notice that the critic head is detached (indicated by the dotted line), which means we do not backpropagate from the critic head into the actor head or the beginning of the model. Only the actor backpropagates through the beginning of the model.

In the following listing we develop the code necessary for distributing multiple instances of the actor-critic model across different processes.

Listing 5.5 Distributing the training

```
MasterNode = ActorCritic()
MasterNode.share_memory()
processes = []
params = {
    'epochs':1000,
    'n_workers':7,
}
```

Creates a global, shared actor-critic model

Sets up a list to store the instantiated processes

The shared_memory() method will allow the parameters of the model to be shared across processes rather than being copied.

```
counter = mp.Value('i',0)
for i in range(params['n_workers']):
    p = mp.Process(target=worker, args=(i,MasterNode,counter,params))
    p.start()
    processes.append(p)
for p in processes:
    p.join()
for p in processes:
    p.terminate()

print(counter.value,processes[1].exitcode)
```

"Joins" each process to wait for it to finish before returning to the main process

Starts a new process that runs the worker function

Makes sure each process is terminated

Prints the global counter value and the first process's exit code (which should be 0)

A shared global counter using multiprocessing's built-in shared object. The 'i' parameter indicates the type is integer.

This is exactly the same setup we had when we demonstrated how to split up an array across multiple processes, except this time we're going to be running a function called worker that will run our CartPole reinforcement learning algorithm.

Next we'll define the worker function, which will run a single agent in an instance of the CartPole environment.

Listing 5.6 The main training loop

```
def worker(t, worker_model, counter, params):
    worker_env = gym.make("CartPole-v1")
    worker_env.reset()
    worker_opt = optim.Adam(lr=1e-4,params=worker_model.parameters())
    worker_opt.zero_grad()
    for i in range(params['epochs']):
        worker_opt.zero_grad()
        values, logprobs, rewards = run_episode(worker_env,worker_model)
        actor_loss,critic_loss,eplen =
    update_params(worker_opt,values,logprobs,rewards)
        counter.value = counter.value + 1
```

Each process runs its own isolated environment and optimizer but shares the model.

We use the collected data from run_episode to run one parameter update step.

The run_episode function plays an episode of the game, collecting data along the way.

counter is a globally shared counter between all the running processes.

The worker function is the function that each individual process will run separately. Each worker (i.e., process) will create its own CartPole environment and its own optimizer but will share the actor-critic model, which is passed in as an argument to the function. Since the model is shared, whenever a worker updates the model parameters, they are updated for all the workers. This is shown at a high-level in figure 5.12.

Since each worker is spawned in a new process that has its own memory, all the data the worker needs should be passed in as an argument to the function explicitly. This also prevents bugs.

In listing 5.7 we define a function to run a single instance of the actor-critic model through one episode in the CartPole environment.

For each process:

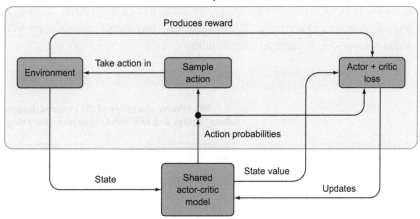

Figure 5.12 **Within each process, an episode of the game is run using the shared model. The loss is computed within each process, but the optimizer acts to update the shared actor-critic model that is used by each process.**

Listing 5.7   Running an episode

Keeps playing the game until the episode ends

Converts the environment state from a numpy array to a PyTorch tensor

Creates lists to store the computed state values (critic), log probabilities (actor), and rewards

Computes the state value and log probabilities over actions

Using the actor's log probabilities over actions, creates and samples from a categorical distribution to get an action

If the last action caused the episode to end, sets the reward to –10 and resets the environment

```
def run_episode(worker_env, worker_model):
    state = torch.from_numpy(worker_env.env.state).float()
    values, logprobs, rewards = [],[],[]
    done = False
    j=0
    while (done == False):
        j+=1
        policy, value = worker_model(state)
        values.append(value)
        logits = policy.view(-1)
        action_dist = torch.distributions.Categorical(logits=logits)
        action = action_dist.sample()
        logprob_ = policy.view(-1)[action]
        logprobs.append(logprob_)
        state_, _, done, info = worker_env.step(action.detach().numpy())
        state = torch.from_numpy(state_).float()
        if done:
            reward = -10
            worker_env.reset()
        else:
            reward = 1.0
        rewards.append(reward)
    return values, logprobs, rewards
```

The run_episode function just runs through a single episode of CartPole and collects the computed state values from the critic, log probabilities over actions from the actor, and rewards from the environment. We store these in lists and use them to compute our loss function later. Since this is an actor-critic method and not Q-learning, we take actions by directly sampling from the policy rather than arbitrarily choosing a policy like epsilon-greedy in Q-learning. There's nothing too out of the ordinary in this function, so let's move on to the updating function.

Listing 5.8   Computing and minimizing the loss

We reverse the order of the rewards, logprobs, and values_ arrays and call .view(-1) to make sure they're flat.

```
def update_params(worker_opt,values,logprobs,rewards,clc=0.1,gamma=0.95):
        rewards = torch.Tensor(rewards).flip(dims=(0,)).view(-1)         ◁───
        logprobs = torch.stack(logprobs).flip(dims=(0,)).view(-1)
        values = torch.stack(values).flip(dims=(0,)).view(-1)
        Returns = []
        ret_ = torch.Tensor([0])
        for r in range(rewards.shape[0]):        ◁───   For each reward (in reverse order),
            ret_ = rewards[r] + gamma * ret_             we compute the return value and
            Returns.append(ret_)                         append it to a returns array.
        Returns = torch.stack(Returns).view(-1)
        Returns = F.normalize(Returns,dim=0)
        actor_loss = -1*logprobs * (Returns - values.detach())
        critic_loss = torch.pow(values - Returns,2)         ◁───   The critic
        loss = actor_loss.sum() + clc*critic_loss.sum()     ◁───   attempts to
        loss.backward()                                            learn to predict
        worker_opt.step()                                          the return.
        return actor_loss, critic_loss, len(rewards)
```

We need to detach the values tensor from the graph to prevent backpropagating through the critic head.

We sum the actor and critic losses to get an overall loss. We scale down the critic loss by the clc factor.

The update_params function is where all the action is, and it's what sets distributed advantage actor-critic apart from the other algorithms we've learned so far. First we take the lists of rewards, log probabilities, and state values and convert them to PyTorch tensors. We then reverse their order because we want to consider the most recent action first, and we make sure they are flattened 1D arrays by calling the .view(-1) method.

The actor_loss is computed as we described earlier in this section with math, using the advantage (technically the baseline, since there's no bootstrapping) rather than the raw reward. Crucially, we must detach the values tensor from the graph when we use the actor_loss, or we will backpropagate through the actor and critic heads, and we only want to update the actor head. The critic loss is a simple squared error between the state values and the returns, and we make sure *not* to detach here since we want to update the critic head. Then we sum the actor and critic losses to get the overall loss. We scale down the critic loss by multiplying by 0.1 because we want the actor to learn faster than the critic. We return the individual losses and the length of the rewards tensor (which indicates how long the episode lasted) to monitor their progress during training.

The way we've set it up here, each worker will update the shared model parameters *asynchronously*, whenever it is done running an episode. We could have designed it such that we wait for all workers to finish running one episode and then sum their gradients together and update the shared parameters synchronously, but this is more complicated, and the asynchronous approach works well in practice.

Put it all together and run it, and you'll get a trained CartPole agent within one minute on a modern computer running on just a few CPU cores. If you plot the loss over time for this, it probably won't be a nice down-trending line like you'd hope because the actor and critic are in competition with one another (figure 5.13). The critic is incentivized to model the returns as best as it can (and the returns depend on what the actor does), but the actor is incentivized to beat the expectations of the critic. If the actor improves faster than the critic, the critic's loss will be high, and vice versa, so there is a somewhat adversarial relationship between the two.

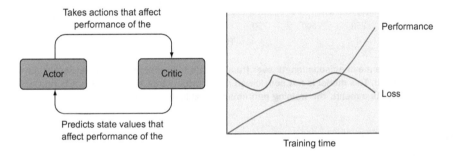

Figure 5.13 The actor and critic have a bit of an adversarial relationship since the actions that the agent take affect the loss of the critic, and the critic makes predictions of state values that get incorporated into the return that affects the training loss of the actor. Hence, the overall loss plot may look chaotic despite the fact that the agent is indeed increasing in performance.

Adversarial training like this is a very powerful technique in many areas of machine learning, not just reinforcement learning. For example, generative adversarial networks (GANs) are an unsupervised method for generating realistic-appearing synthetic samples of data from a training data set using a pair of models that function similarly to an actor and critic. In fact, we will build an even more sophisticated adversarial model in chapter 8.

The take-home here is that if you're using an adversarial model, the loss will be largely uninformative (unless it goes to 0 or explodes toward infinity, in which case something is probably wrong). You have to rely on actually evaluating the objective you care about, which in our case is how well the agent is performing in the game. Figure 5.14 shows the plot of average episode length during the first 120 epochs (about 45 seconds of) training.

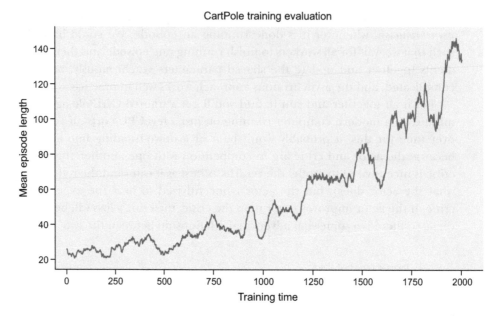

Figure 5.14   The mean episode length over training time for our Monte Carlo distributed advantage actor-critic model. This model is not considered a true critic, since the critic is not bootstrapping during training. As a result, the training performance has high variance.

5.4   *N-step actor-critic*

In the last section, we implemented distributed advantage actor-critic, except that we trained in Monte Carlo mode—we ran a full episode before updating the model parameters. While that makes sense for a simple game like CartPole, usually we want to be able to make more frequent updates. We briefly touched on N-step learning before, but to reiterate, it means we simply calculate our loss and update the parameters after N steps, where N is whatever we choose it to be. If N is 1, this is fully online learning; if N is very large, it will be Monte Carlo again. The sweet spot is somewhere in between.

With Monte Carlo full-episode learning, we don't take advantage of bootstrapping, since there's nothing to bootstrap. We do bootstrap in online learning, as we did with DQN, but with 1-step learning the bootstrap may introduce a lot of bias. This bias may be harmless if it pushes our parameters in the right direction, but in some cases the bias can be so off that we never move in the right direction.

This is why N-step learning is usually better than 1-step (online) learning—the target value for the critic is more accurate, so the critic's training will be more stable and will be able to produce less biased state values. With bootstrapping, we're making a prediction from a prediction, so the predictions will be better if you're able to collect more data before making them. And we like bootstrapping because it improves sample efficiency; you don't need to see as much data (e.g., frames in a game) before updating the parameters in the right direction.

Let's modify our code to do *N*-step learning. The only function we need to modify is run_episode. We need to change it to run for only *N* steps rather than wait for the episode to finish. If the episode finishes before *N* steps, the last return value will be set to 0 (since there is no next state when the game is over) as it was in the Monte Carlo case. However, if the episode hasn't finished by *N* steps, we'll use the last state value as our prediction for what the return would have been had we kept playing—that's where the bootstrapping happens. Without bootstrapping, the critic is just trying to predict the future returns from a state, and it gets the actual returns as training data. With bootstrapping, it is still trying to predict future returns, but it is doing so in part by using its own prediction about future returns (since the training data will include its own prediction).

Listing 5.9 N-step training with CartPole

```
def run_episode(worker_env, worker_model, N_steps=10):
    raw_state = np.array(worker_env.env.state)
    state = torch.from_numpy(raw_state).float()
    values, logprobs, rewards = [],[],[]
    done = False
    j=0
    G=torch.Tensor([0])                              ⬅  The variable G refers to the
                                                         return. We initialize to 0.
    while (j < N_steps and done == False):           ⬅┐  Plays game until N steps
        j+=1                                           │  or when episode is over
        policy, value = worker_model(state)
        values.append(value)
        logits = policy.view(-1)
        action_dist = torch.distributions.Categorical(logits=logits)
        action = action_dist.sample()
        logprob_ = policy.view(-1)[action]
        logprobs.append(logprob_)
        state_, _, done, info = worker_env.step(action.detach().numpy())
        state = torch.from_numpy(state_).float()
        if done:
            reward = -10
            worker_env.reset()
        else:                          ⬅┐  If episode is not done,
            reward = 1.0                 │  sets return to the last
            G = value.detach()           │  state value
        rewards.append(reward)
    return values, logprobs, rewards, G
```

The only things we've changed are the conditions for the while loop (exit by *N* steps), and we've set the return to be the state value of the last step if the episode is not over, thereby enabling bootstrapping. This new run_episode function explicitly returns G, the return, so to get this to work we need to make a couple minor updates to the update_params function and the worker function.

First, add the G parameter to the definition of the update_params function, and change ret_ = G:

```
def update_params(worker_opt,values,logprobs,rewards,G,clc=0.1,gamma=0.95):
    rewards = torch.Tensor(rewards).flip(dims=(0,)).view(-1)
```

```
logprobs = torch.stack(logprobs).flip(dims=(0,)).view(-1)
values = torch.stack(values).flip(dims=(0,)).view(-1)
Returns = []
ret_ = G
    ...
```

The rest of the function is exactly the same and is omitted here.

All we need to change in the `worker` function is to capture the newly returned `G` array and pass it to `update_params`:

```
def worker(t, worker_model, counter, params):
    worker_env = gym.make("CartPole-v1")
    worker_env.reset()
    worker_opt = optim.Adam(lr=1e-4,params=worker_model.parameters())
    worker_opt.zero_grad()
    for i in range(params['epochs']):
        worker_opt.zero_grad()
        values, logprobs, rewards, G = run_episode(worker_env,worker_model)
        actor_loss,critic_loss,eplen =
    update_params(worker_opt,values,logprobs,rewards, G)
        counter.value = counter.value + 1
```

You can run the training algorithm again as before, and everything should work the same except with better performance. You might be surprised at how much more efficient *N*-step learning is. Figure 5.15 shows the plot of episode length over the first 45 seconds of training for this model.

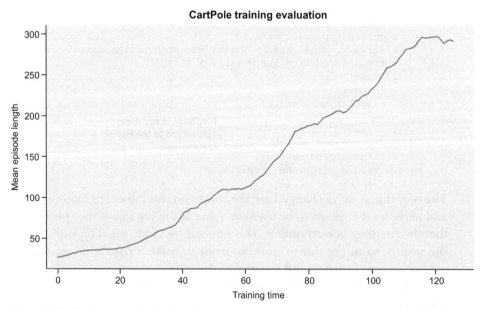

CartPole training evaluation

Figure 5.15 Performance plot for distributed advantage actor-critic with true *N*-step bootstrapping. Compared to our previous Monte Carlo algorithm, the performance is much smoother due to the more stable critic.

Notice in figure 5.15 that the *N*-step model starts getting better right away and reaches an episode length of 300 (after just 45 seconds), compared to only about 140 for the Monte Carlo version. Also notice that this plot is much smoother than the Monte Carlo one. Bootstrapping reduces the variance in the critic and allows it to learn much more rapidly than Monte Carlo.

As a concrete example, imagine the case where you get 3-step rewards of [1,1,–1] for episode 1 and then [1,1,1] for episode 2. The overall return for episode 1 is 0.01 (with $\gamma = 0.99$) and 1.99 for episode 2; that's two orders of magnitude difference in return just based on the random outcome of the episode early in training. That's a lot of variance. Compare that to the same case except with (simulated) bootstrapping, so that the return for each of those episodes also includes the bootstrapped predicted return. With a bootstrapped return prediction of 1.0 for both (assuming the states are similar), the calculated returns are 0.99 and 2.97, which are much closer than without bootstrapping. You can reproduce this example with the following code.

Listing 5.10   Returns with and without bootstrapping

```
#Simulated rewards for 3 steps
r1 = [1,1,-1]
r2 = [1,1,1]
R1,R2 = 0.0,0.0
#No bootstrapping
for i in range(len(r1)-1,0,-1):
    R1 = r1[i] + 0.99*R1
for i in range(len(r2)-1,0,-1):
    R2 = r2[i] + 0.99*R2
print("No bootstrapping")
print(R1,R2)
#With bootstrapping
R1,R2 = 1.0,1.0
for i in range(len(r1)-1,0,-1):
    R1 = r1[i] + 0.99*R1
for i in range(len(r2)-1,0,-1):
    R2 = r2[i] + 0.99*R2
print("With bootstrapping")
print(R1,R2)
>>> No bootstrapping
0.010000000000000009 1.99
With bootstrapping
0.9901 2.9701
```

To recap, in the plain policy gradient method of the previous chapter, we only trained a policy function that would output a probability distribution over all the actions, such that the predicted best action would be assigned the highest probability. Unlike Q-learning where a target value is learned, the policy function is directly reinforced to increase or decrease the probability of the action taken depending on the reward. Often the same action may produce opposite results in terms of reward, causing high variance in the training.

To mitigate this, we introduced a critic model (or in this chapter we used a single, two-headed model) that reduces the variance of the policy function updates by directly modeling the state value. This way, if the actor (policy) takes an action and gets an unusually big or small reward, the critic can moderate this big swing and prevent an unusually large (and possibly destructive) parameter update to the policy. This also leads to the notion of advantage, where instead of training the policy based on raw return (average accumulated rewards), we train based on how much better (or worse) the action was compared to what the critic predicted it would be. This is helpful, because if two actions both lead to the same positive reward, we will naively assume their equivalent actions, but if we compare to what we expected would happen, and one reward performed much better than anticipated, that action should be reinforced more.

As with the rest of the deep learning methods, we generally must use batches of data in order to effectively train. Training with a single example a time introduces too much noise, and the training will likely never converge. To introduce batch training with Q-learning we used an experience replay buffer that could randomly select batches of previous experiences. We could have used experience replay with actor-critic, but it is more common to use distributed training with actor-critic (and, to be clear, Q-learning can also be distributed). Distributed training in actor-critic models is more common because we often want to use a recurrent neural network (RNN) layer as part of our reinforcement learning model in cases where keeping track of prior states is necessary or helpful in achieving the goal. But RNNs need a sequence of temporally related examples, and experience replay relies on a batch of independent experiences. We could store entire trajectories (sequences of experiences) in a replay buffer, but that just adds complexity. Instead, with distributed training and each process running online with its own environment, the models can easily incorporate RNNs.

We didn't cover it here, but there's another way to train an online actor-critic algorithm besides distributed training: simply utilize multiple copies of your environment, and then batch together the states from each independent environment, feeding it into a single actor-critic model that will then produce independent predictions for each environment. This is a viable alternative to distributed training when the environments are not expensive to run. If your environment is a complicated, high-memory- and computer-intensive simulator, it's probably going to be very slow to run multiple copies of it in a single process, so in that case a distributed approach is better.

We have now covered what we consider to be the most foundational parts of reinforcement learning today. You should now be comfortable with the basic mathematical framework of reinforcement learning as a Markov decision process (MDP), and you should be able to able to implement Q-learning, plain policy gradient, and actor-critic models. If you've followed along so far, you should have a good foundation for tackling many other reinforcement learning domains.

In the rest of the book, we'll cover more advanced reinforcement learning methods with the aim of teaching you some of the most advanced RL algorithms of recent times in an intuitive way.

Summary

- Q-learning learns to predict the discounted rewards given a state and action.
- Policy methods learn a probability distribution over actions given a state.
- Actor-critic models combine a Q-learner with a policy learner.
- Advantage actor-critic learns to compute advantages by comparing the expected value of an action to the reward that was actually observed, so if an action is expected to result in a −1 reward but actually results in a +10 reward, its advantage will be higher than an action that is expected to result in +9 and actually results in +10.
- Multiprocessing is running code on multiple different processors that can operate simultaneously and independently.
- Multithreading is like multitasking; it allows you to run multiple tasks faster by letting the operating system quickly switch between them. When one task is idle (perhaps waiting for a file to download), the operating system can continue working on another task.
- Distributed training works by simultaneously running multiple instances of the environment and a single shared instance of the DRL model; after each time step we compute losses for each individual model, collect the gradients for each copy of the model, and then sum or average them together to update the shared parameters. This lets us do mini-batch training without an experience replay buffer.
- N-step learning is in between fully online learning, which trains 1 step at a time, and fully Monte Carlo learning, which only trains at the end of an episode. N-step learning thus has the advantages of both: the efficiency of 1-step learning and the accuracy of Monte Carlo.

Part 2

Above and beyond

After mastering the basics of deep reinforcement learning in part 1, part 2 delves into a variety of more advanced techniques and tackles more sophisticated environments. The chapters in this part can more or less be approached in any order as they do not rely on each other. However, each chapter tends to be more complex than the previous one, so it still may be better to go in sequence.

In chapter 6 we'll introduce an alternative framework for training neural networks using ideas borrowed from the biological sciences. In particular, we'll adapt Charles Darwin's theory of evolution by natural selection for machine learning.

In chapter 7 we'll show that most approaches to reinforcement learning are impoverished in how they represent states of the environment, and we'll fix that by modeling a full probability distribution. In chapter 8 we'll show you how to imbue reinforcement learning agents with a sense of human-like curiosity. In chapter 9 we'll extend what we've learned training individual reinforcement learning agents to scenarios with dozens or hundreds of agents all interacting together.

In chapter 10 we'll tackle one last major project to implement a machine learning model with a crude form of symbolic reasoning. This will allow us to inspect the internal behavior of the neural network and make the model more interpretable. Finally, chapter 11 briefly reviews the core concepts in the book and provides a roadmap for further study.

Alternative optimization methods: Evolutionary algorithms

This chapter covers

- Evolution algorithms for solving optimization problems
- Pros and cons of evolutionary approaches versus previous algorithms
- Solving the CartPole game without backpropagation
- Why evolutionary strategies can scale better than other algorithms

Neural networks were loosely inspired by real biological brains, and convolutional neural networks were also inspired by the biological mechanism of vision. There is a long tradition of advances in technology and engineering being motivated by biological organisms. Nature, through the process of evolution by natural selection, has solved many problems elegantly and efficiently. Naturally, people wondered whether evolution itself could be borrowed and implemented on a computer to generate solutions to problems. As you will see, we can indeed harness evolution to solve problems, and it works surprisingly well and is relatively easy to implement.

In natural evolution, biological traits change and new traits are generated simply by the fact that some traits confer a survival and reproduction advantage that results in those organisms being able to seed more copies of their genes in the next generation. The survival advantage of a gene depends entirely on the environment, which is often unpredictable and dynamic. Our use cases for simulated evolution are much simpler, since we generally want to maximize or minimize a single number, such as the loss when training a neural network.

In this chapter you will learn how to use simulated evolutionary algorithms to train neural networks for use in reinforcement learning without using backpropagation and gradient descent.

6.1   A different approach to reinforcement learning

Why would we even think about abandoning backpropagation? Well, with both DQN and policy gradient approaches we created one agent whose policy depended on a neural network to approximate the Q function or policy function. As shown in figure 6.1, the agent interacts with the environment, collects experiences, and then uses backpropagation to improve the accuracy of its neural network and, hence, its policy. We needed to carefully tune several hyperparameters ranging from selecting the right optimizer function, mini-batch size, and learning rate so that the training would be stable and successful. Since the training of both DQN and policy gradient algorithms relies on stochastic gradient descent, which as the name suggests relies on noisy gradients, there is no guarantee that these models will successfully learn (i.e., converge on a good local or global optimum).

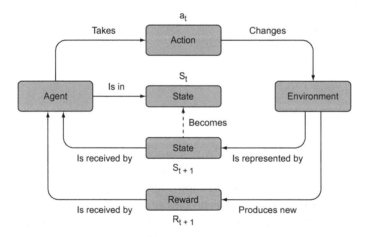

Figure 6.1   For the past algorithms that we covered, our agent interacted with environment, collected experiences, and then learned from those experiences. We repeated the same process over and over for each epoch until the agent stopped learning.

Depending on the environment and the complexity of the network, creating an agent with the right hyperparameters may be incredibly difficult. Moreover, in order to use gradient descent and backpropagation, we need a model that is differentiable. There are certainly interesting and useful models you could construct that might be impossible to train with gradient descent due to the lack of differentiability.

Instead of creating one agent and improving it, we can instead learn from Charles Darwin and use evolution by (un)natural selection. We could spawn multiple different agents with different parameters (weights), observe which ones did the best, and "breed" the best agents such that the descendants could inherit their parents' desirable traits—just like in natural selection. We could emulate biological evolution using algorithms. We wouldn't need to struggle to tune hyperparameters and wait for multiple epochs to see if an agent is learning "correctly." We could just pick the agents that are already performing better (figure 6.2).

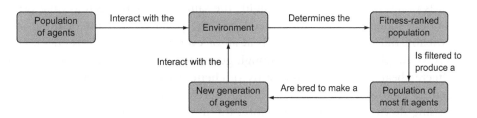

Figure 6.2 Evolutionary algorithms are different from gradient descent-based optimization techniques. With evolutionary strategies, we generate agents and pass the most favorable weights down to the subsequent agents.

This class of algorithms does not require an individual agent to learn. It does not rely on gradient descent and is aptly called a *gradient-free algorithm*. But just because individual agents are not being nudged toward some objective directly does not mean that we are relying on pure chance. The renowned evolutionary biologist Richard Dawkins once said, "Natural selection is anything but random." Similarly, in our quest to build, or more accurately *discover*, the best agent, we will not be relying on pure chance. We will be selecting for the fittest amongst a population with a variance in traits.

6.2 *Reinforcement learning with evolution strategies*

In this section we'll talk about how fitness plays into evolution strategies, and we'll briefly cover the task of selecting the fittest agents. Next, we'll work on how to recombine those agents into new agents and show what happens when we introduce mutations. This evolution is a multiple-generation process, so we'll discuss that and recap the full training loop.

6.2.1 *Evolution in theory*

If you remember from your high school biology class, natural selection selects for the "most fit" individuals from each generation. In biology this represents the individuals that had the greatest reproductive success, and hence passed on their genetic information to subsequent generations. Birds with beak shapes more adept at procuring seeds from trees would have more food and thus be more likely to survive to pass that beak shape gene to their children and grandchildren. But remember, "most fit" is relative to an environment. A polar bear is well adapted to the polar ice caps but would be very unfit in the Amazonian rainforests. You can think of the environment as determining an objective or fitness function that assigns individuals a fitness score based on their performance within that environment; their performance is determined solely by their genetic information.

In biology, each mutation very subtly changes the characteristics of the organism, such that it may be difficult to discern one generation from another. However, allowing these mutations and variations to accumulate over multiple generations allows for perceptible changes. In the evolution of birds' beaks, for example, a population of birds would initially have had roughly the same beak shape. But as time progressed, random mutations were introduced into the population. Most of these mutations probably did not impact the birds at all or even had a deleterious effect, but with a large enough population and enough generations, random mutations occurred that affected beak shapes favorably. Birds with better suited beaks would have an advantage getting food over the other birds, and therefore they'd have a higher likelihood of passing down their genes. Therefore, the next generation would have an increased frequency of the favorably shaped beak gene.

In *evolutionary reinforcement learning*, we are selecting for traits that give our agents the highest reward in a given environment, and by *traits* we mean model parameters (e.g., the weights of a neural network) or entire model structures. An RL agent's fitness can be determined by the expected reward it would receive if it were to perform in the environment.

Let's say agent A played the Atari game Breakout and was able to achieve an average score of 500 while agent B was only able to obtain 300 points. We would say that agent A is more fit than agent B and that we want our optimal agent to be more similar to agent A than B. Remember, the only reason why agent A would be more fit than agent B is because its model parameters were slightly more optimized to the environment.

The objective in evolutionary reinforcement learning is exactly the same as in backpropagation and gradient descent-based training. The only difference is that we use this evolutionary process, which is often referred to as a *genetic algorithm*, to optimize the parameters of a model such as a neural network (figure 6.3).

The process is quite simple, but let's run through the steps of a genetic algorithm in more detail. Let's say we have a neural network that we want to use as an agent to play Gridworld, and we want to train it using a genetic algorithm. Remember, *training* a neural network just means iteratively updating its parameters such that its performance improves. Also recall that given a fixed neural network architecture, the parameters completely determine its behavior, so to copy a neural network we just need to copy its parameters.

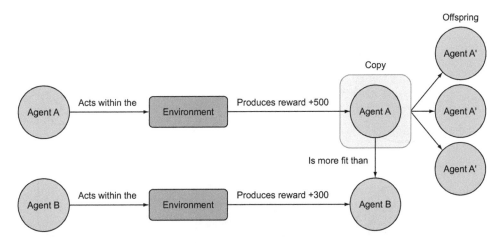

Figure 6.3 In an evolutionary algorithm approach to reinforcement learning, agents compete in an environment, and the agents that are more fit (those that generate more rewards) are preferentially copied to produce offspring. After many iterations of this process, only the most fit agents are left.

Here's how we would train such a neural network using a genetic algorithm (graphically depicted in figure 6.4):

1 We generate an initial population of random parameter vectors. We refer to each parameter vector in the population as an *individual*. Let's say this initial population has 100 individuals.

2 We iterate through this population and assess the fitness of each individual by running the model in Gridworld with that parameter vector and recording the rewards. Each individual is assigned a fitness score based on the rewards it earns. Since the initial population is random, they will all likely perform very poorly, but there will be a few, just by chance, that will perform better than others.

3 We randomly sample a pair of individuals ("parents") from the population, weighted according to their relative fitness score (individuals with higher fitness have a higher probability of being selected) to create a "breeding population."

NOTE There are many different methods of selecting "parents" for the next generation. One way is to simply map a probability of selection onto each individual based on their relative fitness score, and then sample from this distribution. In this way, the most fit will be selected most often, but there will still be a small chance of poor performers being selected. This may help maintain population diversity. Another way is to simply rank all the individuals and take the top N individuals, and use those to mate to fill the next generation. Just about any method that preferentially selects the top performers to mate will work, but some are better than others. There's a tradeoff between selecting the best performers and reducing population diversity—this is very similar to the exploration versus exploitation tradeoff in reinforcement learning.

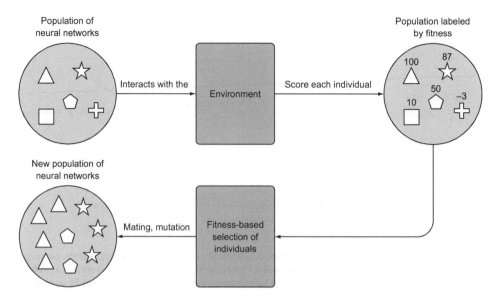

Figure 6.4   A genetic algorithm optimization of neural networks for reinforcement learning. A population of initial neural networks (the RL agents) is tested in the environment, earning rewards. Each individual agent is labeled by how fit it is, which is based on the rewards earned. Individuals are selected for the next generation based on their fitness; more fit individuals are more likely to be included in the next generation. The selected individuals "mate" and are "mutated" to increase genetic diversity.

4   The individuals in the breeding population will then "mate" to produce "offspring" that will form a new, full population of 100 individuals. If the individuals are simply parameter vectors of real numbers, mating vector 1 with vector 2 involves taking a subset from vector 1 and combining it with a complementary subset of vector 2 to make a new offspring vector of the same dimensions. For example, suppose you have vector 1: [1 2 3] and vector 2: [4 5 6]. Vector 1 mates with vector 2 to produce [1 5 6] and [4 2 3]. We simply randomly pair up individuals from the breeding populations and recombine them to produce two new offspring until we fill up a new population. This creates new "genetic" diversity with the best performers.

5   We now have a new population with the top solutions from the last generation, along with new offspring solutions. At this point, we will iterate over our solutions and randomly mutate some of them to make sure we introduce new genetic diversity into every generation to prevent premature convergence on a local optimum. Mutation simply means adding a little random noise to the parameter vectors. If these were binary vectors, mutation would mean randomly flipping a few bits; otherwise we might add some Gaussian noise. The mutation rate needs to be fairly low, or we'll risk ruining the already present good solutions.

6 We now have a new population of mutated offspring from the previous generation. We repeat this process with the new population for *N* number of generations or until we reach *convergence* (which is when the average population's fitness has stopped improving significantly).

6.2.2 *Evolution in practice*

Before we dive into the reinforcement learning application, we'll run a super simple genetic algorithm on an example problem for illustrative purposes. We will create a population of random strings and try to evolve them toward a target string of our choosing, such as "Hello World!"

Our initial population of random strings will look like "gMIgSkybXZyP" and "adlBOM XIrBH." We'll use a function that can tell us how similar these strings are to the target string to give us the fitness scores. We'll then sample pairs of parents from the population weighted by their relative fitness scores, such that individuals with higher fitness scores are more likely to be chosen to become parents. Next we'll mate these parents (also called *crossing* or *recombining*) to produce two offspring strings and add them to the next generation. We'll also mutate the offspring by randomly flipping a few characters in the string. We'll iterate this process and expect that the population will become enriched with strings very close to our target; probably at least one will hit our target exactly (at which point we'll stop the algorithm). This evolutionary process for strings is depicted in figure 6.5.

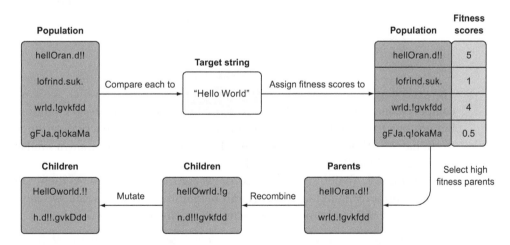

Figure 6.5 A string diagram outlining the major steps in a genetic algorithm for evolving a set of random strings toward a target string. We start with a population of random strings, compare each to the target string, and assign a fitness score to each string based on how similar it is to the target string. We then select high-fitness parents to "mate" (or recombine) to produce children, and then we mutate the children to introduce new genetic variance. We repeat the process of selecting parents and producing children until the next generation is full (when it's the same size as the starting population).

This is perhaps a silly example, but it's one of the simplest demonstrations of a genetic algorithm, and the concepts will directly transfer to our reinforcement learning tasks. Listings 6.1 through 6.4 show the code.

In listing 6.1 we begin by setting up the functions that will instantiate an initial population of random strings and also define a function that can compute a similarity score between two strings, which we will ultimately use as our fitness function.

Listing 6.1 Evolving strings: set up random strings

```python
import random
from matplotlib import pyplot as plt

alphabet = "abcdefghijklmnopqrstuvwxyzABCDEFGHIJKLMNOPQRSTUVWXYZ,.! "
target = "Hello World!"

class Individual:
    def __init__(self, string, fitness=0):
        self.string = string
        self.fitness = fitness

from difflib import SequenceMatcher

def similar(a, b):
    return SequenceMatcher(None, a, b).ratio()

def spawn_population(length=26,size=100):
    pop = []
    for i in range(size):
        string = ''.join(random.choices(alphabet,k=length))
        individual = Individual(string)
        pop.append(individual)
    return pop
```

The list of characters we sample from to produce random strings

The string we're trying to evolve from a random population

Sets up a simple class to store information about each member of the population

Computes a similarity metric between two strings, giving us a fitness score

Produces an initial random population of strings

The preceding code creates an initial population of individuals which are class objects composed of a string field and a fitness score field. Then it creates the random strings by sampling from a list of alphabetic characters. Once we have a population, we need to evaluate the fitness of each individual. For strings, we can compute a similarity metric using a built-in Python module called SequenceMatcher.

In listing 6.2, we define two functions, recombine and mutate. As their names suggest, the former will take two strings and recombine them to create two new strings, and the latter will randomly flip characters in a string to mutate them.

Listing 6.2 Evolving strings: recombine and mutate

```python
def recombine(p1_, p2_):
    p1 = p1_.string
    p2 = p2_.string
    child1 = []
    child2 = []
    cross_pt = random.randint(0,len(p1))
    child1.extend(p1[0:cross_pt])
```

Recombines two parent strings into two new offspring

```
        child1.extend(p2[cross_pt:])
        child2.extend(p2[0:cross_pt])
        child2.extend(p1[cross_pt:])
        c1 = Individual(''.join(child1))
        c2 = Individual(''.join(child2))
        return c1, c2

def mutate(x, mut_rate=0.01):        ◁───┐  Mutates a string by
    new_x_ = []                             randomly flipping
    for char in x.string:                   characters
        if random.random() < mut_rate:
            new_x_.extend(random.choices(alphabet,k=1))
        else:
            new_x_.append(char)
    new_x = Individual(''.join(new_x_))
    return new_x
```

The preceding recombination function takes two parent strings like "hello there" and "fog world" and randomly recombines them by generating a random integer up to the length of the strings and taking the first piece of parent 1 and the second piece of parent 2 to create an offspring, such as "fog there" and "hello world" if the split happened in the middle. If we have evolved a string that contains part of what we want, like "hello" and another string that contains another part of what we want like "world," then the recombination process might give us all of what we want.

The mutation process takes a string like "hellb" and, with some small probability (the mutation rate), will replace a character in the string with a random one. For example, if the mutation rate was 20% (0.2), it is probable that at least one of the 5 characters in "hellb" will be mutated to a random character. Hopefully it will be mutated into "hello" if that is the target. The purpose of mutation is to introduce new information (variance) into the population. If all we did was recombine, it is likely that all the individuals in the population would become too similar too quickly, and we wouldn't find the solution we wanted, because information gets lost each generation if there is no mutation. Note that the mutation rate is critical. If it's too high, the fittest individuals will lose their fitness by mutation, and if it's too low, we won't have enough variance to find the optimal individual. Unfortunately, you have to find the right mutation rate empirically.

In listing 6.3 we define a function that will loop through each individual in a population of strings, compute its fitness score, and associate it with that individual. We also define a function that will create the subsequent generation.

Listing 6.3 Evolving strings: evaluate individuals and create new generation

```
def evaluate_population(pop, target):        ◁───┐  Assigns a fitness score
    avg_fit = 0                                     to each individual in
    for i in range(len(pop)):                       the population
        fit = similar(pop[i].string, target)
        pop[i].fitness = fit
        avg_fit += fit
```

```
        avg_fit /= len(pop)
        return pop, avg_fit

def next_generation(pop, size=100, length=26, mut_rate=0.01):
    new_pop = []
    while len(new_pop) < size:
        parents = random.choices(pop,k=2, weights=[x.fitness for x in pop])
        offspring_ = recombine(parents[0],parents[1])
        child1 = mutate(offspring_[0], mut_rate=mut_rate)
        child2 = mutate(offspring_[1], mut_rate=mut_rate)
        offspring = [child1, child2]
        new_pop.extend(offspring)
    return new_pop
```

> Generates a new generation by recombination and mutation

These are the last two functions we need to complete the evolutionary process. We have a function that evaluates each individual in the population and assigns a fitness score, which just indicates how similar the individual's string is to the target string. The fitness score will vary depending on what the objective is for a given problem. Lastly, we have a function that generates a new population by sampling the most fit individuals in the current population, recombining them to produce offspring, and mutating them.

In listing 6.4 we put everything together and iterate the previous steps to some maximum number of generations. That is, we start with an initial population, go through the process of fitness-scoring individuals and creating a new offspring population, and then repeat this sequence a number of times. After a sufficient number of generations, we expect the final population to be enriched with strings very close to our target string.

Listing 6.4 Evolving strings: putting it all together

```
num_generations = 150
population_size = 900
str_len = len(target)
mutation_rate = 0.00001

pop_fit = []
pop = spawn_population(size=population_size, length=str_len)
for gen in range(num_generations):
    pop, avg_fit = evaluate_population(pop, target)
    pop_fit.append(avg_fit)
    new_pop = next_generation(pop, \
    size=population_size, length=str_len, mut_rate=mutation_rate)
    pop = new_pop
```

> Sets the mutation rate to 0.001%

> Creates the initial random population

> Records population average fitness over training time

If you run the algorithm, it should take a few minutes on a modern CPU. You can find the highest ranked individual in the population as follows:

```
>>> pop.sort(key=lambda x: x.fitness, reverse=True) #sort in place, highest
    fitness first
>>> pop[0].string
"Hello World!"
```

It worked! You can also see the average fitness level of the population increasing each generation in figure 6.6. This is actually a more difficult problem to optimize using an evolutionary algorithm because the space of strings is not continuous; it is hard to take small, incremental steps in the right direction since the smallest step is flipping a character. Hence, if you try making a longer target string, it will take much more time and resources to evolve.

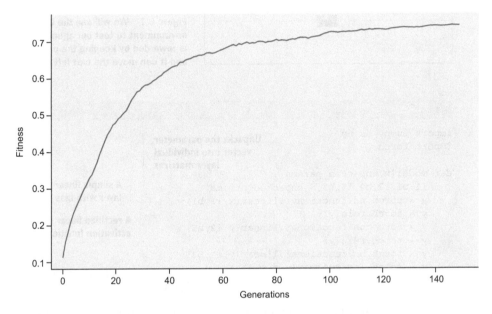

Figure 6.6   This is a plot of average population fitness over the generations. The average population fitness increases fairly monotonically and then plateaus, which looks promising. If the plot was very jagged, the mutation rate might be too high or the population size too low. If the plot converged too quickly, the mutation rate might be too low.

When we're optimizing real-valued parameters in a model, even a small increase in value might improve the fitness, and we can exploit that, which makes optimization faster. But although discrete-valued individuals are harder to optimize in an evolutionary algorithm, they are *impossible* to optimize using vanilla gradient descent and back-propagation, because they are not differentiable.

6.3   *A genetic algorithm for CartPole*

Let's see how this evolution strategy works in a simple reinforcement learning example. We're going to use an evolutionary process to optimize an agent to play CartPole, the environment we introduced in chapter 4 where the agent is rewarded for keeping the pole upright (figure 6.7).

We can represent an agent as a neural network that approximates the policy function—it accepts a state and outputs an action, or more typically a probability distribution over actions. The following listing shows an example of a three-layer network.

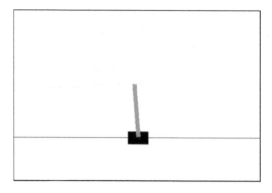

Figure 6.7 We will use the CartPole environment to test our agent. The agent is rewarded by keeping the pole upright, and it can move the cart left or right.

Listing 6.5 Defining an agent

```
import numpy as np
import torch                              Unpacks the parameter
                                          vector into individual
                                              layer matrices
def model(x,unpacked_params):
    l1,b1,l2,b2,l3,b3 = unpacked_params        ◁    A simple linear
    y = torch.nn.functional.linear(x,l1,b1)    ◁    layer with bias
    y = torch.relu(y)                          ◁    A rectified linear unit
    y = torch.nn.functional.linear(y,l2,b2)         activation function
    y = torch.relu(y)
    y = torch.nn.functional.linear(y,l3,b3)
    y = torch.log_softmax(y,dim=0)       ◁    The last layer will output log
    return y                                  probabilities over actions.
```

The function in listing 6.5 defines a 3-layer neural network. The first two layers use rectified linear unit activation functions, and the last layer uses a log-softmax activation function so that we get log probabilities over actions as the final output. Notice that this function expects an input state, x, and unpacked_params, which is a tuple of individual parameter matrices that are used in each layer.

To make the recombination and mutation process easier, we will create a population of parameter vectors (1-tensors) that we must then "unpack" or decompose into individual parameter matrices for use in each layer of the neural network.

Listing 6.6 Unpacking a parameter vector

```
def unpack_params(params, layers=[(25,4),(10,25),(2,10)]):   ◁    The layers parameter
    unpacked_params = []                    ◁                     specifies the shape of
    e = 0                                   Stores each individual each layer matrix.
                                            layer tensor
    for i,l in enumerate(layers):
        s,e = e,e+np.prod(l)
        weights = params[s:e].view(l)    ◁    Unpacks the individual
        s,e = e,e+l[0]                        layer into matrix form
        bias = params[s:e]
        unpacked_params.extend([weights,bias])    ◁    Adds the unpacked
    return unpacked_params                             tensor to the list
```

Iterates through each layer

The preceding function takes a flat parameter vector as the `params` input and a specification of the layers that it contains as the `layers` input, which is a list of tuples; it unpacks the parameter vector into a set of individual layer matrices and bias vectors stored in a list. The default set for `layers` specifies a 3-layer neural network, which therefore consists of 3 weight matrices with dimensions 25×4, 10×25, and 2×10, and 3 bias vectors of dimensions 1×25, 1×10, and 1×2 for a total of $4 * 25 + 25 + 10 * 25 + 10 + 2 * 10 + 2 = 407$ parameters in the flattened parameter vector.

The only reason we're adding this complexity of using flattened parameter vectors and unpacking them for use is that we want to be able to mutate over and recombine the entire set of parameters, which ends up being simpler overall and matches what we did with strings. An alternative approach would be to think of each layer's neural network as an individual chromosome (if you remember the biology)—only matched chromosomes will recombine. Using this approach, you would only recombine parameters from the same layer. This would prevent information from later layers corrupting the earlier layers. We encourage you to try to implement it using this "chromosomal" approach as a challenge once you're comfortable with the way we do it here. You'll need to iterate over each layer, recombine, and mutate them separately.

Next let's add a function to create a population of agents.

Listing 6.7 Spawning a population

```
def spawn_population(N=50,size=407):
    pop = []
    for i in range(N):
        vec = torch.randn(size) / 2.0
        fit = 0
        p = {'params':vec, 'fitness':fit}
        pop.append(p)
    return pop
```

N is the number of individuals in the population; size is the length of the parameter vectors.

Creates a randomly initialized parameter vector

Creates a dictionary to store the parameter vector and its associated fitness score

Each agent will be a simple Python dictionary that stores the parameter vector for that agent and the fitness score for that agent.

Next we implement the function that will recombine two parent agents to produce two new child agents.

Listing 6.8 Genetic recombination

```
def recombine(x1,x2):
    x1 = x1['params']
    x2 = x2['params']
    l = x1.shape[0]
    split_pt = np.random.randint(l)
    child1 = torch.zeros(l)
    child2 = torch.zeros(l)
    child1[0:split_pt] = x1[0:split_pt]
    child1[split_pt:] = x2[split_pt:]
    child2[0:split_pt] = x2[0:split_pt]
    child2[split_pt:] = x1[split_pt:]
```

x1 and x2 are agents, which are dictionaries.

Extracts just the parameter vector

Randomly produces a split or crossover point

The first child is produced by taking the first segment of parent 1 and the second segment of parent 2.

```
c1 = {'params':child1, 'fitness': 0.0}
c2 = {'params':child2, 'fitness': 0.0}
return c1, c2
```

Creates new child agents by packaging the new parameter vectors into dictionaries

This function takes two agents who serve as parents and produces two children or offspring. It does so by taking a random split or crossover point, and then taking the first piece of parent 1 and combining it with the second piece of parent 2, and likewise combines the second piece of parent 1 and the first piece of parent 2. This is exactly the same mechanism we used to recombine strings before.

That was the first stage for populating the next generation; the second stage is to mutate the individuals with some fairly low probability. Mutation is the only source of new genetic information in each generation—recombination only shuffles around information that already exists.

Listing 6.9 Mutating the parameter vectors

rate is the mutation rate, where 0.01 is a 1% mutation rate.

```
def mutate(x, rate=0.01):
    x_ = x['params']
    num_to_change = int(rate * x_.shape[0])
    idx = np.random.randint(low=0,high=x_.shape[0],size=(num_to_change,))
    x_[idx] = torch.randn(num_to_change) / 10.0
    x['params'] = x_
    return x
```

Uses the mutation rate to decide how many elements in the parameter vector to mutate

Randomly resets the selected elements in the parameter vector

We follow basically the same procedure as we did for strings; we randomly change a few elements of the parameter vector. The mutation rate parameter controls the number of elements that we change. We need to control the mutation rate carefully to balance the creation of new information that can be used to improve existing solutions and the destruction of old information.

Next we need to assess the fitness of each agent by actually testing them on the environment (CartPole in our case).

Listing 6.10 Testing each agent in the environment

```
import gym
env = gym.make("CartPole-v0")

def test_model(agent):
    done = False
    state = torch.from_numpy(env.reset()).float()
    score = 0
    while not done:
        params = unpack_params(agent['params'])
        probs = model(state,params)
        action = torch.distributions.Categorical(probs=probs).sample()
        state_, reward, done, info = env.step(action.item())
        state = torch.from_numpy(state_).float()
```

Gets the action probabilities from the model using the agent's parameter vector

Probabilistically selects an action by sampling from a categorical distribution

While game is not lost

```
    score += 1        ◁─┐   Keeps track of the number
  return score          │   of time steps the game is
                        │   not lost as the score
```

The `test_model` function takes an *agent* (a dictionary of a parameter vector and its fitness value) and runs it in the CartPole environment until it loses the game and returns the number of time steps it lasted as its score. We want to breed agents that can last longer and longer in CartPole (therefore achieving a high score).

We need to do this for all the agents in the population.

Listing 6.11 Evaluate all the agents in the population

```
def evaluate_population(pop):
    tot_fit = 0           ◁─┐
    lp = len(pop)
    for agent in pop:       ◁─┐
        score = test_model(agent)   ◁─┐
        agent['fitness'] = score
        tot_fit += score
    avg_fit = tot_fit / lp
    return pop, avg_fit
```

Total fitness for this population; used to later calculate the average fitness of the population

Iterates through each agent in the population

Stores the fitness value

Runs the agent in the environment to assess its fitness

The `evaluate_population` function iterates through each agent in the population and runs `test_model` on them to assess their fitness.

The final main function we need is the `next_generation` function in listing 6.12. Unlike our string genetic algorithm from earlier, where we probabilistically selected parents based on their fitness score, here we employ a different selection mechanism. The *probabilistic selection mechanism* is similar to how we choose actions in a policy gradient method, and it works well there, but for choosing parents in a genetic algorithm, it often ends up leading to too rapid convergence. Genetic algorithms require more exploration than gradient-descent–based methods. In this case we'll use a selection mechanism called *tournament-style selection* (figure 6.8).

In tournament-style selection we select a random subset from the whole population and then choose the top two individuals in this subset as the parents. This ensures we don't always select the same top two parents, but we do end up selecting the better-performing agents more often.

We can change the *tournament size* (the size of the random subset) to control the degree to which we favor choosing the best agents in the current generation, at the risk of losing genetic diversity. In the extreme case, we could set the tournament size to be equal to the size of the population, in which case we would only select the top two individuals in the population. At the other extreme, we could make the tournament size 2, so that we are randomly selecting parents.

In this example we set the tournament size as a percentage of the size of the population. Empirically, tournament sizes of about 20% seem to work fairly well.

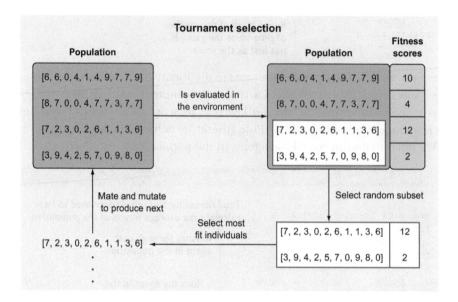

Figure 6.8   In tournament selection we evaluate the fitness of all the individuals in the population as usual, and then we choose a random subset of the full population (in this figure just 2 of 4), and then choose the top individuals (usually 2) in this subset, mate them to produce offspring and mutate them. We repeat this selection process until we fill up the next generation.

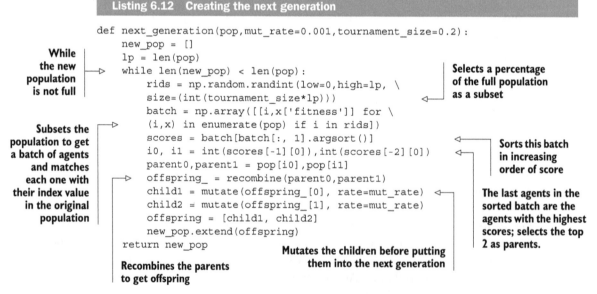

The next_generation function creates a list of random indices to index the population list and create a subset for a tournament batch. We use the enumerate function to keep track of the index positions of each agent in the subset so we can refer back to them in the main population. Then we sort the batch of fitness scores in ascending order and take the last two elements in the list as the top two individuals in that batch. We look up their indices and select the whole agent from the original population list.

Putting it all together, we can train a population of agents to play CartPole in just a handful of generations. You should experiment with the hyperparameters of mutation rate, population size, and number of generations.

Listing 6.13   Training the models

```
num_generations = 25
population_size = 500
mutation_rate = 0.01
pop_fit = []
pop = spawn_population(N=population_size,size=407)
for i in range(num_generations):
    pop, avg_fit = evaluate_population(pop)
    pop_fit.append(avg_fit)
    pop = next_generation(pop, mut_rate=mutation_rate,tournament_size=0.2)
```

- The number of generations to evolve
- The number of individuals in each generation
- Initializes a population
- Evaluates the fitness of each agent in the population
- Populates the next generation

The first generation begins with a population of random parameter vectors, but by chance some of these will be better than the others, and we preferentially select these to mate and produce offspring for the next generation. To maintain genetic diversity, we allow each individual to be mutated slightly. This process repeats until we have individuals who are exceptionally good at playing CartPole. You can see in figure 6.9 that the score steadily increases each generation of evolution.

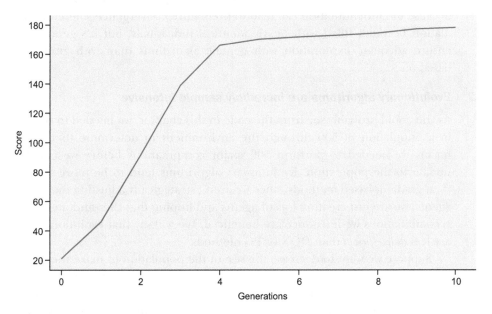

Figure 6.9   The average score of the population over generations in a genetic algorithm used to train agents to play CartPole.

6.4   *Pros and cons of evolutionary algorithms*

The algorithm we implemented in this chapter is a bit different from the previous approaches we've used in this book. There are circumstances where an evolutionary approach works better, such as with problems that would benefit more from exploration; other circumstances make it impractical, such as problems where it is expensive to gather data. In this section we'll discuss the advantages and disadvantages of evolutionary algorithms and where you might benefit from using them over gradient descent.

6.4.1   *Evolutionary algorithms explore more*

One advantage of gradient-free approaches is that they tend to explore more than their gradient-based counterparts. Both DQN and policy gradients followed a similar strategy: collect experiences and nudge the agent to take actions that led to greater rewards. As we discussed, this tends to cause agents to abandon exploring new states if they prefer an action already. We addressed this with DQN by incorporating an epsilon-greedy strategy, meaning there's a small chance the agent will take a random action even if it has a preferred action. With the stochastic policy gradient we relied on drawing a variety of actions from the action probability vector output by our model.

The agents in the genetic algorithm, on the other hand, are not nudged in any direction. We produce a lot of agents in each generation, and with so much random variation between them, most of them will have different policies than each other. There still is an exploration versus exploitation problem in evolutionary strategies because too little mutation can lead to premature convergence where the whole population becomes filled with nearly identical individuals, but it's generally easier to ensure adequate exploration with genetic algorithms than with gradient descent-based ones.

6.4.2   *Evolutionary algorithms are incredibly sample intensive*

As you could probably see from the code in this chapter, we needed to run each agent in a population of 500 through the environment to determine their fitness. That means we needed to perform 500 major computations before we could make an update to the population. Evolutionary algorithms tend to be more sample hungry than gradient-based methods, since we aren't strategically adjusting the weights of our agents; we are just creating lots of agents and hoping that the random mutations and recombinations we introduce are beneficial. We will say that evolutionary algorithms are less *data-efficient* than DQN or PG methods.

Suppose we want to decrease the size of the population to make the algorithm run faster. If we decrease the population size, there are fewer agents to select from when we are picking the two parents. This will make it likely that less fit individuals will make it into the next generation. We rely on a large number of agents being produced in hopes of finding a combination that leads to better fitness. Additionally, as in biology, mutations usually have a negative impact and lead to worse fitness. Having a larger population increases the probability that at least a few mutations will be beneficial.

Being data-inefficient is a problem if collecting data is expensive, such as in robotics or with autonomous vehicles. Having a robot collect one episode of data usually takes a couple of minutes, and we know from our past algorithms that training a simple agent takes hundreds if not thousands of episodes. Imagine how many episodes an autonomous vehicle would need to sufficiently explore its state space (the world). In addition to taking considerably more time, training with physical agents is much more expensive, since you need to purchase the robot and account for any maintenance. It would be ideal if we could train such agents without having to give them physical bodies.

6.4.3 Simulators

Simulators address the preceding concerns. Instead of using an expensive robot or building a car with the necessary sensors, we could instead use computer software to emulate the experiences the environment would provide. For example, when training agents to drive autonomous cars, instead of equipping cars with the necessary sensors and deploying the model on physical cars, we could just train the agents inside software environments, such as the driving game Grand Theft Auto. The agent would receive as input the images of its surroundings, and it would be trained to output driving actions that would get the vehicle to the programmed destination as safely as possible.

Not only are simulators significantly cheaper to train agents with, but agents are able to train much more quickly since they can interact with the simulated environment much faster than in real life. If you need to watch and understand a two-hour movie, it will require two hours of your time. If you focus more intensely, you could probably increase the playback speed by two or three, dropping the amount of time needed to an hour or a bit less. A computer, on the other hand, could be finished before you've viewed the first act. For example, an 8 GPU computer (which could be rented from a cloud service) running ResNet-50, an established deep learning model for image classification, can process over 700 images per second. In a two-hour movie running at 24 frames per second (standard in Hollywood), there are 172,800 frames that need to be processed. This would require four minutes to finish. We could also effectively increase the playback speed for our deep learning model by dropping every few frames, which will drop our processing time to under two minutes. We could also throw more computers at the problem to increase processing power. For a more recent reinforcement learning example, the OpenAI Five bots were able to play 180 years of Dota 2 games each day. You get the picture—computers can process faster than we can, and that's why simulators are valuable.

6.5 Evolutionary algorithms as a scalable alternative

If a simulator is available, the time and financial costs of collecting samples with evolutionary algorithms is less of an issue. In fact, producing a viable agent with evolutionary algorithms can sometimes be faster than gradient-based approaches because we do not have to compute the gradients via backpropagation. Depending on the complexity of the network, this will cut down the computation time by roughly 2–3 times. But there is another advantage of evolutionary algorithms that can allow them to train faster than their gradient counterparts—evolutionary algorithms can scale incredibly well when parallelized. We will discuss this in some detail in this section.

6.5.1 Scaling evolutionary algorithms

OpenAI released a paper called "Evolutionary Strategies as a Scalable Alternative to Reinforcement Learning" by Tim Salimans et al. (2017), in which they described training agents incredibly quickly and efficiently by adding more machines. On a single machine with 18 CPU cores, they were able to make a 3D humanoid learn to walk in 11 hours. But with 80 machines (1,440 CPU cores) they were able to produce an agent in under 10 minutes.

You may be thinking that's obvious—they just threw more machines and money at the problem. But this is actually trickier than it sounds, and other gradient-based approaches struggle to scale to that many machines.

Let's first look at how their algorithm differs from what we did earlier. *Evolutionary algorithm* is an umbrella term for a wide variety of algorithms that take inspiration from biological evolution and rely on iteratively selecting slightly better solutions from a large population to optimize a solution. The approach we implemented to play Cart-Pole is more specifically called a *genetic algorithm*, because it more closely resembles the way biological genes get "updated" from generation to generation through recombination and mutation.

There's another class of evolutionary algorithms confusingly termed *evolutionary strategies* (ES), which employ a less biologically accurate form of evolution, as illustrated in figure 6.10.

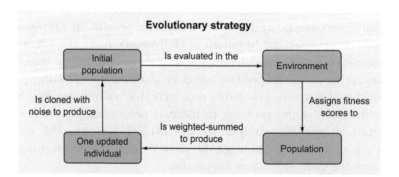

Figure 6.10   In an evolutionary strategy we create a population of individuals by repeatedly adding a small amount of random noise to a parent individual to generate multiple variants of the parent. We then assign fitness scores to each variant by testing them in the environment, and then we get a new parent by taking a weighted sum of all the variants.

If we're training a neural network with an ES algorithm, we start with a single parameter vector θ_t, sample a bunch of noise vectors of equal size (usually from a Gaussian distribution), such as $e_i \sim N(\mu,\sigma)$, where N is a Gaussian distribution with mean vector μ and standard deviation σ. We then create a population of parameter vectors that are mutated versions of θ_t by taking $\theta'_i = \theta + e_i$. We test each of these mutated parameter vectors in the environment and assign them fitness scores based on their performance in the environment. Lastly, we get an updated parameter vector by taking a weighted sum of each of the mutated vectors, where the weights are proportional to their fitness scores (figure 6.11).

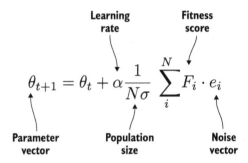

Figure 6.11 In an evolutionary strategy, at each time step we get an updated parameter vector by taking the old parameter vector and adding it to a weighted sum of the noise vectors, where the weights are proportional to the fitness scores.

This evolutionary strategy algorithm is significantly simpler than the genetic algorithm we implemented earlier since there is no mating step. We only perform mutation, and the recombination step does not involve swapping pieces from different parents but is just a simple weighted summation which is very easy to implement and computationally fast. As we'll see, this approach is also easier to parallelize.

6.5.2 Parallel vs. serial processing

When we used a genetic algorithm to train agents to play CartPole, we had to sequentially iterate over each agent and let each agent play CartPole until it lost, in order to determine the fittest agent in each generation before we started the next run. If the agent takes 30 seconds to run through the environment, and we are determining the fitness for 10 agents, this will take 5 minutes. This is known as running a program *serially* (figure 6.12).

Determining each agent's fitness will generally be the longest-running task in an evolutionary algorithm, but each agent can evaluate its own fitness independent of each other. But there's no reason we need to wait for agent 1 to finish playing in the environment before we start evaluating agent 2. We could instead run each agent in the generation on multiple computers at the same time. Each of the 10 agents would go on 10 machines, and we can determine their fitness simultaneously. This means that completing one generation will take ~30 seconds on 10 machines as opposed to 5 minutes on one machine, a 10x speedup. This is known as running the process in *parallel* (figure 6.13).

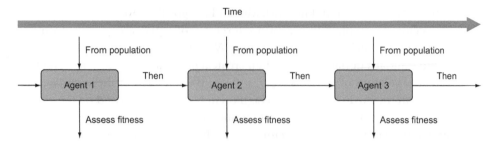

Figure 6.12   Determining the fitness of an agent is often the slowest step in a training loop and requires that we run the agent through the environment (possibly many times). If we are doing this on a single computer, we will be doing this in serial—we have to wait for one to finish running through the environment before we can start determining the fitness of the second agent. The time it takes to run this algorithm is a function of the number of agents *and* the time it takes to run through the environment for a single agent.

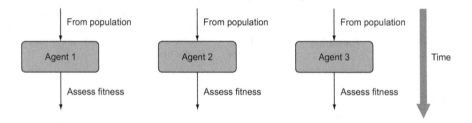

Figure 6.13   If we have multiple machines at our disposal, we can determine the fitness of each agent on its own machine in parallel with each other. We do not have to wait for one agent to finish running through the environment before starting the next one. This will provide a huge speed up if we are training agents with a long episode length. You can see now that this algorithm is only a function of the time it takes to assess the fitness of a single agent, and not the number of agents we are assessing.

6.5.3   Scaling efficiency

Now we can throw more machines and money at the problem, and we won't have to wait nearly as long. In the previous hypothetical example where we added 10 machines and got a 10x speedup—a scaling efficient of 1.0. *Scaling efficiency* is a term used to describe how a particular approach improves as more resources are thrown at it and can be calculated as follows:

$$\text{Scaling Efficiency} = \frac{\text{Multiple of Performance Speed up after adding resources}}{\text{Multiple of Resources Added}}$$

In the real world, processes never have a scaling efficiency of 1. There is always some additional cost to adding more machines that decreases efficiency. More realistically, adding 10 more machines will only give us a 9x speedup. Using the previous scaling efficiency equation we can calculate the scaling efficiency as 0.9 (which is pretty good in the real world).

Ultimately we need to combine the results from assessing the fitness of each agent in parallel so that we can recombine and mutate them. Thus, we need to use true parallel processing followed by a period of sequential processing. This is more generally referred to as *distributed computing* (figure 6.14), since we start with a single processor (often called the *master node*) and distribute tasks to multiple processors to run in parallel, and then collect the results back onto the master node.

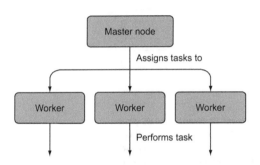

Figure 6.14 A general schematic for how distributed computing works. A master node assigns tasks to worker nodes; the worker nodes perform those tasks and then send their results back to the master node (not shown).

Every step takes a little bit of network time to communicate between machines, which is something we would not encounter if we were running everything on a single machine. Additionally, if just one machine is slower than the others, the other workers will need to wait. To get the maximal scaling efficiency, we want to reduce the amount of communication between nodes as much as possible, both in terms of the number of times nodes need to send data as well as the amount of data that they send.

6.5.4 *Communicating between nodes*

The researchers at OpenAI developed a neat strategy for distributed computing where each node sends only one number (not a whole vector) to each other node, eliminating the need for a separate master node. The idea is that each worker is first initialized with the same parent parameter vector. Then each worker adds a noise vector to its parent to create a slightly different child vector (figure 6.15). Each worker then runs the child vector through the environment to get its fitness score. The fitness score from each worker is sent to all other workers, which just involves sending a single number. Since each worker has the same set of random seeds, each worker can recreate the noise vectors used by all the other workers. Lastly, each worker creates the same new parent vector and the process repeats.

Setting the random seed allows us to consistently generate the same random numbers every time, even on different machines. If you run the code in listing 6.14, you will get the output shown, even though these numbers should be generated "randomly."

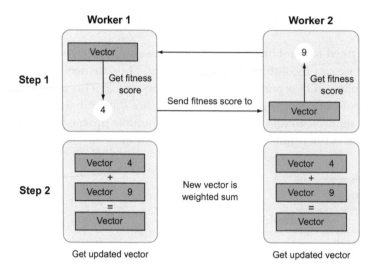

Figure 6.15   The architecture derived from OpenAI's distributed ES paper. Each worker creates a child parameter vector from a parent by adding noise to the parent. Then it evaluates the child's fitness and sends the fitness score to all other agents. Using shared random seeds, each agent can reconstruct the noise vectors used to create the other vectors from the other workers without each having to send an entire vector. Lastly, new parent vectors are created by performing a weighted sum of the child vectors, weighted according to their fitness scores.

Listing 6.14   Setting the random seed

```
import numpy as np
np.random.seed(10)
np.random.rand(4)
>>> array([0.77132064, 0.02075195, 0.63364823, 0.74880388])

np.random.seed(10)
np.random.rand(4)
>> array([0.77132064, 0.02075195, 0.63364823, 0.74880388])
```

Seeding is important; it allows experiments involving random numbers to be reproduced by other researchers. If you do not supply an explicit seed, the system time or some other sort of variable number is used. If we came up with a novel RL algorithm, we would want others to be able to verify our work on their own machines. We would want the agent that another lab generated to be identical, to eliminate any source of error (and therefore doubt). That's why it's important we provide as much detail about our algorithm as possible—the architecture, the hyperparameters used, and sometimes the random seed we used. However, we hope we've developed an algorithm that is robust and that the particular set of random numbers generated doesn't matter to the performance of the algorithm.

6.5.5 *Scaling linearly*

Because the OpenAI researchers reduced the volume of data sent between the nodes, adding nodes did not affect the network significantly. They were able to scale to over a thousand workers linearly.

Scaling linearly means that for every machine added, we receive roughly the same performance boost as we did by adding the previous machine. This is denoted by a straight line on a graph of performance over resources, as seen in figure 6.16.

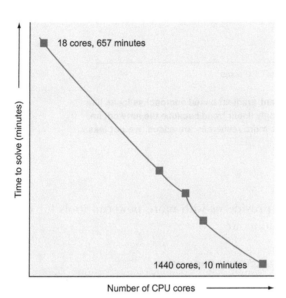

Figure 6.16 Figure recreated from the OpenAI "Evolutionary Strategies as a Scalable Alternative to Reinforcement Learning" paper. The figure demonstrates that as more computing resources were added, the time improvement remained constant.

6.5.6 *Scaling gradient-based approaches*

Gradient-based approaches can be trained on multiple machines as well. However, they do not scale nearly as well as ES. Currently, most distributed training of gradient-based approaches involves training the agent on each worker and then passing the gradients back to a central machine to be aggregated. All the gradients must be passed for each epoch or update cycle, which requires a lot of network bandwidth and strain on the central machine. Eventually the network gets saturated, and adding more workers does not improve training speed as well (figure 6.17).

Evolutionary approaches, on the other hand, do not require backpropagation, so they do not need to send gradient updates to a central server. And with smart techniques like the ones that OpenAI developed, they may only need to send a single number.

Performance scaling for gradient-based training

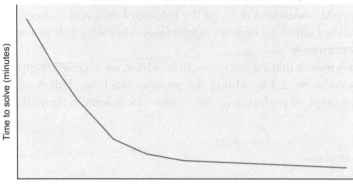

Figure 6.17   **The performance of current gradient-based approaches looks like this. In the beginning, there is a seemingly linear trend because the network has not been saturated. But eventually, as more resources are added, we get less and less of a performance boost.**

Summary

- Evolutionary algorithms provide us with more powerful tools for our toolkit. Based on biological evolution, we
  - Produce individuals
  - Select the best from the current generation
  - Shuffle the genes around
  - Mutate them to introduce some variation
  - Mate them to create new generations for the next population
- Evolutionary algorithms tend to be more data hungry and less data-efficient than gradient-based approaches; in some circumstances this may be fine, notably if you have a simulator.
- Evolutionary algorithms can optimize over nondifferentiable or even discrete functions, which gradient-based methods cannot do.
- Evolutionary strategies (ES) are a subclass of evolutionary algorithms that do not involve biological-like mating and recombination, but instead use copying with noise and weighted sums to create new individuals from a population.

7

Distributional DQN: Getting the full story

This chapter covers

- Why a full probability distribution is better than a single number
- Extending ordinary deep Q-networks to output full probability distributions over Q values
- Implementing a distributional variant of DQN to play Atari Freeway
- Understanding the ordinary Bellman equation and its distributional variant
- Prioritizing experience replay to improve training speed

We introduced Q-learning in chapter 3 as a way to determine the value of taking each possible action in a given state; the values were called action values or Q values. This allowed us to apply a policy to these action values and to choose actions associated with the highest action values. In this chapter we will extend Q-learning to not just determine a point estimate for the action values, but an entire distribution of action values for each action; this is called *distributional Q-learning*. Distributional Q-learning has been shown to result in dramatically better performance on standard benchmarks, and it also allows for more nuanced decision-making, as you will see. Distributional Q-learning algorithms, combined with some other techniques covered in this book, are currently considered a state-of-the-art advance in reinforcement learning.

Most environments we wish to apply reinforcement learning to involve some amount of randomness or unpredictability, where the rewards we observe for a given state-action pair have some variance. In ordinary Q-learning, which we might call *expected-value Q-learning*, we only learn the average of the noisy set of observed rewards. But by taking the average, we throw away valuable information about the dynamics of the environment. In some cases, the rewards observed may have a more complex pattern than just being clustered around a single value. There may be two or more clusters of different reward values for a given state-action; for example, sometimes the same state-action will result in a large positive reward and sometimes in a large negative reward. If we just take the average, we will get something close to 0, which is never an observed reward in this case.

Distributional Q-learning seeks to get a more accurate picture of the distribution of observed rewards. One way to do this would be to keep a record of all the rewards observed for a given state-action pair. Of course, this would require a lot of memory, and for state spaces of high dimensionality it would be computationally impractical. This is why we must make some approximations. But first, let's delve deeper into what expected-value Q-learning is missing, and what distributional Q-learning offers.

7.1   *What's wrong with Q-learning?*

The expected-value type of Q-learning we're familiar with is flawed, and to illustrate this we'll consider a real-world medical example. Imagine we are a medical company, and we want to build an algorithm to predict how a patient with high blood pressure (hypertension) will respond to 4-week course of a new anti-hypertensive drug called Drug X. This will help us decide whether or not to prescribe this drug to an individual patient.

We gather a bunch of clinical data by running a randomized clinical trial in which we take a population of patients with hypertension and randomly assign them to a treatment group (those who will get the real drug) and a control group (those who will get a placebo, an inactive drug). We then record blood pressure over time while the patients in each group are taking their respective drugs. At the end we can see which patients responded to the drug and how much better they did compared to the placebo (figure 7.1).

Once we've collected our data, we can plot a histogram of the change in blood pressure after four weeks on the drug for the treatment and control groups. We might see something like the results in figure 7.2.

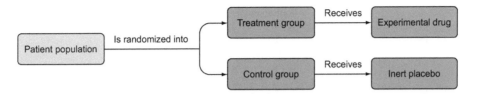

Figure 7.1 In a randomized control trial of a drug, we study the outcome of some treatment compared to a placebo (a nonactive substance). We want to isolate the effect we are trying to treat, so we take a population with some condition and randomly sort them into two groups: a treatment group and a control group. The treatment group gets the experimental drug we are testing, and the control group gets the placebo. After some time, we can measure the outcome for both groups of patients and see if the treatment group, on average, had a better response than the placebo group.

If you first look at the control group histogram in figure 7.2, it appears to be a normal-like distribution centered around –3.0 mmHg (a unit of pressure), which is a fairly insignificant reduction in blood pressure, as you would expect from a placebo. Our algorithm would be correct to predict that for any patient given a placebo, their expected blood pressure change would be –3.0 mmHg on average, even though individual patients had greater or lesser changes than that average value.

Now look at the treatment group histogram. The distribution of blood pressure change is bimodal, meaning there are two peaks, as if we had combined two separate normal distributions. The right-most mode is centered at –2.5 mmHg, much like the control group, suggesting that this subgroup within the treatment group did not benefit from the drug compared to the placebo. However, the left-most mode is centered at –22.3 mmHg, which is a very significant reduction in blood pressure. In fact, it's greater than any currently existing anti-hypertensive drug. This again indicates that there is a subgroup within the treatment group, but this subgroup strongly benefits from the drug.

If you're a physician, and a patient with hypertension walks into your office, all else being equal, should you prescribe them this new drug? If you take the expected value (the average) of the treatment group distribution, you'd only get about –13 mmHg change in blood pressure, which is between the two modes in the distribution. This is still significant compared to the placebo, but it's worse than many existing anti-hypertensives on the market. By that standard, the new drug does not appear to be very effective, despite the fact that a decent number of patients get tremendous benefit from it. Moreover, the expected value of –13 mmHg is very poorly representative of the distribution, since very few patients actually had that level of blood pressure reduction. Patients either had almost no response to the drug or a very robust response; there were very few moderate responders.

Figure 7.3 illustrates the limitations of expected values compared to seeing the full distribution. If you use the expected values of blood pressure changes for each drug, and just pick the drug with the lowest expected value in terms of blood pressure

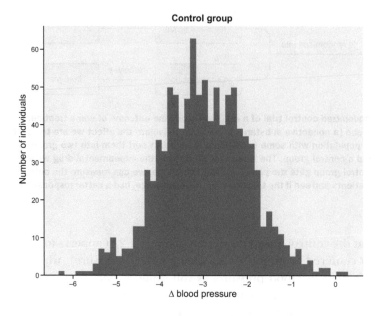

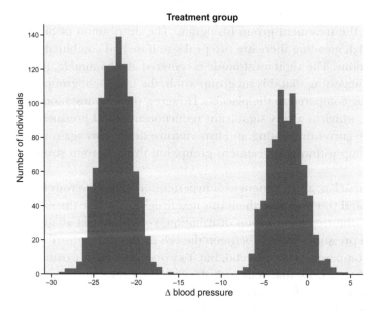

Figure 7.2   Histogram of the measured blood pressure change for the control and treatment groups in a simulated randomized control trial. The *x*-axis is the change in blood pressure from the start (before treatment) to after treatment. We want blood pressure to decrease, so negative numbers are good. We count the number of patients who have each value of blood pressure change, so the peak at –3 for the control group means that most of those patients had a blood pressure drop of 3 mmHg. You can see that there are two subgroups of patients in the treatment group: one group had a significant reduction in blood pressure, and another group had minimal to no effect. We call this a bimodal distribution, where *mode* is another word for "peak" in the distribution.

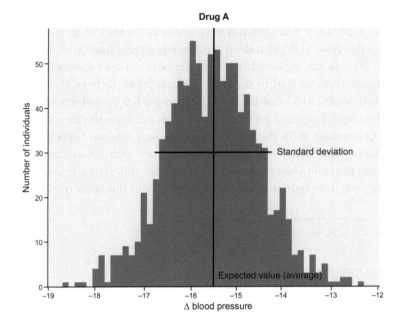

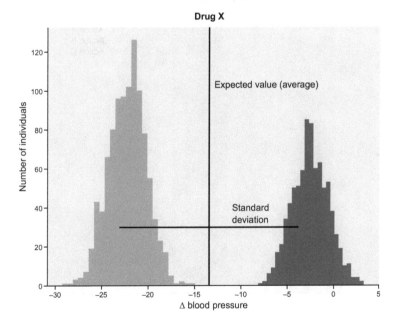

Figure 7.3   Here we compare simulated Drug A to Drug X to see which lowers blood
pressure the most. Drug A has a lower average (expected) value of –15.5 mmHg and
a lower standard deviation, but Drug X is bimodal with one mode centered at –22.5
mmHg. Notice that for Drug X virtually no patients had a blood pressure change that
fell near the average value.

change (ignoring patient-specific complexities, such as side effects), you will be acting optimally at the population level, but not necessarily at the individual level.

So what does this have to do with deep reinforcement learning? Well, Q-learning, as you've learned, gives us the expected (average, time-discounted) state-action values. As you might imagine, this can lead to the same limitations we've been discussing in the case of drugs, with multimodal distributions. Learning a full probability distribution of state-action values would give us a lot more power than just learning the expected value, as in ordinary Q-learning. With the full distribution, we could see if there is multimodality in the state-action values and how much variance there is in the distribution. Figure 7.4 models the action-value distributions for three different actions, and you can see that some actions have more variance than others. With this additional information,

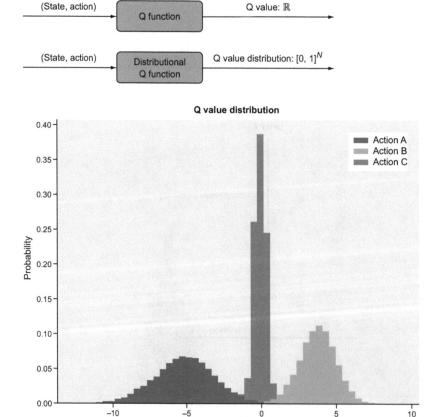

Figure 7.4   Top: An ordinary Q function takes a state-action pair and computes the associated Q value. Middle: A distributional Q function takes a state-action pair and computes a probability distribution over all possible Q values. Probabilities are bounded in the interval [0,1], so it returns a vector with all elements in [0,1] and their sum is 1. Bottom: An example Q value distribution produced by the distributional Q function for three different actions for some state. Action A is likely to lead to an average reward of –5, whereas action B is likely to lead to an average reward of +4.

we can employ risk-sensitive policies—policies that aim not merely to maximize expected rewards but also to control the amount of risk we take in doing so.

Most convincingly, an empirical study was done that evaluated several popular variants and improvements to the original DQN algorithm, including a distributional variant of DQN, to see which were most effective alone and which were most important in combination ("Rainbow: Combining Improvements in Deep Reinforcement Learning" by Hessel et al., 2017). It turns out that distributional Q-learning was the best-performing algorithm overall, among all the individual improvements to DQN that they tested. They combined all the techniques together in a "Rainbow" DQN, which was shown to be far more effective than any individual technique. They then tested to see which components were most crucial to the success of Rainbow, and the results were that distributional Q-learning, multistep Q-learning (covered in chapter 5), and prioritized replay (which will be briefly covered in section 7.7) were the most important to the Rainbow algorithm's performance.

In this chapter you will learn how to implement a distributional deep Q-network (Dist-DQN) that outputs a probability distribution over state-action values for each possible action given a state. We saw some probability concepts in chapter 4, where we employed a deep neural network as a policy function that directly output a probability distribution over actions, but we will review these concepts and go into even more depth here, as these concepts are important to understand in order to implement Dist-DQN. Our discussion of probability and statistics may seem a bit too academic at first, but it will become clear why we need these concepts for a practical implementation.

This chapter is the most conceptually difficult chapter in the whole book as it contains a lot of probability concepts that are difficult to grasp at first. There is also more math here than in any other chapter. Getting through this chapter is a big accomplishment; you will learn or review a lot of fundamental topics in machine learning and reinforcement learning that will give you a greater grasp of these fields.

7.2   *Probability and statistics revisited*

While the mathematics behind probability theory is consistent and uncontroversial, the interpretation of what it means to say something as trivial as "the probability of a fair coin turning up heads is 0.5" is actually somewhat contentious. The two major camps are called *frequentists* and *Bayesians*.

A frequentist says the probability of a coin turning up heads is whatever proportion of heads are observed if one could flip the coin an infinite number of times. A short sequence of coin flips might yield a proportion of heads as high as 0.8, but as you keep flipping, it will tend toward 0.5 exactly, in the infinite limit.

Hence, probabilities are just frequencies of events. In this case, there are two possible outcomes, heads or tails, and each outcome's probability is its frequency after an infinite number of trials (coin flips). This is, of course, why probabilities are values between 0 (impossible) and 1 (certain), and the probabilities for all possible outcomes must sum to 1.

This is a simple and straightforward approach to probability, but it has significant limitations. In the frequentist setting, it is difficult or perhaps impossible to make sense of a question like "what is the probability that Jane Doe will be elected to city council?" since it is impossible in practice and theory for such an election to happen an infinite number of times. Frequentist probability doesn't make much sense for these kinds of one-off events. We need a more powerful framework to handle these situations, and that is what Bayesian probability gives us.

In the Bayesian framework, probabilities represent degrees of belief about various possible outcomes. You can certainly have a belief about something that can only happen once, like an election, and your belief about what is likely to happen can vary depending on how much information you have about a particular situation, and new information will cause you to update your beliefs (see table 7.1).

Table 7.1   Frequentist versus Bayesian probabilities

Frequentist	Bayesian
Probabilities are frequencies of individual outcomes	Probabilities are degrees of belief
Computes the probability of the data given a model	Computes the probability of a model given the data
Uses hypothesis testing	Uses parameter estimation or model comparison
Is computationally easy	Is (usually) computationally difficult

The basic mathematical framework for probability consists of a *sample space*, Ω, which is the set of all possible outcomes for a particular question. In the case of an election, for example, the sample space is the set of all candidates eligible to be elected. There is a probability distribution (or measure) function, $P:\Omega \to [0,1]$, where P is a function from the sample space to real numbers in the interval from 0 to 1. You could plug in $P(candidate\ A)$ and it will spit out a number between 0 and 1 indicating the probability of candidate A winning the election.

> **NOTE** Probability theory is more complicated than what we've articulated here and involves a branch of mathematics called *measure theory*. For our purposes, we do not need to delve any deeper into probability theory than we already have. We will stick with an informal and mathematically nonrigorous introduction to the probability concepts we need.

The *support* of a probability distribution is another term we will use. The support is just the subset of outcomes that are assigned nonzero probabilities. For example, temperatures can't be less than 0 Kelvin, so negative temperatures would be assigned probability 0; the support of the probability distribution over temperatures would be from 0 to positive infinity. Since we generally don't care about outcomes that are impossible, you'll often see "support" and "sample space" used interchangeably, even though they may not be the same.

7.2.1 *Priors and posteriors*

If we were to ask you "what is the probability of each candidate in a 4-way race winning?" without specifying who the candidates were or what the election was about, you might refuse to answer, citing insufficient information. If we really pressed you, you might say that since you know nothing else, each candidate has a ¼ chance of winning. With that answer, you've established a *prior probability distribution* that is uniform (each possible outcome has the same probability) over the candidates.

In the Bayesian framework, probabilities represent beliefs, and beliefs are always tentative in situations when new information can become available, so a prior probability distribution is just the distribution you start with before receiving some new information. After you receive new information, such as some biographical information about the candidates, you might update your prior distribution based on that new information—this updated distribution is now called your *posterior probability distribution*. The distinction between prior and posterior distribution is contextual, since your posterior distribution will become a new prior distribution right before you receive another set of new information. Your beliefs are continually updated as a succession of prior distributions to posterior distributions (see figure 7.5), and this process is generically called *Bayesian inference.*

Bayesian inference

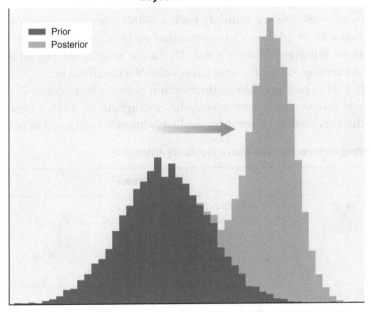

Figure 7.5   Bayesian inference is the process of starting with a prior distribution, receiving some new information, and using that to update the prior into a new, more informed distribution called the posterior distribution.

7.2.2   *Expectation and variance*

There are a number of questions we can ask a probability distribution. We can ask what the single "most likely" outcome is, which we commonly think of as the *mean* or *average* of the distribution. You're probably familiar with the calculation of the mean as taking the sum of all the results and dividing by the number of results. For example, the mean of the 5-day temperature forecast of [18, 21, 17, 17, 21]°C is [18 + 21 + 17 + 17 + 21]/5 = 94/5 = 18.8°C. This is the average predicted temperature over a sample of 5 days in Chicago, Illinois, USA.

Consider if instead we asked five people to give us their prediction for tomorrow's temperature in Chicago and they happened to give us the same numbers, [18, 21, 17, 17, 21]°C. If we wanted the average temperature for tomorrow, we would follow the same procedure, adding the numbers up and dividing by the number of samples (five) to get the average predicted temperature for tomorrow. But what if person 1 was a meteorologist, and we had a lot more confidence in their prediction compared to the other four people that we randomly polled on the street? We would probably want to weight the meteorologist's prediction higher than the others. Let's say we think that their prediction is 60% likely to be true, and the other four are merely 10% likely to be true (notice 0.6 + 4 * 0.10 = 1.0), this is a *weighted average*; it's computed by multiplying each sample by its weight. In this case, that works out as follows: [(0.6 * 18) + 0.1 * (21 + 17 + 17 + 21)] = 18.4°C.

Each temperature is a possible outcome for tomorrow, but not all outcomes are equally likely in this case, so we multiply each possible outcome by its probability (weight) and then sum. If all the weights are equal and sum to 1, we get an ordinary average calculation, but many times it is not. When the weights are not all the same, we get a weighted average called the *expectation value* of a distribution.

The expected value of a probability distribution is its "center of mass," the value that is most likely on average. Given a probability distribution, $P(x)$, where x is the sample space, the expected value for discrete distributions is calculated as follows.

Table 7.2   Computing an expected value from a probability distribution

Math	Python
$\mathbb{E}[P] = \sum x \cdot P(x)$	```\n>>> x = np.array([1,2,3,4,5,6])\n>>> p = np.array([0.1,0.1,0.1,0.1,0.2,0.4])\n>>> def expected_value(x,p):\n>>> return x @ p\n>>> expected_value(x,p)\n4.4\n```

The expected value operator (where *operator* is another term for *function*) is denoted $\mathbb{E}$, and it's a function that takes in a probability distribution and returns its expected value. It works by taking a value, x, multiplying by its associated probability, $P(x)$, and summing for all possible values of x.

In Python, if $P(x)$ is represented as a numpy array of probabilities, probs, and another numpy array of outcomes (the sample space), the expected value is

```
>>> import numpy as np
>>> probs = np.array([0.6, 0.1, 0.1, 0.1, 0.1])
>>> outcomes = np.array([18, 21, 17, 17, 21])
>>> expected_value = 0.0
>>> for i in range(probs.shape[0]):
>>>         expected_value += probs[i] * outcomes[i]

>>> expected_value
18.4
```

Alternatively, the expected value can be computed as the inner (dot) product between the probs array and the outcomes array, since the inner product does the same thing—it multiplies each corresponding element in the two arrays and sums them all.

```
>>> expected_value = probs @ outcomes
>>> expected_value
18.4
```

A discrete probability distribution means that its sample space is a finite set, or in other words, only a finite number of possible outcomes can occur. A coin toss, for example, can only have one of two outcomes.

However, tomorrow's temperature could be any real number (or if measured in Kelvin, it could be any real number from 0 to infinity), and the real numbers or any subset of the real numbers is infinite since we can continually divide them: 1.5 is a real number, and so is 1.500001, and so forth. When the sample space is infinite, this is a *continuous probability distribution.*

In a continuous probability distribution, the distribution does not tell you the probability of a particular outcome, because with an infinite number of possible outcomes, each individual outcome must have an infinitely small probability in order for the sum to be 1. Thus, a continuous probability distribution tells you the *probability density* around a particular possible outcome. The probability density is the sum of probabilities around a small interval of some value—it's the probability that the outcome will fall within some small interval. The difference between discrete and continuous distributions is depicted in figure 7.6. That's all we'll say about continuous distributions for now because in this book we'll really only deal with discrete probability distributions.

Another question we can ask of a probability distribution is its spread or *variance.* Our beliefs about something can be more or less confident, so a probability distribution can be narrow or wide respectively. The calculation of variance uses the expectation operator and is defined as $Var(X) = \sigma^2 = \mathbb{E}[(X - \mu)^2]$, but don't worry about remembering this equation—we will use built-in numpy functions to compute variance. Variance is either denoted $Var(X)$ or σ^2 (sigma squared) where $\sqrt{\sigma^2} = \sigma$ is the standard deviation, so the variance is the standard deviation squared. The μ in this

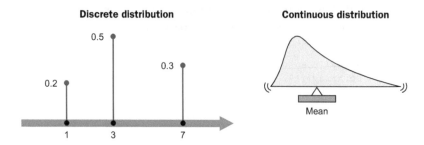

Figure 7.6   Left: A discrete distribution is like a numpy array of probabilities associated with another numpy array of outcome values. There is a finite set of probabilities and outcomes. Right: A continuous distribution represents an infinite number of possible outcomes, and the y axis is the probability density (which is the probability that the outcome takes on a value within a small interval).

equation is the standard symbol for mean, which again is $\mu = \mathbb{E}[X]$, where X is a *random variable* of interest.

A random variable is just another way of using a probability distribution. A random variable is associated with a probability distribution, and a probability distribution can yield random variables. We can create a random variable, T, for tomorrow's temperature. It is a random variable since it is an unknown value but it can only take on specific values that are valid with respect to its underlying probability distribution. We can use random variables wherever a normal deterministic variable might be used, but if we add a random variable with a deterministic variable, we will get a new random variable.

For example, if we think tomorrow's temperature is just going to be today's temperature plus some random noise, we can model this as $T = t_0 + e$, where e is a random variable of noise. The noise might have *normal (Gaussian) distribution* centered around 0 with a variance of 1. Thus T will be a new normal distribution with mean t_0 (today's temperature), but it will still have a variance of 1. A normal distribution is the familiar bell-shaped curve.

Table 7.3 shows a few common distributions. The normal distribution gets wider or narrower depending on the variance parameter, but otherwise it looks the same for any set of parameters. In contrast, the beta and gamma distributions can look quite different depending on their parameters—two different versions of each of these are shown. Random variables are typically denoted with a capital letter like X. In Python, we might set up a random variable using numpy's `random` module:

```
>>> t0 = 18.4
>>> T = lambda: t0 + np.random.randn(1)
>>> T()
array([18.94571853])
>>> T()
array([18.59060686])
```

Table 7.3   Common probability distributions

Normal distribution	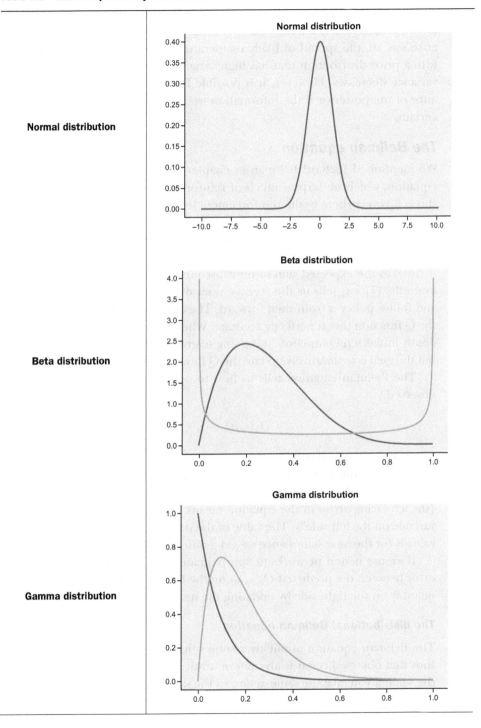
Beta distribution	
Gamma distribution	

Here we made T an anonymous function that accepts no arguments and just adds a small random number to 18.4 every time it is called. The variance of T is 1, which means that most of the values that T returns will be within 1 degree of 18.4. If the variance was 10, the spread of likely temperatures would be greater. Generally we start with a prior distribution that has high variance, and as we get more information the variance decreases. However, it is possible for new information to increase the variance of the posterior if the information we get is very unexpected and makes us less certain.

7.3   The Bellman equation

We mentioned Richard Bellman in chapter 1, but here we will discuss the Bellman equation, which underpins much of reinforcement learning. The Bellman equation shows up everywhere in the reinforcement learning literature, but if all you want to do is write Python, you can do that without understanding the Bellman equation. This section is optional; it's for those interested in a bit more mathematical background.

As you'll recall, the Q function tells us the value of a state-action pair, and value is defined as the expected sum of time-discounted rewards. In the Gridworld game, for example, $Q_\pi(s,a)$ tells us the average rewards we will get if we take action a in state s and follow policy π from then forward. The optimal Q function is denoted Q^* and is the Q function that is perfectly accurate. When we first start playing a game with a randomly initialized Q function, it is going to give us very inaccurate Q value predictions, but the goal is to iteratively update the Q function until it gets close to the optimal Q^*.

The Bellman equation tells us how to update the Q function when rewards are observed,

$$Q_\pi(s_t, a_t) \leftarrow r_t + \gamma \cdot V_\pi(s_{t+1}),$$

where $V_\pi(s_{t+1}) = max[Q_\pi(s_{t+1}, a)]$

So the Q value of the current state, $Q_\pi(s_t, a)$, should be updated to be the observed reward r_t plus the value of the next state $V_\pi(s_{t+1})$ multiplied by the discount factor γ (the left-facing arrow in the equation means "assign the value on the right side to the variable on the left side"). The value of the next state is simply whatever the highest Q value is for the next state (since we get a different Q value for each possible action).

If we use neural networks to approximate the Q function, we try to minimize the error between the predicted $Q_\pi(s_t, a_t)$ on the left side of the Bellman equation and the quantity on the right side by updating the neural network's parameters.

7.3.1   The distributional Bellman equation

The Bellman equation implicitly assumes that the environment is deterministic and thus that observed rewards are deterministic (i.e., the observed reward will be always the same if you take the same action in the same state). In some cases this is true, but in other cases it is not. All the games we have used and will use (except for Gridworld) involve at least some amount of randomness. For example, when we downsample the frames of a game, two originally different states will get mapped into the same down-sampled state, leading to some unpredictability in observed rewards.

In this case, we can make the deterministic variable r_t into a random variable $R(s_t, a)$ that has some underlying probability distribution. If there is randomness in how states evolve into new states, the Q function must be a random variable as well. The original Bellman equation can now be represented as

$$Q(s_t, a_t) \leftarrow \mathbb{E}[R(s_t, a)] + \gamma \cdot \mathbb{E}[Q(S_{t+1}, A_{t+1})]$$

Again, the Q function is a random variable because we interpret the environment as having stochastic transitions. Taking an action may not lead to the same next state, so we get a probability distribution over next states and actions. The expected Q value of the next state-action pair is the most likely Q value given the most likely next state-action pair.

If we get rid of the expectation operator, we get a full distributional Bellman equation:

$$Z(s_t, a_t) \leftarrow R(s_t, a_t) + \gamma \cdot Z(S_{t+1}, A_{t+1})$$

Here we use Z to denote the distributional Q value function (which we will also refer to as the *value distribution*). When we do Q-learning with the original Bellman equation, our Q function will learn the expected value of the value distribution because that is the best it can do, but in this chapter we will use a slightly more sophisticated neural network that will return a value distribution and thus can learn the distribution of observed rewards rather than just the expected value. This is useful for the reasons we described in the first section—by learning a distribution we have a way to utilize risk-sensitive policies that take into consideration the variance and possible multimodality of the distribution.

7.4 Distributional Q-learning

We've now covered all the preliminaries necessary to implement a distributional deep Q-network (Dist-DQN). If you didn't completely understand all of the material in the previous sections, don't worry; it will become more clear when we start writing the code.

In this chapter we are going to use one of the simplest Atari games in the OpenAI Gym, Freeway (figure 7.7), so that we can train the algorithm on a laptop CPU. Unlike other chapters, we're also going to use the RAM version of the game. If you look at the available game environments at https://gym.openai.com/envs/#atari, you will see that each game has two versions, with one being labeled with "RAM."

Freeway is a game where you control a chicken with actions of UP, DOWN, or NO-OP ("no-operation" or do nothing). The objective is to move the chicken across the freeway, avoiding oncoming traffic, to get to the other side, where you get a reward of +1. If you don't get all three chickens across the road in a limited amount of time, you lose the game and get a negative reward.

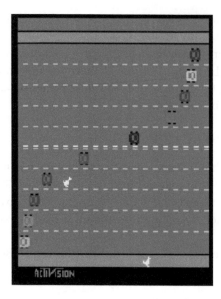

Figure 7.7   Screenshot from the Atari game Freeway. The objective is to move the chicken across the freeway, avoiding oncoming traffic.

In most cases in this book, we train our DRL agents using the raw pixel representation of the game and thus use convolutional layers in our neural network. In this case, though, we're introducing new complexity by making a distributional DQN, so we'll avoid convolutional layers to keep the focus on the topic at hand and keep the training efficient.

The RAM version of each game is essentially a compressed representation of the game in the form of a 128-element vector (the positions and velocities of each game character, etc.). A 128-element vector is small enough to process through a few fully connected (dense) layers. Once you are comfortable with the simple implementation we'll use here, you can use the pixel version of the game and upgrade the Dist-DQN to use convolutional layers.

7.4.1   *Representing a probability distribution in Python*

If you didn't read the optional section 7.3, the only important thing you missed is that instead of using a neural network to represent a Q function, $Q_\pi(s,a)$, that returns a single Q value, we can instead denote a value distribution, $Z_\pi(s,a)$, that represents a random variable of Q values given a state-action pair. This probabilistic formalism subsumes the deterministic algorithms we've been using in prior chapters, since a deterministic outcome can always be represented by a *degenerate* probability distribution (figure 7.8), where all the probability is assigned to a single outcome.

Let's first start with how we're going to represent and work with value distributions. As we did in the section on probability theory, we will represent a discrete probability distribution over rewards using two numpy arrays. One numpy array will be the possible outcomes (i.e., the *support* of the distribution), and the other will be an equal-sized

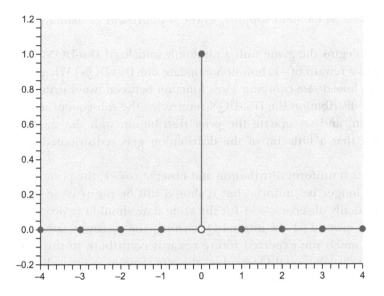

Figure 7.8 This is a *degenerate* distribution, since all the possible values are assigned a probability of 0 except for one value. The outcome values that are *not* assigned 0 probability are called the probability distribution's *support*. The degenerate distribution has a support of 1 element (in this case, the value 0).

array storing the probabilities for each associated outcome. Recall, if we take the inner product between the support array and the probability array, we get the expected reward of the distribution.

One problem with the way we're representing the value distribution, $Z(s,a)$, is that since our array is a finite size, we can only represent a finite number of outcomes. In some cases, the rewards are usually restricted within some fixed, finite range, but in the stock market, for example, the amount of money you can make or lose is theoretically unlimited. With our method, we have to choose a minimum and maximum value that we can represent. This limitation has been solved in a follow-up paper by Dabney et al., "Distributional Reinforcement Learning with Quantile Regression" (2017). We will briefly discuss their approach at the end of the chapter.

For Freeway, we restrict the support to be between −10 and +10. All time steps that are *nonterminal* (i.e., those that don't result in a winning or losing state) give a reward of −1 to penalize taking too much time crossing the road. We reward +10 if the chicken successfully crosses the road and −10 if the game is lost (if the chicken doesn't cross the road before the timer runs out). When the chicken gets hit by a car, the game isn't necessarily lost; the chicken just gets pushed down away from the goal.

Our Dist-DQN will take a state, which is a 128-element vector, and will return 3 separate but equal-sized tensors representing the probability distribution over the support for each of the 3 possible actions (UP, DOWN, NO-OP) given the input state. We will use a 51-element support, so the support and probability tensors will be 51 elements.

If our agent begins the game with a randomly initialized Dist-DQN, takes action UP, and receives a reward of –1, how do we update our Dist-DQN? What is the target distribution and how do we compute a loss function between two distributions? Well, we use whatever distribution the Dist-DQN returns for the subsequent state, s_{t+1}, as a prior distribution, and we update the prior distribution with the single observed reward, r_t, such that a little bit of the distribution gets redistributed around the observed r_t.

If we start with a uniform distribution and observe $r_t = -1$, the posterior distribution should no longer be uniform, but it should still be pretty close (figure 7.9). Only if we repeatedly observe $r_t = -1$ for the same state should the distribution start to strongly peak around –1. In normal Q-learning, the discount rate, γ (gamma), controlled how much the expected future rewards contribute to the value of the current state. In distributional Q-learning, the γ parameter controls how much we update the prior toward the observed reward, which achieves a similar function (figure 7.10).

If we discount the future a lot, the posterior will be strongly centered around the recently observed reward. If we weakly discount the future, the observed reward will only mildly update the prior distribution, $Z(S_{t+1}, A_{t+1})$. Since Freeway has sparse positive rewards in the beginning (because we need to take many actions before we observe our first win), we will set gamma so we only make small updates to the prior distribution.

In listing 7.1 we set up an initial uniform discrete probability distribution and show how to plot it.

Listing 7.1   Setting up a discrete probability distribution in numpy

```
import torch
import numpy as np
from matplotlib import pyplot as plt

vmin,vmax = -10.,10.
nsup=51
support = np.linspace(vmin,vmax,nsup)
probs = np.ones(nsup)
probs /= probs.sum()
z3 = torch.from_numpy(probs).float()
plt.bar(support,probs)
```

Sets the minimum and maximum values of the support of the distribution

Sets the number of elements of the support

Creates the support tensor, a tensor of evenly spaced values from –10 to +10

Plots the distribution as a bar plot

Uniform distribution

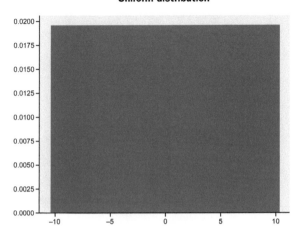

Normal-ish distribution

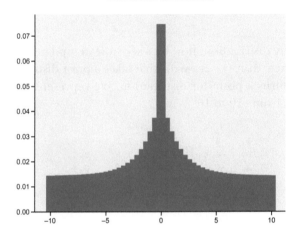

Normal-like distribution

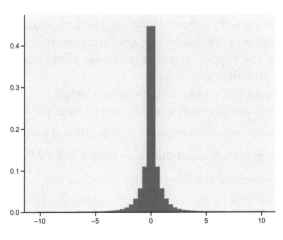

Figure 7.9 We've created a function that takes a discrete distribution and updates it based on observed rewards. This function is performing a kind of approximate Bayesian inference by updating a prior distribution into a posterior distribution. Starting from a uniform distribution (on top, we observe some rewards and we get a peaked distribution at 0 (shown in the middle), and then we observe even more rewards (all zeros), and the distribution becomes a narrow, normal-like distribution (as shown on the bottom).

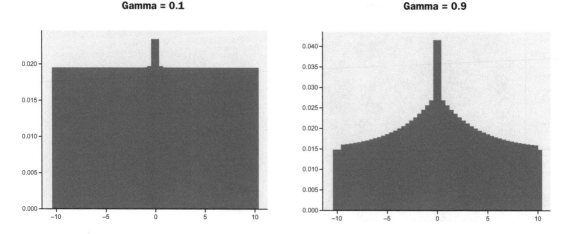

Figure 7.10 **This figure shows how a uniform distribution changes with lower or higher values for gamma (the discount factor).**

We have defined a uniform probability distribution; now let's see how we update the distribution. We want a function, `update_dist(z, reward)`, that takes a prior distribution and an observed reward and returns a posterior distribution. We represent the support of the distribution as a vector from –10 to 10:

```
>>> support
array([-10. ,  -9.6,  -9.2,  -8.8,  -8.4,  -8. ,  -7.6,  -7.2,  -6.8,
        -6.4,  -6. ,  -5.6,  -5.2,  -4.8,  -4.4,  -4. ,  -3.6,  -3.2,
        -2.8,  -2.4,  -2. ,  -1.6,  -1.2,  -0.8,  -0.4,   0. ,   0.4,
         0.8,   1.2,   1.6,   2. ,   2.4,   2.8,   3.2,   3.6,   4. ,
         4.4,   4.8,   5.2,   5.6,   6. ,   6.4,   6.8,   7.2,   7.6,
         8. ,   8.4,   8.8,   9.2,   9.6,  10. ])
```

We need to be able to find the closest support element in the support vector to an observed reward. For example, if we observe $r_t = -1$, we'll want to map that to either –1.2 or –0.8 since those are the closest (equally close) support elements. More importantly, we want the indices of these support elements so that we can get their corresponding probabilities in the probability vector. The support vector is static—we never update it. We only update the corresponding probabilities.

You can see that each support element is 0.4 away from its nearest neighbors. The numpy `linspace` function creates a sequence of evenly spaced elements, and the spacing is given by $\frac{v_{max} - v_{min}}{N - 1}$, where N is the number of support elements. If you plug 10, –10, and $N = 51$ into that formula, you get 0.4. We call this value dz (for delta Z), and we use it to find the closest support element index value by the equation $b_j = \frac{r - v_{min}}{dz}$, where b_j is the index value. Since b_j may be a fractional number, and indices need to be non-negative integers, we simply round the value to the nearest whole number with `np.round(...)`. We also need to clip any values outside the minimum and maximum support range. For example, if the observed $r_t = -2$ then $b_j = \frac{-2 - (-10)}{0.4} = \frac{-2 + 10}{0.4} = 20$. You can see that the support element with index 20 is –2, which in this case exactly corresponds to the observed reward (no rounding needed). We can then find the corresponding probability for the –2 support element using the index.

Once we find the index value of the support element corresponding to the observed reward, we want to redistribute some of the probability mass to that support and the nearby support elements. We have to take care that the final probability distribution is a real distribution and sums to 1. We will simply take some of the probability mass from the neighbors on the left and right and add it to the element that corresponds to the observed reward. Then those nearest neighbors will steal some probability mass from their nearest neighbor, and so on, as shown in figure 7.11. The amount of probability mass stolen will get exponentially smaller the farther we go from the observed reward.

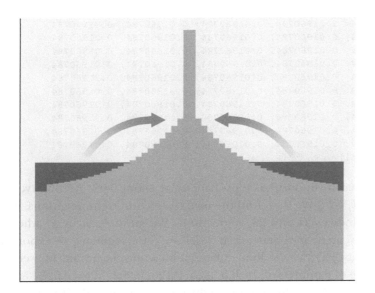

Figure 7.11 The `update_dist` function redistributes probability from neighbors toward the observed reward value.

In listing 7.2 we implement the function that takes a set of supports, the associated probabilities, and an observation, and returns an updated probability distribution by redistributing the probability mass toward the observed value.

Listing 7.2 Updating a probability distribution

```
def update_dist(r,support,probs,lim=(-10.,10.),gamma=0.8):
    nsup = probs.shape[0]
```

```
vmin,vmax = lim[0],lim[1]
dz = (vmax-vmin)/(nsup-1.)
bj = np.round((r-vmin)/dz)
bj = int(np.clip(bj,0,nsup-1))
m = probs.clone()
j = 1
for i in range(bj,1,-1):
    m[i] += np.power(gamma,j) * m[i-1]
    j += 1
j = 1
for i in range(bj,nsup-1,1):
    m[i] += np.power(gamma,j) * m[i+1]
    j += 1
m /= m.sum()
return m
```

Calculates the support spacing value

Calculates the index value of the observed reward in the support

Rounds and clips the value to make sure it is a valid index value for the support

Starting from the immediate left neighbor, steals part of its probability

Starting from the immediate right neighbor, steals part of its probability

Divides by the sum to make sure it sums to 1

Let's walk through the mechanics of this to see how it works. We start with a uniform prior distribution:

```
>>> probs
array([0.01960784, 0.01960784, 0.01960784, 0.01960784, 0.01960784,
       0.01960784, 0.01960784, 0.01960784, 0.01960784, 0.01960784,
       0.01960784, 0.01960784, 0.01960784, 0.01960784, 0.01960784,
       0.01960784, 0.01960784, 0.01960784, 0.01960784, 0.01960784,
       0.01960784, 0.01960784, 0.01960784, 0.01960784, 0.01960784,
       0.01960784, 0.01960784, 0.01960784, 0.01960784, 0.01960784,
       0.01960784, 0.01960784, 0.01960784, 0.01960784, 0.01960784,
       0.01960784, 0.01960784, 0.01960784, 0.01960784, 0.01960784,
       0.01960784, 0.01960784, 0.01960784, 0.01960784, 0.01960784,
       0.01960784, 0.01960784, 0.01960784, 0.01960784, 0.01960784,
       0.01960784])
```

You can see that each support has a probability of about 0.02. We observe $r_t = -1$, and we calculate $b_j \approx 22$. We then find the nearest left and right neighbors, denoted m_l and m_r, to be indices 21 and 23, respectively. We multiply m_l by γ^j, where j is a value that we increment by 1 starting at 1, so we get a sequence of exponentially decreasing gammas: $\gamma^1, \gamma^2, \ldots \gamma^j$. Remember, gamma must be a value between 0 and 1, so the sequence of gammas will be 0.5, 0.25, 0.125, 0.0625 if $\gamma = 0.5$. So at first we take $0.5 * 0.02 = 0.01$ from the left and right neighbors and add it to the existing probability at $b_j = 22$, which is also 0.02. So the probability at $b_j = 22$ will become $0.01 + 0.01 + 0.02 = 0.04$.

Now the left neighbor, m_l, steals probability mass from its own left neighbor at index 20, but it steals less because we multiply by γ^2. The right neighbor, m_r, does the same by stealing from its neighbor on the right. Each element in turn steals from either its left or right neighbor until we get to the end of the array. If gamma is close to 1, like 0.99, a lot of probability mass will be redistributed to the support close to r_t.

Let's test our distribution update function. We'll give it an observed reward of –1 starting from a uniform distribution.

Listing 7.3   Redistributing probability mass after a single observation

```
ob_reward = -1
Z = torch.from_numpy(probs).float()
Z = update_dist(ob_reward,torch.from_numpy(support).float(), \
    Z,lim=(vmin,vmax),gamma=0.1)
plt.bar(support,Z)
```

You can see in figure 7.12 that the distribution is still fairly uniform, but now there is a distinct "bump" centered at –1. We can control how big this bump is with the discount factor γ. On your own, try changing gamma to see how it changes the update.

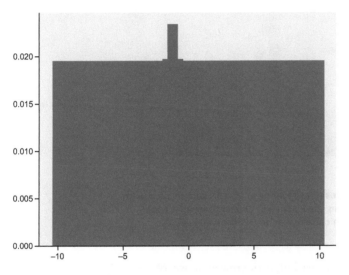

Figure 7.12   This is the result of updating an initially uniform probability distribution after observing a single reward. Some probability mass is redistributed toward the support element corresponding to the observed reward.

Now let's see how the distribution changes when we observe a sequence of varying rewards. (We have just made up this sequence of rewards; they do not come from the Freeway game.) We should be able to observe multimodality.

Listing 7.4   Redistributing probability mass with a sequence of observations

```
ob_rewards = [10,10,10,0,1,0,-10,-10,10,10]
for i in range(len(ob_rewards)):
    Z = update_dist(ob_rewards[i], torch.from_numpy(support).float(), Z, \
                    lim=(vmin,vmax), gamma=0.5)
plt.bar(support, Z)
```

You can see in figure 7.13 that there are now four peaks of varying heights corresponding to the four different kinds of rewards observed, namely 10, 0, 1, and –10. The highest peak (mode of the distribution) corresponds to 10, since that was the most frequently observed reward.

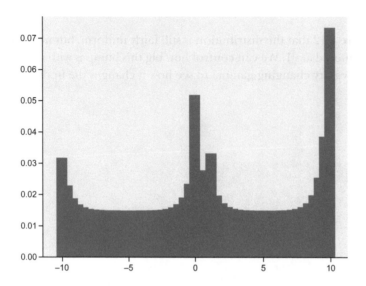

Figure 7.13   This is the result of updating an initially uniform probability distribution after observing a sequence of different rewards. Each "peak" in the distribution corresponds to an observed reward.

Now let's see how the variance decreases if we observe the same reward multiple times, starting from a uniform prior.

> **Listing 7.5   Decreased variance with sequence of same reward**

```
ob_rewards = [5, 5, 5, 5, 5, 5, 5, 5, 5, 5, 5, 5, 5, 5, 5, 5, 5, 5, 5]
for i in range(len(ob_rewards)):
    Z = update_dist(ob_rewards[i], torch.from_numpy(support).float(), \
                    Z, lim=(vmin,vmax), gamma=0.7)
plt.bar(support, Z)
```

You can see in figure 7.14 that the uniform distribution transforms into a normal-like distribution centered at 5 with much lower variance. We will use this function to generate the target distribution that we want the Dist-DQN to learn to approximate. Let's build the Dist-DQN now.

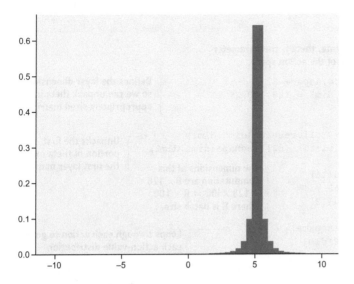

Figure 7.14   The result of updating an initially uniform probability distribution after observing the same reward multiple times. The uniform distribution converges toward a normal-like distribution.

7.4.2   *Implementing the Dist-DQN*

As we briefly discussed earlier, the Dist-DQN will take a 128-element state vector, pass it through a couple of dense feedforward layers, and then it will use a `for` loop to multiply the last layer by 3 separate matrices to get 3 separate distribution vectors. We will lastly apply the softmax function to ensure it is a valid probability distribution. The result is a neural network with 3 different output "heads." We collect these 3 output distributions into a single 3×51 matrix and return that as the final output of the Dist-DQN. Thus, we can get the individual action-value distributions for a particular action by indexing a particular row of the output matrix. Figure 7.15 shows the overall architecture and tensor transformations. In listing 7.6 we define the function that implements the Dist-DQN.

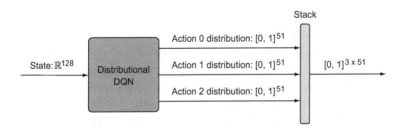

Figure 7.15   The Dist-DQN accepts a 128-element state vector and produces 3 separate 51-element probability distribution vectors, which then get stacked into a single 3×51 matrix.

Listing 7.6   The Dist-DQN

x is the 128-element vector state, theta is the parameter vector, and aspace is the size of the action space.

```
def dist_dqn(x,theta,aspace=3):
    dim0,dim1,dim2,dim3 = 128,100,25,51
    t1 = dim0*dim1
    t2 = dim2*dim1
    theta1 = theta[0:t1].reshape(dim0,dim1)
    theta2 = theta[t1:t1 + t2].reshape(dim1,dim2)
    l1 = x @ theta1
    l1 = torch.selu(l1)
    l2 = l1 @ theta2
    l2 = torch.selu(l2)
    l3 = []
    for i in range(aspace):
        step = dim2*dim3
        theta5_dim = t1 + t2 + i * step
        theta5 = theta[theta5_dim:theta5_dim+step].reshape(dim2,dim3)
        l3_ = l2 @ theta5
        l3.append(l3_)
    l3 = torch.stack(l3,dim=1)
    l3 = torch.nn.functional.softmax(l3,dim=2)
    return l3.squeeze()
```

Defines the layer dimensions so we can unpack theta into appropriately sized matrices

Unpacks the first portion of theta into the first layer matrix

The dimensions of this computation are B × 128 × 128 × 100 = B × 100, where B is batch size.

The dimensions of this computation are B × 100 × 100 × 25 = B × 25.

Loops through each action to generate each action-value distribution

The dimensions of this computation are B × 25 × 25 × 51 = B × 51.

The dimensions of the last layer are B × 3 × 51.

In this chapter we will do gradient descent manually, and to make this easier we have our Dist-DQN accept a single parameter vector called theta that we will unpack and reshape into multiple separate layer matrices of the appropriate sizes. This is easier since we can just do gradient descent on a single vector rather than on multiple separate entities. We also will use a separate target network as we did in chapter 3, so all we need to do is keep a copy of theta and pass that into the same dist_dqn function.

The other novelty here is the multiple output heads. We're used to a neural network returning a single output vector, but in this case we want it to return a matrix. To do that, we set up a loop where we multiply l2 by each of three separate layer matrices, resulting in three different output vectors that we stack into a matrix. Other than that, it is a very simple neural network with a total of five dense layers.

Now we need a function that will take the output of our Dist-DQN, a reward, and an action, and generate the target distribution we want our neural network to get closer to. This function will use the update_dist function we used earlier, but it only wants to update the distribution associated with the action that was actually taken. Also, as you learned in chapter 3, we also need a different target when we've reached a terminal state. At the terminal state, the expected reward is the observed reward, since there are no future rewards by definition. That means the Bellman update reduces to $Z(s_t, a_t) \leftarrow R(S_t, A_t)$. Since we only observe a single reward, and there is no prior distribution to update, the target becomes what is called a *degenerate distribution*. That's just a fancy term for a distribution where all the probability mass is concentrated at a single value.

Listing 7.7 Computing the target distribution

```
def get_target_dist(dist_batch,action_batch,reward_batch,support,lim=(- \
        10,10),gamma=0.8):
    nsup = support.shape[0]
    vmin,vmax = lim[0],lim[1]
    dz = (vmax-vmin)/(nsup-1.)
    target_dist_batch = dist_batch.clone()
    for i in range(dist_batch.shape[0]):
        dist_full = dist_batch[i]
        action = int(action_batch[i].item())
        dist = dist_full[action]
        r = reward_batch[i]
        if r != -1:
            target_dist = torch.zeros(nsup)
            bj = np.round((r-vmin)/dz)
            bj = int(np.clip(bj,0,nsup-1))
            target_dist[bj] = 1.
        else:
            target_dist = update_dist(r,support,dist,lim=lim,gamma=gamma)
        target_dist_batch[i,action,:] = target_dist

    return target_dist_batch
```

Loops through the batch dimension

If the reward is not –1, it is a terminal state and the target is a degenerate distribution at the reward value.

If the state is nonterminal, the target distribution is a Bayesian update of the prior given the reward.

Only changes the distribution for the action that was taken

The get_target_dist function takes a batch of data of shape $B \times 3 \times 51$ where B is the batch dimension, and it returns an equal-sized tensor. For example, if we only have one example in our batch, $1 \times 3 \times 51$, and the agent took action 1 and observed a reward of –1, this function would return a $1 \times 3 \times 51$ tensor, except that the 1×51 distribution associated with index 1 (of dimension 1) will be changed according to the update_dist function using the observed reward of –1. If the observed reward was instead 10, the 1×51 distribution associated with action 1 would be updated to be a degenerate distribution where all elements have 0 probability except the one associated with the reward of 10 (index 50).

7.5 *Comparing probability distributions*

Now that we have a Dist-DQN and a way to generate target distributions, we need a loss function that will calculate how different the predicted action-value distribution is from the target distribution; then we can backpropagate and do gradient descent as usual, to update the Dist-DQN parameters to be more accurate next time. We often use the mean squared error (MSE) loss function when trying to minimize the distance between two batches of scalars or vectors, but this is not an appropriate loss function between two probability distributions. But there are many possible choices for a loss function between probability distributions. We want a function that will measure how different or distant two probability distributions are and that will minimize that distance.

In machine learning, we are usually trying to train a parametric model (e.g., a neural network) to predict or produce data that closely matches empirical data from some data set. Thinking probabilistically, we can conceive of a neural network as generating synthetic data and trying to train the neural network to produce more and more realistic data—data that closely resembles some empirical data set. This is how we train *generative* models (models that generate data); we update their parameters so that the data they generate looks very close to some training (empirical) data set.

For example, let's say we want to build a generative model that produces images of celebrities' faces (figure 7.16). In order to do this, we need some training data, so we use the freely available CelebA data set that contains hundreds of thousands of high quality photographs of various celebrities such as Will Smith and Britney Spears. Let's call our generative model *P* and this empirical data set *Q*.

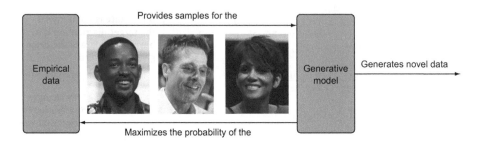

Figure 7.16   A generative model can be a probabilistic model that trains by maximizing the probability that it generates samples that are similar to some empirical data set. Training happens in an iterative loop where the empirical data is supplied to the generative model, which tries to maximize the probability of the empirical data. Before training, the generative model will assign low probability to examples taken from the training data set, and the objective is for the generative model to assign high probability to examples drawn from the data set. After a sufficient number of iterations, the generative model will have assigned high probability to the empirical data, and we can then sample from this distribution to generate new, synthetic data.

The images in data set Q were sampled from the real world, but they are just a small sample of the infinite number of photographs that already exist but are not in the data set and that could have been taken but were not. For example, there may just be one headshot photo of Will Smith in the data set, but another photo of Will Smith taken at a different angle could just as easily have been part of the data set. A photo of Will Smith with a baby elephant on top of his head, while not impossible, would be less likely to be included in the data set because it is less likely to exist (who would put a baby elephant on their head?).

There are naturally more and less likely photos of celebrities, so the real world has a probability distribution over images of celebrities. We can denote this true probability distribution of celebrity photos as $Q(x)$, where x is some arbitrary image, and $Q(x)$ tells us the probability of that image existing in the world. If x is a specific image in data set Q, then $Q(x) = 1.0$, since that image definitely exists in the real world. However, if we plug in an image that's not in the data set but likely exists in the real world outside of our small sample, then $Q(x)$ might equal 0.9.

When we randomly initialize our generative model *P*, it will output random-looking images that look like white noise. We can think of our generative model as a random variable, and every random variable has an associated probability distribution that we denote *P*(*x*), so we can also ask our generative model what the probability of a specific image is given its current set of parameters. When we first initialize it, it will think all images are more or less equally probable, and all will be assigned a fairly low probability. So if we ask *P*("Will Smith photo") it will return some tiny probability, but if we ask *Q*("Will Smith photo"), we'll get 1.0.

In order to train our generative model *P* to generate realistic celebrity photos using data set *Q*, we need to ensure the generative model assigns high probability to the data in *Q* and also to data not in *Q* but that plausibly could be. Mathematically, we want to maximize this ratio:

$$LR = \frac{P(x)}{Q(x)}$$

We call this the *likelihood ratio* (LR) between *P*(*x*) and *Q*(*x*). *Likelihood* in this context is just another word for *probability*.

If we take the ratio for an example image of Will Smith that exists in *Q* using an untrained *P*, we might get

$$LR = \frac{P(x = \text{Will Smith})}{Q(x = \text{Will Smith})} = \frac{0.0001}{1.0} = 0.0001$$

This is a tiny ratio. We want to backpropagate into our generative model and do gradient descent to update its parameters so that this ratio is maximized. This likelihood ratio is the objective function we want to maximize (or minimize its negative).

But we don't want to do this just for a single image; we want the generative model to maximize the total probability of all the images in data set *Q*. We can find this total probability by taking the product of all the individual examples (because the probability of *A and B* is the probability of *A times* the probability of *B* when *A* and *B* are independent and come from the same distribution). So our new objective function is the product of the likelihood ratios for each piece of data in the data set. We have several math equations coming up but we're just using them to explain the underlying probability concepts; don't spend any time trying to remember them.

Table 7.4 The likelihood ratio in math and Python

Math	Python

$LR = \prod_i \frac{P(x_i)}{Q(x_i)}$	```
	p = np.array([0.1,0.1])
	q = np.array([0.6,0.5])
	def lr(p,q):
	    return np.prod(p/q)
	``

One problem with this objective function is that computers have a hard time multiplying a bunch of probabilities, since they are tiny floating-point numbers that when multiplied together create even smaller floating-point numbers. This results in numerical inaccuracies and ultimately numerical underflow, since computers have a finite range of numbers they can represent. To improve this situation, we generally use log probabilities (equivalently, log likelihoods) because the logarithm function turns tiny probabilities into large numbers ranging from negative infinity (when the probability approaches 0) up to a maximum of 0 (when the probability is 1).

Logarithms also have the nice property that $\log(a \cdot b) = \log(a) + \log(b)$, so we can turn multiplication into addition, and computers can handle that a lot better without risking numerical instability or overflows. We can transform the previous product log-likelihood ratio equation into this:

Table 7.5   The log-likelihood ratio in math and Python

Math	Python
| $LR = \sum_i \log\left(\dfrac{P(x_i)}{Q(x_i)}\right)$ | ```python
p = np.array([0.1,0.1])
q = np.array([0.6,0.5])
def lr(p,q):
    return np.sum(np.log(p/q))
``` |

This log-probability version of the equation is simpler and better for computation, but another problem is that we want to weight individual samples differently. For example, if we sample an image of Will Smith from the data set, it should have a higher probability than an image of some less famous celebrity, since the less famous celebrity probably has fewer photos taken of them. We want our model to put more weight on learning images that are more probable out in the real world or, in other words, with respect to the empirical distribution $Q(x)$. We will weight each log-likelihood ratio by its $Q(x)$ probability.

Table 7.6   The weighted log-likelihood ratio in math and Python

Math	Python
| $LR = \sum_i Q(x_i) \cdot \log\left(\dfrac{P(x_i)}{Q(x_i)}\right)$ | ```python
p = np.array([0.1,0.1])
q = np.array([0.6,0.5])
def lr(p,q):
    x = q * np.log(p/q)
    x = np.sum(x)
    return x
``` |

We now have an objective function that measures how likely a sample from the generative model is, compared to the real-world distribution of data, weighted by how likely the sample is in the real world.

There's one last minor problem. This objective function must be maximized because we want the log-likelihood ratio to be high, but by convenience and convention we prefer to have objective functions that are error or loss functions to be minimized. We can remedy this by adding a negative sign, so a high likelihood ratio becomes a small error or loss.

Table 7.7 The Kullback-Leibler divergence

Math	Python
$$D_{KL}(Q \| P) = -\sum_i Q(x_i) \cdot \log\left(\frac{P(x_i)}{Q(x_i)}\right)$$	```python p = np.array([0.1,0.1]) q = np.array([0.6,0.5]) def lr(p,q): x = q * np.log(p/q) x = -1 * np.sum(x) return x ```

You may notice we switched out *LR* for some strange symbols: $D_{KL}(Q\|P)$. It turns out the objective function we just created is a very important one in all of machine learning; it's called the *Kullback-Leibler divergence* (KL divergence for short). The KL divergence is a kind of error function between probability distributions; it tells you how different two probability distributions are.

Often we are trying to minimize the distance between a model-generated probability distribution and some empirical distribution from real data, so we want to minimize the KL divergence. As you just saw, minimizing the KL divergence is equivalent to maximizing the joint log-likelihood ratio of the generated data compared to the empirical data. One important thing to note is that the KL divergence is not symmetric, i.e., $D_{KL}(Q\|P) \neq D_{KL}(P\|Q)$, and this should be clear from its mathematical definition. The KL divergence contains a ratio, and no ratio can equal its inverse unless both are 1, i.e., $\frac{a}{b} \neq \frac{b}{a}$ unless $a = b$.

Although the KL divergence makes a perfect objective function, we can simplify it just a bit for our purposes. Recall that $\log(a/b) = \log(a) - \log(b)$ in general. So we can rewrite the KL divergence as

$$D_{KL}(Q\|P) = -\Sigma_i Q(x) \cdot \log(P(x_i)) - \log(Q(x_i))$$

Note that in machine learning, we only want to optimize the model (update the parameters of the model to reduce the error); we cannot change the empirical distribution $Q(x)$. Therefore, we really only care about the weighted log probability on the left side:

$$H(Q,P) = -\Sigma_i Q(x) \cdot \log(P(x_i))$$

This simplified version is called the cross-entropy loss and is denoted $H(Q,P)$. This is the actual loss function that we will use in this chapter to get the error between our predicted action-value distribution and a target (empirical) distribution.

In listing 7.8 we implement the cross-entropy loss as a function that takes a batch of action-value distributions and computes the loss between that and a target distribution.

Listing 7.8   The cross-entropy loss function

```
def lossfn(x,y):
    loss = torch.Tensor([0.])
    loss.requires_grad=True
    for i in range(x.shape[0]):
        loss_ = -1 * torch.log(x[i].flatten(start_dim=0)) @
y[i].flatten(start_dim=0)
        loss = loss + loss_
    return loss
```

Loss between prediction distribution x and target distribution y

Loops through batch dimension

Flattens along action dimension to get a concatenated sequence of the distributions

---

The `lossfn` function takes a prediction distribution, x, of dimensions $B \times 3 \times 51$ and a target distribution, y, of the same dimensions, and then it flattens the distribution over the action dimension to get a $B \times 153$ matrix. Then it loops through each 1×153 row in the matrix and computes the cross entropy between the 1×153 prediction distribution and the 1×153 target distribution. Rather than explicitly summing over the product of x and y, we can combine these two operations and get the result in one shot by using the inner product operator, `@`.

We could choose to just compute the loss between the specific action-value distribution for the action that was taken, but we compute the loss for all three action-value distributions so that the Dist-DQN learns to keep the other two actions not taken unchanged; it only updates the action-value distribution that was taken.

7.6   *Dist-DQN on simulated data*

Let's test all the parts so far with a simulated target distribution to see if our Dist-DQN can successfully learn to match the target distribution. In listing 7.9 we take an initially uniform distribution, run it through our Dist-DQN, and update it using a synthetic vector of two reward observations.

Listing 7.9   Testing with simulated data

```
aspace = 3
tot_params = 128*100 + 25*100 + aspace*25*51
theta = torch.randn(tot_params)/10.
theta.requires_grad=True
theta_2 = theta.detach().clone()

vmin,vmax= -10,10
gamma=0.9
lr = 0.00001
update_rate = 75
support = torch.linspace(-10,10,51)
state = torch.randn(2,128)/10.
```

Defines the action space to be of size 3

Defines the total number of Dist-DQN parameters based on layer sizes

Randomly initializes a parameter vector for Dist-DQN

Clones theta to use as a target network

Synchronizes the main and target Dist-DQN parameters every 75 steps

Randomly initializes two states for testing

Creates
synthetic
action
data

Initializes a
prediction batch

Creates
synthetic
reward data

```
action_batch = torch.Tensor([0,2])
reward_batch = torch.Tensor([0,10])
losses = []
pred_batch = dist_dqn(state,theta,aspace=aspace)
target_dist = get_target_dist(pred_batch,action_batch,reward_batch, \
                              support, lim=(vmin,vmax),gamma=gamma)

plt.plot((target_dist.flatten(start_dim=1)[0].data.numpy()),color='red',label
    ='target')
plt.plot((pred_batch.flatten(start_dim=1)[0].data.numpy()),color='green',labe
    l='pred')
plt.legend()
```

Initializes a target batch

The purpose of the preceding code is to test the Dist-DQN's ability to learn the distribution for two samples of synthetic data. In our synthetic data, action 0 is associated with a reward of 0, and action 2 is associated with a reward of 10. We expect the Dist-DQN to learn that state 1 is associated with action 1 and state 2 with action 2 and learn the distributions. You can see, in figure 7.17, with the randomly initialized parameter

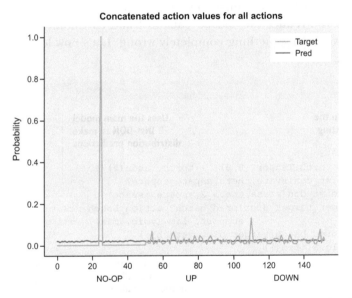

Figure 7.17 This shows the predicted action-value distributions produced by an untrained Dist-DQN and the target distribution after observing a reward. There are three separate action-value distributions of length 51 elements, but here they've been concatenated into one long vector to illustrate the overall fit between the prediction and target. The first 51 elements correspond to the action-value distribution of the NO-OP operation, the second 51 elements correspond to the action-value distribution of the UP action, and the last 51 elements correspond to the DOWN distribution. You can see the prediction is a completely flat (uniform) distribution for all three actions, whereas the target distribution has a mode (a peak) for action 0 and some noisy peaks for the other two actions. The goal is to get the prediction to match the target distribution.

vector, that the prediction distribution for all three actions (remember, we flattened it along the action dimension) is pretty much a uniform distribution, whereas the target distribution has a peak within action 0 (since we plotted only the first sample). After training, the prediction and target distributions should match fairly well.

The reason why a target network is so important is very clear with Dist-DQN. Remember, a target network is just a copy of the main model that we update after some lag time. We use the target network's prediction to create the target for learning, but we only use the main model parameters to do gradient descent. This stabilizes the training because without a target network the target distribution will change after each parameter update from gradient descent.

Yet gradient descent is trying to move the parameters toward better matching the target distribution, so there is a circularity (hence instability) that can lead to the target distribution dramatically changing as a result of this dance between the Dist-DQN's predictions and the target distribution. By using a lagged copy of the Dist-DQN prediction (via a lagged copy of the parameters, which is the target network), the target distribution does not change every iteration and is not immediately affected by the continual updates from the main Dist-DQN model. This significantly stabilizes the training. If you reduce the update_rate to 1 and try training, you will see that the target evolves into something completely wrong. Let's now look at how to train the Dist-DQN.

Listing 7.10 Dist-DQN training on synthetic data

Adds some random noise to the rewards to mitigate overfitting

Uses the main model Dist-DQN to make distribution predictions

Uses the target network Dist-DQN to make distribution predictions (using lagged parameters)

```
for i in range(1000):
    reward_batch = torch.Tensor([0,8]) + torch.randn(2)/10.0
    pred_batch = dist_dqn(state,theta,aspace=aspace)
    pred_batch2 = dist_dqn(state,theta_2,aspace=aspace)
    target_dist = get_target_dist(pred_batch2,action_batch,reward_batch, \
                  support, lim=(vmin,vmax),gamma=gamma)
    loss = lossfn(pred_batch,target_dist.detach())
    losses.append(loss.item())
    loss.backward()
    # Gradient Descent
    with torch.no_grad():
        theta -= lr * theta.grad
    theta.requires_grad = True

    if i % update_rate == 0:
        theta_2 = theta.detach().clone()
fig,ax = plt.subplots(1,2)
ax[0].plot((target_dist.flatten(start_dim=1)[0].data.numpy()),color='red',lab
    el='target')
ax[0].plot((pred_batch.flatten(start_dim=1)[0].data.numpy()),color='green',la
    bel='pred')
ax[1].plot(losses)
```

Uses the main model's distribution prediction in the loss function

Uses the target network's distributions to create the target distribution for learning

Synchronizes the target network parameters with the main model parameters

The top graphic in figure 7.18 shows that the target and prediction from Dist-DQN now match almost exactly after training (you may not even be able to see that there are two overlapping distributions anymore). It works! The loss plot on the bottom of figure 7.18 has those spikes from each time the target network is synchronized to the

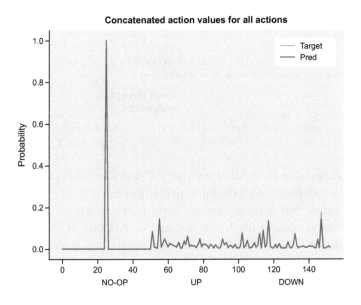

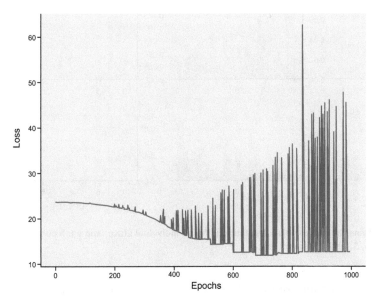

Figure 7.18 Top: The concatenated action-value distributions for all three actions after training. Bottom: Loss plot over training time. The baseline loss is decreasing, but we see ever-increasing spikes.

main model and the target distribution suddenly changes, leading to a higher than normal loss at that time step. We can also look at the learned distributions for each action for each sample in the batch. The following listing shows how to do this.

Listing 7.11   Visualizing the learned action-value distributions

```
tpred = pred_batch
cs = ['gray','green','red']
num_batch = 2
labels = ['Action {}'.format(i,) for i in range(aspace)]
fig,ax = plt.subplots(nrows=num_batch,ncols=aspace)
```

Loops through experiences in batch ⟶
```
for j in range(num_batch):
    for i in range(tpred.shape[1]):
        ax[j,i].bar(support.data.numpy(),tpred[j,i,:].data.numpy(),\
            label='Action {}'.format(i),alpha=0.9,color=cs[i])
```
⟵ **Loops through each action**

In figure 7.19 you can see that in the first sample, the distribution on the left associated with action 0 has collapsed into a degenerate distribution at 0, just like the simulated data. Yet the other two actions remain fairly uniform with no clear peaks. Similarly, in the second sample in the batch, the action 2 (DOWN) distribution is a degenerate distribution at 10, as the data was also degenerate (a sequence of identical samples), and the other two actions remain fairly uniform.

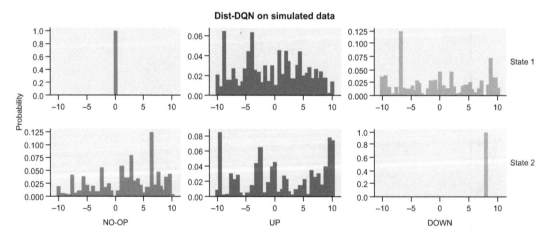

Figure 7.19   Each row contains the action-value distributions for an individual state, and each column in a row is the distribution for actions 0, 1, and 2 respectively.

This Dist-DQN test has almost everything we will use in a real experiment with Atari Freeway. There are just two functions we need before we get to playing Freeway. One will preprocess the states returned from the OpenAI Gym environment. We will get a 128-element numpy array with elements ranging from 0 to 255, and we'll need to convert it to a PyTorch tensor and normalize the values to be between 0 and 1 to moderate the size of the gradients.

We also need a policy function that decides which actions to take, given the predicted action-value distributions. With access to a full probability distribution over action values, we can utilize more sophisticated risk-sensitive policies. In this chapter, we will use a simple policy of choosing actions based on their expected value, in order to keep complexity to a minimum. Although we are learning a full probability distribution, we will choose actions based on their expected value, just like in ordinary Q-learning.

Listing 7.12 Preprocessing states and selecting actions

```
def preproc_state(state):
    p_state = torch.from_numpy(state).unsqueeze(dim=0).float()
    p_state = torch.nn.functional.normalize(p_state,dim=1)    # Normalizes state values to be between 0 and 1
    return p_state

def get_action(dist,support):
    actions = []
    for b in range(dist.shape[0]):    # Loops through batch dimension of distribution
        expectations = [support @ dist[b,a,:] for a in range(dist.shape[1])]    # Computes the expectation values for each action-value distribution
        action = int(np.argmax(expectations))    # Computes the action associated with the highest expectation value
        actions.append(action)
    actions = torch.Tensor(actions).int()
    return actions
```

Recall, we can compute the expected (or expectation) value of a discrete distribution by simply taking the inner product of the support tensor with the probability tensor. We do this for all three actions and select the one that has the highest expected value. Once you get comfortable with the code here, you can try coming up with a more sophisticated policy, perhaps one that takes into consideration the variance (i.e., the confidence) of each action-value distribution.

7.7 Using distributional Q-learning to play Freeway

We're finally ready to use the Dist-DQN algorithm to play the Atari game Freeway. We don't need any other major functionality besides what we've already described. We will have a main Dist-DQN model and a copy—the target network to stabilize training. We will use an epsilon-greedy strategy with a decreasing epsilon value over epochs: with probability epsilon the action selection will be random, otherwise the action will be selected by the `get_action` function, which chooses based on the highest expected value. We will also use an experience replay mechanism, just like with an ordinary DQN.

We will also introduce a very basic form of *prioritized replay*. With normal experience replay, we store all the experiences the agent has in a fixed-size memory buffer, and new experiences displace old ones at random; then we randomly sample a batch from this memory buffer for training. In a game like Freeway, though, where almost all actions result in a –1 reward and we rarely get a +10 or –10 reward, the experience replay memory is going to be heavily dominated by data that all says basically the same thing. It's not very informative to the agent, and the truly significant experiences such as winning or losing the game get strongly diluted, significantly slowing learning.

To alleviate this problem, whenever we take an action that leads to a winning or losing state of the game (i.e., when we get a reward of –10 or +10), we add multiple copies of this experience to the replay buffer to prevent it from being diluted by all the –1 reward experiences. Hence, we *prioritize* certain highly informative experiences over other less informative experiences because we really want our agent to learn which actions lead to success or failure rather than just game continuation.

If you access the code for this chapter on this book's GitHub at http://mng.bz/JzKp, you will find the code we used to record frames of the live game play during training. We also recorded the real-time changes in the action-value distributions so you can see how the game play affects the predicted distributions and vice versa. We do not include that code here in the book, as it would take too much space. In listing 7.13 we initialize the hyperparameters and variables we'll need for our Dist-DQN algorithm.

Listing 7.13   Dist-DQN plays Freeway, preliminaries

```python
import gym
from collections import deque
env = gym.make('Freeway-ram-v0')
aspace = 3
env.env.get_action_meanings()

vmin,vmax = -10,10
replay_size = 200
batch_size = 50
nsup = 51
dz = (vmax - vmin) / (nsup-1)
support = torch.linspace(vmin,vmax,nsup)       ⟵ Experience replay
                                                  buffer using the deque
replay = deque(maxlen=replay_size)             ⟵ data structure

Learning  ⟶ lr = 0.0001
rate
           gamma = 0.1          Starting epsilon
Discount   epochs = 1300        for epsilon-greedy
factor     eps = 0.20        ⟵  policy              Prioritized-replay; duplicates
                                                    highly informative experiences in
Ending/  ⟶ eps_min = 0.05                           the replay this many times
minimum    priority_level = 5  ⟵
epsilon    update_freq = 25    ⟵ Updates the target
                                  network every 25 steps

Randomly   #Initialize DQN parameter vector
initializes tot_params = 128*100 + 25*100 + aspace*25*51   ⟵ The total number of
parameters ⟶ theta = torch.randn(tot_params)/10.             parameters for Dist-DQN
for Dist-DQN theta.requires_grad=True
           theta_2 = theta.detach().clone()   ⟵ Initializes parameters for
                                                 target network
```

```
losses = []
cum_rewards = []
renders = []
state = preproc_state(env.reset())
```

Stores each win (successful freeway crossing) as a 1 in this list

These are all the settings and starting objects we need before we get to the main training loop. All of it is roughly the same as what we did for the simulation test, except we have a prioritized replay setting that controls how many copies of a highly informative experience (such as a win) we should add to the replay. We also use an epsilon-greedy strategy, and we will start with an initially high epsilon value and decrease it during training to a minimum value to maintain a minimal amount of exploration.

Listing 7.14 The main training loop

```
from random import shuffle
for i in range(epochs):
    pred = dist_dqn(state,theta,aspace=aspace)
    if i < replay_size or np.random.rand(1) < eps:
        action = np.random.randint(aspace)
    else:
        action = get_action(pred.unsqueeze(dim=0).detach(),support).item()
    state2, reward, done, info = env.step(action)
    state2 = preproc_state(state2)
    if reward == 1: cum_rewards.append(1)
    reward = 10 if reward == 1 else reward
    reward = -10 if done else reward
    reward = -1 if reward == 0 else reward
    exp = (state,action,reward,state2)
    replay.append(exp)

    if reward == 10:
        for e in range(priority_level):
            replay.append(exp)

    shuffle(replay)
    state = state2

    if len(replay) == replay_size:
        indx = np.random.randint(low=0,high=len(replay),size=batch_size)
        exps = [replay[j] for j in indx]
        state_batch = torch.stack([ex[0] for ex in exps],dim=1).squeeze()
        action_batch = torch.Tensor([ex[1] for ex in exps])
        reward_batch = torch.Tensor([ex[2] for ex in exps])
        state2_batch = torch.stack([ex[3] for ex in exps],dim=1).squeeze()
        pred_batch = dist_dqn(state_batch.detach(),theta,aspace=aspace)
        pred2_batch = dist_dqn(state2_batch.detach(),theta_2,aspace=aspace)
        target_dist = get_target_dist(pred2_batch,action_batch,reward_batch, \
                                support, lim=(vmin,vmax),gamma=gamma)
        loss = lossfn(pred_batch,target_dist.detach())
        losses.append(loss.item())
        loss.backward()
        with torch.no_grad():
```

Epsilon-greedy action selection

Takes selected action in the environment

Changes reward to +10 if environment produced reward of 1 (successful freeway crossing)

Adds experience to replay memory

Changes reward to –10 if game is over (no crossings after a long time)

If reward is 10, that indicates a successful crossing, and we want to amplify this experience.

Changes reward to –1 if original reward was 0 (game is just continuing) to penalize doing nothing

Prepares experience as a tuple of the starting state, the observed reward, the action taken, and the subsequent state

Once replay buffer is full, begins training

Gradient descent

```
            theta -= lr * theta.grad
        theta.requires_grad = True                    Synchronizes the target
                                                       network parameters to the
    if i % update_freq == 0:                  ◁───     main model parameters
        theta_2 = theta.detach().clone()
                                                       Decrements epsilon as a
    if i > 100 and eps > eps_min:             ◁───    function of the epoch number
        dec = 1./np.log2(i)
        dec /= 1e3
        eps -= dec                  Resets the environment
                                    if the game is over
    if done:                                  ◁───
        state = preproc_state(env.reset())
        done = False
```

Almost all of this is the same kind of code we used for the ordinary DQN a few chapters ago. The only changes are that we're dealing with Q distributions rather than single Q values and that we use prioritized replay. If you plot the losses, you should get something like figure 7.20.

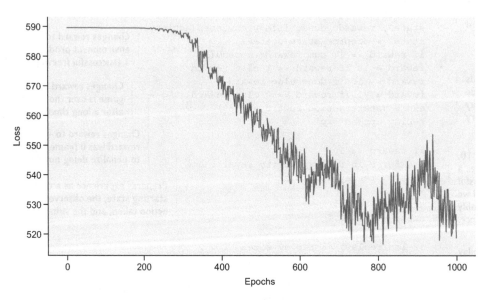

Figure 7.20   The loss plot for training Dist-DQN on the Atari game Freeway. The loss gradually declines but has significant "spikiness" due to the periodic target network updates.

The loss plot in figure 7.20 generally goes down but has "spikiness" due to the updates of the target network, just like we saw with the simulated example. If you investigate the cum_rewards list, you should get a list of ones [1, 1, 1, 1, 1, 1] indicating how many successful chicken crossings occurred. If you're getting four or more, that indicates a successfully trained agent.

Figure 7.21 shows a mid-training game screenshot alongside the corresponding predicted action-value distributions (again, refer to the GitHub code to see how to do this).

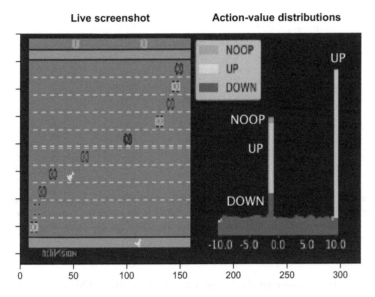

Figure 7.21 Left: Screenshot of live gameplay in Atari Freeway. Right: The corresponding action-value distributions of each of the each actions overlaid. The spike on the right corresponds to the UP action and the spike on the left corresponds mostly to the NO-OP action. Since the right spike is larger, the agent is more likely to take the UP action, which seems like the right thing to do in this case. It is difficult to see, but the UP action also has a spike on top of the NO-OP spike on the left, so the UP action-value distribution is bimodal, suggesting that taking the UP action might lead to either a –1 reward or a +10 reward, but the +10 reward is more likely since that spike is taller.

In figure 7.21 you can see that the action-value distribution for the UP action has two modes (peaks): one at –1 and the other at +10. The expectation value of this distribution is much higher than the other actions, so this action will be selected.

Figure 7.22 shows a few of the learned distributions in the experience replay buffer, to give you a better view of the distributions. Each row is a sample from the replay buffer associated with a single state. Each figure in a row is the action-value distribution for the NO-OP, UP, and DOWN actions respectively. Above each figure is the expected value of that distribution. You can see that in all the samples, the UP action has the highest expected value, and it has two clear peaks: one at –1 and another at +10. The distributions for the other two actions have a lot more variance, because once the agent learns that going up is the best way to win, there are fewer and fewer experiences using the other two actions, so they remain relatively uniform. If we continued training for longer, they would eventually converge to a peak at –1 and possibly a smaller peak at –10, since with epsilon greedy we will still be taking a few random actions.

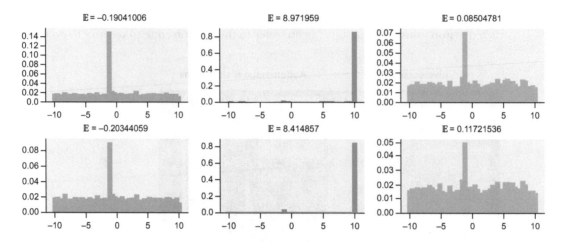

Figure 7.22 Each column has the action-value distributions for a particular action for a given state (row). The number above each plot is the expectation value for that distribution, which is the weighted average value for that distribution. The distributions look fairly similar by eye, but the expected values are distinct enough to result in significantly different action selections.

Distributional Q-learning is one of the biggest improvements to Q-learning in the past few years, and it's still being actively researched. If you compare Dist-DQN to ordinary DQN, you should find you get better overall performance with Dist-DQN. It is not well understood why Dist-DQN performs so much better, especially given that we are only choosing actions based on expected values, but a few reasons are likely. One is that training a neural network to predict multiple things at the same time has been shown to improve generalization and overall performance. In this chapter, our Dist-DQN learned to predict three full probability distributions rather than a single action value, so these auxiliary tasks force the algorithm to learn more robust abstractions.

We also discussed a significant limitation in the way we've implemented Dist-DQN, namely that we're using discrete probability distributions with finite support, so we can only represent action values within a very small range, from –10 to 10. We could make this range wider at the cost of more computational processing, but we can never represent an arbitrarily small or large value with this approach. The way we've implemented it is to use a fixed set of supports but learn the set of associated probabilities.

One fix to this problem is to instead use a fixed set of probabilities over a variable (learned) set of supports. For example, we can fix our probability tensor to range from 0.1 to 0.9, e.g., `array([0.1, 0.2, 0.3, 0.4, 0.5, 0.6, 0.7, 0.8, 0.9])`, and we instead have our Dist-DQN predict the set of associated supports for these fixed probabilities. That is, we're asking our Dist-DQN to learn what support value has a probability of 0.1, and 0.2, and so on. This is called *quantile regression* because these fixed probabilities end up representing quantiles of the distribution (figure 7.23). We learn the supports at and below the 50th percentile (probability 0.5), the 60th percentile, and so on.

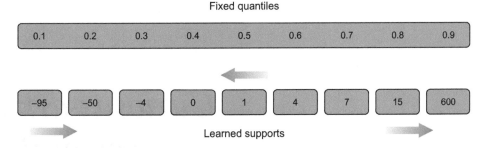

Figure 7.23   In quantile regression, rather than learning what probabilities are assigned to a fixed set of supports, we learn a set of supports that correspond to a fixed set of probabilities (quantiles). Here you can see that the median value is 1 since it is at the 50th percentile.

With this approach, we still have a discrete probability distribution, but we can now represent any possible action value—it can be arbitrarily small or large and we have no fixed range.

Summary

- The advantages of distributional Q-learning include improved performance and a way to utilize risk-sensitive policies.
- Prioritized replay can speed learning by increasing the proportion of highly informative experiences in the experience replay buffer.
- The Bellman equation gives us a precise way to update a Q function.
- The OpenAI Gym includes alternative environments that produce RAM states, rather than raw video frames. The RAM states are easier to learn since they are usually of much lower dimensionality.
- Random variables are variables that can take on a set of outcomes weighted by an underlying probability distribution.
- The entropy of a probability distribution describes how much information it contains.
- The KL divergence and cross-entropy can be used to measure the loss between two probability distributions.
- The support of a probability distribution is the set of values that have nonzero probability.
- Quantile regression is a way to learn a highly flexible discrete distribution by learning the set of supports rather than the set of probabilities.

Curiosity-driven exploration

The fundamental reinforcement learning algorithms we have studied so far, such as deep Q-learning and policy gradient methods are very powerful techniques in a lot of situations, but they fail dramatically in other environments. Google's DeepMind pioneered the field of deep reinforcement learning back in 2013 when they used deep Q-learning to train an agent to play multiple Atari games at superhuman performance levels. But the performance of the agent was highly variable across different types of games. At one extreme, their DQN agent played the Atari game Breakout vastly better than a human, but at the other extreme the DQN was much worse than a human at playing Montezuma's Revenge (figure 8.1), where it could not even pass the first level.

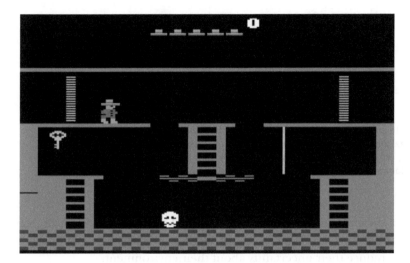

Figure 8.1   Screenshot from the Montezuma's Revenge Atari game. The player must navigate through obstacles to get a key before any rewards are received.

NOTE   The paper that brought great attention to the field of deep reinforcement learning was "Human-level control through deep reinforcement learning" by Volodymyr Mnih and collaborators at Google DeepMind in 2015. The paper is fairly readable and contains the details you'd need to replicate their results.

What's the difference between the environments that explains these disparities in performance? The games that DQN was successful at all gave relatively frequent rewards during game play and did not require significant long-term planning. Montezuma's Revenge, on the other hand, only gives a reward after the player finds a key in the room, which also contains numerous obstacles and enemies. With a vanilla DQN, the agent starts exploring essentially at random. It will take random actions and wait to observe rewards, and those rewards reinforce which actions are best to take given the environment. But in the case of Montezuma's Revenge, it is extremely unlikely that the agent will find the key and get a reward with this random exploration policy, so it will never observe a reward and will never learn.

This problem is called the *sparse reward problem*, since the rewards in the environment are sparsely distributed (figure 8.2). If the agent doesn't observe enough reward signals to reinforce its actions, it can't learn.

Animal and human learning offer us the only natural examples of intelligent systems, and we can turn to them for inspiration. Indeed, researchers trying to tackle this sparse reward problem noticed that humans not only maximize extrinsic rewards

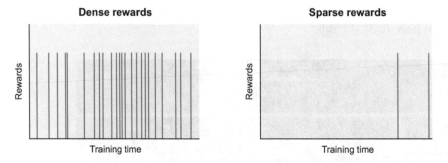

Figure 8.2 In environments with dense rewards, the rewards are received fairly frequently during the training time, making it easy to reinforce actions. In sparse reward environments, rewards may only be received after many sub-goals are completed, making it difficult or impossible for an agent to learn based on reward signals alone.

(those from the environment), like food and sex, but they also demonstrate an intrinsic curiosity, a motivation to explore just for the sake of understanding how things work and to reduce their uncertainty about their environment.

In this chapter you will we learn about methods for successfully training reinforcement learning agents in sparse reward environments by using principles from human intelligence, specifically our innate curiosity. You will see how curiosity can drive the development of basic skills that the agent can use to accomplish sub-goals and find the sparse rewards. In particular, you will see how a curiosity-powered agent can play the Atari game Super Mario Bros. and learn how to navigate the dynamic terrain just by curiosity alone.

NOTE The code for this chapter is in this book's GitHub repository in the chapter 8 folder: http://mng.bz/JzKp.

8.1   *Tackling sparse rewards with predictive coding*

In the world of neuroscience, and particularly computational neuroscience, there is a framework for understanding neural systems at a high level called the *predictive coding model.* In this model, the theory says that all neural systems from individual neurons up to large-scale neural networks are running an algorithm that attempts to predict inputs, and hence tries to minimize the *prediction error* between what it expects to experience and what it actually experiences. So at a high level, as you're going about your day, your brain is taking in a bunch of sensory information from the environment, and it's training to predict how the sensory information will evolve. It's trying to stay one step ahead of the actual raw data coming in.

If something surprising (i.e., unexpected) happens, your brain experiences a large prediction error and then presumably does some parameter updating to prevent that from happening again. For example, you might be talking to someone you just met, and your brain is constantly trying to predict the next word that person will say before they say it. Since this is someone you don't know, your brain will probably have a relatively high average prediction error, but if you become best friends, you'll probably be quite good at finishing their sentences. This is not something you try to do; whether you want to or not, your brain is trying to reduce its prediction error.

Curiosity can be thought of as a kind of desire to reduce the uncertainty in your environment (and hence reduce prediction errors). If you were a software engineer and you saw some online posts about this interesting field called machine learning, your curiosity to read a book like this would be based on the goal of reducing your uncertainty about machine learning.

One of the first attempts to imbue reinforcement learning agents with a sense of curiosity involved using a prediction error mechanism. The idea was that in addition to trying to maximize extrinsic (i.e., environment-provided) rewards, the agent would also try to predict the next state of the environment given its action, and it would try to reduce its prediction error. In very familiar areas of an environment, the agent would learn how it works and would have a low prediction error. By using this prediction error as another kind of reward signal, the agent would be incentivized to visit areas of the environment that were novel and unknown. That is, the higher the prediction error is, the more surprising a state is, and therefore the agent should be incentivized to visit these high prediction error states. Figure 8.3 shows the basic framework for this approach.

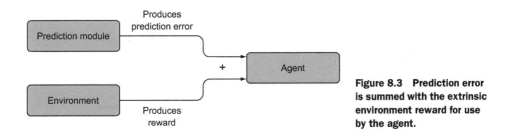

Figure 8.3 Prediction error is summed with the extrinsic environment reward for use by the agent.

The idea is to sum the prediction error (which we will call the *intrinsic reward*) with the extrinsic reward and use that total as the new reward signal for the environment. Now the agent is incentivized to not only figure out how to maximize the environment reward but also to be curious about the environment. The prediction error is calculated as shown in figure 8.4.

The intrinsic reward is based on the prediction error of states in the environment. This works fairly well on the first pass, but people eventually realized that it runs into another problem, often called the "noisy TV problem" (figure 8.5). It turns out that if you train these agents in an environment that has a constant source of randomness, such as a TV screen playing random noise, the agent will have a constantly high prediction error and will be unable to reduce it. It just stares at the noisy TV

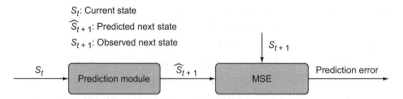

S_t: Current state

$\widehat{S}_{t+1}$: Predicted next state

S_{t+1}: Observed next state

Figure 8.4 The prediction module takes in a state, S_t, (and action a_t, not shown) and produces a prediction for the subsequent state, $\widehat{S}_{t+1}$ (pronounced "S hat t+1", where the hat symbol suggests an approximation). This prediction, along with the true next state, are passed to a mean-squared error function (or some other error function), which produces the prediction error.

indefinitely, since it is highly unpredictable and thus provides a constant source of intrinsic rewards. This is more than just an academic problem, since many real-world environments have similar sources of randomness (e.g., a tree's leaves rustling in the wind).

Figure 8.5 The noisy TV problem is a theoretical and practical problem where a reinforcement learning agent with a naive sense of curiosity will become entranced by a noisy TV, forever staring at it. This is because it is intrinsically rewarded by unpredictability, and white noise is very unpredictable.

At this point, it seems like prediction error has a lot of potential, but the noisy TV problem is a big flaw. Perhaps we shouldn't pay attention to the absolute prediction error but instead to the rate of change of prediction error. When the agent transitions to an unpredictable state, it will experience a transient surge of prediction error, but then it goes away. Similarly, if the agent encounters a noisy TV, at first it is highly unpredictable and therefore has a high prediction error, but the high prediction error is maintained, so the rate of change is zero.

This formulation is better, but it still has some potential issues. Imagine that an agent is outside and sees a tree with leaves blowing in the wind. The leaves are blowing around randomly, so this is a high prediction error. The wind stops blowing, and the prediction error goes down, since the leaves are not moving anymore. Then the wind starts blowing again, and prediction error goes up. In this case, even if we're using a prediction error rate, the rate will be fluctuating along with the wind. We need something more robust.

We want to use this prediction error idea, but we don't want it to be vulnerable to trivial randomness or unpredictability in the environment that doesn't matter. How do we add in the "doesn't matter" constraint to the prediction error module? Well, when we say that something doesn't matter, we mean that it does not affect us or is perhaps uncontrollable. If leaves are randomly blowing in the wind, the agent's actions don't affect the leaves, and the leaves don't affect the actions of the agent. It turns out we can implement this idea as a separate module, in addition to the state prediction module—that's the subject of this chapter. This chapter is based on elucidating and implementing the idea from a paper by Deepak Pathak et al. titled "Curiosity-driven Exploration by Self-supervised Prediction" (2017), which successfully resolves the issues we've been discussing.

We will follow this paper pretty closely because it was one of the biggest contributions to solving the sparse reward problem, and this paper led to a flurry of related research. It also turns out to describe one of the easiest algorithms to implement, among the many others in this area. In addition, one of the goals of this book is to not only teach you the foundational knowledge and skills of reinforcement learning, but to give you a solid-enough mathematics background to be able to read and understand reinforcement learning papers and implement them on your own. Of course, some papers require advanced mathematics, and they are outside the scope of this book, but many of the biggest papers in the field require only some basic calculus, algebra, and linear algebra—things that you probably know if you have made it this far. The only real barrier is getting past the mathematical notation, which we hope to make easier here. We want to teach you how to fish rather than just giving you fish, as the saying goes.

8.2 *Inverse dynamics prediction*

We've described how we could use the prediction error as a curiosity signal. The prediction error module from the last section is implemented as a function, $f:(S_t, a_t) \rightarrow \hat{S}_{t+1}$, that takes a state and the action taken and returns the predicted next state (figure 8.6). It is predicting the future (forward) state of the environment, so we call it the *forward-prediction model*.

Remember, we want to only predict aspects of the state that actually matter, not parts that are trivial or noise. The way we build in the "doesn't matter" constraint to the prediction model is to add another model called an *inverse model*, $g:(S_t, S_{t+1}) \rightarrow \hat{a}_t$. This is a function, g, that takes a state and the next state, and then returns a prediction for which action was taken that led to the transition from s_t to s_{t+1}, as shown in figure 8.7.

S_t: State at time t

a_t: Action at time t

$\widehat{S}_{t+1}$: Predicted next state

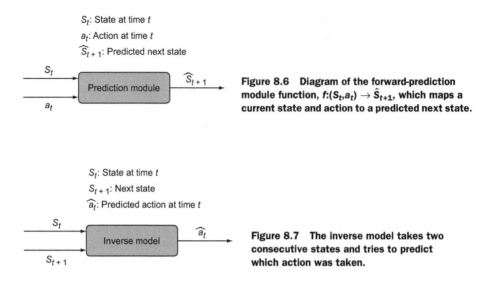

Figure 8.6   **Diagram of the forward-prediction module function, $f{:}(S_t, a_t) \rightarrow \hat{S}_{t+1}$, which maps a current state and action to a predicted next state.**

S_t: State at time t

S_{t+1}: Next state

$\widehat{a_t}$: Predicted action at time t

Figure 8.7   **The inverse model takes two consecutive states and tries to predict which action was taken.**

On its own, this inverse model is not really useful; there's an additional model that is tightly coupled to the inverse model called the *encoder model*, denoted ϕ. The encoder function, $\phi{:}S_t \rightarrow \tilde{S}_t$, takes a state and returns an encoded state $\tilde{S}_t$ such that the dimensionality of $\tilde{S}_t$ is significantly lower than the raw state S_t (figure 8.8). The raw state might be an RGB video frame with height, width, and channel dimensions, and ϕ will encode that state into a low-dimensional vector. For example, a frame might be 100 pixels by 100 pixels by 3 color channels for a total of 30,000 elements. Many of those pixels will be redundant and not useful, so we want our encoder to encode this state into say a 200-element vector with high-level non-redundant features.

S_t: State at time t

$\phi(S_t)$: Encoded state

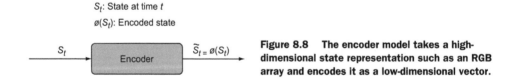

Figure 8.8   **The encoder model takes a high-dimensional state representation such as an RGB array and encodes it as a low-dimensional vector.**

NOTE   A variable with the tilde symbol over it, such as $\tilde{S}_t$, denotes some sort of transformed version of the underlying variable, which may have different dimensionality. A variable with the hat symbol over it, such as $\hat{S}_t$, denotes an approximation (or prediction) of the underlying state and has the same dimensionality.

The encoder model is trained via the inverse model because we actually use the encoded states as inputs to the forward and inverse models *f* and *g* rather than the raw states. That is, the forward model becomes a function, $f: \phi(S_t) \times a_t \rightarrow \hat{\phi}(S_{t+1})$, where $\hat{\phi}(S_{t+1})$ refers to a prediction of the encoded state, and the inverse model becomes a function, $g: \phi(S_t) \times \hat{\phi}(S_{t+1}) \rightarrow \hat{a}_t$ (figure 8.9). The notation $P: a \times b \rightarrow c$ means that we define some function P that takes a pair (a,b) and transforms it into a new object c.

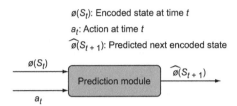

$\emptyset(S_t)$: Encoded state at time t

a_t: Action at time t

$\widehat{\emptyset}(S_{t+1})$: Predicted next encoded state

Figure 8.9 **The forward-prediction module actually uses encoded states, not the raw states. Encoded states are denoted $\phi(S_t)$ or $\tilde{S}_t$.**

The encoder model isn't trained directly—it is *not* an autoencoder. It is only trained through the inverse model. The inverse model is trying to predict the action that was taken to transition from one state to the next using the encoded states as inputs, and in order to minimize its own prediction error, its error will backpropagate through to the encoder model as well as itself. The encoder model will then learn to encode states in a way that is useful for the task of the inverse model. Importantly, although the forward model also uses the encoded states as inputs, we do *not* backpropagate from the forward model to the encoder model. If we did, the forward model would coerce the encoder model into mapping all states into a single fixed output, since that would be the easiest to predict.

Figure 8.10 shows the overall graph structure: the forward pass of the components and also the backward (backpropagation) pass to update the model parameters. It is worth repeating that the inverse model backpropagates back through to the encoder model, and the encoder model is only trained together with the inverse model. We must use PyTorch's detach() method to detach the forward model from the encoder so it won't backpropagate into the encoder. The purpose of the encoder is not to give us a low-dimensional input for improved performance but to learn to encode the state using a representation that only contains information relevant for predicting actions. This means that aspects of the state that are randomly fluctuating and have no impact on the agent's actions will be stripped from this encoded representation. This, in theory, should avoid the noisy TV problem.

Notice that for both the forward and inverse models we need access to the data for a full transition, i.e., we need (S_t, a_t, S_{t+1}). This is not an issue when we use an experience replay memory, as we did in chapter 3 about deep Q-learning, since the memory will store a bunch of these kinds of tuples.

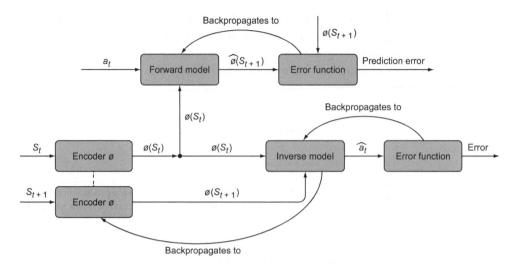

Figure 8.10 The curiosity module. First the encoder will encode states S_t and S_{t+1} into low-dimensional vectors, $\phi(S_t)$ and $\phi(S_{t+1})$ respectively. These encoded states are passed to the forward and inverse models. Notice that the inverse model backpropagates to the encoded model, thereby training it through its own error. The forward model is trained by backpropagating from its own error function, but it does *not* backpropagate through to the encoder like the inverse model does. This ensures that the encoder learns to produce state representations that are only useful for predicting which action was taken. The black circle indicates a copy operation that copies the output from the encoder and passes the copies to the forward and inverse models.

8.3   *Setting up Super Mario Bros.*

Together, the forward, inverse, and encoder models form the *intrinsic curiosity module* (ICM), which we will discuss in detail later in this chapter. The components of the ICM function together for the sole purpose of generating an intrinsic reward that drives curiosity in the agent. The ICM generates a new intrinsic reward signal based on information from the environment, so it is independent of how the agent model is implemented. The ICM can be used for any type of environment, but it will be most useful in sparse reward environments.

We could use whatever agent model implementation we want, such as a distributed actor-critic model (covered in chapter 5). In this chapter we will use a Q-learning model to keep things simple and focus on implementing the ICM. We will use Super Mario Bros. as our testbed.

Super Mario Bros. does not really suffer from the sparse reward problem. The particular environment implementation we will use provides a reward in part based on forward progress through the game, so positive rewards are almost continuously provided. However, Super Mario Bros. is still a great choice to test the ICM because we can choose to "turn off" the extrinsic (environment-provided) reward signal; we can see how well the agent explores the environment just based on curiosity, and we can see how well correlated the extrinsic and intrinsic rewards are.

The implementation of Super Mario Bros. we will use has 12 discrete actions that can be taken at each time step, including a NO-OP (no-operation) action. Table 8.1 lists all the actions.

Table 8.1 Actions in Super Mario Bros.

Index	Action
0	NO-OP / Do nothing
1	Right
2	Right + Jump
3	Right + Run
4	Right + Jump + Run
5	Jump
6	Left
7	Left + Run
8	Left + Jump
9	Left + Jump + Run
10	Down
11	Up

You can install Super Mario Bros. by itself with `pip`:

```
>>> pip install gym-super-mario-bros
```

After it is installed, you can test the environment (e.g., try running this code in a Jupyter Notebook) by playing a random agent and taking random actions. To review how to use the OpenAI Gym, please refer back to chapter 4. In the following listing we instantiate the Super Mario Bros. environment and test it by taking random actions.

Listing 8.1 Setting up the Super Mario Bros. environment

There are two sets of action-spaces we can import: one with 5 actions (simple) and one with 12 (complex).

This wrapper module will make the action-space smaller by combining actions together.

```
import gym
from nes_py.wrappers import JoypadSpace
import gym_super_mario_bros
from gym_super_mario_bros.actions import SIMPLE_MOVEMENT, COMPLEX_MOVEMENT
env = gym_super_mario_bros.make('SuperMarioBros-v0')
env = JoypadSpace(env, COMPLEX_MOVEMENT)
```

Wraps the environment's action space to be 12 discrete actions

```
done = True
for step in range(2500):          ◄─────┐  Tests the environment by
    if done:                             │  taking random actions
        state = env.reset()
    state, reward, done, info = env.step(env.action_space.sample())
    env.render()
env.close()
```

If everything went well, a little window should pop up displaying Super Mario Bros., but it will be taking random actions and not making any forward progress through the level. By the end of this chapter you will have trained an agent that makes consistent forward progress and has learned to avoid or jump on enemies and to jump over obstacles. This, only using the intrinsic curiosity-based reward.

In the OpenAI Gym interface, the environment is instantiated as a class object called env and the main method you need to use is its step(...) method. The step method takes an integer representing the action to be taken. As with all OpenAI Gym environments, this one returns state, reward, done, and info data after each action is taken. The state is a numpy array with dimensions (240, 256, 3) representing an RGB video frame. The reward is bounded between –15 and 15 and is based on the amount of forward progress. The done variable is a Boolean that indicates whether or not the game is over (e.g., whether Mario dies). The info variable is a Python dictionary with the metadata listed in table 8.2.

Table 8.2 The metadata returned after each action in the `info` variable (source: https://github.com/Kautenja/gym-super-mario-bros)

Key	Type	Description
coins	int	The number of collected coins
flag_get	bool	True if Mario reached a flag or ax
life	int	The number of lives left, i.e., {3, 2, 1}
score	int	The cumulative in-game score
stage	int	The current stage, i.e., {1, ..., 4}
status	str	Mario's status, i.e., {'small', 'tall', 'fireball'}
time	int	The time left on the clock
world	int	The current world, i.e., {1, ..., 8}
x_pos	int	Mario's x position in the stage

We will only need to use the x_pos key. In addition to getting the state after calling the step method, you can also retrieve the state at any point by calling env.render ("rgb_array"). That's basically all you need to know about the environment in order to train an agent to play it.

8.4 Preprocessing and the Q-network

The raw state is an RGB video frame with dimensions (240, 256, 3), which is unnecessarily high-dimensional and would be computationally costly for no advantage. We will convert these RGB states into grayscale and resize them to 42 × 42 to allow our model to train much faster.

Listing 8.2 Downsample state and convert to grayscale

```
import matplotlib.pyplot as plt                      The scikit-image library
from skimage.transform import resize        ◁——      has an image-resizing
import numpy as np                                   function built in.

def downscale_obs(obs, new_size=(42,42), to_gray=True):
    if to_gray:
        return resize(obs, new_size, anti_aliasing=True).max(axis=2)   ◁——
    else:
        return resize(obs, new_size, anti_aliasing=True)
                              To convert to grayscale, we simply take the maximum
                              values across the channel dimension for good contrast.
```

The downscale_obs function accepts the state array (obs), a tuple indicating the new size in height and width, and a Boolean for whether to convert to grayscale or not. We set it to True by default since that is what we want. We use the scikit-image library's resize function, so you may need to install it if you don't have it already (go to the download page at https://scikit-image.org/). It's a very useful library for working with image data in the form of multidimensional arrays.

You can use matplotlib to visualize a frame of the state:

```
>>> plt.imshow(env.render("rgb_array"))
>>> plt.imshow(downscale_obs(env.render("rgb_array")))
```

The downsampled image will look pretty blurry, but it still contains enough visual information to play the game.

We need to build a few other data processing functions to transform these raw states into a useful form. We will not just pass a single 42 × 42 frame to our models; we will instead pass the last three frames of the game (in essence, adding a channel dimension) so the states will be a 3 × 42 × 42 tensor (figure 8.11). Using the last three frames gives our model access to velocity information (i.e., how fast and in which direction objects are moving) rather than just positional information.

When the game first starts, we only have access to the first frame, so we prepare the initial state by concatenating the same state three times to get the 3 × 42 × 42 initial state. After this initial state, we can replace the last frame in the state with the most recent frame from the environment, replace the second frame with the old last one, and replace the first frame with the old second. Basically, we have a fixed length first-in-first-out data structure where we append to the right, and the left automatically pops off. Python has a built-in data structure called deque in the collections library that can implement this behavior when the maxlen attribute is set to 3.

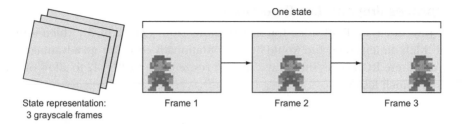

State representation:
3 grayscale frames

Frame 1   Frame 2   Frame 3

Figure 8.11 Each state given to the agent is a concatenation of the three most recent (grayscale) frames in the game. This is necessary so that the model can have access to not just the position of objects, but also their direction of movement.

We will use three functions to prepare the raw states in a form that our agent and encoder models will use. The prepare_state function resizes the image, converts to grayscale, converts from numpy to PyTorch tensor, and adds a batch dimension using the .unsqueeze(dim=) method. The prepare_multi_state function takes a tensor of dimensions Batch x Channel x Height x Width and updates the channel dimension with new frames. This function will only be used during the testing of the trained model; during training we will use a deque data structure to continuously append and pop frames. Lastly the prepare_initial_state function prepares the state when we first start the game and don't have a history of two prior frames. This function will copy the one frame three times to create a Batch x 3 x Height x Width tensor.

Listing 8.3   Preparing the states

```
import torch
from torch import nn
from torch import optim
import torch.nn.functional as F
from collections import deque

def prepare_state(state):
    return torch.from_numpy(downscale_obs(state,
        to_gray=True)).float().unsqueeze(dim=0)


def prepare_multi_state(state1, state2):
    state1 = state1.clone()
    tmp = torch.from_numpy(downscale_obs(state2, to_gray=True)).float()
    state1[0][0] = state1[0][1]
    state1[0][1] = state1[0][2]
    state1[0][2] = tmp
    return state1


def prepare_initial_state(state,N=3):
    state_ = torch.from_numpy(downscale_obs(state, to_gray=True)).float()
    tmp = state_.repeat((N,1,1))
    return tmp.unsqueeze(dim=0)
```

Downscales state and converts to grayscale, converts to a PyTorch tensor, and finally adds a batch dimension

Given an existing 3-frame state1 and a new single frame 2, adds the latest frame to the queue

Creates a state with three copies of the same frame and adds a batch dimension

8.5   *Setting up the Q-network and policy function*

As we mentioned, we will use a deep Q-network (DQN) for the agent. Recall that a DQN takes a state and produces action values, i.e., predictions for the expected rewards for taking each possible action. We use these action values to determine a policy for action selection. For this particular game there are 12 discrete actions, so the output layer of our DQN will produce a vector of length 12 where the first element is the predicted value of taking action 0, and so on.

Remember that action values are (in general) unbounded in either direction; they can be positive or negative if the rewards can be positive or negative (which they can be in this game), so we do not apply any activation function on the last layer. The input to the DQN is a tensor of shape `Batch x 3 x 42 x 42`, where, remember, the channel dimension (3) is for the most recent three frames of game play.

For the DQN, we use an architecture consisting of four convolutional layers and two linear layers. The *exponential linear unit* (ELU) activation function is used after each convolutional layer and the first linear layer (but there's no activation function after the last linear layer). The architecture is diagrammed in figure 8.12. As an exercise you can add a *long short-term memory* (LSTM) or *gated recurrent unit* (GRU) layer that can allow the agent to learn from long-term temporal patterns.

Our DQN will learn to predict the expected rewards for each possible action given the state (i.e., action values or Q values), and we use these action values to decide which action to take. Naively we should just take the action associated with the highest value, but our DQN will not produce accurate action values in the beginning, so we need to have a policy that allows for some exploration so the DQN can learn better action-value estimates.

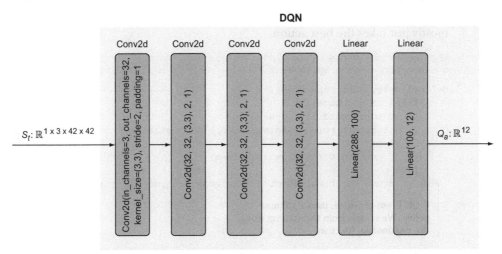

Not shown: ELU activation function applied after each layer except the output layer.

Figure 8.12   The DQN architecture we will use. The state tensor is the input, and it is passed through four convolutional layers and then two linear layers. The ELU activation function is applied after the first five layers but not the output layer because the output needs to be able to produce arbitrarily scaled Q values.

Earlier we discussed using the epsilon-greedy policy, where we take a random action with probability ε and take the action with the highest value with probability $(1 - \varepsilon)$. We usually set ε to be some reasonably small probability like 0.1, and often we'll slowly decrease ε during training so that it becomes more and more likely to choose the highest value action.

We also discussed sampling from a softmax function as our policy. The softmax function essentially takes a vector input with arbitrary real numbers and outputs a same-sized vector where each element is a probability, so all elements sum to 1. It therefore creates a discrete probability distribution. If the input vector is a set of action values, the softmax function will return a discrete probability distribution over the actions based on their action values, such that the action with the highest action value will be assigned the highest probability. If we sample from this distribution, the actions with the highest values will be chosen more often, but other actions will also be chosen. The problem with this approach is that if the best action (according to the action values) is only slightly better than other options, the worse actions will still be chosen with a fairly high frequency. For example, in the following example we take an action-value tensor for five actions and apply the softmax function from PyTorch's functional module.

```
>>> torch.nn.functional.softmax(th.Tensor([3.6, 4, 3, 2.9, 3.5]))
tensor([0.2251, 0.3358, 0.1235, 0.1118, 0.2037])
```

As you can see, the best action (index 1) is only slightly better than the others, so all the actions have pretty high probability, and this policy is not that much different from a uniformly random policy. We will use a policy that begins with a softmax policy to encourage exploration, and after a fixed number of game steps we will switch to an epsilon-greedy strategy, which will continue to give us some exploration capacity but mostly just takes the best action.

Listing 8.4 The policy function

```
def policy(qvalues, eps=None):
    if eps is not None:
        if torch.rand(1) < eps:
            return torch.randint(low=0,high=7,size=(1,))
        else:
            return torch.argmax(qvalues)
    else:
        return torch.multinomial(F.softmax(F.normalize(qvalues)), num_samples=1)
```

The policy function takes a vector of action values and an epsilon (eps) parameter.

If eps is not provided, uses a softmax policy. We sample from the softmax using the multinomial function.

The other big component we need for the DQN is an *experience replay memory*. Gradient-based optimization does not work well if you only pass one sample of data at a time because the gradients are too noisy. In order to average over the noisy gradients, we need to take sufficiently large samples (called batches or mini-batches) and average or sum the gradients over all the samples. Since we only see one sample of data at a time when playing a game, we instead store the experiences in a "memory" store and then sample mini-batches from the memory for training.

We will build an experience replay class that contains a list to store tuples of experiences, where each tuple is of the form (S_t, a_t, r_t, S_{t+1}). The class will also have methods to add a memory and sample a mini-batch.

Listing 8.5 Experience replay

```
from random import shuffle
import torch
from torch import nn
from torch import optim
import torch.nn.functional as F

class ExperienceReplay:
    def __init__(self, N=500, batch_size=100):
        self.N = N
        self.batch_size = batch_size
        self.memory = []
        self.counter = 0

    def add_memory(self, state1, action, reward, state2):
        self.counter +=1
        if self.counter % 500 == 0:
            self.shuffle_memory()

        if len(self.memory) < self.N:
            self.memory.append( (state1, action, reward, state2) )
        else:
            rand_index = np.random.randint(0,self.N-1)
            self.memory[rand_index] = (state1, action, reward, state2)

    def shuffle_memory(self):
        shuffle(self.memory)

    def get_batch(self):
        if len(self.memory) < self.batch_size:
            batch_size = len(self.memory)
        else:
            batch_size = self.batch_size
        if len(self.memory) < 1:
            print("Error: No data in memory.")
            return None

        ind = np.random.choice(np.arange(len(self.memory)), \
        batch_size,replace=False)
        batch = [self.memory[i] for i in ind] #batch is a list of tuples
        state1_batch = torch.stack([x[0].squeeze(dim=0) for x in batch],dim=0)
        action_batch = torch.Tensor([x[1] for x in batch]).long()
        reward_batch = torch.Tensor([x[2] for x in batch])
        state2_batch = torch.stack([x[3].squeeze(dim=0) for x in batch],dim=0)
        return state1_batch, action_batch, reward_batch, state2_batch
```

N is the maximum size of the memory list.

batch_size is the number of samples to generate from the memory with the get_batch(...) method.

Every 500 iterations of adding a memory, shuffles the memory list to promote a more random sample

If the memory is not full, adds to the list; otherwise replaces a random memory with the new one

Uses Python's built-in shuffle function to shuffle the memory list

Randomly samples a mini-batch from the memory list

Creates an array of random integers representing indices

The experience replay class essentially wraps a list with extra functionality. We want to be able to add tuples to the list, but only up to a maximum number, and we want to be able to sample from the list. When we sample with the get_batch(...) method, we create an array of random integers representing indices in the memory list. We index into the memory list with these indices, retrieving a random sample of memories. Since each sample is a tuple, (S_t, a_t, r_t, S_{t+1}), we want to separate out the different components and stack them together into a S_t tensor, a_t tensor, and so on, where the first dimension of the array is the batch size. For example, the S_t tensor we want to return should be of dimension batch_size $\times$ 3 (channels) $\times$ 42 (height) $\times$ 42 (width). PyTorch's stack(...) function will concatenate a list of individual tensors into a single tensor. We also make use of the squeeze(...) and unsqueeze(...) methods to remove and add dimensions of size 1.

With all of that set up, we have just about everything we need to train a vanilla DQN besides the training loop itself. In the next section we will implement the intrinsic curiosity module.

8.6   *Intrinsic curiosity module*

As we described earlier, the intrinsic curiosity module (ICM) is composed of three independent neural network models: the forward model, inverse model, and the encoder (figure 8.13). The forward model is trained to predict the next (encoded) state, given the current (encoded) state and an action. The inverse model is trained to predict the action that was taken, given two successive (encoded) states, $\phi(S_t)$ and $\phi(S_{t+1})$. The encoder simply transforms a raw three-channel state into a single low-dimensional vector. The inverse model acts indirectly to train the encoder to encode states in a way that only preserves information relevant to predicting the action.

The input and output types of each component of the ICM are shown in figure 8.14. The forward model is a simple two-layer neural network with linear layers. The input to the forward model is constructed by concatenating the state $\phi(S_t)$ with the action a_t. The encoded state $\phi(S_t)$ is a tensor $B \times 288$ and the action a_t: $B \times 1$ is a batch of integers indicating the action index, so we make a one-hot encoded vector by creating a vector of size 12 and setting the respective a_t index to 1. Then we concatenate these two tensors to create a batch $\times$ 288 + 12 = batch $\times$ 300 dimensional tensor. We

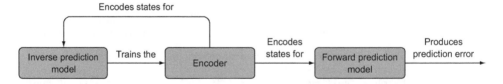

Figure 8.13   A high-level overview of the intrinsic curiosity module (ICM). The ICM has three components that are each separate neural networks. The encoder model encodes states into a low-dimensional vector, and it is trained indirectly through the inverse model, which tries to predict the action that was taken given two consecutive states. The forward model predicts the next encoded state, and its error is the prediction error that is used as the intrinsic reward.

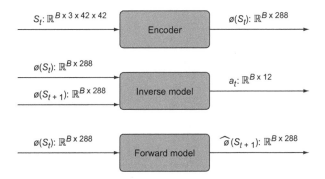

Figure 8.14 This figure shows the type and dimensionality of the inputs and outputs of each component of the ICM.

use the rectified linear unit (ReLU) activation unit after the first layer, but we do not use an activation function after the output layer. The output layer produces a $B \times 288$ tensor.

The inverse model is also a simple two-layer neural network with linear layers. The input is two encoded states, S_t and S_{t+1}, concatenated to form a tensor of dimension batch $\times$ 288 + 288 = batch $\times$ 576. We use a ReLU activation function after the first layer. The output layer produces a tensor of dimension batch $\times$ 12 with a softmax function applied, resulting in a discrete probability distribution over actions. When we train the inverse model, we compute the error between this discrete distribution over actions and a one-hot encoded vector of the true action taken.

The encoder is a neural network composed of four convolutional layers (with an identical architecture to the DQN), with an ELU activation function after each layer. The final output is then flattened to get a flat 288-dimensional vector output.

The whole point of the ICM is to produce a single quantity, the forward-model prediction error (figure 8.15). We literally take the error produced by the loss function and use that as the intrinsic reward signal for our DQN. We can add this intrinsic

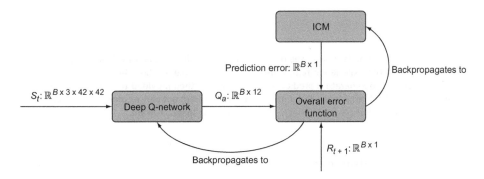

Figure 8.15 The DQN and the ICM contribute to a single overall loss function that is given to the optimizer to minimize with respect to the DQN and ICM parameters. The DQN's Q-value predictions are compared to the observed rewards. The observed rewards, however, are summed together with the ICM's prediction error to get a new reward value.

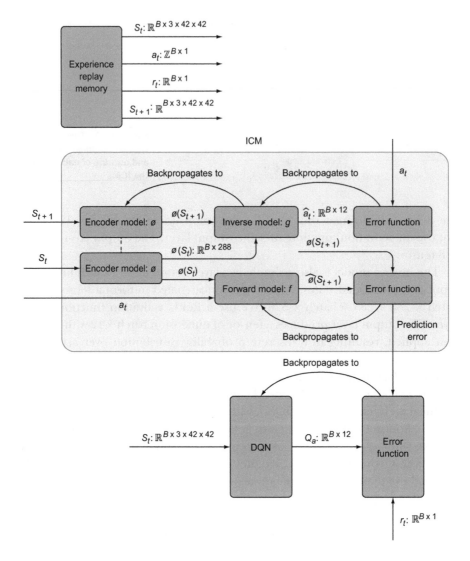

**Figure 8.16 A complete view of the overall algorithm, including the ICM. First we generate
B samples from the experience replay memory and use these for the ICM and DQN. We run
the ICM forward to generate a prediction error, which is then provided to the DQN's error
function. The DQN learns to predict action values that reflect not only extrinsic (environment
provided) rewards but also an intrinsic (prediction error-based) reward.**

reward to the extrinsic reward to get the final reward signal, $r_t = r_i + r_e$. We can scale
the intrinsic or extrinsic rewards to control the proportions of the total reward.

Figure 8.16 shows the ICM in more detail, including the agent model (DQN). Let's
look at the code for the components of the ICM.

Listing 8.6   ICM components

```
class Phi(nn.Module):                    ←┐  Phi is the encoder network.
    def __init__(self):
        super(Phi, self).__init__()
        self.conv1 = nn.Conv2d(3, 32, kernel_size=(3,3), stride=2, padding=1)
        self.conv2 = nn.Conv2d(32, 32, kernel_size=(3,3), stride=2, padding=1)
        self.conv3 = nn.Conv2d(32, 32, kernel_size=(3,3), stride=2, padding=1)
        self.conv4 = nn.Conv2d(32, 32, kernel_size=(3,3), stride=2, padding=1)

    def forward(self,x):
        x = F.normalize(x)
        y = F.elu(self.conv1(x))
        y = F.elu(self.conv2(y))
        y = F.elu(self.conv3(y))
        y = F.elu(self.conv4(y)) #size [1, 32, 3, 3] batch, channels, 3 x 3
        y = y.flatten(start_dim=1) #size N, 288
        return y

class Gnet(nn.Module):               ←┘  Gnet is the inverse model.
    def __init__(self):
        super(Gnet, self).__init__()
        self.linear1 = nn.Linear(576,256)
        self.linear2 = nn.Linear(256,12)

    def forward(self, state1,state2):
        x = torch.cat( (state1, state2) ,dim=1)
        y = F.relu(self.linear1(x))
        y = self.linear2(y)
        y = F.softmax(y,dim=1)
        return y

class Fnet(nn.Module):                   ←┐  Fnet is the forward model.
    def __init__(self):
        super(Fnet, self).__init__()
        self.linear1 = nn.Linear(300,256)
        self.linear2 = nn.Linear(256,288)

    def forward(self,state,action):
        action_ = torch.zeros(action.shape[0],12)
        indices = torch.stack( (torch.arange(action.shape[0]),
    action.squeeze()), dim=0)
        indices = indices.tolist()
        action_[indices] = 1.
        x = torch.cat( (state,action_) ,dim=1)
        y = F.relu(self.linear1(x))
        y = self.linear2(y)
        return y
```

The actions are stored as integers in the replay memory, so we convert to a one-hot encoded vector.

None of these components have complicated architectures. They're fairly mundane, but together they form a powerful system. Now we need to include our DQN model, which is a simple set of a few convolutional layers.

Listing 8.7   Deep Q-network

```
class Qnetwork(nn.Module):
    def __init__(self):
        super(Qnetwork, self).__init__()
        self.conv1 = nn.Conv2d(in_channels=3, out_channels=32,
    kernel_size=(3,3), stride=2, padding=1)
        self.conv2 = nn.Conv2d(32, 32, kernel_size=(3,3), stride=2, padding=1)
        self.conv3 = nn.Conv2d(32, 32, kernel_size=(3,3), stride=2, padding=1)
        self.conv4 = nn.Conv2d(32, 32, kernel_size=(3,3), stride=2, padding=1)
        self.linear1 = nn.Linear(288,100)
        self.linear2 = nn.Linear(100,12)

    def forward(self,x):
        x = F.normalize(x)
        y = F.elu(self.conv1(x))
        y = F.elu(self.conv2(y))
        y = F.elu(self.conv3(y))
        y = F.elu(self.conv4(y))
        y = y.flatten(start_dim=2)
        y = y.view(y.shape[0], -1, 32)
        y = y.flatten(start_dim=1)
        y = F.elu(self.linear1(y))
        y = self.linear2(y)            ⟵ The output is of
        return y                          shape N x 12.
```

We've covered the ICM components; now let's put them together. We're going to define a function that accepts (S_t, a_t, S_{t+1}) and returns the forward-model prediction error and the inverse-model error. The forward-model error will be used not only to backpropagate and train the forward model but also as the intrinsic reward for the DQN. The inverse-model error is only used to backpropagate and train the inverse and encoder models. First we'll look at the hyperparameter setup and the instantiation of the models.

Listing 8.8   Hyperparameters and model instantiation

```
params = {
    'batch_size':150,
    'beta':0.2,
    'lambda':0.1,
    'eta': 1.0,
    'gamma':0.2,
    'max_episode_len':100,
    'min_progress':15,
    'action_repeats':6,
    'frames_per_state':3
}

replay = ExperienceReplay(N=1000, batch_size=params['batch_size'])
Qmodel = Qnetwork()
encoder = Phi()
forward_model = Fnet()
```

```
inverse_model = Gnet()
forward_loss = nn.MSELoss(reduction='none')
inverse_loss = nn.CrossEntropyLoss(reduction='none')
qloss = nn.MSELoss()
all_model_params = list(Qmodel.parameters()) + list(encoder.parameters())
all_model_params += list(forward_model.parameters()) +
    list(inverse_model.parameters())
opt = optim.Adam(lr=0.001, params=all_model_params)
```

We can add the parameters from each model into a single list and pass that into a single optimizer.

Some of the parameters in the `params` dictionary will look familiar, such as `batch_size`, but the others probably don't. We'll go over them, but first let's take a look at the overall loss function.

Here's the formula for the overall loss for all four models (including the DQN):

$$minimize[\lambda \cdot Q_{loss} + (1 - \beta)F_{loss} + \beta \cdot G_{loss}]$$

This formula adds the DQN loss to the forward and inverse model losses, each scaled by a coefficient. The DQN loss has a free-scaling parameter, λ, whereas the forward and inverse model losses share a scaling parameter, β, so that they're inversely related. This is the only loss function we backpropagate through, so at each training step we backpropagate through all four models starting from this single loss function.

The `max_episode_len` and `min_progress` parameters are used to set the minimum amount of forward progress Mario must make or we'll reset the environment. Sometimes Mario will get stuck behind an obstacle and will just keep taking the same action forever, so if Mario doesn't move forward enough in a reasonable amount of time, we just assume he's stuck.

During training, if the policy function says to take action 3 (for example), we will repeat that action six times (set according to the `action_repeats` parameter) instead of just once. This helps the DQN learn the value of actions more quickly. During testing (i.e., inference), we only take the action once. The gamma parameter is the same gamma parameter from the DQN chapter. When training the DQN, the target value is not just the current reward r_t but the highest predicted action value for the next state, so the full target is $r_t + \gamma \cdot max(Q(S_{t+1}))$. Lastly, the `frames_per_state` parameter is set to 3 since each state is the last three frames of the game play.

> **Listing 8.9 The loss function and reset environment**

```
def loss_fn(q_loss, inverse_loss, forward_loss):
    loss_ = (1 - params['beta']) * inverse_loss
    loss_ += params['beta'] * forward_loss
    loss_ = loss_.sum() / loss_.flatten().shape[0]
    loss = loss_ + params['lambda'] * q_loss
    return loss

def reset_env():
    """
```

```
    Reset the environment and return a new initial state
    """
    env.reset()
    state1 = prepare_initial_state(env.render('rgb_array'))
    return state1
```

Finally, we get to the actual ICM function.

Listing 8.10 The ICM prediction error calculation

**Encodes state1 and state2
using the encoder model**

**Runs the forward model using the encoded
states, but we detach them from the graph**

```
def ICM(state1, action, state2, forward_scale=1., inverse_scale=1e4):
    state1_hat = encoder(state1)
    state2_hat = encoder(state2)
    state2_hat_pred = forward_model(state1_hat.detach(), action.detach())
    forward_pred_err = forward_scale * forward_loss(state2_hat_pred, \
                       state2_hat.detach()).sum(dim=1).unsqueeze(dim=1)
    pred_action = inverse_model(state1_hat, state2_hat)
    inverse_pred_err = inverse_scale * inverse_loss(pred_action, \
                                       action.detach().flatten())
                                       .unsqueeze(dim=1)
    return forward_pred_err, inverse_pred_err
```

**The inverse model
returns a softmax probability
distribution over actions.**

It must be repeated how important it is to properly detach nodes from the graph when running the ICM. Recall that PyTorch (and pretty much all other machine learning libraries) builds a computational graph where nodes are *operations* (computations), and *connections* (also called edges) between nodes are the tensors that flow in and out of individual operations. By calling the .detach() method, we disconnect the tensor from the computational graph and treat it just like raw data; this prevents PyTorch from backpropagating through that edge. If we don't detach the state1_hat and state2_hat tensors when we run the forward model and its loss, the forward model will backpropagate into the encoder and will corrupt the encoder model.

We've now approached the main training loop. Remember, since we're using experience replay, training only happens when we sample from the replay buffer. We'll set up a function that samples from the replay buffer and computes the individual model errors.

Listing 8.11 Mini-batch training using experience replay

**We reshape these tensors to add a single
dimension to be compatible with the models.**

```
def minibatch_train(use_extrinsic=True):
    state1_batch, action_batch, reward_batch, state2_batch = replay.get_batch()
    action_batch = action_batch.view(action_batch.shape[0],1)
    reward_batch = reward_batch.view(reward_batch.shape[0],1)

    forward_pred_err, inverse_pred_err = ICM(state1_batch, action_batch,
        state2_batch)
```

**Runs
the ICM**

Scales the forward-prediction error using the eta parameter

Computes the action values for the next state

```
i_reward = (1. / params['eta']) * forward_pred_err
reward = i_reward.detach()
if use_explicit:
    reward += reward_batch
qvals = Qmodel(state2_batch)
reward += params['gamma'] * torch.max(qvals)
reward_pred = Qmodel(state1_batch)
reward_target = reward_pred.clone()
indices = torch.stack( (torch.arange(action_batch.shape[0]), \
action_batch.squeeze()), dim=0)
indices = indices.tolist()
reward_target[indices] = reward.squeeze()
q_loss = 1e5 * qloss(F.normalize(reward_pred), \
F.normalize(reward_target.detach()))
return forward_pred_err, inverse_pred_err, q_loss
```

Starts totaling up the reward; makes sure to detach the i_reward tensor

The use_explicit Boolean variable lets us decide whether or not to use explicit rewards in addition to the intrinsic reward.

Since the action_batch is a tensor of integers of action indices, we convert this to a tensor of one-hot encoded vectors.

Now let's tackle the main training loop, shown in listing 8.12. We initialize the first state using the prepare_initial_state(...) function we defined earlier, which just takes the first frame and repeats it three times along the channel dimension. We also set up a deque instance, to which we will append each frame as we observe them. The deque is set to a maxlen of 3, so only the most recent three frames are stored. We convert the deque first to a list and then to a PyTorch tensor of dimensions $1 \times 3 \times 42 \times 42$ before passing it to the Q-network.

Listing 8.12 The training loop

```
epochs = 3500
env.reset()
state1 = prepare_initial_state(env.render('rgb_array'))
eps=0.15
losses = []
episode_length = 0
switch_to_eps_greedy = 1000
state_deque = deque(maxlen=params['frames_per_state'])
e_reward = 0.
last_x_pos = env.env.env._x_position
ep_lengths = []
use_explicit = False
for i in range(epochs):
    opt.zero_grad()
    episode_length += 1
    q_val_pred = Qmodel(state1)
    if i > switch_to_eps_greedy:
        action = int(policy(q_val_pred,eps))
    else:
        action = int(policy(q_val_pred))
    for j in range(params['action_repeats']):
        state2, e_reward_, done, info = env.step(action)
        last_x_pos = info['x_pos']
        if done:
            state1 = reset_env()
            break
```

We need to keep track of the last x position in order to reset if there's no forward progress.

Runs the DQN forward to get action-value predictions

After the first 1,000 epochs, switches to the epsilon-greedy policy

Repeats whatever action the policy says 6 times, to speed up learning

If Mario is not making sufficient forward progress, restarts the game and tries again

```
        e_reward += e_reward_
        state_deque.append(prepare_state(state2))
    state2 = torch.stack(list(state_deque),dim=1)
    replay.add_memory(state1, action, e_reward, state2)
    e_reward = 0
    if episode_length > params['max_episode_len']:
        if (info['x_pos'] - last_x_pos) < params['min_progress']:
            done = True
        else:
            last_x_pos = info['x_pos']
    if done:
        ep_lengths.append(info['x_pos'])
        state1 = reset_env()
        last_x_pos = env.env.env._x_position
        episode_length = 0
    else:
        state1 = state2
    if len(replay.memory) < params['batch_size']:
        continue
    forward_pred_err, inverse_pred_err, q_loss = \
      minibatch_train(use_extrinsic=False)
    loss = loss_fn(q_loss, forward_pred_err, inverse_pred_err)
    loss_list = (q_loss.mean(), forward_pred_err.flatten().mean(),\
                      inverse_pred_err.flatten().mean())
    losses.append(loss_list)
    loss.backward()
    opt.step()
```

Converts the deque object into a tensor

Adds the single experience to the replay buffer

Gets the errors for one mini-batch of data from the replay buffer

Computes the overall loss

While it's a bit lengthy, this training loop is pretty simple. All we do is prepare a state, input to the DQN, get action values (Q values), input to the policy, get an action to take, and then call the env.step(action) method to perform the action. We then get the next state and some other metadata. We add this full experience as a tuple, (S_t, a_t, r_t, S_{t+1}), to the experience replay memory. Most of the action is happening in the mini-batch training function we already covered.

That is the main code you need to build an end-to-end DQN and ICM to train on Super Mario Bros. Let's test it out by training for 5,000 epochs, which takes about 30 minutes or so running on a MacBook Air (with no GPU). We will train with use_extrinsic=False in the mini-batch function, so it is learning only from the intrinsic reward. You can plot the individual losses for each of the ICM components and the DQN with the following code. We will log-transform the loss data to keep them on a similar scale.

```
>>> losses_ = np.array(losses)
>>> plt.figure(figsize=(8,6))
>>> plt.plot(np.log(losses_[:,0]),label='Q loss')
>>> plt.plot(np.log(losses_[:,1]),label='Forward loss')
>>> plt.plot(np.log(losses_[:,2]),label='Inverse loss')
>>> plt.legend()
>>> plt.show()
```

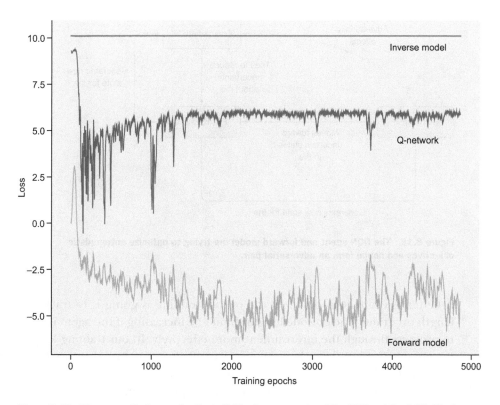

Figure 8.17   These are the losses for the individual components of the ICM and the DQN. The losses do not smoothly decrease like we're used to with a single supervised neural network because the DQN and ICM are trained adversarially.

As shown in figure 8.17, the DQN loss initially drops and then slowly increases and plateaus. The forward loss seems to slowly decrease but is pretty noisy. The inverse model looks sort of flatlined, but if you were to zoom in, it does seem to very slowly decrease over time. The loss plots look a lot nicer if you set `use_extrinsic=True` and use the extrinsic rewards. But don't feel let down by the loss plots. If we test the trained DQN, you will see that it does a lot better than the loss plots suggest. This is because the ICM and DQN are behaving like an adversarial dynamic system since the forward model is trying to lower its prediction error, but the DQN is trying to maximize the prediction error by steering the agent toward unpredictable states of the environment (figure 8.18).

If you look at the loss plot for a *generative adversarial network* (GAN), the generator and discriminator loss look somewhat similar to our DQN and forward model loss with `use_extrinsic=False`. The losses do not smoothly decrease like you're used to when you train a single machine learning model.

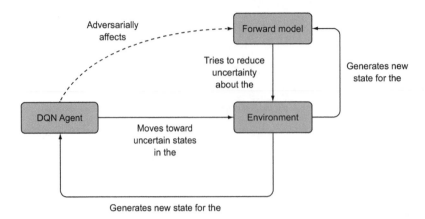

Figure 8.18   The DQN agent and forward model are trying to optimize antagonistic objectives and hence form an adversarial pair.

A better assessment of how well the overall training is going is to track the episode length over time. The episode length should be increasing if the agent is learning how to progress through the environment more effectively. In our training loop, whenever the episode finishes (i.e., when the done variable becomes True because the agent dies or doesn't make sufficient forward progress), we save the current info['x_pos'] to the ep_lengths list. We expect that the maximum episode lengths will get longer and longer over training time.

```
>>> plt.figure()
>>> plt.plot(np.array(ep_lengths), label='Episode length')
```

In figure 8.19 we see that early on the biggest spike is getting to the 150 mark (i.e., the x position in the game), but over training time the farthest distance the agent is able to reach (represented by the height of the spikes) steadily increases, although there is some randomness.

The episode length plot looks promising, but let's render a video of our trained agent playing Super Mario Bros. If you're running this on your own computer, the OpenAI Gym provides a render function that will open a new window with live game play. Unfortunately, this won't work if you're using a remote machine or cloud virtual machine. In those cases, the easiest alternative is to run a loop of the game, saving each observation frame to a list, and once the loop terminates, convert it to a numpy array. You can then save this numpy array of video frames as a video and play it in a Jupyter Notebook.

```
>>> import imageio;
>>> from IPython.display import Video;
>>> imageio.mimwrite('gameplay.mp4', renders, fps=30);
>>> Video('gameplay.mp4')
```

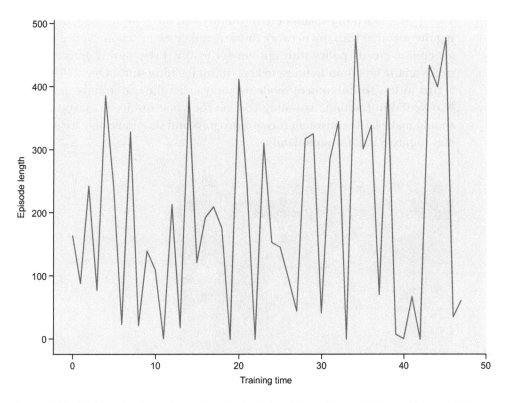

Figure 8.19 Training time is on the *x* axis and episode length is on the *y* axis. We see bigger and bigger spikes over training time, which is what we expect.

In listing 8.13 we use the built-in OpenAI Gym render method to view the game in real-time.

Listing 8.13 Testing the trained agent

```
eps=0.1
done = True
state_deque = deque(maxlen=params['frames_per_state'])
for step in range(5000):
    if done:
        env.reset()
        state1 = prepare_initial_state(env.render('rgb_array'))
    q_val_pred = Qmodel(state1)
    action = int(policy(q_val_pred,eps))
    state2, reward, done, info = env.step(action)
    state2 = prepare_multi_state(state1,state2)
    state1=state2
    env.render()
env.close()
```

There's not much to explain here if you followed the training loop; we're just extracting the part that runs the network forward and takes an action. Notice that we still use an epsilon-greedy policy with epsilon set to 0.1. Even during inference, the agent needs a little bit of randomness to keep it from getting stuck. One difference to notice is that in test (or inference) mode, we only enact the action once and not six times like we did in training. Assuming you get the same results as us, your trained agent should make fairly consistent forward progress and should be able to jump over obstacles (figure 8.20). Congratulations!

Figure 8.20 The Mario agent trained only from intrinsic rewards successfully jumping over a chasm. This demonstrates it has learned basic skills without any explicit rewards to do so. With a random policy, the agent would not even be able to move forward, let alone learn to jump over obstacles.

If you're not getting the same results, try changing the hyperparameters, particularly the learning rate, mini-batch size, maximum episode length, and minimum forward progress. Training for 5,000 epochs with intrinsic rewards works, but in our experience it's sensitive to these hyperparameters. Of course, 5,000 epochs is not very long, so training for longer will result in more interesting behavior.

How will this work in other environments?

We trained our DQN agent with an ICM-based reward on a single environment, Super Mario Bros, but the paper "Large-Scale Study of Curiosity-Driven Learning" by Yuri Burda et al. (2018) demonstrated how effective intrinsic rewards alone can be. They ran a number of experiments using curiosity-based rewards across multiple games, finding that a curious agent could progress through 11 levels in Super Mario Bros. and could learn to play Pong, among other games. They used essentially the same ICM we just built, except they used a more sophisticated actor-critic model called *proximal policy optimization* (PPO) rather than DQN.

An experiment you can try is to replace the encoder network with a *random projection*. A random projection just means multiplying the input data by a randomly initialized matrix (e.g., a randomly initialized neural network that is fixed and not trained). The Burda et al. 2018 paper demonstrated that a random projection works almost as well as the trained encoder.

8.7　*Alternative intrinsic reward mechanisms*

In this chapter we described the serious problem faced by RL agents in environments with sparse rewards. We considered the solution to be imbuing agents with a sense of curiosity, and we implemented an approach from the Pathak et al. 2017 paper, one of the most widely cited papers in reinforcement learning research in recent years. We chose to demonstrate this approach not just because it is popular, but because it builds on what we've learned in previous chapters without introducing too many new notions. Curiosity-based learning (which goes by many names) is a very active area of research, and there are many alternative approaches, some of which we think are better than the ICM.

Many of the other exciting methods use Bayesian inference and information theory to come up with novel mechanisms to drive curiosity. The prediction error (PE) approach we used in this chapter is just one implementation under a broader PE umbrella. The basic idea, as you now know, is that the agent wants to reduce its PE (or in other words, its uncertainty about the environment), but it must do so by actively seeking out novelty lest it be surprised by something unexpected.

Another umbrella is that of agent *empowerment*. Rather than seeking to minimize prediction error and make the environment more predictable, empowerment strategies optimize the agent to maximize its control over the environment (figure 8.21). One paper in this area is "Variational Information Maximisation for Intrinsically Motivated Reinforcement Learning" by Shakir Mohamed and Danilo Jimenez Rezende (2015). We can make the informal statement about maximizing control over the environment into a precise mathematical statement (which we will only approximate here).

The premise relies on the quantity called *mutual information* (MI). We will not define it mathematically here, but informally, MI measures how much information is shared between two sources of data called *random variables* (because usually we deal with data that has some amount of randomness or uncertainty). Another less tautological definition is that MI measures how much your uncertainty about one quantity, x, is reduced given another quantity, y.

Information theory was first developed with real-world communication problems in mind, where one problem is how to best encode messages across a possibly noisy communication channel so that the received message is the least corrupted (figure 8.22). Suppose we have an original message x that we want to send across a noisy communication line (e.g., using radio waves), and we want to maximize the mutual information

Prediction error approaches   **Empowerment approaches**

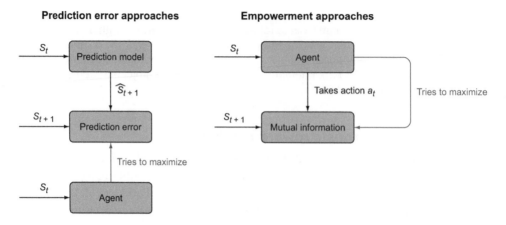

Figure 8.21 The two main approaches for solving the sparse reward problem with curiosity-like methods are prediction error methods, like the one we used in this chapter, and empowerment methods. Rather than trying to maximize the prediction error between a given state and the next predicted state, empowerment methods aim to maximize the mutual information (MI) between the agent's actions and the next states. If the MI between the agent's action and the next state is high, that means the agent has a high level of control (or power) over the resulting next states (i.e., if you know which action the agent took, you can predict the next state well). This incentivizes the agent to learn how to maximally control the environment.

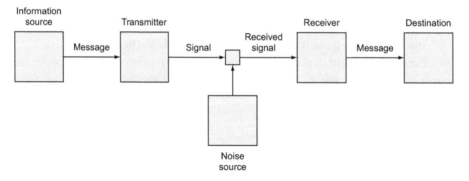

Figure 8.22 Claude Shannon developed communication theory, which was born from the need to encode messages efficiently and robustly across noisy communication channels as depicted here. The goal is to encode the message such that the mutual information between the received message and the sent message is maximal.

between x and the received message y. We do this by developing some way of encoding x, which might be a textual document, into a pattern of radio waves that minimizes the probability of the data being corrupted by noise. Once someone else receives the decoded message, y, they can be assured that their received message is very close to the original message.

In our example, x and y were both some sort of written message, but x and y need not be the same type of quantities. For example, we can ask what the mutual information is between the one-year stock price history of a company and its annual revenue: If we start with a very uncertain estimate about the annual revenue of a company, and then we learn the one-year stock price history, how much is our uncertainty reduced? If it's reduced a lot, the MI is high.

That example involved different quantities, but both used the units of dollars—that need not be the case either. We could ask what the MI is between the daily temperature and the sales of ice cream shops.

In the case of agent empowerment in reinforcement learning, the objective is to maximize the mutual information between an action (or sequence of actions) and the resulting future state (or states). Maximizing this objective means that if you know what action the agent took, you will have a high confidence about what the resulting state was. This means the agent has a high degree of control over the environment, since it can reliably reach states given its actions. Hence, a maximally empowered agent has maximal degrees of freedom.

This is different than the prediction-error approach because minimizing PE directly encourages exploration, whereas maximizing empowerment may induce exploratory behavior as a means to learn empowering skills, but only indirectly. Consider a young woman, Sarah, who decides to travel the world and explore as much as possible. She is reducing her uncertainty about the world. Compare her to Bill Gates, who by being extraordinarily rich, has a high degree of power. He may not be interested in traveling as much as Sarah, but he can if he wants, and no matter where he is at any time, he can go where he wants to go.

Both empowerment and curiosity objectives have their use cases. Empowerment-based objectives have been shown to be useful for training agents to acquire complex skills without any extrinsic reward (e.g., robotic tasks or sports games), whereas curiosity-based objectives tend to be more useful for exploration (e.g., games like Super Mario Bros. where the goal is to progress through levels). In any case, these two metrics are more similar than they are different.

Summary

- The sparse reward problem is when an environment rarely produces a useful reward signal, which severely challenges the way ordinary DRL attempts to learn.
- The sparse reward problem can be solved by creating synthetic reward signals that we call curiosity rewards.
- A curiosity module creates synthetic rewards based on how unpredictable the next state of the environment is, encouraging the agent to explore more unpredictable parts of the environment.
- The intrinsic curiosity module (ICM) consists of three independent neural networks: a forward-prediction model, an inverse model, and an encoder.

- The encoder encodes high-dimensional states into a low-dimensional vector with high-level features (which removes noise and trivial features).
- The forward-prediction model predicts the next encoded state, and its error provides the curiosity signal.
- The inverse model trains the encoder by taking two successive encoded states and predicting the action that was taken.
- Empowerment is a closely related but alternative approach to curiosity-based learning. In empowerment, the agent is incentivized to learn how to maximize the amount of control it has over the environment.

Multi-agent
reinforcement learning

This chapter covers

- Why ordinary Q-learning can fail in the multi-agent setting
- How to deal with the "curse of dimensionality" with multiple agents
- How to implement multi-agent Q-learning models that can perceive other agents
- How to scale multi-agent Q-learning by using the mean field approximation
- How to use DQNs to control dozens of agents in a multi-agent physics simulation and game

So far, the reinforcement learning algorithms we have covered—Q-learning, policy gradients, and actor-critic algorithms—have all been applied to control a single agent in an environment. But what about situations where we want to control multiple agents that can interact with each other? The simplest example of this would be a two-player game where each player is implemented as a reinforcement learning agent. But there are other situations in which we might want to model hundreds or thousands of individual agents all interacting with each other, such as a traffic simulation. In this chapter you will learn how to adapt what you've learned so far into this multi-agent scenario by implementing an algorithm called *mean field Q-learning* (MF-Q), first described in a paper titled "Mean Field Multi-Agent Reinforcement Learning" by Yaodong Yang et al. (2018).

9.1   *From one to many agents*

In the case of games, the environment might contain other agents that we do not control, often called *non-player characters* (NPCs). For example, in chapter 8 we trained an agent to play Super Mario Bros., which has many NPCs. These NPCs are controlled by some other unseen game logic, but they can and often do interact with the main player. From the perspective of our deep Q-network (DQN) agent, these NPCs are nothing more than patterns in the state of the environment that change over time. Our DQN is not directly aware of the actions of the other players. This is not an issue because these NPCs do not learn; they have fixed policies. As you'll see in this chapter, sometimes we want to go beyond mere NPCs and actually model the behavior of many interacting agents that learn (figure 9.1), and this requires a bit of a reformulation of the basic reinforcement learning framework you've learned about so far in this book.

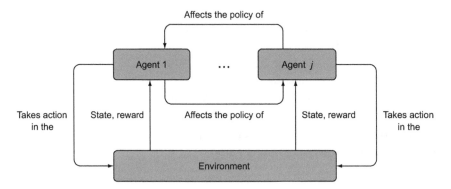

Figure 9.1   In the multi-agent setting, each agent's actions not only affect the evolution of the environment, but also the policies of other agents, leading to highly dynamic agent interactions. The environment will produce a state and reward, which each agent 1 through *j* use to take actions using their own policies. However, each agent's policy will affect all the other agents' policies.

For example, imagine that we directly want to control the actions of many interacting agents in some environment using a deep reinforcement learning algorithm. For example, there are games with multiple players grouped into teams, and we may want to develop an algorithm that can play a bunch of players on a team against another team. Or we may want to control the actions of hundreds of simulated cars to model traffic patterns. Or maybe we're economists and we want to model the behavior of thousands of agents in a model of an economy. This is a different situation than having

NPCs because, unlike NPCs, these other agents all learn, and their learning is affected by each other.

The most straightforward way to extend what we know already into a multi-agent setting is to instantiate multiple DQNs (or some other similar algorithm) for the various agents, and each agent sees the environment as it is and takes actions. If the agents we are trying to control all use the same policy, which is a reasonable assumption in some cases (e.g., in a multi-player game where each player is identical), then we could even re-use a single DQN (i.e., a single set of parameters) to model multiple agents.

This approach is called *independent Q-learning* (IL-Q), and it works reasonably well, but it misses the fact that interactions between agents affect the decision-making of each. With an IL-Q algorithm, each agent is completely unaware of what other agents are doing and how other agents' actions might affect itself. Each agent only gets a state representation of the environment, which includes the current state of each other agent, but it essentially treats the activity of other agents in the environment as noise since the behavior of other agents is, at most, only partially predictable (figure 9.2).

Independent Q-learning

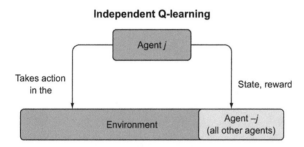

Figure 9.2 In independent Q-learning, an agent does not directly perceive the actions of other agents but rather pretends they are part of the environment. This is an approximation that loses the convergence guarantees that Q-learning has in the single-agent setting, since the other agents make the environment nonstationary.

In the ordinary Q-learning we've done so far, where there's only a single agent in the environment, we know the Q function will converge to the optimal value, so we will converge on an optimal policy (it is mathematically guaranteed to converge in the long run). This is because in the single-agent setting, the environment is *stationary*, meaning the distribution of rewards for a given action in a given state is always the same (figure 9.3). This stationary feature is violated in the multi-agent setting since the rewards an individual agent receives will vary not only based on its own actions but on the actions of other agents. This is because all agents are reinforcement learning agents that learn through experience; their policies are constantly changing in response to changes in the environment. If we use IL-Q in this nonstationary environment, we lose the convergence guarantee, and this can impair the performance of independent Q-learning significantly.

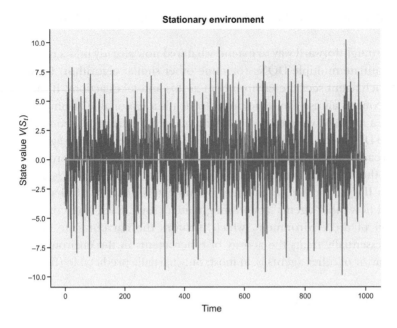

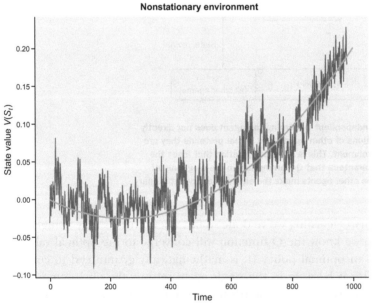

Figure 9.3   In a stationary environment, the expected (i.e., average) value over time for
a given state will remain constant (stationary). Any particular state transition may have a
stochastic component, hence the noisy-looking time series, but the mean of the time series is
constant. In a nonstationary environment, the expected value for a given state transition will
change over time, which is depicted in this time series as a changing mean or baseline over
time. The Q function is trying to learn the expected value for state-actions, and it can only
converge if the state-action values are stationary, but in the multi-agent setting, the expected
state-action values can change over time due to the evolving policies of other agents.

A normal Q function is a function $Q(s,a): S \times A \rightarrow R$ (figure 9.4); it's a function from a state-action pair to a reward (some real number). We can remedy the problems with IL-Q by making a slightly more sophisticated Q function that incorporates knowledge of the actions of other agents, $Q_j(s,a_j,a_{-j}): S \times A_j \times A_{-j} \rightarrow R$. This is a Q function for the agent indexed by j that takes a tuple of the state, agent j's action, and all the other agents' actions (denoted $-j$, pronounced "not j") to the predicted reward for this tuple (again, just a real number). It is known that a Q function of this sort regains the convergence guarantee that it will eventually learn the optimal value and policy functions, and thus this modified Q function is able to perform much better.

Unfortunately, this new Q function is intractable when the number of agents is large because the joint action-space a_{-j} is extremely large and grows exponentially with the number of agents. Remember how we encode an action? We use a vector with length equal to the number of actions. If we want to encode a single action, we make this a *one-hot vector* where all elements are 0 except at the position corresponding to the action, which is set to 1. For example, in the Gridworld environment the agent has four actions (up, down, left, right), so we encode actions as a length 4 vector, where [1,0,0,0] could be encoded as "up" and [0,1,0,0] could be "down" and so forth.

Figure 9.4 The Q function takes a state and produces state-action values (Q values), which are then used by the policy function to produce an action. Alternatively, we can directly train a policy function that operates on a state and returns a probability distribution over actions.

Remember, the policy $\pi(s): S \rightarrow A$ is a function that takes a state and returns an action. If it is a deterministic policy, it will have to return one of these one-hot vectors; if it is a stochastic policy, it returns a probability distribution over the actions, e.g., [0.25,0.25,0.2,0.3]. The exponential growth is due to the fact that if we want to unambiguously encode a joint action—for example, the joint action of two agents with four actions each in Gridworld—then we have to use a $4^2 = 16$ length one-hot vector instead of just a 4 length vector. This is because there are 16 different possible combinations of actions between two agents with 4 actions each: [Agent 1: Action 1, Agent 2: Action 4], [Agent 1: Action 3, Agent 2: Action 3] and so on (see figure 9.5).

If we want to model the joint action of 3 agents, we have to use a $4^3 = 64$ length vector. So, in general for Gridworld, we have to use a 4^N length vector, where N is the number of agents. For any environment, the size of the joint action vector will be $|A|^N$ where $|A|$ refers to the size of the action space (i.e., the number of discrete actions). That is an exponentially growing vector in the number of agents, and this is impractical

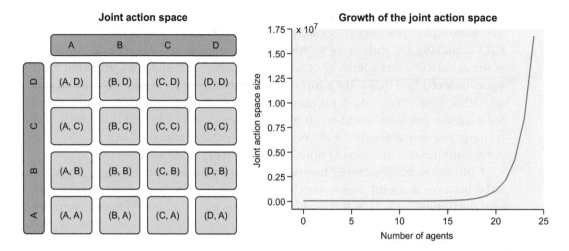

Figure 9.5   If each agent has an action space of size 4 (i.e., it is represented by a 4 element one-hot vector), the joint action space of two agents is $4^2 = 16$, or 4^N where N is the number of agents. This means the growth of the joint action space is exponential in the number of agents. The figure on the right shows the joint action space size for agents with individual action spaces of size 2. Even with just 25 agents, the joint action space becomes a 33,554,432 element one-hot vector, which is computationally impractical to work with.

and intractable for any significant number of agents. Exponential growth is always a bad thing, since it means your algorithm can't scale. This exponentially large joint action space is the main new complication that *multi-agent reinforcement learning* (MARL) brings, and it is the problem we'll spend this chapter solving.

9.2   *Neighborhood Q-learning*

You might be wondering if there is a more efficient and compact way of representing actions and joint actions that might get around this issue of an impractically large joint-action space, but unfortunately there is no unambiguous way to represent an action using a more compact encoding. Try thinking of how you could communicate, unambiguously, which actions a group of agents took using a single number, and you'll realize you can't do it better than with an exponentially growing number.

At this point, MARL doesn't seem practical, but we can change that by making some approximations to this idealized joint-action Q function. One option is to recognize that in most environments, only agents in close proximity to each other will have any significant effect on each other. We don't necessarily need to model the joint actions of *all* the agents in the environment; we can approximate this by only modeling the joint actions of agents within the same *neighborhood*. In a sense, we divide the full joint-action space into a set of overlapping subspaces and only compute Q values for these much smaller subspaces. We might call this method *neighborhood Q-learning* or *subspace Q-learning* (figure 9.6).

Neighborhood MARL

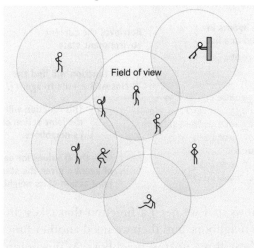

Figure 9.6 In neighborhood MARL, each agent has a field of view (FOV) or neighborhood, and it can only see the actions of the other agents within this neighborhood. However, it may still get the full state information about the environment.

By constraining the size of the neighborhood, we stop the exponential growth of the joint-action space to the fixed size we set for the neighborhood. If we have a multi-agent Gridworld with 4 actions for each agent and 100 agents total, the full joint-action space is 4^100, which is an intractable size; no computer could possibly compute with (or even store) such a large vector. However, if we use subspaces of the joint-action space and set the size of each subspace (neighborhood) to 3 (so the size of each subspace is $4^3 = 64$), this is a much bigger vector than with a single agent, but it's definitely something we can compute with. In this case, if we're computing the Q values for agent 1, we find the 3 agents closest in distance to agent 1 and build a joint-action one-hot vector of length 64 for these 3 agents. That's what we give to the Q function (figure 9.7). So for each of the 100 agents, we would build these subspace joint-action vectors, and use them to compute Q values for each agent. Then we would use those Q values to take actions as usual.

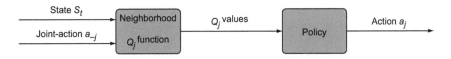

Figure 9.7 The neighborhood Q function for agent *j* accepts the current state and the joint-action vector for the other agents within its neighborhood (or field of view), denoted a_{-j}. It produces Q values that get passed to the policy function that chooses the action to take.

Let's write some pseudocode for how this works.

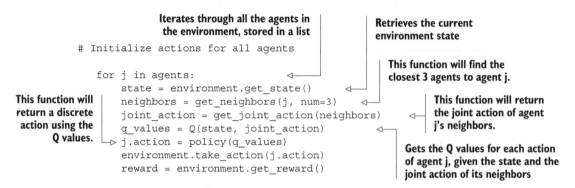

Listing 9.1   Pseudocode for neighborhood Q-learning, part 1

Iterates through all the agents in the environment, stored in a list

Retrieves the current environment state

```
# Initialize actions for all agents

for j in agents:
    state = environment.get_state()
    neighbors = get_neighbors(j, num=3)
    joint_action = get_joint_action(neighbors)
    q_values = Q(state, joint_action)
    j.action = policy(q_values)
    environment.take_action(j.action)
    reward = environment.get_reward()
```

This function will find the closest 3 agents to agent j.

This function will return a discrete action using the Q values.

This function will return the joint action of agent j's neighbors.

Gets the Q values for each action of agent j, given the state and the joint action of its neighbors

The pseudocode in listing 9.1 shows that we need a function that takes the current agent *j* and finds its nearest three neighbors, and then we need another function that will build the joint action using these three nearest neighbors. At this point, we have another problem: how do we build the joint action without already knowing the actions of the other agents? In order to compute the Q values for agent *j* (and thus take an action), we need to know the actions that agents −*j* are taking (we use −*j* to denote the agents that are *not* agent *j*, but in this case only the nearest neighbors). In order to figure out the actions of agents −*j*, however, we would need to compute all of their Q values, and then it seems like we get into an infinite loop and never get anywhere.

To avoid this problem, we start by initializing all the actions for the agents randomly, and then we can compute the joint actions using these random actions. But if that's all we did, using joint actions wouldn't be much help, since they're random. In the pseudocode in listing 9.2 we address the problem by rerunning this process a few times (that's the `for m in range(M)` part, where M is some small number like 5). The first time we run this, the joint action will be random, but then all the agents will have taken an action based on their Q functions, so the second time it will be slightly less random, and if we keep doing this a few more times, the initial randomness will be sufficiently diluted and we can take the actions at the end of this iteration in the real environment.

Listing 9.2   Pseudocode for neighborhood Q-learning, part 2

```
# Initialize actions for all agents

for m in range(M):
    for j in agents:
        state = environment.get_state()
        neighbors = get_neighbors(j, num=3)
        joint_actions = get_joint_action(neighbors)
        q_values = Q(state, joint_actions)
        j.action = policy(q_values)
```

Iterates through the process of computing joint actions and Q values a few times to dilute the initial randomness

```
for j in agents:
    environment.take_action(j.action)
    reward = environment.get_reward()
```
Needs to loop through agents again to take the final actions that were computed in the previous loop

Listings 9.1 and 9.2 show the basic structure of how we will implement neighborhood Q-learning, but one detail we've left out is exactly how to construct the joint-action space for the neighboring agents. We build a joint action from a set of individual actions by using the *outer product* operation from linear algebra. The simplest way to express this is to "promote" an ordinary vector to a matrix. For example, we have a length 4 vector and we could promote it to a 4×1 matrix. In PyTorch and numpy we can do this using the `reshape` method on a tensor, e.g., `torch.Tensor([1,0,0,0]).reshape(1,4)`. The result we get when multiplying two matrices depends on their dimensions and the order in which we multiply them. If we take an A: 1×4 matrix and multiply it by another matrix B: 4×1, then we get a 1×1 result, which is a *scalar* (a single number). This would be the *inner product* of two vectors (promoted to matrices), since the largest dimensions are sandwiched in between the two singlet dimensions. The outer product is just the reverse of this, where the two large dimensions are on the outside and the two singlet dimensions are on the inside, resulting in a $4 \times 1 \otimes 1 \times 4 = 4 \times 4$ matrix.

If we have two agents in Gridworld with individual actions [0,0,0,1] ("right") and [0,0,1,0] ("left"), their joint action can be computed by taking the outer product of these vectors. Here's how we do it in numpy:

```
>>> np.array([[0,0,0,1]]).T @ np.array([[0,1,0,0]])
array([[0, 0, 0, 0],
       [0, 0, 0, 0],
       [0, 0, 0, 0],
       [0, 1, 0, 0]])
```

The result is a 4×4 matrix, with a total of 16 elements as we would expect from our discussion in the previous section. The dimension of the result of the outer product between two matrices is $\dim(A) * \dim(B)$, where A and B are vectors and "dim" refers to the size (dimension) of the vector. The outer product is the reason why the joint-action space grows exponentially. Generally, we need our neural network Q function to operate on inputs that are vectors, so since the outer product gives us a matrix result, we simply flatten it into a vector:

```
>>> z = np.array([[0,0,0,1]]).T @ np.array([[0,1,0,0]])
>>> z.flatten()
array([0, 0, 0, 0, 0, 0, 0, 0, 0, 0, 0, 0, 0, 1, 0, 0])
```

Hopefully, you can appreciate that the neighborhood Q-learning approach is not much more complicated than ordinary Q-learning. We just need to give it an additional input, which is the joint-action vector of each agent's nearest neighbors. Let's figure out the details by tackling a real problem.

9.3   *The 1D Ising model*

In this section we're going to apply MARL to solve a real physics problem that was first described in the early 1920s by physicist Wilhelm Lenz and his student Ernst Ising. But first, a brief physics lesson. Physicists were trying to understand the behavior of magnetic materials such as iron by mathematical models. A piece of iron that you can hold in your hand is a collection of iron atoms that are grouped together by metallic bonding. An atom is composed of a nucleus of protons (positively charged), neutrons (no charge), and an outer "shell" of electrons (negatively charged). Electrons, like other elementary particles, have a property called *spin*, which is quantized such that an electron can only have a spin-up or spin-down at any time (figure 9.8).

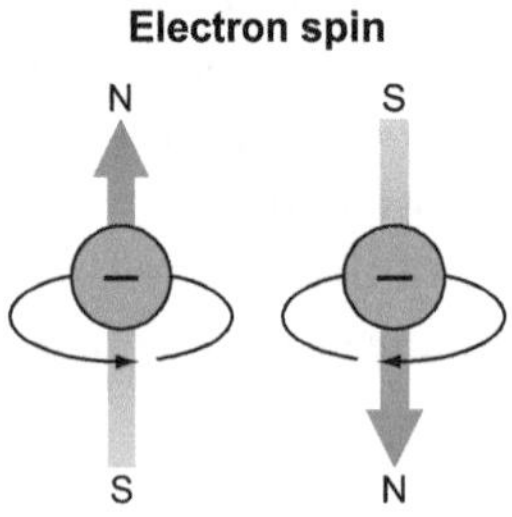

Electron spin

Figure 9.8   Electrons are negatively charged elementary particles that surround the nucleus of every atom. They have a property called *spin*, and it can either be spin-up or spin-down. Since they are charged particles, they generate a magnetic field, and the direction they spin determines the orientation of the poles (north or south) of the magnetic field.

The spin property can be thought of as the electron rotating either clockwise or counter-clockwise; this is not literally true, but it suffices for our purposes. When a charged object rotates, it creates a magnetic field, so if you took a rubber balloon, gave it a static charge by rubbing it on the carpet, and then spun it around, you would have yourself a balloon magnet (albeit an extremely weak magnet). Electrons likewise create a magnetic field by virtue of their spin and electric charge, so electrons really are very tiny magnets, and since all iron atoms have electrons, the entire piece of iron can become a big magnet if all of its electrons are aligned in the same direction (i.e., all spin-up or all spin-down).

There's one added complexity though. Although individual electrons have a tendency to align themselves, a sufficiently large group of aligned electrons actually becomes unstable. This is because as the number of aligned electrons grows larger,

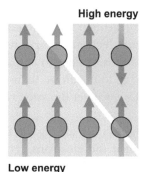

High energy

Low energy

Figure 9.9 When electrons are packed together, they prefer to have their spins aligned in the same direction because it is a lower energy configuration than when their spins are anti-aligned, and all physical systems tend toward lower energy (all else being equal).

the magnetic field grows and creates some internal strain on the material. So what really happens is that electrons will form clusters, called *domains*, in which all the electrons are aligned (either spin up or down), but other domains also form. For example, there might be a domain of 100 electrons aligned spin-up next to another domain of 100 electrons all aligned spin-down. So at the very local level, electrons minimize their energy by being aligned, but when too many are aligned and the magnetic field becomes too strong, the overall energy of the system grows, causing the electrons to align only into relatively small domains.

Presumably the interactions between trillions of electrons in the bulk material result in the complex organization of electrons into domains, but it is very difficult to model that many interactions. So physicists made a simplifying assumption that a given electron is only affected by its nearest neighbors, which is exactly the same assumption we've made with neighborhood Q-learning (figure 9.10).

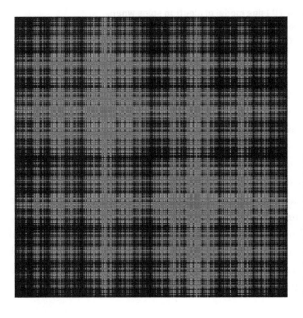

Figure 9.10 This is a high-resolution Ising model where each pixel represents an electron. The lighter pixels are spin-up, and black is spin-down. You can see that the electrons organize into domains where all the electrons within a domain are aligned, but nearby electrons in an adjacent domain are anti-aligned with respect to the first domain. This organization reduces the energy of the system.

Remarkably, we can model the behavior of many electrons and observe the large-scale emergent organization with multi-agent reinforcement learning. All we need to do is interpret the energy of an electron as its "reward." If an electron changes its spin to align with its neighbor, we will give it a positive reward; if it decides to anti-align, we give it a negative reward. When all the electrons are trying to maximize their rewards, this is the same as trying to minimize their energy, and we will get the same result the physicists get when they use energy-based models.

You might wonder why these modeled electrons wouldn't just all align in the same direction rather than form domains like a real magnet if the electrons get positive rewards for being aligned. Our model is not completely realistic, but it does end up forming domains because with a sufficiently large number of electrons, it becomes increasingly improbable for all of them to align in the same direction, given that there is some randomness to the process (figure 9.11).

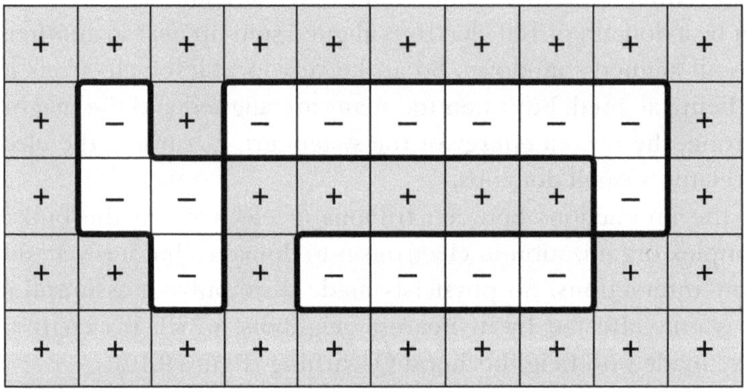

Figure 9.11   This is a depiction of a 2D Ising model of electron spins where + is spin-up and – is spin-down. There is a domain of electrons that are all spin-down (highlighted in black), and these are surrounded by a shell of spin-up electrons.

As you'll see, we can also model the temperature of the system by changing the amount of exploration and exploitation. Remember, exploration involves randomly choosing actions, and a high temperature involves random changes as well. They're quite analogous.

Modeling the behavior of electron spins may seem unimportant, but the same basic modeling technique used for electrons can be used to solve problems in genetics, finance, economics, botany, and sociology, among others. It also happens to be one of the simplest ways to test out MARL, so that's our main motivation here.

The only thing we need to do to create an Ising model is to create a grid of binary digits where 0 represents spin-down and 1 represents spin-up. This grid could be of any dimensions. We could have a one-dimensional grid (a vector), a two-dimensional grid (a matrix), or some high-order tensor.

Over the next few code listings we will first solve the 1D Ising model, since it is so easy that we don't need to use any fancy mechanisms like experience replay or distributed algorithms. We won't even use PyTorch's built-in optimizers—we will write out the gradient descent manually in just a few lines of code. In listing 9.3 we'll define some functions to create the electron grid.

Listing 9.3   1D Ising model: Create the grid and produce rewards

```python
import numpy as np
import torch
from matplotlib import pyplot as plt

def init_grid(size=(10,)):
    grid = torch.randn(*size)
    grid[grid > 0] = 1
    grid[grid <= 0] = 0
    grid = grid.byte()          ◁——— Converts the floating-
    return grid                       point numbers into a byte
                                      object to make it binary

def get_reward(s,a):   ◁——┐  This function takes neighbors
    r = -1                 │  in s and compares them to
    for i in s:            │  agent a; if they match, the
        if i == a:         │  reward is higher.
            r += 0.9
    r *= 2.
    return r
```

We have two functions in listing 9.3; the first creates a randomly initialized 1D grid (a vector) by first creating a grid of numbers drawn from a standard normal distribution. Then we set all the negative numbers to be 0 and all the positive numbers to be 1, and we will get approximately the same number of 1s and 0s in the grid. We can visualize the grid using matplotlib:

```python
>>> size = (20,)
>>> grid = init_grid(size=size)
>>> grid
tensor([1, 0, 0, 0, 0, 1, 0, 0, 1, 0, 0, 1, 0, 0, 0, 1, 0, 1, 0, 0],
       dtype=torch.uint8)

>>> plt.imshow(np.expand_dims(grid,0))
```

As you can see in figure 9.12, the 1s are lightly shaded and the 0s are dark. We have to use the `np.expand_dims(...)` function to make the vector into a matrix by adding a singlet dimension, since `plt.imshow` only works on matrices or 3-tensors.

The second function in listing 9.3 is our reward function. It accepts a list, s, of binary digits, and a single binary digit, a, and then compares how many values in s match a. If all of the values match, the reward is maximal, and if none of them match, the reward is negative. The input s will be the list of neighbors. In this case, we will use the two nearest neighbors, so for a given agent its neighbors will be the agents to its

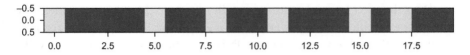

Figure 9.12   This is a 1D Ising model representing the electron spins for electrons arranged in a single row.

left and right on the grid. If an agent is at the end of the grid, its right neighbor will be the first element in the grid, so we wrap around to the beginning. This makes the grid into a circular grid.

Each element in the grid (either 1 or 0) represents an electron being spin-up or spin-down. In reinforcement learning jargon, the electrons are individual *agents* in the environment. Agents need to have value functions and policies, so they cannot merely be a binary number. The binary number on the grid represents the action of the agent, choosing to be either spin-up or spin-down. Hence, we need to model our agents using a neural network. We will use a Q-learning approach rather than the policy gradient method. In listing 9.4 we define a function that will create parameter vectors to be used in a neural network.

Listing 9.4   The 1D Ising model: Generate neural network parameters

```
def gen_params(N,size):
    ret = []                          ◁───┐   This function
    for i in range(N):                     │   generates a list of
        vec = torch.randn(size) / 10.      │   parameter vectors for
        vec.requires_grad = True           │   a neural network.
        ret.append(vec)
    return ret
```

Since we will be using a neural network to model the Q function, we need to generate the parameters for it. In our case, we will use a separate neural network for each agent, although this is unnecessary; each agent has the same policy, so we could re-use the same neural network. We'll do this just to show how it works; for the later examples we will use a shared Q function for agents with identical policies.

Since the 1D Ising model is so simple, we will write the neural network manually by specifying all the matrix multiplications rather than using PyTorch's built-in layers. We need to make a Q function that accepts a state vector and a parameter vector, and in the function body we unpack the parameter vector into multiple matrices that form each layer of the network.

Listing 9.5   The 1D Ising model: Defining the Q function

```
def qfunc(s,theta,layers=[(4,20),(20,2)],afn=torch.tanh):
    l1n = layers[0]
    l1s = np.prod(l1n)        ◁──┤   Takes the first tuple in layers and multiplies those numbers
                                  │   to get the subset of the theta vector to use as the first layer
```

```
theta_1 = theta[0:l1s].reshape(l1n)
l2n = layers[1]
l2s = np.prod(l2n)
theta_2 = theta[l1s:l2s+l1s].reshape(l2n)
bias = torch.ones((1,theta_1.shape[1]))
l1 = s @ theta_1 + bias
l1 = torch.nn.functional.elu(l1)
l2 = afn(l1 @ theta_2)
return l2.flatten()
```

Reshapes the theta vector subset into a matrix for use as the first layer of the neural network

This is the first layer computation. The s input is a joint-action vector of dimensions (4,1).

We can also input an activation function to use for the last layer; the default is tanh since our reward ranges [-1,1].

This is the Q function implemented as simple 2-layer neural network (figure 9.13). It expects a state vector, s, that is the binary vector of neighbors states, and a parameter vector, theta. It also needs the keyword parameter, `layers`, which is a list of the form `[(s1,s2),(s3,s4)...]` that indicates the shape of the parameter matrix for each layer. All Q functions return Q values for each possible action; in this case they are for down or up (two actions). For example, it might return the vector [-1,1], indicating the expected reward for changing the spin to down is –1 and the expected reward for changing the spin to up is +1.

Joint-action Parameters

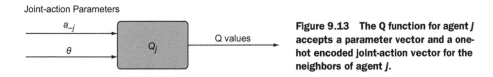

Figure 9.13   The Q function for agent *J* accepts a parameter vector and a one-hot encoded joint-action vector for the neighbors of agent *J*.

The advantage of using a single parameter vector is that it is easy to store all the parameters for multiple neural networks as a list of vectors. We just let the neural network unpack the vector into layer matrices. We use the `tanh` activation function because its output is in the interval [-1,1], and our reward is in the interval [-2,2], so a +2 reward will strongly push the Q value output toward +1. However, we want to be able to re-use this Q function for our later projects, so we provide the activation function as an optional keyword parameter, `afn`. In listing 9.6 we define some helper functions to produce state information from the environment (which is the grid).

Listing 9.6   The 1D Ising model: Get the state of the environment

```
def get_substate(b):
    s = torch.zeros(2)
    if b > 0:
        s[1] = 1
    else:
        s[0] = 1
    return s

def joint_state(s):
    s1_ = get_substate(s[0])
```

Takes a single binary number and turns it into a one-hot encoded action vector like [0,1].

If the input is 0 (down), the action vector is [1,0]; otherwise it is [0,1].

s is a vector with 2 elements where s[0] = left neighbor, s[1] = right neighbor.

Gets the action vectors for each element in s

```
s2_ = get_substate(s[1])
ret = (s1_.reshape(2,1) @ s2_.reshape(1,2)).flatten()      ←——┐
return ret                                                     │
```

**Creates the joint-action space using the
outer-product, then flattens into a vector**

The functions in listing 9.6 are two auxiliary functions we need to prepare the state information for the Q function. The `get_substate` function takes a single binary number (0 for spin-down and 1 for spin-up) and turns it into a one-hot encoded action vector, where 0 becomes [1,0] and 1 becomes [0,1] for an action space of [down, up]. The grid only contains a series of binary digits representing the spin of each agent, but we need to turn those binary digits into action vectors and then take the outer product to get a joint-action vector for the Q function. In listing 9.7 we put some of the pieces we've made together to create a new grid and a set of parameter vectors that, in effect, comprises the set of agents on the grid.

Listing 9.7   The 1D Ising model: Initialize the grid

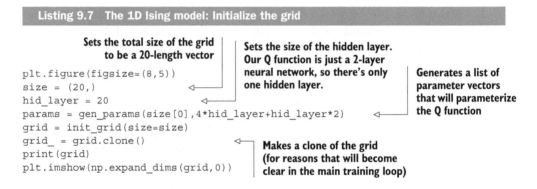

**Sets the total size of the grid
to be a 20-length vector**

**Sets the size of the hidden layer.
Our Q function is just a 2-layer
neural network, so there's only
one hidden layer.**

**Generates a list of
parameter vectors
that will parameterize
the Q function**

```
plt.figure(figsize=(8,5))
size = (20,)                                        ←——┘
hid_layer = 20                                      ←——
params = gen_params(size[0],4*hid_layer+hid_layer*2)   ←——
grid = init_grid(size=size)
grid_ = grid.clone()                         ←——┐
print(grid)                                       │
plt.imshow(np.expand_dims(grid,0))               │
```

**Makes a clone of the grid
(for reasons that will become
clear in the main training loop)**

If you run the listing 9.7 code, you should get something like figure 9.14, but yours will look different since it is randomly initialized.

```
tensor([0, 0, 1, 0, 0, 1, 1, 0, 1, 0, 0, 1, 0, 0, 1, 0, 1, 0, 1, 0],
       dtype=torch.uint8)
```

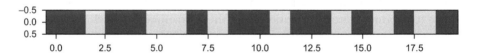

Figure 9.14   A 1D Ising model of electrons arranged in a single row.

You will notice that the spins are pretty randomly distributed between up (1) and down (0). When we train our Q function, we expect to get the spins to align themselves in the same direction. They may not *all* align in the same direction, but they should at least cluster into domains that are all aligned. Let's get into the main training loop now that we have all of the necessary functions defined.

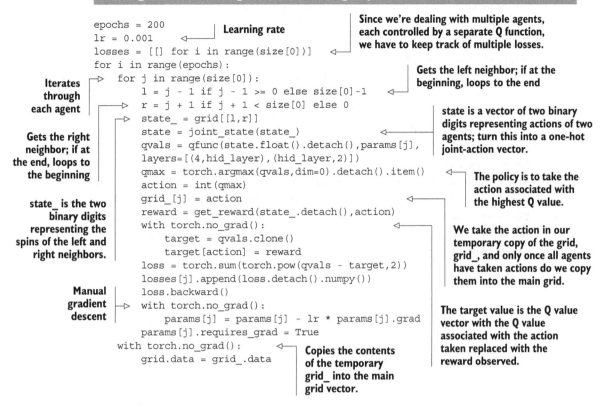

Listing 9.8 The 1D Ising model: The training loop

```
epochs = 200
lr = 0.001                  ◄─── Learning rate
losses = [[] for i in range(size[0])]
for i in range(epochs):
    for j in range(size[0]):
        l = j - 1 if j - 1 >= 0 else size[0]-1
        r = j + 1 if j + 1 < size[0] else 0
        state_ = grid[[l,r]]
        state = joint_state(state_)
        qvals = qfunc(state.float().detach(),params[j],
        layers=[(4,hid_layer),(hid_layer,2)])
        qmax = torch.argmax(qvals,dim=0).detach().item()
        action = int(qmax)
        grid_[j] = action
        reward = get_reward(state_.detach(),action)
        with torch.no_grad():
            target = qvals.clone()
            target[action] = reward
        loss = torch.sum(torch.pow(qvals - target,2))
        losses[j].append(loss.detach().numpy())
        loss.backward()
        with torch.no_grad():
            params[j] = params[j] - lr * params[j].grad
        params[j].requires_grad = True
    with torch.no_grad():
        grid.data = grid_.data
```

Since we're dealing with multiple agents, each controlled by a separate Q function, we have to keep track of multiple losses.

Learning rate

Iterates through each agent

Gets the left neighbor; if at the beginning, loops to the end

Gets the right neighbor; if at the end, loops to the beginning

state_ is the two binary digits representing the spins of the left and right neighbors.

state is a vector of two binary digits representing actions of two agents; turn this into a one-hot joint-action vector.

The policy is to take the action associated with the highest Q value.

We take the action in our temporary copy of the grid, grid_, and only once all agents have taken actions do we copy them into the main grid.

Manual gradient descent

The target value is the Q value vector with the Q value associated with the action taken replaced with the reward observed.

Copies the contents of the temporary grid_ into the main grid vector.

In the main training loop, we iterate through all 20 agents (which are representing electrons), and for each one we find its left and right neighbors, get their joint-action vector, and use that to compute Q values for the two possible actions of spin-down and spin-up. The 1D Ising model, as we've set it up, isn't just a line of grid cells but rather a circular chain of grid cells such that all agents have a left and right neighbor (figure 9.15).

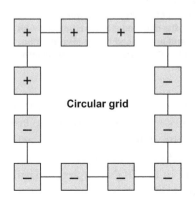

Circular grid

Figure 9.15 We are representing the 1D Ising model with a single binary vector, but it is actually a circular grid because we treat the leftmost electron as being immediately next to the rightmost electron.

Each agent has its own associated parameter vector that we use to parameterize the Q function, so each agent is controlled by a separate deep Q-network (although it is only a 2-layer neural network, so not really "deep"). Again, since each agent has the same optimal policy, which is to align the same way as its neighbors, we could have used a single DQN to control them all. We will use this approach in our subsequent projects, but we thought it was useful to show how straightforward it is to model each agent separately. In other environments, where agents may have differing optimal policies, you would need to use separate DQNs for each one.

We've simplified this main training function a bit to avoid distractions (figure 9.16). First, notice that the policy we use is a greedy policy. The agent takes the action that has the highest Q value every time; there's no epsilon-greedy policy where we sometimes take a random action. In general, some sort of exploration strategy is necessary, but this is such a simple problem that it still works. In the next section, we will solve a 2D Ising model on a square grid, and in that case we will use a softmax policy where the temperature parameter will model the actual physical temperature of the system of electrons we are trying to model.

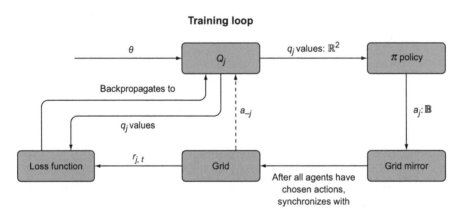

Figure 9.16 This is a string diagram for the main training loop. For each agent, j, the corresponding Q function accepts a parameter vector and the joint-action vector for agent j, denoted a_{-j}. The Q function outputs a 2-element Q value vector that is input to the policy function, and it chooses an action (a binary digit) that then gets stored in a mirror (clone) of the grid environment. After all agents have chosen actions, the mirrored grid synchronizes with the main grid. The rewards are generated for each agent and are passed to the loss function, which computes a loss and backpropagates the loss into the Q function, and ultimately into the parameter vector for updating.

The other simplification we made is that the target Q value is set to be r_{t+1} (the reward after taking the action). Normally it would be $r_{t+1} + \gamma * V(S_{t+1})$, where the last term is the discount factor gamma times the value of the state after taking the action. The $V(S_{t+1})$ is calculated by just taking the maximum Q value of the subsequent state S_{t+1}. This is the bootstrapping term we learned about in the DQN chapter. We will include this term in the 2D Ising model later in this chapter.

If you run the training loop and plot the grid again, you should see something like this:

```
>>> fig,ax = plt.subplots(2,1)
>>> for i in range(size[0]):
        ax[0].scatter(np.arange(len(losses[i])),losses[i])
>>> print(grid,grid.sum())
>>> ax[1].imshow(np.expand_dims(grid,0))
```

The first plot in figure 9.17 is a scatter plot of the losses over each epoch for each agent (each color is a different agent). You can see that the losses all fall and plateau around 30 epochs. The bottom plot is our Ising model grid, of course, and you can see that it has organized into two domains that are all completely aligned with each other. The lighter part in the middle is a group of agents that are aligned in the up (1) direction, and the rest are aligned in the down (0) direction. This is much better than the random distribution we started off with, so our MARL algorithm definitely worked in solving this 1D Ising model.

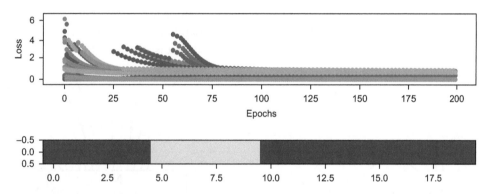

Figure 9.17 **Top: The losses for each agent over the training epochs. You can see that they all decrease and at a minimum at around 30 epochs or so. Bottom: The 1D Ising model after maximizing rewards (minimizing energy). You can see that all the electrons are clustered together into domains where they are all oriented the same way.**

We have successfully "solved" the 1D Ising model. Let's add a bit more complexity by moving on to a 2D Ising model. In addition to addressing some of the simplifications we've made, we'll introduce a new approach to neighborhood Q-learning called *mean field Q-learning*.

9.4 Mean field Q-learning and the 2D Ising model

You just saw how a neighborhood Q-learning approach is able to solve the 1D Ising model fairly rapidly. This is because, rather than using the full joint-action space that would have been a $2^{20} = 1{,}048{,}576$ element joint-action vector, which is intractable, we just used each agent's left and right neighbors. That reduced the size down to a $2^2 = 4$ element joint-action vector, which is very manageable.

In a 2D grid, if we want to do the same thing and just get the joint-action space of an agent's immediate neighbors, there are 8 neighbors, so the joint-action space is a $2^8 = 256$ element vector. Computing with a 256 element vector is definitely doable, but doing it for say 400 agents in a 20×20 grid will start to get costly. If we wanted to use a 3D Ising model, the number of immediate neighbors would be 26 and the joint-action space is $2^{26} = 67,108,864$; now we're into intractable territory again.

As you can see, the neighborhood approach is much better than using the full joint-action space, but with more complex environments, even the joint-action space of immediate neighbors is too large when the number of neighbors is large. We need to make an even bigger simplifying approximation. Remember, the reason why the neighborhood approach works in the Ising model is because an electron's spin is most affected by the magnetic field of its nearest neighbors. The magnetic field strength decreases proportionally to the square of the distance from the field source, so it is reasonable to ignore distant electrons.

We can make another approximation by noting that when two magnets are brought together, the resulting field is a kind of sum of these two magnets (figure 9.18). We can replace the knowledge of there being two separate magnets with an approximation of there being one magnet with a magnetic field that is the sum of the two components.

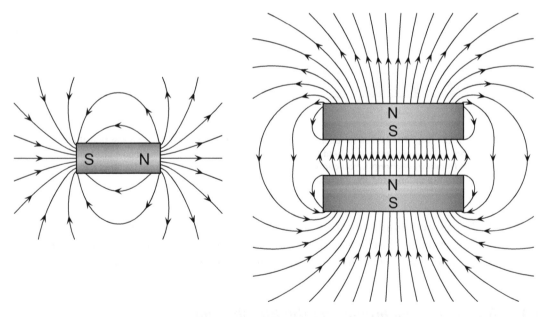

Figure 9.18 Left: A single bar magnet and its magnetic field lines. Recall that a magnet has two magnetic poles, often called North (N) and South (S). Right: Put two bar magnets close together, and their combined magnetic field is a bit more complicated. When we're modeling how the electron spins behave in a 2D or 3D grid, we care about the overall magnetic field generated by the contributations of all the electrons in a neighborhood; we don't need to know what the magnetic field is for each individual electron.

It is not the individual magnetic fields of the nearest electrons that matter so much as their sum, so rather than giving our Q function the spin information about each neighboring electron, we can instead give it the sum of their spins. For example, in the 1D grid, if the left neighbor has an action vector of [1,0] (down) and the right neighbor has an action vector of [0,1] (up), the sum would be [1,0] + [0,1] = [1,1].

Machine learning algorithms perform better when data is normalized within a fixed range like [0,1], partly due to the fact that the activation functions only output data within a limited output range (the *codomain*), and they can be "saturated" by inputs that are too large or too small. For example, the tanh function has a codomain (the range of values that it can possibly output) in the interval [−1,+1], so if you give it two really large but non-equal numbers, it will output numbers very close to 1. Since computers have limited precision, the output values both might end up rounding to 1 despite being based on different inputs. If we had normalized these inputs to be within [−1,1], for example, tanh might return 0.5 for one input and 0.6 for the other, a meaningful difference.

So rather than just giving the sum of the individual action vectors to our Q function, we will give it the sum divided by the total value of all the elements, which will normalize the elements in the resulting vector to be between [0,1]. For example, we will compute [1,0] + [0,1] = [1,1]/2 = [0.5,0.5]. This normalized vector will sum to 1, and each element will be between [0,1], so what does that remind you of? A probability distribution. We will, in essence, compute a probability distribution over the actions of the nearest neighbors, and give that vector to our Q function.

Computing the mean field action vector
In general, we compute the mean field action vector with this formula,

$$a_{-j} = \frac{1}{N} \sum_{i=0}^{N} a_i$$

where a_{-j} is just a notation for the mean field of the neighboring agents around agent j, and a_i refers to the action vector for agent i, which is one of agent j's neighbors. So we sum all the action vectors in the neighborhood of size N for agent j, and then we divide by the size of the neighborhood to normalize the results. If the math doesn't suit you, you will see how this works in Python soon.

This approach is called a *mean field approximation*, or in our case, *mean field Q-learning* (MF-Q). The idea is that we compute a kind of average magnetic field around each electron rather than supplying the individual magnetic fields of each neighbor (figure 9.19). The great thing about this approach is that the mean field vector is only as long as an individual action vector, no matter how big our neighborhood size is or how many total agents we have.

This means that our mean field vector for each agent will only be a 2-element vector for the 1D Ising model and also for the 2D and higher dimensional Ising models.

Mean field approximation

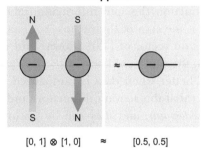

$[0, 1] \otimes [1, 0] \quad \approx \quad [0.5, 0.5]$

Figure 9.19 The joint action for a pair of electron spins is the outer product between their individual action vectors, which is a 4-element one-hot vector. Rather than using this exact joint action, we can approximate it by taking the average of these two action vectors, resulting in what's called the *mean field approximation*. For two electrons together, with one spin-up and the other spin-down, the mean field approximation results in reducing this two electron system to a single "virtual" electron with an indeterminate spin of [0.5,0.5].

Our environment can be arbitrarily complex and high-dimensional, and it will still be computationally easy.

Let's see how mean field Q-learning (MF-Q) works on the 2D Ising model. The 2D Ising model is exactly the same as the 1D version, except now it's a 2D grid (i.e., a matrix). The agent in the top-left corner will have its left neighbor be the agent in the top-right corner, and its neighbor above will be the agent in the bottom-left corner, so the grid is actually wrapped around the surface of a sphere (figure 9.20).

Figure 9.20 We represent the 2D Ising model as a 2D square grid (i.e., a matrix), but we design it so that there are no boundaries, and the agents that appear to be on a boundary are actually immediately adjacent to the agents on the opposite side of the grid. Thus the 2D grid is really a 2D grid wrapped around the surface of a sphere.

Listing 9.9   Mean field Q-learning: The policy function

We will use the deque data structure as an experience replay storage list, since it can be set to have a maximum size.

We will use the shuffle function to shuffle the experience replay buffer.

```
from collections import deque
from random import shuffle

def softmax_policy(qvals,temp=0.9):
    soft = torch.exp(qvals/temp) / torch.sum(torch.exp(qvals/temp))
    action = torch.multinomial(soft,1)
    return action
```

This policy function takes in a Q value vector and returns an action, either 0 (down) or 1 (up).

This is the softmax function definition.

The softmax function converts the Q values into a probability distribution over the actions. We use the multinomial function to randomly select an action weighted by the probabilities.

The first new function we're going to use for the 2D Ising model is the softmax function. You saw this before in chapter 2 when we introduced the idea of a policy function. A policy function is a function, $\pi:S \rightarrow A$, from the space of states to the space of actions. In other words, you give it a state vector and it returns an action to take. In chapter 4 we used a neural network as a policy function and directly trained it to output the best actions. In Q-learning, we have the intermediate step of first computing action values (Q values) for a given state, and then we use those action values to decide which action to take. So in Q-learning, the policy function takes in Q values and returns an action.

DEFINITION The softmax function is defined mathematically as

$$P_t(a) = \frac{\exp(q_t(a)/\tau)}{\sum\limits_{i=1}^{n} \exp(q_t(i)/\tau)},$$

where $P_t(a)$ is the probability distribution over actions, $q_t(a)$ is a Q-value vector, and τ is the temperature parameter.

As a reminder, the softmax function takes in a vector with arbitrary numbers and then "normalizes" this vector to be a probability distribution, so that all the elements are positive and sum to 1, and each element after the transformation is proportional to the element before the transformation (i.e., if an element was the largest in the vector, it will be assigned the largest probability). The softmax function has one additional input, the temperature parameter, denoted with the Greek symbol tau, τ.

If the temperature parameter is large, it will minimize the difference in probabilities between the elements, and if the temperature is small, differences in the input will be magnified. For example, the vector `softmax([10,5,90], temp=100) = [0.2394, 0.2277, 0.5328]` and `softmax([10,5,90], temp=0.1) = [0.0616, 0.0521, 0.8863]`. With a high temperature, even though the last element, 90, is 9 times larger than the second-largest element, 10, the resulting probability distribution assigns it a probability of 0.53, which is only about twice as big as the second-largest probability. When the temperature approaches infinity, the probability distribution will be uniform (i.e., all probabilities are equal). When the temperature approaches 0, the probability distribution will become a *degenerate distribution* where all the probability mass is at a single point. By using this as a policy function, when $\tau \rightarrow \infty$, the actions will be selected completely randomly, and when $\tau \rightarrow 0$, the policy becomes the `argmax` function (which we used in the previous section with the 1D Ising model).

The reason this parameter is called "temperature" is because the softmax function is also used in physics to model physical systems like the spins of a system of electrons, where the temperature changes the behavior of the system. There's a lot of cross-pollination between physics and machine learning. In physics it's called the *Boltzmann distribution*, where it "gives the probability that a system will be in a certain state as a function of that state's energy and the temperature of the system" (Wikipedia). In some reinforcement learning academic papers you might see the softmax policy referred to as the Boltzmann policy, but now you know it's the same thing.

We are using a reinforcement learning algorithm to solve a physics problem, so the temperature parameter of the softmax function actually corresponds to the temperature of the electron system we are modeling. If we set the temperature of the system to be very high, the electrons will spin randomly and their tendency to align to neighbors will be overcome by the high temperature. If we set the temperature too low, the electrons will be stuck and won't be able to change much. In listing 9.10 we introduce a function to find the coordinates of agents and another function to generate the rewards in the new 2D environment.

Listing 9.10   Mean field Q-learning: Coordinate and reward functions

Finds x coordinate

Finds y coordinate

Takes a single index value from the flattened grid and converts it back into [x,y] coordinates

This is the reward function for the 2D grid.

The reward is based on how different the action is from the mean field action.

Scales the reward to be between [–1,+1] using the tanh function

```
def get_coords(grid,j):
    x = int(np.floor(j / grid.shape[0]))
    y = int(j - x * grid.shape[0])
    return x,y

def get_reward_2d(action,action_mean):
    r = (action*(action_mean-action/2)).sum()/action.sum()
    return torch.tanh(5 * r)
```

It is inconvenient to work with [x,y] coordinates to refer to agents in the 2D grid. We generally refer to agents using a single index value based on flattening the 2D grid into a vector, but we need to be able to convert this flat index into [x,y] coordinates, and that is what the get_coords function does. The get_reward_2d function is our new reward function for the 2D grid. It computes the difference between an action vector and a mean field vector. For example, if the mean field vector is [0.25,0.75] and the action vector is [1,0], the reward should be lower than if the action vector were [0,1]:

```
>>> get_reward_2d(torch.Tensor([1,0]),torch.Tensor([0.25, 0.75]))
tensor(-0.8483)

>>> get_reward_2d(torch.Tensor([0,1]),torch.Tensor([0.25, 0.75]))
tensor(0.8483)
```

Now we need to create a function that will find an agent's nearest neighbors and then compute the mean field vector for these neighbors.

Listing 9.11   Mean field Q-learning: Calculate the mean action vector

Converts vectorized index j into grid coordinates [x,y], where [0,0] is top left

```
def mean_action(grid,j):
    x,y = get_coords(grid,j)
```

```
action_mean = torch.zeros(2)        ◁─┐    This will be the action mean
for i in [-1,0,1]:                  ◁─┘    vector that we will add to.
    for k in [-1,0,1]:
        if i == k == 0:                    Two for loops allow us to find each of
            continue                       the 8 nearest neighbors of agent j.
        x_,y_ = x + i, y + k
        x_ = x_ if x_ >= 0 else grid.shape[0] - 1
        y_ = y_ if y_ >= 0 else grid.shape[1] - 1
        x_ = x_ if x_ < grid.shape[0] else 0
        y_ = y_ if y_ < grid.shape[1] else 0
        cur_n = grid[x_,y_]
        s = get_substate(cur_n)     ◁─┤    Converts each neighbor's binary
        action_mean += s                   spin into an action vector
action_mean /= action_mean.sum()    ◁─┐    Normalizes the action vector to
return action_mean                         be a probability distribution
```

This function accepts an agent index, j (a single integer, the index based on the flattened grid) and returns that agent's eight nearest (surrounding) neighbors' mean action on the grid. We find the eight nearest neighbors by getting the agent's coordinates, such as [5,5], and then we just add every combination of [x,y] where $x,y \in \{0,1\}$. So we'll do [5,5] + [1,0] = [6,5] and [5,5] + [-1,1] = [4,6], etc.

These are all the additional functions we need for the 2D case. We'll re-use the init_grid function and gen_params functions from earlier. Let's initialize the grid and parameters.

```
>>> size = (10,10)
>>> J = np.prod(size)
>>> hid_layer = 10
>>> layers = [(2,hid_layer),(hid_layer,2)]
>>> params = gen_params(1,2*hid_layer+hid_layer*2)
>>> grid = init_grid(size=size)
>>> grid_ = grid.clone()
>>> grid__ = grid.clone()
>>> plt.imshow(grid)
>>> print(grid.sum())
```

We're starting with a 10×10 grid to make it run faster, but you should try playing with larger grid sizes. You can see in figure 9.21 that the spins are randomly distributed on the initial grid, so we hope that after we run our MARL algorithm it will look a lot more organized—we hope to see clusters of aligned electrons. We've reduced the hidden layer size to 10, to further reduce the computational cost. Notice that we're only generating a single parameter vector; we're going to be using a single DQN to control all of the 100 agents, since they have the same optimal policy. We're creating two copies of the main grid for reasons that will be clear once we get to the training loop.

For this example, we are going to add some of the complexities we left out of the 1D case, since this is a harder problem. We will be using an experience replay mechanism to store experiences and train on mini-batches of these experiences. This reduces the variance in the gradients and stabilizes the training. We will also use the

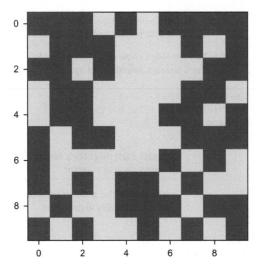

Figure 9.21 This is a randomly initialized 2D Ising model. Each grid square represents an electron. The light-colored grid squares represent electrons oriented with spin-up and the dark squares are spin-down.

proper target Q values, $r_{t+1} + \gamma * V(S_{t+1})$, so we need to calculate Q values twice per iteration: once to decide which action to take, and then again to get $V(S_{t+1})$. In listing 9.12 we jump into the main training loop of the 2D Ising model.

Listing 9.12   Mean field Q-learning: The main training loop

> **num_iter controls how many times we iterate to get rid of the initial randomness from the mean field actions.**

> **Makes a list of lists to store the losses for each agent**

> **replay_size controls the total number of experiences we store in the experience replay list.**

```
epochs = 75
lr = 0.0001
num_iter = 3
losses = [ [] for i in range(size[0])]
replay_size = 50
replay = deque(maxlen=replay_size)
batch_size = 10
gamma = 0.9
losses = [[] for i in range(J)]

for i in range(epochs):
    act_means = torch.zeros((J,2))
    q_next = torch.zeros(J)
    for m in range(num_iter):
        for j in range(J):
            action_mean = mean_action(grid_,j).detach()
            act_means[j] = action_mean.clone()
            qvals = qfunc(action_mean.detach(),params[0],layers=layers)
            action = softmax_policy(qvals.detach(),temp=0.5)
            grid__[get_coords(grid_,j)] = action
            q_next[j] = torch.max(qvals).detach()
        grid_.data = grid__.data
    grid.data = grid_.data
    actions = torch.stack([get_substate(a.item()) for a in grid.flatten()])
    rewards = torch.stack([get_reward_2d(actions[j],act_means[j]) for j in
        range(J)])
```

The discount factor

The experience replay is a deque collection, which is basically a list with a maximum size.

Sets the batch size to 10, so we get a random subset of 10 experiences from the replay and train with that

Stores the mean field actions for all the agents

Stores the Q values for the next state after taking an action

Since mean fields are initialized randomly, we iterate a few times to dilute the initial randomness.

Iterates through all agents in the grid

```
exp = (actions,rewards,act_means,q_next)
replay.append(exp)
shuffle(replay)
if len(replay) > batch_size:
    ids = np.random.randint(low=0,high=len(replay),size=batch_size)
    exps = [replay[idx] for idx in ids]
    for j in range(J):
        jacts = torch.stack([ex[0][j] for ex in exps]).detach()
        jrewards = torch.stack([ex[1][j] for ex in exps]).detach()
        jmeans = torch.stack([ex[2][j] for ex in exps]).detach()
        vs = torch.stack([ex[3][j] for ex in exps]).detach()
        qvals = torch.stack([
                qfunc(jmeans[h].detach(),params[0],layers=layers) \
                            for h in range(batch_size)])
        target = qvals.clone().detach()
        target[:,torch.argmax(jacts,dim=1)] = jrewards + gamma * vs
        loss = torch.sum(torch.pow(qvals - target.detach(),2))
        losses[j].append(loss.item())
        loss.backward()
        with torch.no_grad():
            params[0] = params[0] - lr * params[0].grad
        params[0].requires_grad = True
```

Annotations:
- Collects an experience and adds to the experience replay buffer
- Once the experience replay buffer has more experiences than the batch size parameter, starts training
- Generates a list of random indices to subset the replay buffer

That's a lot of code, but it's only a little more complicated than what we had for the 1D Ising model. The first thing to point out is that since the mean field of each agent depends on its neighbors, and the neighbors' spins are randomly initialized, all the mean fields will be random to begin with too. To help convergence, we first allow each agent to select an action based on these random mean fields, and we store the action in the temporary grid copy, grid__, so that the main grid doesn't change until all agents have made a final decision about which action to take. After each agent has made a tentative action in grid__, we update the second temporary grid copy, grid_ which is what we're using to calculate the mean fields. In the next iteration, the mean fields will change, and we allow the agents to update their tentative actions. We do this a few times (controlled by the num_iter parameter) to allow the actions to stabilize around a near optimal value based on the current version of the Q function. Then we update the main grid and collect all the actions, rewards, mean fields, and q_next values ($V(S_{t+1})$) and add them to the experience replay buffer.

Once the replay buffer has more experiences than the batch size parameter, we can begin training on mini-batches of experiences. We generate a list of random index values and use these to subset some random experiences in the replay buffer. Then we run one step of gradient descent as usual. Let's run the training loop and see what we get.

```
>>> fig,ax = plt.subplots(2,1)
>>> ax[0].plot(np.array(losses).mean(axis=0))
>>> ax[1].imshow(grid)
```

It worked! You can see from figure 9.22 that all but three of the electrons (agents) have their spins aligned in the same direction, which minimizes the energy of the system (and maximizes the reward). The loss plot looks chaotic partly because we're using a single DQN to model each agent, so the DQN is sort of in a battle against itself when one agent is trying to align to its neighbor but its neighbor is trying to align to another agent. Some instability can happen.

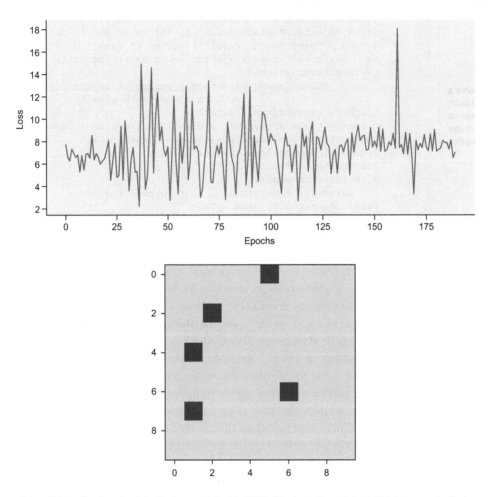

Figure 9.22   The top graph is the loss plot for the DQN. The loss doesn't look like it is converging, but we can see that it does indeed learn to minimize the energy of the system (maximize reward) as a whole in the bottom panel.

In the next section we will push our multi-agent reinforcement learning skills to the next level by tackling a harder problem with two teams of agents battling against each other in a game.

9.5   *Mixed cooperative-competitive games*

If you think of the Ising model as a multiplayer game, it would be considered a pure cooperative multiplayer game, since all the agents have the same objective and their reward is maximized when they work together to all align in the same direction. In contrast, chess would be a pure competitive game, because when one player is winning the other player is losing; it is zero-sum. Team-based games, like basketball or football, are called *mixed cooperative-competitive games,* since the agents on the same team need to cooperate in order to maximize their rewards, but when one team as a whole is winning, the other team must be losing, so at the team-to-team level it is a competitive game.

In this section we are going to use an open source Gridworld-based game that is specially designed for testing multi-agent reinforcement learning algorithms in cooperative, competitive, or mixed cooperative-competitive scenarios (figure 9.23). In our case, we will set up a mixed cooperative-competitive scenario with two teams of Gridworld agents that can move around in the grid and can also attack other agents on the opposing team. Each agent starts with 1 "health point" (HP), and when they're attacked the HP decreases little by little until it gets to 0, at which point the agent dies and is cleared off the grid. Agents get rewards for attacking and killing agents on the opposing team.

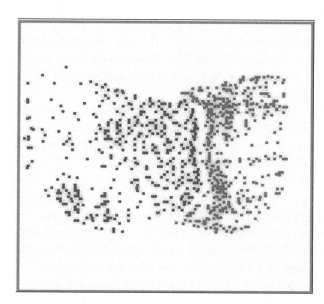

Figure 9.23   Screenshot from the MAgent multiplayer Gridworld game with two opposing teams of Gridworld agents. The objective is for each team to kill the other.

Since all the agents on one team share the same objective and hence the optimal policy, we can use a single DQN to control all the agents on one team, and a different DQN to control the agents on the other team. It's basically a battle between two

DQNs, so this would be a perfect opportunity to try out different kinds of neural networks and see which is better. To keep things simple, though, we'll use the same DQN for each team.

You'll need to install the MAgent library from https://github.com/geek-ai/MAgent by following the instructions on the readme page. From this point on, we'll assume you have it installed and that you can successfully run `import magent` in your Python environment.

Listing 9.13   Creating the MAgent environment

```
import magent                                          ⊲─┐  Imports the cityblock distance function
import math                                                from scipy to compute distances
from scipy.spatial.distance import cityblock  ⊲─┘  between agents on the grid

map_size = 30                                                    Sets up the environment
env = magent.GridWorld("battle", map_size=map_size)  ⊲─┤  in "battle" mode with a
env.set_render_dir("MAgent/build/render")  ⊲─┐         30 x 30 grid

team1, team2 = env.get_handles()  ⊲─┐    Sets up our ability to view
                                              the game after training
      Initializes the two team objects ┘
```

MAgent is highly customizable, but we will be using the built-in configuration called "battle" to set up a two-team battle scenario. MAgent has an API similar to OpenAI Gym but there are some important differences. First, we have to set up "handles" for each of the two teams. These are objects, `team1` and `team2`, that have methods and attributes relevant to each team. We generally pass these handles to a method of the environment object, `env`. For example, to get a list of the coordinates of each agent on team 1, we use `env.get_pos(team1)`.

We're going to use the same technique to solve this environment as we did for the 2D Ising model, but with two DQNs. We'll use a softmax policy and experience replay buffer. Things will get a bit complicated because the number of agents changes over training, since agents can die and be removed from the grid.

With the Ising model, the state of the environment was the joint actions; there was no additional state information. In MAgent we additionally have the positions and health points of agents as state information. The Q function will be $Q_j(s_t, a_{-j})$ where a_{-j} is the mean field for the agents within agent j's *field of view* (FOV) or neighborhood. By default, each agent has a FOV of the 13×13 grid around itself. Thus, each agent will have a state of this binary 13×13 FOV grid that shows a 1 where there are other agents. However, MAgent separates the FOV matrix by teams, so each agent has two 13 $\times$ 13 FOV grids: one for its own team and one for the other team. We will need to combine these into a single state vector by flattening and concatenating them together. MAgent also provides the health points of the agents in the FOV, but for simplicity we will not use these.

We've initialized the environment, but we haven't initialized the agents on the grid. We now have to decide how many agents and where to place them on the grid for each team.

Listing 9.14 Adding the agents

```
hid_layer = 25                                        Generates two parameter
in_size = 359                                         vectors to parameterize
act_space = 21                                                  two DQNs
layers = [(in_size,hid_layer),(hid_layer,act_space)]
params = gen_params(2,in_size*hid_layer+hid_layer*act_space)  ◁──┐
map_size = 30
width = height = map_size          Sets the number of agents
n1 = n2 = 16              ◁────────  for each team to 16
gap = 1             ◁──┐
epochs = 100           │ Sets the initial gap distance
replay_size = 70       │ between each team's agents
batch_size = 25
                                     Loops to position agents
                                     on team 1 on the left side
                                                   of the grid
side1 = int(math.sqrt(n1)) * 2
pos1 = []
for x in range(width//2 - gap - side1, width//2 - gap - side1 + side1, 2):  ◁──┐
    for y in range((height - side1)//2, (height - side1)//2 + side1, 2):
        pos1.append([x, y, 0])

                                                       Loops to position
                                                       agents on team 2
side2 = int(math.sqrt(n2)) * 2                         on the right side
pos2 = []                                              of the grid
for x in range(width//2 + gap, width//2 + gap + side2, 2):  ◁──┘
    for y in range((height - side2)//2, (height - side2)//2 + side2, 2):
        pos2.append([x, y, 0])

                                            Adds the agents to the grid
                                            for team 1 using the position
env.reset()                                 lists we just created
env.add_agents(team1, method="custom", pos=pos1)  ◁──┘
env.add_agents(team2, method="custom", pos=pos2)
```

Here we've set up our basic parameters. We're creating a 30 × 30 grid with 16 agents for each team to keep the computational cost low, but if you have a GPU, feel free to make a bigger grid with more agents. We initialize two parameter vectors, one for each team. Again we're only using a simple two-layer neural network as the DQN. We can now visualize the grid.

```
>>> plt.imshow(env.get_global_minimap(30,30)[:,:,:].sum(axis=2))
```

Team 2 is on the left and team 1 on the right (figure 9.24). All the agents are initialized in a square pattern, and the teams are separated by just one grid square. Each agent's action space is a 21-length vector, depicted in figure 9.25. In listing 9.15 we introduce a function to find the neighboring agents of a particular agent.

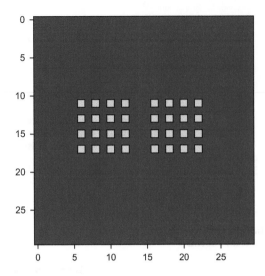

Figure 9.24 The starting positions for the two teams of agents in the MAgent environment. The light squares are the individual agents.

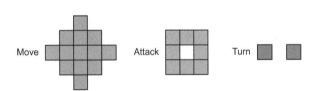

Figure 9.25 This depicts the action space for agents in the MAgent library. Each agent can move in 13 different directions or attack in 8 directions immediately around it. The turn actions are disabled by default, so the action space is 13 + 8 = 21.

Listing 9.15 Finding the neighbors

```
def get_neighbors(j,pos_list,r=6):
    neighbors = []
    pos_j = pos_list[j]
    for i,pos in enumerate(pos_list):
        if i == j:
            continue
        dist = cityblock(pos,pos_j)
        if dist < r:
            neighbors.append(i)
    return neighbors
```

Given [x,y] positions of all agents in pos_list, returns indices of agents that are within the radius of agent j

We need this function to find the neighbors in the FOV of each agent to be able to calculate the mean action vector. We can use env.get_pos(team1) to get a list of coordinates for each agent on team 1, and then we can pass this into the get_neighbors function along with an index, j, to find the neighbors of agent j.

```
>>> get_neighbors(5,env.get_pos(team1))
[0, 1, 2, 4, 6, 7, 8, 9, 10, 13]
```

So agent 5 has 10 other agents on team 1 within its 13×13 FOV.

We now need to create a few other helper functions. The actions that the environment accepts and returns are integers 0 to 20, so we need to be able to convert this to a one-hot action vector and back to integer form. We also need a function that will get the mean field vector for the neighbors around an agent.

> **Listing 9.16 Calculating the mean field action**

```
def get_onehot(a,l=21):          ◁─┐  Converts integer representation
    x = torch.zeros(21)               of action into one-hot vector
    x[a] = 1                          representation
    return x


def get_scalar(v):          ◁─┐  Converts one-hot vector action
    return torch.argmax(v)        into integer representation


def get_mean_field(j,pos_list,act_list,r=7,l=21):      ◁─┐  Gets the mean field
    neighbors = get_neighbors(j,pos_list,r=r)   ◁─┐         action of agent j; pos_list
    mean_field = torch.zeros(l)                            is what is returned by
    for k in neighbors:            Finds all the          env.get_pos(team1), and
        act_ = act_list[k]         neighbors of the       l is action space
        act = get_onehot(act_)     agents using pos_list  dimension
        mean_field += act
    tot = mean_field.sum()                                           Makes sure we
    mean_field = mean_field / tot if tot > 0 else mean_field  ◁─┤   don't divide
    return mean_field                                                by zero
```

The `get_mean_field` function first calls the `get_neighbors` function to get the coordinates of all the agents for agent j. The `get_mean_field` function then uses these coordinates to get the agents' action vectors, add them, and divide by the total number of agents to normalize. The `get_mean_field` function expects the corresponding action vector `act_list` (a list of integer-based actions) where indices in `pos_list` and `act_list` match to the same agent. The parameter r refers to the radius in grid squares around agent j that we want to include as neighbors, and l is the size of the action space, which is 21.

Unlike the Ising model examples, we're going to create separate functions to select actions for each agent and to do training, since this is a more complex environment and we want to modularize a bit more. After each step in the environment, we get an observation tensor for all the agents simultaneously.

The observation returned by `env.get_observation(team1)` is actually a tuple with two tensors. The first tensor is shown in the top portion of figure 9.26. It is a complex high-order tensor, whereas the second tensor in the tuple has some additional information that we will ignore. From now on, when we say *observation* or *state*, we mean the first tensor as depicted in figure 9.26.

Figure 9.26 shows that this observation tensor is arranged in slices. The observation is an $N \times 13 \times 13 \times 7$ tensor where N is the number of agents (in our case 16). Each 13×13 slice of the tensor for a single agent shows the FOV with the location of the wall (slice 0), team 1 agents (slice 1), team 1 agents' HPs (slice 2), and so forth.

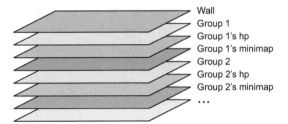

Figure 9.26 **The structure of the observation tensor. It is an *N* x 13 x 13 x 7 tensor where *N* is the number of agents on the team.**

We will only be using slices 1 and 4 for the locations of the agents on team 1 and team 2 within the FOV. So, a single agent's observation tensor will be $13 \times 13 \times 2$, and we will flatten this into a vector to get a 338-length state vector. We'll then concatenate this state vector with the mean field vector, which is length 21, to get a $338 + 21 = 359$ length vector that will be given to the Q function. It would be ideal to use a two-headed neural network like we did in chapter 7. That way one head could process the state vector and the other could process the mean field action vector, and we could then recombine the processed information in a later layer. We did not do that here for simplicity, but is a good exercise for you to try. In listing 9.27 we define a function to choose the action for an agent, given its observation (the mean field of its neighboring agents).

Listing 9.17 Choosing actions

```
def infer_acts(obs,param,layers,pos_list,acts,act_space=21,num_iter=5,temp=0.5):
    N = acts.shape[0]
    mean_fields = torch.zeros(N,act_space)
    acts_ = acts.clone()
    qvals = torch.zeros(N,act_space)

    for i in range(num_iter):
        for j in range(N):
            mean_fields[j] = get_mean_field(j,pos_list,acts_)

        for j in range(N):
            state = torch.cat((obs[j].flatten(),mean_fields[j]))
            qs = qfunc(state.detach(),param,layers=layers)
            qvals[j,:] = qs[:]
            acts_[j] = softmax_policy(qs.detach(),temp=temp)
    return acts_, mean_fields, qvals

def init_mean_field(N,act_space=21):
    mean_fields = torch.abs(torch.rand(N,act_space))
    for i in range(mean_fields.shape[0]):
        mean_fields[i] = mean_fields[i] / mean_fields[i].sum()
    return mean_fields
```

Gets the number of agents

Clones the action vector to avoid changing in place

Alternates a few times to converge on action

Uses the mean field actions and state to compute Q values and select actions using a softmax policy

Loops through the agents and computes their neighborhood mean field action vectors

Randomly initializes the mean field vectors

This is the function we will use to choose all the actions for each agent after we get an observation. It utilizes a mean field Q function parameterized by `param` and `layers` to sample actions for all agents using the softmax policy. The `infer_acts` function takes the following parameters (vector dimensions in parentheses for each):

- `obs` is the observation tensor, $N \times 13 \times 13 \times 2$.
- `mean_fields` is tensor containing all the mean field actions for each agent, $N \times 21$.
- `pos_list` is list of positions for each agent returned by `env.get_pos(...)`.
- `acts` is a vector of integer-represented actions of each agent (N,).
- `num_iter` is the number of times to alternative between action sampling and policy updates.
- `temp` is the softmax policy temperature, to control the exploration rate.

The function returns a tuple:

- `acts_` is a vector of integer actions sampled from policy (N,).
- `mean_fields_` is a tensor of mean field vectors for each agent (N,21).
- `qvals` is a tensor of Q values for each action for each agent (N,21).

Lastly, we need the function that does the training. We will give this function our parameter vector and experience replay buffer and let it do the mini-batch stochastic gradient descent.

Listing 9.18 The training function

Subsets the experience replay buffer to get a mini-batch of data

Generates a random list of indices to subset the experience replay

Collects all states from the mini-batch into single tensor

Collects all actions from the mini-batch into a single tensor

Loops through each experience in the mini-batch

Computes Q values for each experience in the replay

Collects all rewards from the mini-batch into a single tensor

Collects all mean field actions from the mini-batch into a single tensor

Collects all state values from the mini-batch into a single tensor

Computes the target Q values

Stochastic gradient descent

```python
def train(batch_size,replay,param,layers,J=64,gamma=0.5,lr=0.001):
    ids = np.random.randint(low=0,high=len(replay),size=batch_size)
    exps = [replay[idx] for idx in ids]
    losses = []
    jobs = torch.stack([ex[0] for ex in exps]).detach()
    jacts = torch.stack([ex[1] for ex in exps]).detach()
    jrewards = torch.stack([ex[2] for ex in exps]).detach()
    jmeans = torch.stack([ex[3] for ex in exps]).detach()
    vs = torch.stack([ex[4] for ex in exps]).detach()
    qs = []
    for h in range(batch_size):
        state = torch.cat((jobs[h].flatten(),jmeans[h]))
        qs.append(qfunc(state.detach(),param,layers=layers))
    qvals = torch.stack(qs)
    target = qvals.clone().detach()
    target[:,jacts] = jrewards + gamma * torch.max(vs,dim=1)[0]
    loss = torch.sum(torch.pow(qvals - target.detach(),2))
    losses.append(loss.detach().item())
    loss.backward()
    with torch.no_grad():
        param = param - lr * param.grad
    param.requires_grad = True
    return np.array(losses).mean()
```

This function works pretty much the same way we did experience replay with the 2D Ising model in listing 9.12, but the state information is more complicated.

The `train` function trains a single neural network using stored experiences in an experience replay memory buffer. It has the following inputs and outputs:

- Inputs:
  - `batch_size` (int)
  - `replay`, list of tuples (`obs_1_small`, `acts_1`, `rewards1`, `act_means1`, `qnext1`)
  - `param` (vector) neural network parameter vector
  - `layers` (list) contains shape of neural network layers
  - `J` (int) number of agents on this team
  - `gamma` (float in [0,1]) discount factor
  - `lr` (float) learning rate for SGD
- Returns:
  - `loss` (float)

We've now set up the environment, set up the agents for the two teams, and defined several functions to let us train the two DQNs we're using for mean field Q-learning. Now we get into the main loop of game play. Be warned, there is a lot of code in the next few listings, but most of it is just boilerplate and isn't critical for understanding the overall algorithm.

Let's first set up our preliminary data structures, like the replay buffers. We will need separate replay buffers for team 1 and team 2. In fact, we will need almost everything separate for team 1 and team 2.

Listing 9.19   Initializing the actions

```
N1 = env.get_num(team1)            ◁─┐  Stores the number of
N2 = env.get_num(team2)              │  agents on each team
step_ct = 0
acts_1 = torch.randint(low=0,high=act_space,size=(N1,))    ◁─┐ Initializes the actions
acts_2 = torch.randint(low=0,high=act_space,size=(N2,))      │ for all the agents

replay1 = deque(maxlen=replay_size)    ◁─┐ Creates replay buffer using
replay2 = deque(maxlen=replay_size)      │ a deque data structure

qnext1 = torch.zeros(N1)           ◁─┐ Creates tensors to store the Q(s')
qnext2 = torch.zeros(N2)             │ values, where s' is the next state

act_means1 = init_mean_field(N1,act_space)    ◁─┐ Initializes the mean
act_means2 = init_mean_field(N2,act_space)      │ fields for each agent

rewards1 = torch.zeros(N1)         ◁─┐ Creates tensors to store the
rewards2 = torch.zeros(N2)           │ rewards for each agent

losses1 = []
losses2 = []
```

The variables in listing 9.19 allow us to keep track of the actions (integers), mean field action vectors, rewards, and next state Q values for each agent so that we can package these into experiences and add them into the experience replay system. In listing 9.20 we define a function to take actions on behalf of a particular team of agents and another function to store experiences in the replay buffer.

Listing 9.20   Taking a team step and adding to the replay

Gets the list of coordinates for each agent on a team

Gets observation tensor from team 1, which is a 16 x 13 x 13 x 7 tensor

Gets the list of indices for the agents that are still alive

Subsets the observation tensor to only get the positions of the agents

Decides which actions to take using the DQN for each agent

Loops through each agent

```
def team_step(team,param,acts,layers):
    obs = env.get_observation(team)              ◄─┘
    ids = env.get_agent_id(team)                 ◄─
    obs_small = torch.from_numpy(obs[0][:,:,:,[1,4]])   ◄─
    agent_pos = env.get_pos(team)
    acts, act_means, qvals = infer_acts(obs_small,\
                                param,layers,agent_pos,acts)
    return acts, act_means, qvals, obs_small, ids

def add_to_replay(replay,obs_small, acts,rewards,act_means,qnext):    ◄─
    for j in range(rewards.shape[0]):
        exp = (obs_small[j], acts[j],rewards[j],act_means[j],qnext[j])
        replay.append(exp)
    return replay
```

Adds each individual agent's experience separately to the replay buffer

The `team_step` function is the workhouse of the main loop. We use it to collect all the data from the environment and to run the DQN to decide which actions to take. The `add_to_replay` function takes the observation tensor, action tensor, reward tensor, action mean field tensor, and the next state Q value tensor and adds each individual agent experience to the replay buffer separately.

The rest of the code is all within a giant `while` loop, so we will break it into parts, but just remember that it's all part of the same loop. Also remember that all this code is together in Jupyter Notebooks on this book's GitHub page at http://mng.bz/JzKp. It contains all of the code we used to create the visualizations, and more comments. We finally get to the main training loop of the algorithm in listing 9.21.

Listing 9.21   Training loop

Instantiates the chosen actions in the environment

Uses the team_step method to collect environment data and choose actions for the agents using the DQN

While the game is not over

```
for i in range(epochs):
    done = False
    while not done:                    ◄─
        acts_1, act_means1, qvals1, obs_small_1, ids_1 = \
        team_step(team1,params[0],acts_1,layers)    ◄─
        env.set_action(team1, acts_1.detach().numpy().astype(np.int32))
```

```
    acts_2, act_means2, qvals2, obs_small_2, ids_2 = \
    team_step(team2,params[0],acts_2,layers)
            env.set_action(team2, acts_2.detach().numpy().astype(np.int32))
```

Takes a step in the environment, which will generate a new observation and rewards ▷
```
    done = env.step()

    _, _, qnext1, _, ids_1 = team_step(team1,params[0],acts_1,layers)   ◁
    _, _, qnext2, _, ids_2 = team_step(team2,params[0],acts_2,layers)
```
Reruns team_step to get the Q values for the next state in the environment

Renders the environment for viewing later ▷
```
    env.render()

    rewards1 = torch.from_numpy(env.get_reward(team1)).float()   ◁
    rewards2 = torch.from_numpy(env.get_reward(team2)).float()
```
Collects the rewards into a tensor for each agent

The while loop runs as long as the game is not over; the game ends when all the agents on one team die. Within the team_step function, we first get the observation tensor and subset the part we want as we described before, resulting in a $13 \times 13 \times 2$ tensor. We also get ids_1, which are the indices for the agents that are still alive on team 1. We also need to get the coordinate positions of each agent on each team. Then we use our infer_acts function to choose actions for each agent and instantiate them in the environment, and finally take an environment step, which will generate new observations and rewards. Let's continue in the while loop.

Listing 9.22   Adding to the replay (still in `while` loop from listing 9.21)

Adds to experience replay ▷
```
    replay1 = add_to_replay(replay1, obs_small_1,
    acts_1,rewards1,act_means1,qnext1)
    replay2 = add_to_replay(replay2, obs_small_2,
    acts_2,rewards2,act_means2,qnext2)
```
Builds a zipped list of IDs to keep track of which agents died and will be cleared from the grid

Shuffles the replay buffer ▷
```
    shuffle(replay1)
    shuffle(replay2)

    ids_1_ = list(zip(np.arange(ids_1.shape[0]),ids_1))   ◁
    ids_2_ = list(zip(np.arange(ids_2.shape[0]),ids_2))
```

Clears the dead agents off the grid ▷
```
    env.clear_dead()

    ids_1  = env.get_agent_id(team1)   ◁
    ids_2  = env.get_agent_id(team2)
```
Now that the dead agents are cleared, gets the new list of agent IDs

```
    ids_1_ = [i for (i,j) in ids_1_ if j in ids_1]   ◁
    ids_2_ = [i for (i,j) in ids_2_ if j in ids_2]
```
Subsets the old list of IDs based on which agents are still alive

```
    acts_1 = acts_1[ids_1_]   ◁
    acts_2 = acts_2[ids_2_]
```
Subsets the action list based on the agents that are still alive

```
    step_ct += 1
    if step_ct > 250:
        break
```

<table>
<tr><td>

If the replay
buffers are
sufficiently
full, starts
training

</td><td>

```
if len(replay1) > batch_size and len(replay2) > batch_size:
    loss1 = train(batch_size,replay1,params[0],layers=layers,J=N1)
    loss2 = train(batch_size,replay2,params[1],layers=layers,J=N1)
    losses1.append(loss1)
    losses2.append(loss2)
```

</td></tr>
</table>

In this last part of the code, all we do is collect all the data into a tuple and append it to the experience replay buffers for training. The one complexity of MAgent is that the number of agents decreases over time as they die, so we need to do some house-keeping with our arrays to make sure we're keeping the data matched up with the right agents over time.

If you run the training loop for just a handful of epochs, the agents will start demonstrating some skill in battle, since we made the grid very small and only have 16 agents on each team. You can view a video of the recorded game by following the instructions here: http://mng.bz/aRdz. You should see the agents charge at each other and a few get killed before the video ends. Figure 9.27 is a screenshot toward the end of our video showing one of the teams clearly beating the other team by attacking them in a corner.

Figure 9.27 Screenshot of the MAgent battle game after training with mean field Q-learning. The dark team has forced the light team into the corner and it's attacking them.

Summary

- Ordinary Q-learning does not work well in the multi-agent setting because the environment becomes nonstationary as agents learn new policies.
- A nonstationary environment means that the expected value of rewards changes over time.
- In order to handle this nonstationarity, the Q function needs to have access to the joint-action space of other agents, but this joint-action space scales

exponentially with the number of agents, which becomes intractable for most practical problems.

- Neighborhood Q-learning can mitigate the exponential scaling by only computing over the joint-action space of the immediate neighbors of a given agent, but even this can be too large if the number of neighbors is large.

- Mean field Q-learning (MF-Q) scales linearly with the number of agents because we only compute a mean action rather than a full joint-action space.

Interpretable reinforcement learning: Attention and relational models

10

This chapter covers

- Implementing a relational reinforcement algorithm using the popular self-attention model
- Visualizing attention maps to better interpret the reasoning of an RL agent
- Reasoning about model invariance and equivariance
- Incorporating double Q-learning to improve the stability of training

Hopefully by this point you have come to appreciate just how powerful the combination of deep learning and reinforcement learning is for solving tasks previously thought to be the exclusive domain of humans. Deep learning is a class of powerful learning algorithms that can comprehend and reason through complex patterns and data, and reinforcement learning is the framework we use to solve control problems.

Throughout this book we've used games as a laboratory for experimenting with reinforcement learning algorithms as they allow us to assess the ability of these algorithms in a very controlled setting. When we build an RL agent that learns to play a game well, we are generally satisfied our algorithm is working. Of course, reinforcement learning has many more applications outside of playing games; in some of these other domains, the raw performance of the algorithm using some metric (e.g., the accuracy percentage on some task) is not useful without knowing *how* the algorithm is making its decision.

For example, machine learning algorithms employed in healthcare decisions need to be explainable, since patients have a right to know *why* they are being diagnosed with a particular disease or why they are being recommended a particular treatment. Although conventional deep neural networks can be trained to achieve remarkable feats, it is often unclear what process is driving their decision-making.

In this chapter we will introduce a new deep learning architecture that goes some way to unraveling this problem. Moreover, it not only offers interpretability gains but also performance gains in many cases. This new class of models is called *attention models* because they learn how to *attend to* (or focus on) only the salient aspects of an input. More specifically for our case, we will be developing a *self-attention model*, which is a model that allows each feature within an input to learn to attend to various other features in the input. This form of attention is closely related to the class of neural networks termed *graph neural networks*, which are neural networks explicitly designed to operate on graph structured data.

10.1   Machine learning interpretability with attention and relational biases

A *graph* (also called a network) is a data structure that is composed of a set of *nodes* and *edges* (connections) between nodes (figure 10.1). The nodes could represent anything: people in a social network, publications in a publication citation network, cities connected by highways, or even images where each pixel is a node and adjacent pixels are connected by edges. A graph is a very generic structure for representing data with relational structure, which is almost all the data we see in practice. Whereas *convolutional neural networks* are designed to process grid-like data, such as images, and *recurrent neural networks* are well-poised for sequential data, graph neural networks are more generic in that they can handle any data that can be represented as a graph. Graph neural networks have opened up a whole new set of possibilities for machine learning and they are an active area of research (figure 10.2).

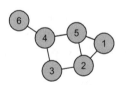

Figure 10.1   A simple graph. Graphs are composed of nodes (the number-labeled circles) and edges (the lines) between nodes that represent relationships between nodes. Some data is naturally represented with this kind of graph structure, and traditional neural network architectures are unable to process this kind of data. Graph neural networks (GNNs), on the other hand, can directly operate on graph-structured data.

Self-attention models (SAMs) can be used to construct graph neural networks, but our goal is not to operate on explicitly graph-structured data; we will instead be working with image data, as usual, but we will use a self-attention model to learn a graph

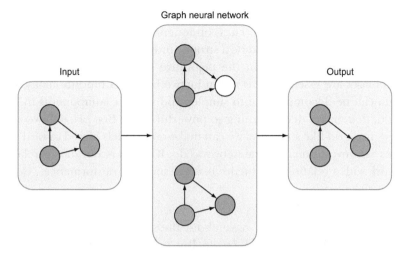

Figure 10.2 A graph neural network can directly operate on a graph, compute over the nodes and edges, and return an updated graph. In this example, the graph neural network decides to remove the edge connecting the bottom two nodes. This is an abstract example, but the nodes could represent real world variables and the arrows represent causal direction, so the algorithm would be learning to infer causal pathways between variables.

representation of the features within the image. In a sense, we hope the SAM will convert a raw image into a graph structure, and that the graph structure it constructs will be somewhat interpretable. If we train a SAM on a bunch of images of people playing basketball, for example, we might hope it learns to associate the people with the ball, and the ball with the basket. That is, we want it to learn that the ball is a node, the basket is a node, and the players are nodes and to learn the appropriate edges between the nodes. Such a representation would give us much more insight into the mechanics of our machine learning model than would a conventional convolutional neural network or the like.

Different neural network architectures such as convolutional, recurrent, or attention have different *inductive biases* that can improve learning when those biases are accurate. *Inductive reasoning* is when you observe some data and infer a more general pattern or rule from it. *Deductive reasoning* is what we do in mathematics when we start with some premises and by following logical rules assumed to be true, we can make a conclusion with certainty.

For example, the syllogism "All planets are round. Earth is a planet. Therefore, the Earth is round" is a form of deductive reasoning. There is no uncertainty about the conclusion if we assume the premises to be true.

Inductive reasoning, on the other hand, can only lead to probabilistic conclusions. Inductive reasoning is what you do when you play a game like chess. You cannot deduce what the other player is going to do; you have to rely on the available evidence and make an inference. Biases are essentially your expectations before you have seen any data. If you always expected your chess opponent, no matter who it was, to make a particular opening move, that would be a strong (inductive) bias.

Biases are often talked about in the pejorative sense, but in machine learning architectural biases are essential. It is the inductive bias of compositionality, i.e., that complex data can be decomposed into simpler and simpler components in a hierarchical fashion, that makes deep learning so powerful in the first place. If we know the data is images in a grid-like structure, we can make our models biased toward learning local features as convolutional neural networks do. If we know our data is relational, a neural network with a relational inductive bias will improve performance.

10.1.1 *Invariance and equivariance*

Biases are the prior knowledge we have about the structure of the data we wish to learn, and they make learning much faster. But there's more to it than just biases. With a convolutional neural network (CNN), the bias is toward learning local features, but CNNs also have the property of translation *invariance*. A function is said to be invariant to a particular transformation of its input when such a transformation does not change the output. For example, the addition function is invariant to the order of its inputs $add(x,y) = add(y,x)$, whereas the subtraction operator does not share this order invariance (this particular invariant property has its own special name: *commutativity*). In general, a function, $f(x)$, is invariant with respect to some transformation, $g(x)$, to its input, x, when $f(g(x)) = f(x)$. CNNs are functions in which a translation (movement up, down, left, or right) of an object in an image will not impact the behavior of the CNN classifier; it is invariant to translation (top panel of figure 10.3).

If we use a CNN to detect the location of an object in an image, it is no longer invariant to translation but rather *equivariant* (bottom panel of figure 10.3). *Equivariance* is when $f(g(x)) = g(f(x))$, for some transformation function g. This equation says that if we take an image with a face in the center, apply a translation so the face is now in the top-left corner, and then run it through a CNN face detector, the result is the same as if we had just run the original centered image through the face detector and then translated the output to the top-left corner. The distinction is subtle, and often invariance and equivariance are used interchangeably since they are related.

Ideally, we want our neural network architectures to be invariant to many kinds of transformations our input data might suffer. In the case of images, we generally want our machine learning model to be invariant to translations, rotations, smooth deformations (e.g., stretching or squeezing), and to noise. CNNs are only invariant or equivariant to translations but are not necessarily robust against rotations or smooth deformations.

In order to get the kind of invariance we want, we need a *relational model*—a model that is capable of identifying objects and relating them to one another. If we have an image of a cup on top of a table, and we train a CNN to identify the cup, it will perform

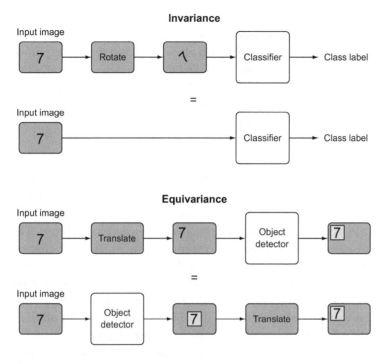

Figure 10.3 Invariance: Rotational invariance is a property of the function such that a rotation transformation of the input does not change the output of the function. Equivariance: Translational equivariance for a function is when applying the translation to the input results in the same output as when you apply the translation after the function has already been performed on the unaltered input.

well. But if we were to rotate the image 90 degrees, it would likely fail because it is not rotation-invariant, and our training data did not include rotated images. However, a (purely) relational model should, in principle, have no problem with this because it can learn to do relational reasoning. It can learn that "cups are on tables," and this relational description does not depend on a particular viewing angle. Hence, machine learning models with relational reasoning abilities can model powerful and generic relations between objects. *Attention models* are one way of achieving this and the topic of this chapter.

10.2 *Relational reasoning with attention*

There are many possible ways of implementing a relational model. We know what we want: a model that can learn how objects in input data are related to one another. We also want the model to learn higher-level features over such objects, just like a CNN does. We also want to maintain the composability of ordinary deep learning models so we can stack together multiple layers (such as CNN layers) to learn more and more abstract features. And perhaps most important of all, we need this to be computationally efficient so we can train this relational model on large amounts of data.

A generic model called *self-attention* meets all of these requirements, although it is less scalable than the other models we've looked at so far. Self-attention, as the name suggests, involves an attention mechanism in which the model can learn to attend to a subset of the input data. But before we get to self-attention, let's first talk about ordinary attention.

10.2.1 *Attention models*

Attention models are loosely inspired by human and animal forms of attention. With human vision, we cannot see or focus on the entire field of view in front of us; our eyes make saccadic (rapid, jerky) movements to scan across the field of view, and we can consciously decide to focus on a particularly salient area within our view. This allows us to focus on processing the relevant aspects of a scene, which is an efficient use of resources. Moreover, when we're engaged in thought and reasoning, we can only attend to a few things at once. We also naturally tend to employ relational reasoning when we say things like "he is older than her" or "the door closed behind me;" we are relating the properties or behavior of certain objects in the world to others. Indeed, words in human language generally only convey meaning when related to other words. In many cases, there is no absolute frame of reference; we can only describe things as they relate to other things that we know.

Absolute (nonrelational) attention models are designed to function like our eyes in that they try to learn how to extract only the relevant parts of the input data for efficiency and interpretability (you can see what the model is learning to attend to when making a decision), whereas the self-attention model we will build here is a way of introducing relational reasoning into the model; the goal is not necessarily to distill the data.

The simplest form of absolute attention for an image classifier would be a model that actively crops the image, selecting subregions from the image and only processing those (figure 10.4). The model would have to learn what to focus on, but this would tell us what parts of the image it is using to make its classification. This is difficult to implement because cropping is nondifferentiable. In order to crop a 28×28 pixel image, we would need our model to produce integer-valued coordinates that form the rectangular subregion to subset, but integer-valued functions are noncontinuous and thus nondifferentiable, meaning we can't apply gradient descent-based training algorithms.

We could train such a model using a genetic algorithm, as you learned in chapter 6, or we could use reinforcement learning. In the reinforcement learning case, the model would produce an integer set of coordinates, crop the image based on those coordinates, process the subregion, and make a classification decision. If it classifies correctly, it would get a positive reward, or it would get a negative reward for an incorrect classification. In this way, we could employ the REINFORCE algorithm you learned earlier to train the model to perform an otherwise nondifferentiable function. This

Figure 10.4   An example of absolute attention where a function might simply look at subregions of an image and only process those one at a time. This can significantly reduce the computational burden, since the dimensionality of each segment is much smaller than the whole image.

procedure is described in the paper "Recurrent Models of Visual Attention" by Volodymyr Mnih et al. (2014). This form of attention is termed *hard* attention because it is nondifferentiable.

There is also *soft* attention, which is a differentiable form of attention that simply applies a filter to minimize or maintain certain pixels in the image by multiplying each pixel in the image by a soft attention value between 0 and 1. The attention model can then learn to set certain pixels to 0 or maintain certain relevant pixels (figure 10.5). Since the attention values are real numbers and not integers, this form of attention is differentiable, but it loses the efficiency of a hard attention model, since it still needs to process the entire image rather than just a portion of it.

In a self-attention model (SAM), the process is quite different and more complicated. Remember, the output of a SAM is essentially a graph, except that each node is constrained to only be connected with a few other nodes (hence the "attention" aspect).

Figure 10.5   An example of soft attention where a model would learn which pixels to keep and which pixels to ignore (i.e., set to 0). Unlike the hard-attention model, the soft-attention model needs to process the entire image at once, which can be computationally demanding.

10.2.2 *Relational reasoning*

Before we get into the details of self-attention, let's first sketch out how a general *relational reasoning module* ought to work. Any machine learning model is typically fed some raw data in the form of a vector or higher-order tensor, or perhaps a sequence of such tensors, as in language models. Let's use an example from language modeling, or *natural language processing* (NLP), because it is a bit easier to grasp than processing raw images. Let's consider the task of translating a simple sentence from English into Chinese.

English	Chinese
I ate food.	我吃饭了.

Each word, w_i, in English is encoded as a fixed-length one-hot vector, $w_i : \mathbb{B}^n$, with dimensionality n. The dimensionality determines the maximal vocabulary size. For example, if $n = 10$, the model can only handle a vocabulary of 10 words in total, so usually it is much larger, such as $n \approx 40000$. Likewise, each word in Chinese is encoded as a fixed-length vector. We want to build a translation model that can translate each word of English into Chinese.

The first approaches to this problem were based on recurrent neural networks, which are inherently sequential models, as they are capable of storing data from each input. A recurrent neural network, at a high level, is a function that maintains an internal state that is updated with each input that it sees (figure 10.6).

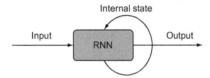

Figure 10.6 A recurrent neural network (RNN) is capable of maintaining an internal state that is updated with each new input it receives. This allows RNNs to model sequential data such as time series or language.

Most RNN language models work by first having an encoder model that consumes a single English word at a time, and once done gives its internal state vector to a different decoder RNN that outputs individual Chinese words one at a time. The problem with RNNs is that they are not easily parallelized because you must maintain an internal state, which depends on the sequence length (figure 10.7). If sequence lengths vary across inputs and outputs, you have to synchronize all the sequences until they're done processing.

While many thought that language models needed recurrence to work well, given the natural sequential nature of language, researchers found that a relatively simple attention model with no recurrence at all could perform even better and is trivially parallelizable, making it easier to train faster and with more data. These are the so-called *transformer models*, which rely on self-attention. We will not get into their details—we'll just sketch out the basic mechanism here.

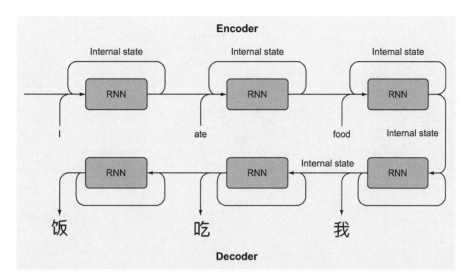

Figure 10.7 **Schematic of an RNN language model. Two separate RNNs are used, an encoder and a decoder. The encoder takes an input sentence word by word and, once complete, sends its internal state to the decoder RNN, which produces each word in the target sentence until it halts.**

The idea is that a Chinese word, c_i, can be translated as a function of the weighted combination of a context of English words, e_i. The context is simply a fixed-length collection of words that are in proximity to a given English word. Given the sentence "My dog Max chased a squirrel up the tree and barked at it," a context of three words for the word "squirrel" would be the subsentence "Max chased a squirrel up the tree" (i.e., we include the three words on either side of the target word).

For the English phrase "I ate food" in figure 10.7, we would use all three words. The first Chinese word would be produced by taking a weighted sum of all the English words in the sentence: $c_i = f(\Sigma a_i \cdot e_i)$, where a_i is the (attention) weight, which is a number between 0 and 1 such that $\Sigma a_i = 1$. The function f would be a neural network, such as a simple feedforward neural network. The function as a whole would need to learn the neural network weights in f as well as the attention weights, a_i. The attention weights would be produced by some other neural network function.

After successful training, we can inspect these attention weights and see which English words are attended to when translating to a given Chinese word. For example, when producing the Chinese word 我, the English word "I" would have a high attention weight associated with it, whereas the other words would be mostly ignored.

This general procedure is called *kernel regression*. To take an even simpler example, let's say we have a data set that looks like figure 10.8, and we want to make a machine learning model that can take an unseen x and predict an appropriate y, given this training data. There are two broad classes of how to do this: *nonparametric* and *parametric* methods.

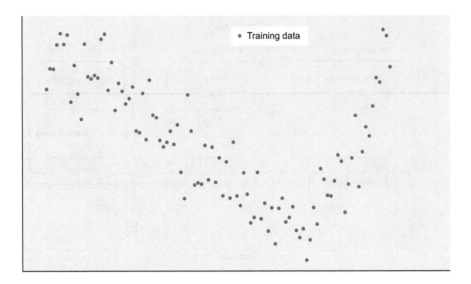

Figure 10.8   Scatter plot of a nonlinear data set on which we might want to train a regression algorithm.

Neural networks are *parametric models* because they have a fixed set of adjustable parameters. A simple polynomial function like $f(x) = ax^3 + bx^2 + c$ is a parametric model because we have three parameters (a,b,c) that we can train to fit this function to some data.

A *nonparametric model* is a model that either has no trainable parameters or has the ability to dynamically adjust the number of parameters it has, based on the training data. Kernel regression is an example of a nonparametric model for prediction; the simplest version of kernel regression is to simply find the nearest x_i points in the training data, X, to some new input, x, and then return the corresponding $y \in Y$ in the training data that is the average (figure 10.9).

In this case, however, we have to choose how many points qualify as being the nearest neighbors to the input x, and it is problematic since all of these nearest neighbors contribute equally to the outcome. Ideally, we could weight (or attend to) all the points in the data set according to how similar they are to the input, and then take the weighted sum of their corresponding y_i to make a prediction. We'd need some function, $f: X \to A$: a function that takes an input $x \in X$ and returns a set of attention weights $a \in A$ that we could use to perform this weighted sum. This procedure is essentially exactly what we'll do in attention models, except that the difficulty lies in deciding how to efficiently compute the attention weights.

In general, a *self-attention model* seeks to take a collection of objects and learn how each of those objects is related to the other objects via attention weights. In graph theory, a graph is a data structure, $G = (N,E)$, i.e., a collection of nodes, N, and edges (connections or relations) between nodes, E. The collection, N, might just be a set of

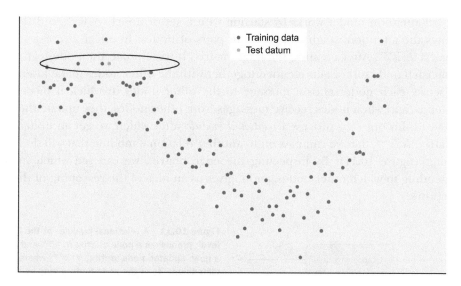

Figure 10.9 One way to perform nonparametric kernel regression to predict the *y* component of a new *x* value is to find the most similar (i.e., the closest) *x*'s in the training data and then take the average of their respective *y* components.

node labels such as {0,1,2,3,...}, or each node might contain data, and thus each node might be represented by some feature vector. In the latter case, we can store our collection of nodes as a matrix $N: \mathbb{R}^{n \times f}$, where f is the feature dimension, such that each row is a feature vector for that node.

The collection of edges, *E*, can be represented by an *adjacency matrix, $E: \mathbb{R}^{n \times n}$*, where each row and column are nodes, such that a particular value in row 2, column 3 represents the strength of the relationship between node 2 and node 3 (right panel of figure 10.10). This is the very basic setup for a graph, but graphs can get more complicated where even the edges have feature vectors associated with them. We will not attempt that here.

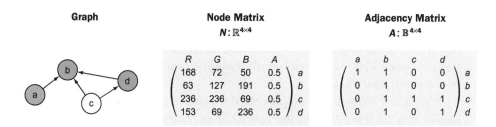

Figure 10.10 The graph structure on the left can be represented quantitatively with a node feature matrix that encodes the individual node features and an adjacency matrix that encodes the edges (i.e., connections or arrows) between nodes. A 1 in the *a* row in the *b* column indicates that node *a* has an edge from *a* to *b*. The node features could be something like an RGBA value if the nodes represented pixels.

A self-attention model works by starting with a set of nodes, $N: \mathbb{R}^{n \times f}$, and then computes the attention weights between all pairs of nodes. In effect, it creates an edge matrix $E: \mathbb{R}^{n \times n}$. After creating the edge matrix, it will update the node features such that each node sort of gets blended together with the other nodes that it attends to. In a sense, each node sends a message to the other nodes to which it most strongly attends, and when nodes receive messages from other nodes, they update themselves. We call this one-step process a *relational module*, after which we get an updated node matrix, $N: \mathbb{R}^{n \times f}$, that we can pass on to another relational module that will do the same thing (figure 10.11). By inspecting the edge matrix, we can see which nodes are attending to which other nodes, and it gives us an idea of the reasoning of the neural network.

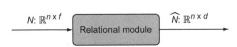

Figure 10.11   A relational module, at the highest level, processes a node matrix, $N: \mathbb{R}^{n \times f}$, and outputs a new, updated node matrix, $\tilde{N}: \mathbb{R}^{n \times d}$, where the dimensionality of the node feature may be different.

In a *self-attention language model*, each word from one language is attending to all the words in context of the other language, but the attention weights (or edges) represent to what degree each word is attending to (i.e., related to) each other word. Hence, a self-attention language model can reveal the meaning of a translated Chinese word with respect to the words in an English sentence. For example, the Chinese word 吃 means "eat," so this Chinese word would have a large attention weight to "eat" but would only weakly be attending to the other words.

Self-attention makes more intuitive sense when used in language models, but in this book we've mostly dealt with machine learning models that operate on visual data, such as pixels from a video frame. Visual data, however, is not naturally structured as a collection of objects or nodes that we can directly pass into a relational module. We need a way of turning a bunch of pixels into a set of objects. One way to do it would be to simply call each individual pixel an object. To make things more computationally efficient, and to be able to process the image into more meaningful objects, we can first pass the raw image through a few convolutional layers that will return a tensor with dimensions (C, H, W) for channels, height, and width. In this way, we can define the objects in the convolved image as vectors across the channel dimension, i.e., each object is a vector of dimension C, and there will be $N = H * W$ number of objects (figure 10.12).

After a raw image has been processed through a few trained CNN layers, we would expect that each position in the feature maps corresponds to particular salient features in the underlying image. For example, we hope the CNNs might learn to detect objects in the image that we can then pass into our relational module to process relations between objects. Each convolutional filter learns a particular feature for each spatial position, so taking all these learned features for a particular (x,y) grid position in an image yields a single vector for that position that encodes all the learned

Convolutional filters

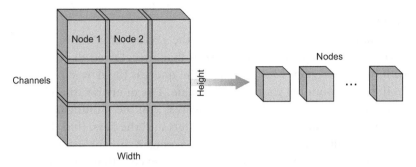

Figure 10.12 **A convolutional layer returns a series of convolutional "filters" stored in a 3-tensor with shape channels (i.e., the number of filters) by height by width. We can turn this into a set of nodes by taking slices along the channel dimension where each node is then a channel-length vector, for a total of height times width number of nodes. We package these into a new matrix of dimension $N \times C$, where N is the number of nodes and C is the channel dimension.**

features. We can do this for all the grid positions to collect a set of putative objects in the image, which we can represent as nodes in a graph, except that we do not know the connectivity between the nodes yet. That is what our relational reasoning module will attempt to do.

10.2.3 Self-attention models

There are many possible ways to build a relational module, but as we've discussed, we will implement one based on a self-attention mechanism. We have described the idea at a high level, but it is time we got into the details of implementation. The model we'll build is based on the one described in the paper "Deep reinforcement learning with relational inductive biases" by Vinicius Zambaldi et al. (2019) from DeepMind.

We already discussed the basic framework of a node matrix $N:\mathbb{R}^{n \times f}$ and an edge matrix $E:\mathbb{R}^{n \times n}$, and we discussed the need to process a raw image into a node matrix. Just like with kernel regression, we need some way of computing the distance (or inversely, the similarity) between two nodes. There is no single option for this, but one common approach is to simply take the *inner product* (also called *dot product*) between the two nodes' feature vectors as their similarity.

The dot product between two equal-length vectors is computed by multiplying corresponding elements in each vector and then summing the result. For example, the inner product between vectors $a = (1,-2,3)$ and $b = (-1,5,-2)$ is denoted $\langle a,b \rangle$ and is calculated as $\langle a,b \rangle = \Sigma a_i b_i$, which in this case is $1 \cdot -1 + -2 \cdot 5 + 3 \cdot -2 = -1 - 10 - 6 = -17$. The sign of each element in a and b are opposite, so the resulting inner product is a negative number indicating strong disagreement between the vectors. In contrast, if $a = (1,-2,3)$, $b = (2,-3,2)$ then $\langle a,b \rangle = 14$, which is a big positive number, since the two vectors are more similar element by element. Hence, the dot product gives us an easy way to compute the similarity between a pair of vectors, such as nodes in our node matrix. This approach leads to what is called (scaled) *dot product attention*; the scaled part will come into play later.

Once we have our initial set of nodes in the node matrix N, we will project this matrix into three new separate node matrices that are referred to as *keys*, *queries*, and *values*. With the kernel regression example, the query is the new x for which we want to predict the corresponding y, which is the value. The query is x, the y is the value. In order to find the value, we must locate the nearest x_i in the training data, which is the key. We measure the similarity between the query and the keys, find the keys that are most similar to the query, and then return the average value for that set of keys.

This is exactly what we will do in self-attention, except that the queries, keys, and values will all come from the same origin. We multiply the original node matrix by three separate projection matrices to produce a query matrix, a key matrix, and a value matrix. The projection matrices will be learned during training just like any other parameters in the model. During training, the projection matrices will learn how to produce queries, keys, and values that will lead to optimal attention weights (figure 10.13).

Let's take a single pair of nodes to make this concrete. Say we have a node (which is a feature vector), $a:\mathbb{R}^{10}$, and another node, $b:\mathbb{R}^{10}$. To calculate the self-attention of these two nodes, we first will project these nodes into a new space by multiplying by some projection matrices, i.e., $a_Q = a^T Q$, $a_K = a^T K$, $a_V = a^T V$, where the superscript T

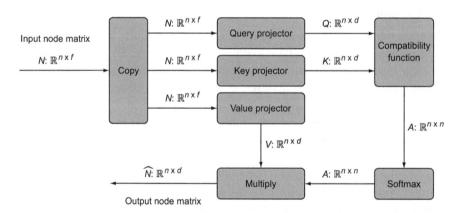

Figure 10.13 A high-level view of a self-attention-based relational module. The input to a relational module is a node matrix $N:\mathbb{R}^{n \times f}$ with n nodes each with an f-dimensional feature vector. The relational module then copies this matrix for a total of three copies, and projects each one into a new matrix via a simple linear layer without an activation function, creating separate query, key, and value matrices. The query and key matrices are input to a compatibility function, which is any function that computes how compatible (similar in some way) each node is to each other node, resulting in a set of unnormalized attention weights, $A:\mathbb{R}^{n \times n}$. This matrix is then normalized via the softmax function across the rows, such that each row's values will sum to 1. The value matrix and normalized attention matrix are then multiplied, $\hat{N} = AV$. The output of the relational module is then usually passed through one or more linear layers (not depicted).

indicates transposition, such that the node vector is now a column vector, e.g., $a^T:\mathbb{R}^{1\times 10}$, and the corresponding matrix is $Q:\mathbb{R}^{10\times d}$, such that $a_Q = a^T Q:\mathbb{R}^d$. We now have three new versions of a that may be of some different dimensionality from the input, e.g., $a_Q, a_K, a_V:\mathbb{R}^{20}$. We do the same for the node b. We can calculate how related a is to itself first by multiplying (via the inner product) its query and key together. Remember, we compute *all* pairwise interactions between nodes, including self-interactions. Unsurprisingly, objects are likely to be related to themselves, although not necessarily, since the corresponding queries and keys (after projection) may be different.

After we multiply the query and key together for object a, we get an unnormalized attention weight, $w_{a,a} = \langle a_Q, a_K \rangle$, which is a single scalar value for the self-attention between a and a (itself). We then do the same for the pairwise interaction between a and b, and b and a, and b and b, so we get a total of four attention weights. These could be arbitrarily small or large numbers, so we normalize all the attention weights using the softmax function, which as you may recall, takes a bunch of numbers (or a vector) and normalizes all the values to be in the interval [0,1] and forces them to sum to 1 so that they form a proper discrete probability distribution. This normalization forces the attention mechanism to only attend to what is absolutely necessary for the task. Without this normalization, the model could easily attend to everything, and it would remain un-interpretable.

Once we have the normalized attention weights, we can collect them into an attention weight matrix. In our simple example with two objects, a and b, this would be a 2×2 matrix. We can then multiply the attention matrix by each value vector, which will increase or decrease the elements in each vector value according to the attention weights. This will give us a set of new and updated node vectors. Each node has been updated based on the strength of its relationships to other nodes.

Rather than multiplying individual vectors together one at a time, we can instead multiply entire node matrices together. Indeed, we can efficiently combine the three steps of key-query multiplication (to form an attention matrix), then attention-matrix with value-matrix multiplication, and finally normalization, into an efficient matrix multiplication,

$$\hat{N} = softmax(QK^T)\, V$$

where $Q:\mathbb{R}^{n\times f}$, $K^T:\mathbb{R}^{f\times n}$, $V:\mathbb{R}^{n\times f}$, where n is the number of nodes, f is the dimension of the node feature vector, Q is the query matrix, K is the key matrix, and V is the value matrix.

You can see that the result of QK^T will be a $n \times n$ dimensional matrix, which is an adjacency matrix as we described earlier, but in this context we call it the attention (weight) matrix. Each row and column represent a node. If the value in row 0 and column 1 is high, we know that node 0 attends strongly to node 1. The normalized attention (i.e., adjacency) weight matrix $A = softmax(QK^T):\mathbb{R}^{n\times n}$ tells us all the pairwise interactions between nodes. We then multiply this by the value matrix, which will update each node's feature vector according to its interactions with other nodes, such that the final result is an updated node matrix, $\hat{N}:\mathbb{R}^{n \times f}$. We can then pass this updated node matrix through a linear layer to do additional learning over the node features and apply a nonlinearity to model more complex features. We call this whole procedure a *relational module* or *relational block*. We can stack these relational modules sequentially to learn higher order and more complex relations.

In most cases, the final output of our neural network model needs to be a small vector, such as for Q values in DQN. After we've processed the input through 1 or more relational modules, we can reduce the matrix down to a vector by either doing a MaxPool operation or an AvgPool operation. For a node matrix $\hat{N}:\mathbb{R}^{n \times f}$, either of these pooling operations applied over the n dimension would result in a f-dimensional vector. MaxPool just takes the maximum value along the n dimension. We can then run this pooled vector through one or more linear layers before returning the final result as our Q values.

10.3 *Implementing self-attention for MNIST*

Before we delve into the difficulties of reinforcement learning, let's try building a simple self-attention network to classify MNIST digits. The famous MNIST data set is 60,000 hand-drawn images of digits, where each image is 28 × 28 pixels in grayscale. The images are labeled according to the digit that is depicted. The goal is to train a machine learning model to accurately classify the digits.

This data set is very easy to learn, even with a simple one-layer neural network (a linear model). A multilayer CNN can achieve in the 99% accuracy range. While easy, it is a great data set to use as a "sanity check," just to make sure your algorithm can learn anything at all.

We will first test out our self-attention model on MNIST, but we ultimately plan to use it as our deep Q-network in game playing, so the only difference between a DQN and an image classifier is that the dimensionality of the inputs and outputs will be different—everything in between can remain the same.

10.3.1 *Transformed MNIST*

Before we build the model itself, we need to prepare the data and create some functions to preprocess the data so that it is in the right form for our model. For one, the raw MNIST images are grayscale pixel arrays with values from 0 to 255, so we need to normalize those values to be between 0 and 1, or the gradients during training will be too variable and training will be unstable. Because MNIST is so easy, we can also strain our model a bit more by adding noise and perturbing the images randomly (e.g., random translations and rotations). This will also allow us to assess translational and rotational invariance. These preprocessing functions are defined in the following listing.

Listing 10.1   Preprocessing functions

```
import numpy as np
from matplotlib import pyplot as plt
import torch
```

```
from torch import nn
import torchvision as TV
```

Downloads and loads the
MNIST training data

```
mnist_data = TV.datasets.MNIST("MNIST/", train=True, transform=None,\
                                target_transform=None, download=True) <──
mnist_test = TV.datasets.MNIST("MNIST/", train=False, transform=None,\
                                target_transform=None, download=True) <──
```

**Downloads and loads the MNIST
testing data for validation**

**Adds
random
spots to
the image**

```
def add_spots(x,m=20,std=5,val=1):
    mask = torch.zeros(x.shape)
    N = int(m + std * np.abs(np.random.randn()))
    ids = np.random.randint(np.prod(x.shape),size=N)
    mask.view(-1)[ids] = val
    return torch.clamp(x + mask,0,1)

def prepare_images(xt,maxtrans=6,rot=5,noise=10):
    out = torch.zeros(xt.shape)
    for i in range(xt.shape[0]):
        img = xt[i].unsqueeze(dim=0)
        img = TV.transforms.functional.to_pil_image(img)
        rand_rot = np.random.randint(-1*rot,rot,1) if rot > 0 else 0
        xtrans,ytrans = np.random.randint(-maxtrans,maxtrans,2)
        img = TV.transforms.functional.affine(img, rand_rot,
    (xtrans,ytrans),1,0)
        img = TV.transforms.functional.to_tensor(img).squeeze()
        if noise > 0:
            img = add_spots(img,m=noise)
        maxval = img.view(-1).max()
        if maxval > 0:
            img = img.float() / maxval
        else:
            img = img.float()
        out[i] = img
    return out
```

**Preprocesses the images
and perform random
transformations of
rotation and translation**

The add_spots function takes an image and adds random noise to it. This function is used by the prepare_images function, which normalizes the image pixels between 0 and 1 and performs random minor transformations such as adding noise, translating (shifting) the image, and rotating the image.

Figure 10.14 shows an example of an original and perturbed MNIST digit. You can see that the image is translated up and to the right and has random dots sprinkled in. This makes the learning task more difficult because our model must learn translational, noise, and rotational invariant features in order to successfully classify. The prepare_images function has parameters that let you tune how much the image will be perturbed, so you can control the difficulty of the problem.

10.3.2 *The relational module*

Now we can dive into the relational neural network itself. Until now, all of the projects in this book were designed to be compelling enough to illustrate an important concept but simple enough to be able to run on a modern laptop without needing a GPU.

Original image

Transformed image

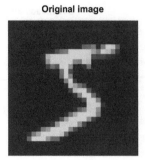 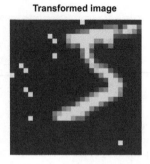

Figure 10.14   Left: Original MNIST digit for the number "5". Right: Transformed version that is translated to the top right and with random noise sprinkled in.

The computational demands of the self-attention module, however, are significantly greater than any of the other models we have built so far in the book. You can still try running this model on your laptop, but it will be significantly faster if you have a CUDA-enabled GPU. If you don't have a GPU, you can easily launch a cloud-based Jupyter Notebook using Amazon SageMaker, Google Cloud, or Google Colab (which is free as of this writing).

> **NOTE**   The code we show in this book will not include the necessary (but very minor) modifications necessary to run on a GPU. Please refer to this book's GitHub page at http://mng.bz/JzKp to see how to enable the code to run on a GPU, or consult the PyTorch documentation at https://pytorch.org/docs/stable/notes/cuda.html.

In listing 10.2 we define a class that is the relational module. It is a single, but complex, neural network that includes an initial set of convolutional layers followed by the key, query, and value matrix multiplications.

Listing 10.2   Relational module

```
class RelationalModule(torch.nn.Module):
    def __init__(self):
        super(RelationalModule, self).__init__()
        self.ch_in = 1
        self.conv1_ch = 16          ◁┐  Defines the number
        self.conv2_ch = 20          │  of channels for each
        self.conv3_ch = 24          │  convolutional layer
        self.conv4_ch = 30
        self.H = 28                 ◁┐  self.H and self.W are the
        self.W = 28                 │  height and width of the
        self.node_size = 36         │  input image, respectively.
        self.lin_hid = 100
        self.out_dim = 10
        self.sp_coord_dim = 2          The number of objects or nodes, which
        self.N = int(16**2)         ◁┤  is just the number of pixels after passing
                                       through the convolutions
        self.conv1 = nn.Conv2d(self.ch_in,self.conv1_ch,kernel_size=(4,4))
        self.conv2 = nn.Conv2d(self.conv1_ch,self.conv2_ch,kernel_size=(4,4))
```

The dimension of the nodes after passing through the relational module

The dimensionality of each node vector is the number of channels in the last convolution plus 2 spatial dimensions.

Layer normalization improves learning stability.

```
self.conv3 = nn.Conv2d(self.conv2_ch,self.conv3_ch,kernel_size=(4,4))
self.conv4 = nn.Conv2d(self.conv3_ch,self.conv4_ch,kernel_size=(4,4))

self.proj_shape = (self.conv4_ch+self.sp_coord_dim,self.node_size)
self.k_proj = nn.Linear(*self.proj_shape)
self.q_proj = nn.Linear(*self.proj_shape)
self.v_proj = nn.Linear(*self.proj_shape)

self.norm_shape = (self.N,self.node_size)
self.k_norm = nn.LayerNorm(self.norm_shape, elementwise_affine=True)
self.q_norm = nn.LayerNorm(self.norm_shape, elementwise_affine=True)
self.v_norm = nn.LayerNorm(self.norm_shape, elementwise_affine=True)

self.linear1 = nn.Linear(self.node_size, self.node_size)
self.norm1 = nn.LayerNorm([self.N,self.node_size],
    elementwise_affine=False)
self.linear2 = nn.Linear(self.node_size, self.out_dim)
```

The basic setup of our model is an initial block of four convolutional layers that we use to preprocess the raw pixel data into higher-level features. Our ideal relational model would be completely invariant to rotations and smooth deformations, and by including these convolutional layers that are only translation-invariant, our whole model is now less robust to rotations and deformations. However, the CNN layers are more computationally efficient than relational modules, so doing some preprocessing with CNNs usually works out well in practice.

After the CNN layers, we have three linear projection layers that project a set of nodes into a higher-dimensional feature space. We also have some LayerNorm layers (discussed in more detail shortly), and a couple of linear layers at the end. Overall, it's not a complicated architecture, but the details are in the forward pass of the model.

Listing 10.3   The forward pass (continued from listing 10.2)

```
def forward(self,x):
        N, Cin, H, W = x.shape
        x = self.conv1(x)
        x = torch.relu(x)
        x = self.conv2(x)
        x = x.squeeze()
        x = torch.relu(x)
        x = self.conv3(x)
        x = torch.relu(x)
        x = self.conv4(x)
        x = torch.relu(x)

        _,_,cH,cW = x.shape
        xcoords = torch.arange(cW).repeat(cH,1).float() / cW
        ycoords = torch.arange(cH).repeat(cW,1).transpose(1,0).float() / cH
        spatial_coords = torch.stack([xcoords,ycoords],dim=0)
        spatial_coords = spatial_coords.unsqueeze(dim=0)
        spatial_coords = spatial_coords.repeat(N,1,1,1)
        x = torch.cat([x,spatial_coords],dim=1)
```

Appends the (x,y) coordinates of each node to its feature vector and normalizes to within the interval [0, 1]

```
x = x.permute(0,2,3,1)
x = x.flatten(1,2)

K = self.k_proj(x)          ◁┐  Projects the input node
K = self.k_norm(K)           │  matrix into key, query,
                             │  and value matrices
Q = self.q_proj(x)
Q = self.q_norm(Q)

V = self.v_proj(x)                        Batch matrix
V = self.v_norm(V)                        multiplies the query
A = torch.einsum('bfe,bge->bfg',Q,K)  ◁──┘ and key matrices
A = A / np.sqrt(self.node_size)
A = torch.nn.functional.softmax(A,dim=2)
with torch.no_grad():
    self.att_map = A.clone()
E = torch.einsum('bfc,bcd->bfd',A,V)  ◁┐  Batch matrix multiplies
E = self.linear1(E)                    │  the attention weight
E = torch.relu(E)                      │  matrix and the value
E = self.norm1(E)                      │  matrix
E = E.max(dim=1)[0]
y = self.linear2(E)
y = torch.nn.functional.log_softmax(y,dim=1)
return y
```

Let's see how this forward pass corresponds to the schematic back in figure 10.13. There are a few novelties used in this code that have not come up elsewhere in this book and that you may be unaware of. One is the use of the LayerNorm layer in PyTorch, which unsurprisingly stands for *layer normalization*.

LayerNorm is one form of neural network normalization; another popular one is called *batch normalization* (or just BatchNorm). The problem with unnormalized neural networks is that the magnitude of the inputs to each layer in the neural network can vary dramatically, and the range of values that the inputs can take can change from batch to batch. This increases the variability of the gradients during training and leads to instability, which can significantly slow training. Normalization seeks to keep all inputs at each major step of computation to within a relatively fixed, narrow range (i.e., with some constant mean and variance). This keeps gradients more stable and can make training much faster.

As we have been discussing, self-attention (and the broader class of relational or graph) models are capable of feats that ordinary feedforward models struggle with due to their inductive bias of data being relational. Unfortunately, because the model involves a softmax in the middle, this can make training unstable and difficult as the softmax restricts outputs to within a very narrow range that can become saturated if the input is too big or small. Thus it is critical to include normalization layers to reduce these problems, and in our experiments LayerNorm improves training performance substantially, as expected.

10.3.3 *Tensor contractions and Einstein notation*

The other novelty in this code is the use of the `torch.einsum` function. Einsum is short for *Einstein summation* (also called *Einstein notation*); it was introduced by Albert Einstein as a new notation for representing certain kinds of operations with tensors. While we could have written the same code without Einsum, it is much simpler with it, and we encourage its use when it offers improved code readability.

To understand it, you must recall that tensors (in the machine learning sense, where they are just multidimensional arrays) may have 0 or more dimensions that are accessed by corresponding indices. Recall that a scalar (single number) is a 0-tensor, a vector is a 1-tensor, a matrix is a 2-tensor, and so on. The number corresponds to how many indices each tensor has. A vector has one index because each element in a vector can be addressed and accessed by a single nonnegative integer index value. A matrix element is accessed by two indices, its row and column positions. This generalizes to arbitrary dimensions.

If you've made it this far, you're familiar with operations like the inner (dot) product between two vectors and matrix multiplication (either multiplying a matrix with a vector or another matrix). The generalization of these operations to arbitrary order tensors (e.g., the "multiplication" of two 3-tensors) is called a *tensor contraction*. Einstein notation makes it easy to represent and compute any arbitrary tensor contraction, and with self-attention, we're attempting to contract two 3-tensors (and later two 4-tensors) so it becomes necessary to use Einsum or we would have to reshape the 3-tensor into a matrix, do normal matrix multiplication, and then reshape it back into a 3-tensor (which is much less readable than just using Einsum).

This is the general formula for a tensor contraction of two matrices:

$$C_{i,k} = \sum_j A_{i,j} B_{j,k}$$

The output on the left, $C_{i,k}$, is the resulting matrix from multiplying matrices $A: i \times j$ and $B: j \times k$ (where i,j,k are the dimensions) such that dimension j for each matrix is the same size (which we know is required to do matrix multiplication). What this tells us is that element $C_{0,0}$, for example, is equal to $\Sigma A_{0,j} B_{j,0}$ for all j. The first element in the output matrix C is computed by taking each element in the first row of A, multiplying it by each element in the first column of B, and then summing these all together. We can figure out each element of C by this process of summing over a particular *shared index* between two tensors. This summation over a shared index is the process of tensor contraction, since we start with, for example, two input tensors with two indices each (for a total of four indices) and the output has two indices because two of the four get contracted away. If we did a tensor contraction over two 3-tensors, the result would be a 4-tensor.

Einstein notation can also easily represent a batch matrix multiplication in which we have two collections of matrices and we want to multiply the first two matrices together, the second two together, etc., until we get a new collection of multiplied matrices.

Tensor contraction: example

Let's tackle a concrete example of a tensor contraction; we'll contract two matrices using Einstein notation.

$$A = \begin{bmatrix} 1 & -2 & 4 \\ -5 & 9 & 3 \end{bmatrix}$$

$$B = \begin{bmatrix} -3 & -3 \\ 5 & 9 \\ 0 & 7 \end{bmatrix}$$

Matrix A is a 2×3 matrix and matrix B is 3×2. We will label the dimensions of these matrices using arbitrary characters. For example, we'll label matrix $A : i \times j$ with dimensions (indices) i and j, and matrix $B : j \times k$ with indices j and k. We could have labeled the indices using any characters, but we want to contract over the shared dimensions of $A_j = B_j = 3$, so we label them with the same characters.

$$C = \begin{bmatrix} x_{0,0} & x_{0,1} \\ x_{1,0} & x_{1,1} \end{bmatrix}$$

This C matrix represents the output. Our goal is to figure out the values of the x values, which are labeled by their indexed positions. Using the previous tensor contraction formula, we can figure out $x_{0,0}$ by finding row 0 of matrix A and column 0 of matrix $B : A_{0,j} = [1,-2,4]$ and $B_{j,0} = [-3,5,0]^T$. Now we loop over the j index, multiplying each element of $A_{0,j}$ with $B_{j,0}$ and then summing them together to get a single number, which will be $x_{0,0}$ In this case, $x_{0,0} = \Sigma A_{0,j} \cdot B_{j,0} = (1 \cdot -3) + (-2 \cdot 5) + (4 \cdot 0) = -3 - 10 = -13$. That was the calculation just for one element in the output matrix, element $C_{0,0}$. We do this same process for all elements in C and we get all the values. Of course, we never do this by hand, but this is what is happening under the hood when we do a tensor contraction, and this process generalizes to tensors of higher order than just matrices.

Most of the time you will see Einstein notation written without the summation symbol, where it is assumed we sum over the shared index. That is, rather than explicitly writing $C_{i,k} = \Sigma A_{i,j} \cdot B_{j,k}$, we often just write $C_{i,k} = A_{i,j} B_{j,k}$ and omit the summation.

This is the Einsum equation for batch matrix multiplication,

$$C_{b,i,k} = \sum_j A_{b,i,j} B_{b,j,k}$$

where the b dimension is the batch dimension and we just contract over the shared j dimension. We will use Einsum notation to do batch matrix multiplication, but we can also use it to contract over multiple indices at once when using higher-order tensors than matrices.

In listing 10.3 we used `A = torch.einsum('bfe,bge->bfg',Q,K)` to compute batched matrix multiplication of the Q and K matrices. Einsum accepts a string that contains the instructions for which indices to contract over, and then the tensors that will be contracted. The string `'bfe,bge->bfg'` associated with tensors Q and K means that Q is a tensor with three dimensions labeled, `bfe`, and K is a tensor with three dimensions labeled, `bge`, and that we want to contract these tensors to get an output tensor with three dimensions labeled, `bfg`. We can only contract over dimensions that are the same size and are labeled the same, so in this case we contract over the e dimension, which is the node feature dimension, leaving us with two copies of the node dimension, which is why the output is of dimension $b \times n \times m$. When using Einsum, we can label the dimensions of each tensor with any alphabetic characters, but we must make sure that the dimension we wish to contract over is labeled with the same character for both tensors.

After the batch matrix multiplication, and we have the unnormalized adjacency matrix, we did `A = A / np.sqrt(self.node_size)` to rescale the matrix to reduce excessively large values and improve training performance; this is why we earlier referred to this is as *scaled* dot product attention.

In order to get the Q, K, and V matrices, as we discussed earlier, we took the output of the last convolutional layer which is a tensor of dimensions batch $\times$ channels $\times$ height $\times$ width, and we collapse the height and width dimensions into a single dimension of (height $\times$ width = n) for the number of nodes, since each pixel position will become a potential node or object in the node matrix. Thus we get an initial node matrix of $N: b \times c \times n$ that we reshape into $N: b \times n \times c$.

By collapsing the spatial dimensions into a single dimension, the spatial arrangement of the nodes is scrambled and the network would struggle to discover that certain nodes (which were originally nearby pixels) are related spatially. That is why we add two extra channel dimensions that encode the (x,y) position of each node before it was collapsed. We normalize the positions to be in the interval [0, 1], since normalization almost always helps with performance.

Adding these absolute spatial coordinates to the end of each node's feature vector helps maintain the spatial information, but it is not ideal since these coordinates are in reference to an external coordinate system, which means we're dampening some of the invariance to spatial transformations that a relational module should have, in theory. A more robust approach is to encode *relative* positions with respect to other nodes, which would maintain spatial invariance. However, this approach is more complicated, and we can still achieve good performance and interpretability with the absolute encoding.

We then pass this initial node matrix through three different linear layers to project it into three different matrices with a potentially different channel dimension (which we will call *node-feature dimension* from this point), as shown in figure 10.15.

Once we multiply the query and key matrices, we get an unnormalized attention weight matrix, $A: b \times n \times n$, where b = batch and n = the number of nodes. We then normalize it by applying softmax across the rows (dimension 1, counting from 0) such that each row sums to 1. This forces each node to only pay attention to a small number of other nodes, or to spread its attention very thinly across many nodes.

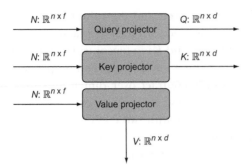

Figure 10.15 **The projection step in self-attention. The input nodes are projected into a (usually) higher-dimensional feature space by simple matrix multiplication.**

Then we multiply the attention matrix by the value matrix to get an updated node matrix, such that each node is now a weighted combination of all the other nodes. So if node 0 pays strong attention to nodes 5 and 9 but ignores the others, once we multiply the attention matrix with the value matrix, node 0 will be updated to be a weighted combination of nodes 5 and 9 (and itself, because nodes generally pay some attention to themselves). This general operation is termed *message passing* because each node sends a message (i.e., its own feature vector) to the nodes to which it is connected.

Once we have our updated node matrix, we can reduce it down to a single vector by either averaging or max-pooling over the node dimension to get a single *d*-dimensional vector that should summarize the graph as a whole. We can pass that through a few ordinary linear layers before getting our final output, which is just a vector of Q values. Thus we are building a relational deep Q-network (Rel-DQN).

10.3.4 *Training the relational module*

You might have noticed the last function call in the code is actually `log_softmax`, which is not something we would use for Q-learning. But before we get to Q-learning, we will test our relational module on classifying MNIST digits and compare it to a conventional nonrelational convolutional neural network. Given that our relational module has the ability to model long-distance relationships in a way that a simple convolutional neural network cannot, we would expect our relational module to perform better in the face of strong transformations. Let's see how it does.

Listing 10.4 MNIST training loop

```
agent = RelationalModule()          ◁─┐  Creates an instance of
epochs = 1000                         │  our relational module
batch_size=300
lr = 1e-3
opt = torch.optim.Adam(params=agent.parameters(),lr=lr)
lossfn = nn.NLLLoss()
for i in range(epochs):
    opt.zero_grad()
    batch_ids = np.random.randint(0,60000,size=batch_size)  ◁─┐ Randomly selects
    xt = mnist_data.train_data[batch_ids].detach()            │ a subset of the
                                                              │ MNIST images
```

Perturbs the images in the batch using the prepare_images function we created, using max rotation of 30 degrees

```
xt = prepare_images(xt,rot=30).unsqueeze(dim=1)
yt = mnist_data.train_labels[batch_ids].detach()
pred = agent(xt)
pred_labels = torch.argmax(pred,dim=1)
acc_ = 100.0 * (pred_labels == yt).sum() / batch_size
correct = torch.zeros(batch_size,10)
rows = torch.arange(batch_size).long()
correct[[rows,yt.detach().long()]] = 1.
loss = lossfn(pred,yt)
loss.backward()
opt.step()
```

The predicted image class is the output vector's argmax.

Calculates prediction accuracy within the batch

This is a pretty straightforward training loop to train our MNIST classifier. We omitted the code necessary to store the losses for later visualization, but the unabridged code can be found in this book's GitHub repository. We told the prepare_images function to randomly rotate the images by up to 30 degrees in either direction, which is a significant amount.

Figure 10.16 shows how the relational module performed after 1,000 epochs (which is not long enough to reach maximum accuracy). The plots look good, but this is just performance on the training data.

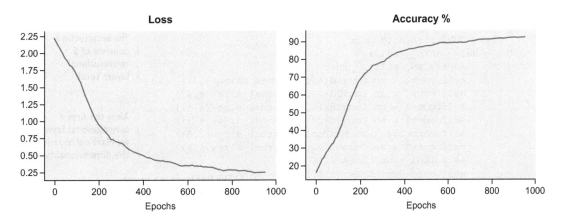

Figure 10.16 The loss and accuracy over training epochs for the relational module on classifying MNIST digits

To really know how well it performs, we need to run the model on the test data, which is a separate set of data that the model has never seen before. We'll run it on 500 examples from the test data to calculate its accuracy.

Listing 10.5 MNIST test accuracy

```
def test_acc(model,batch_size=500):
    acc = 0.
    batch_ids = np.random.randint(0,10000,size=batch_size)
    xt = mnist_test.test_data[batch_ids].detach()
    xt = prepare_images(xt,maxtrans=6,rot=30,noise=10).unsqueeze(dim=1)
```

```
    yt = mnist_test.test_labels[batch_ids].detach()
    preds = model(xt)
    pred_ind = torch.argmax(preds.detach(),dim=1)
    acc = (pred_ind == yt).sum().float() / batch_size
    return acc, xt, yt

acc2, xt2, yt2 = test_acc(agent)
print(acc2)
>>> 0.9460
```

We get nearly 95% accuracy at test time with the relational module after just 1,000 epochs of testing. Again, 1,000 epochs with a batch size of 300 is not enough to reach maximal accuracy. Maximal accuracy with any decent neural network on (unperturbed) MNIST should be around the 98–99% mark. But we're not going for maximum accuracy here; we're just making sure it works and that it performs better than a convolutional neural network with a similar number of parameters.

We used the following simple CNN as a baseline, which has 88,252 trainable parameters compared to the relational module's 85,228. The CNN actually has about 3,000 more parameters than our relational module, so it has a bit of an advantage.

Listing 10.6   Convolutional neural network baseline for MNIST

```
class CNN(torch.nn.Module):
    def __init__(self):
        super(CNN, self).__init__()
        self.conv1 = nn.Conv2d(1,10,kernel_size=(4,4))      ◁──  The architecture
        self.conv2 = nn.Conv2d(10,16,kernel_size=(4,4))           consists of 5
        self.conv3 = nn.Conv2d(16,24,kernel_size=(4,4))           convolutional
        self.conv4 = nn.Conv2d(24,32,kernel_size=(4,4))           layers total.
        self.maxpool1 = nn.MaxPool2d(kernel_size=(2,2))     ◁──  After the first 4
        self.conv5 = nn.Conv2d(32,64,kernel_size=(4,4))           convolutional layers,
        self.lin1 = nn.Linear(256,128)                            we MaxPool to reduce
        self.out = nn.Linear(128,10)                              the dimensionality.
    def forward(self,x):                                ◁──  The last layer is a linear
        x = self.conv1(x)                                     layer after we flatten the
        x = nn.functional.relu(x)                             output from the CNN.
        x = self.conv2(x)
        x = nn.functional.relu(x)
        x = self.maxpool1(x)
        x = self.conv3(x)
        x = nn.functional.relu(x)
        x = self.conv4(x)
        x = nn.functional.relu(x)
        x = self.conv5(x)
        x = nn.functional.relu(x)
        x = x.flatten(start_dim=1)
        x = self.lin1(x)                                ┌──  Lastly, we apply the
        x = nn.functional.relu(x)                       │    log_softmax function
        x = self.out(x)                                 │    to classify the digits
        x = nn.functional.log_softmax(x,dim=1)      ◁──┘    probabilistically.
        return x
```

Instantiate this CNN and swap it in for the relational module in the previous training loop to see how it compares. We get a test accuracy of only 87.80% with this CNN, demonstrating that our relational module is outperforming a CNN architecture, controlling for the number of parameters. Moreover, if you crank up the transformation level (e.g., add more noise, rotate even more), the relational module will maintain a higher accuracy than the CNN. As we noted earlier, our particular implementation of the relational module is not practically invariant to rotations and deformations because, in part, we've added the absolute coordinate positions; it's not all relational, but it has the ability to compute long-distance relations between features in the image, as opposed to a CNN that can just compute local features.

We wanted to introduce relational modules not merely because they might get better accuracy on some data set, but because they are more interpretable than traditional neural network models. We can inspect the learned relationships in the attention weight matrix to see which parts of the input the relational module is using to classify images or predict Q values as shown in figure 10.17.

Original image   **Attention weight matrix**

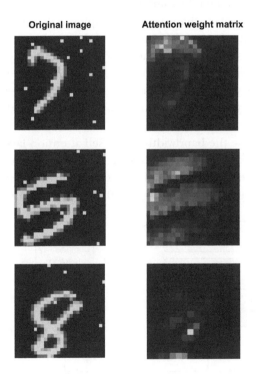

Figure 10.17 Left column: Original input MNIST images (after transformation). Right column: Corresponding self-attention weights showing where the model is paying the most attention.

We visualize this attention map by just reshaping the attention map into a square image:

```
>>> plt.imshow(agent.att_map[0].max(dim=0)[0].view(16,16))
```

The attention weight matrix is a *batch* $\times$ n $\times$ n matrix where n is the number of nodes, which is $16^2 = 256$ in our example, since after the convolutional layers the spatial extent is reduced from the original 28×28. Notice in the top two examples of figure 10.17 that attention maps highlight the contour of the digit but with more intensity at certain parts. If you look through a number of these attention maps, you'll notice that the model tends to pay most attention to the inflection and crossover points of the digit. For the digit 8, it can successfully classify this image as the number 8 just by paying attention to the center of the 8 and the bottom part. You can also notice that in none of the examples is attention given to the added spots of noise in the input; attention is only given to the real digit part of the image, demonstrating that the model is learning to separate the signal from the noise to a large degree.

10.4   *Multi-head attention and relational DQN*

We've demonstrated that our relational model performs well on the simple task of classifying MNIST digits and furthermore that by visualizing the learned attention maps we can get a sense of what data the model is using to make its decisions. If the trained model keeps misclassifying a particular image, we can inspect its attention map and see if perhaps it is getting distracted by some noise.

One problem with the self-attention mechanism we've employed so far is that it severely constrains the amount of data that can be transmitted due to the softmax. If the input had hundreds or thousands of nodes, the model would only be able to put attention weight on a very small subset of those, and it may not be enough. We want to be able to bias the model toward learning relationships, which the softmax helps promote, but we don't want to necessarily limit the amount of data that can pass through the self-attention layer.

In effect, we need a way to increase the bandwidth of the self-attention layer without fundamentally altering its behavior. To address this issue, we'll allow our model to have multiple attention *heads*, meaning that the model learns multiple attention maps that operate independently and are later combined (figure 10.18). One attention head

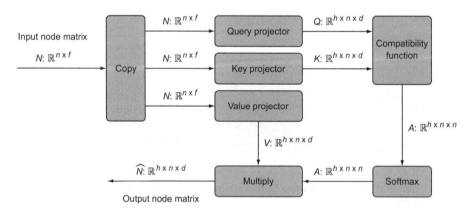

Figure 10.18   Multi-head dot product attention (MHDPA). Rather than use a single attention matrix, we can have multiple attention matrices called *heads* that can independently attend to different aspects of an input. The only difference is adding a new head dimension to the query, key and value tensors.

might focus on a particular region or features of the input, whereas another head would focus elsewhere. This way we can increase the bandwidth through the attention layer but we can still keep the interpretability and relational learning intact. In fact, multi-head attention can improve interpretability because within each attention head, each node can more strongly focus on a smaller subset of other nodes rather than having to spread its attention more thinly. Thus, multi-head attention can give us a better idea of which nodes are strongly related.

With multi-head attention, the utility of Einsum becomes even more obvious as we will be operating on 4-tensors of dimension *batch × head × number of nodes × features*. Multi-head attention will not be particularly useful for MNIST because the input space is already small and sparse enough that a single attention head has enough bandwidth and interpretability. Hence, this is a good time to introduce our reinforcement learning task for this chapter. Because the relational module is the most computationally expensive model we've implemented in this book so far, we want to use a simple environment that still demonstrates the power of relational reasoning and interpretability in reinforcement learning.

We will be coming full circle and returning to a Gridworld environment that we first encountered in chapter 3. But the Gridworld environment we will be using in this chapter is much more sophisticated. We'll be using the MiniGrid library found on GitHub at https://github.com/maximecb/gym-minigrid; it is implemented as an OpenAI Gym environment. It includes a wide variety of different kinds of Gridworld environments of varying complexity and difficulty. Some of these Gridworld environments are so difficult (largely due to sparse rewards) that only the most cutting-edge reinforcement learning algorithms are capable of making headway. Install the package using `pip`:

```
>>> pip3 install gym-minigrid
```

We will be using a somewhat difficult environment in which the Gridworld agent must navigate to a key, pick it up, use it to open a door, and then navigate to a goal-post in order to receive a positive reward (figure 10.19). This is a lot of steps before it ever sees a reward, so we will encounter the sparse reward problem. This would actually be a great opportunity to employ curiosity-based learning, but we will restrict ourselves to the smallest version of the grid, the MiniGrid, so that even a random agent would eventually find the goal, so we can successfully train without curiosity. For the larger grid variants of this environment, curiosity or related approaches would be almost necessary.

There are a few other complexities to the MiniGrid set of environments. One is that they are partially observable environments, meaning the agent cannot see the whole grid but only a small region immediately surrounding it. Another is that the agent does not simply move left, right, up, and down but has an orientation. The agent can only move forward, turn left, or turn right; it is always oriented in a particular direction and must turn around before moving backward, for example. The agent's

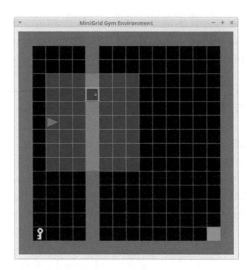

Figure 10.19   The MiniGrid-DoorKey environment. In this environment, the agent (the triangle) must first navigate to the key, pick it up, navigate to the door (the hollow square), open it, and then navigate to the solid square. Each game initializes the objects on the grid randomly, and the agent only has a partial view of the grid indicated by the highlighted region around it.

partial view of the environment is *egocentric*, meaning the agent sees the grid as if it were facing it. When the agent changes direction without moving position, its view changes. The state we receive from the environment is a $7 \times 7 \times 3$ tensor, so the agent only sees a 7×7 subregion of the grid in front of it; the last (channel) dimension of the state encodes which object (if any) is present at that position.

This Gridworld environment is a good testbed for our relational module because in order to successfully learn how to play, the agent must learn how to relate the key to the lock and the lock to being able to access the goal, which is all a form of relational reasoning. In addition, the game is naturally represented by a set of objects (or nodes), since each "pixel" position in the grid really is an actual object, unlike in the MNIST example. This means we can see exactly which objects the agent is paying attention to. We might hope it learns to pay most attention to the key, door, and goal square, and that the key is related to the door. If this turns out to be the case, it suggests the agent is learning not too differently than how a human would learn how to relate the objects on the grid.

Overall we will repurpose the relational module we created earlier for the MNIST example as a relational DQN, so we really only need to change the output to a normal activation function rather than the `log_softmax` we used for classification. But first, let's get back to implementing multi-head attention. As operating on higher-order tensors gets more complicated, we will get help from a package called Einops that extends the capabilities of PyTorch's built-in Einsum function. You can install it using `pip`:

```
>>> pip install einops
>>> from einops import rearrange
```

There are only two important functions in this package (`rearrange` and `reduce`), and we will only use one, the `rearrange` function. `rearrange` basically lets us reshape the dimensions of a higher-order tensor more easily and readably than the built-in PyTorch functions, and it has a syntax similar to Einsum. For example, we can reorder the dimensions of a tensor like this:

```
>>> x = torch.randn(5,7,7,3)
>>> rearrange(x, "batch h w c -> batch c h w").shape
torch.Size([5, 3, 7, 7])
```

Or if we had collapsed the spatial dimensions h and w into a single dimension N for nodes, we can undo this:

```
>>> x = torch.randn(5,49,3)
>>> rearrange(x, "batch (h w) c -> batch h w c", h=7).shape
torch.Size([5, 7, 7, 3])
```

In this case, we tell it that the input has three dimensions but the second dimension is secretly two dimensions (h, w) that were collapsed, and we want to extract them out into separate dimensions again. We only need to tell it the size of h or w, and it can infer the size of the other dimension.

The main change for multi-head attention is that when we project the initial node matrix $N : \mathbb{R}^{b \times n \times f}$ into key, query, and value matrices, we add an extra head dimension: $Q, K, V : \mathbb{R}^{b \times h \times n \times d}$, where b is the batch dimension, and h is the head dimension. We will (arbitrarily) set the number of heads to be 3 for this example, so $h = 3$, $n = 7 * 7 = 49$, $d = 64$, where n is the number of nodes (which is just the total number of grid positions in view), and d is the dimensionality of the node feature vectors, which is just something we choose empirically to be 64, but smaller or larger values might work just as well.

We will need to do a tensor contraction between the query and key tensors to get an attention tensor, $A : \mathbb{R}^{b \times h \times n \times n}$, pass it through a softmax, contract this with the value tensor, collapse the head dimension with the last n dimension, and contract the last (collapsed) dimension with a linear layer to get our updated node tensor, $N : \mathbb{R}^{b \times n \times d}$, which we can then pass through another self-attention layer or collapse all the nodes into a single vector and pass it through some linear layers to the final output. We will stick with a single-attention layer for all examples.

First we'll go over some specific lines in the code that are different from the single-head attention model; the full model is reproduced in listing 10.7. In order to use PyTorch's built-in linear layer module (which is just a matrix multiplication plus a bias vector), we will create a linear layer where the last dimension size is expanded by the number of attention heads.

```
>>> self.proj_shape = (self.conv4_ch+self.sp_coord_dim,self.n_heads *
    self.node_size)
>>> self.k_proj = nn.Linear(*self.proj_shape)
>>> self.q_proj = nn.Linear(*self.proj_shape)
>>> self.v_proj = nn.Linear(*self.proj_shape)
```

We make three separate, ordinary linear layers just as we did for the single-head attention model, but this time we'll expand the last dimension by multiplying it by the number of attention heads. The input to these projection layers is a batch of initial node matrices, $N: \mathbb{R}^{b \times n \times c}$, and the c dimension is equal to the output channel dimension of the last convolutional layer plus the two spatial coordinates that we append. The linear layer thus contracts over the channel dimension to give us query, key, and value matrices, $Q, K, V: \mathbb{R}^{b \times n \times (h \cdot d)}$, so we will use the Einops `rearrange` function to expand out the last dimension into head and d dimensions.

```
>>> K = rearrange(self.k_proj(x), "b n (head d) -> b head n d",
      head=self.n_heads)
```

We will extract out the separate head and d dimension and simultaneously reorder the dimensions so that the head dimension comes after the batch dimension. Without Einops, this would be more code and not nearly as readable.

For this example, we will also abandon the dot (inner) product as the compatibility function (recall, this is the function that determines the similarity between the query and keys) and instead use something called *additive attention* (figure 10.20). The dot product attention would work fine, but we wanted to illustrate that it is not the only kind of compatibility function, and the additive function is actually a bit more stable and expressive.

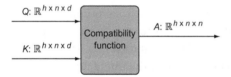

Figure 10.20   **The compatibility function computes the similarity between each key and query vector, resulting in an adjacency matrix.**

With dot product attention, we compute the compatibility (i.e., the similarity) between each query and key by simply taking the dot product between each vector. When the two vectors are similar element-wise, the dot product will yield a large positive value, and when they are dissimilar, it may yield a value near zero or a big negative value. This means the output of the (dot product) compatibility function is unbounded in both directions, and we can get arbitrarily large or small values. This can be problematic when we then pass it through the softmax function, which can easily saturate. By *saturate* we mean that when a particular value in an input vector is dramatically larger than other values in the vector, the softmax may assign all its probability mass to that single value, setting all the others to zero, or vice versa. This can make our gradients too large or too small for particular values and destabilize training.

Additive attention can solve this problem at the expense of introducing additional parameters. Instead of simply multiplying the Q and K tensors together, we'll instead pass them both through independent linear layers, add them together, and then apply an activation function, followed by another linear layer (figure 10.21). This allows for a more complex interaction between Q and K without as much risk of

Additive attention

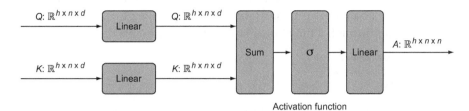

Figure 10.21   **Additive attention is an alternative to dot product attention that can be more stable. Instead of multiplying the queries and keys together, we first pass them independently through linear layers and then add them together, apply a nonlinear function, and pass through another linear layer to change the dimensionality.**

causing numerical instability, since addition will not exaggerate numerical differences like multiplication does. First we need to add three new linear layers for the additive attention.

```
>>> self.k_lin = nn.Linear(self.node_size, self.N)
>>> self.q_lin = nn.Linear(self.node_size, self.N)
>>> self.a_lin = nn.Linear(self.N, self.N)
```

In the forward method we define the actual computation steps for additive attention:

```
>>> A = torch.nn.functional.elu(self.q_lin(Q) + self.k_lin(K))
>>> A = self.a_lin(A)
>>> A = torch.nn.functional.softmax(A, dim=3)
```

As you can see, we pass Q through a linear layer and K through its own linear layer, add them together, and then apply a nonlinear activation function. Then we pass this result through another linear layer and lastly apply the softmax across the node rows, which finally yields the attention weight tensor.

Now we do the same as before and contract the attention tensor with the V tensor along the last n dimension to get a tensor with dimensions $b \times h \times n \times d$, which is a multi-headed node matrix.

```
>>> E = torch.einsum('bhfc,bhcd->bhfd',A,V)
```

What we want at the end of the self-attention module is an updated node matrix with dimensions $b \times n \times d$, so we will concatenate or collapse the head dimension and d dimension, and then pass this through a linear layer to reduce the dimensionality back down to size d.

```
>>> E = rearrange(E, 'b head n d -> b n (head d)')
>>> E = self.linear1(E)
>>> E = torch.relu(E)
>>> E = self.norm1(E)
```

The final shape of this is now $b \times n \times d$, which is exactly what we want. Since we're only going to use a single self-attention module, we want to reduce this 3-tensor into a 2-tensor of just a batch of vectors, so we will maxpool over the n dimension, and then pass the result through a final linear layer, which represents the Q values.

```
>>> E = E.max(dim=1)[0]
>>> y = self.linear2(E)
>>> y = torch.nn.functional.elu(y)
```

That's it. We just went through all the core lines of code, but let's see it all together and test it out.

Listing 10.7   Multi-head relational module

```python
class MultiHeadRelationalModule(torch.nn.Module):
    def __init__(self):
        super(MultiHeadRelationalModule, self).__init__()
        self.conv1_ch = 16
        self.conv2_ch = 20
        self.conv3_ch = 24
        self.conv4_ch = 30
        self.H = 28
        self.W = 28
        self.node_size = 64
        self.lin_hid = 100
        self.out_dim = 5
        self.ch_in = 3
        self.sp_coord_dim = 2
        self.N = int(7**2)
        self.n_heads = 3

        self.conv1 =
    nn.Conv2d(self.ch_in,self.conv1_ch,kernel_size=(1,1),padding=0)     ◄─┐  We use 1 x 1 convolutions to
        self.conv2 =                                                       preserve the spatial organization
    nn.Conv2d(self.conv1_ch,self.conv2_ch,kernel_size=(1,1),padding=0)     of the objects in the grid.
        self.proj_shape = (self.conv2_ch+self.sp_coord_dim,self.n_heads *
    self.node_size)
        self.k_proj = nn.Linear(*self.proj_shape)
        self.q_proj = nn.Linear(*self.proj_shape)
        self.v_proj = nn.Linear(*self.proj_shape)           ┐  Sets up linear
                                                               layers for additive
        self.k_lin = nn.Linear(self.node_size,self.N)    ◄──┘  attention
        self.q_lin = nn.Linear(self.node_size,self.N)
        self.a_lin = nn.Linear(self.N,self.N)

        self.node_shape = (self.n_heads, self.N,self.node_size)
        self.k_norm = nn.LayerNorm(self.node_shape, elementwise_affine=True)
        self.q_norm = nn.LayerNorm(self.node_shape, elementwise_affine=True)
        self.v_norm = nn.LayerNorm(self.node_shape, elementwise_affine=True)

        self.linear1 = nn.Linear(self.n_heads * self.node_size, self.node_size)
        self.norm1 = nn.LayerNorm([self.N,self.node_size],
            elementwise_affine=False)
        self.linear2 = nn.Linear(self.node_size, self.out_dim)
```

```
def forward(self,x):
    N, Cin, H, W = x.shape
    x = self.conv1(x)
    x = torch.relu(x)
    x = self.conv2(x)
    x = torch.relu(x)
    with torch.no_grad():
        self.conv_map = x.clone()          ◁──  Saves a copy of the
    _,_,cH,cW = x.shape                          post-convolved input
    xcoords = torch.arange(cW).repeat(cH,1).float() / cW    for later visualization
    ycoords = torch.arange(cH).repeat(cW,1).transpose(1,0).float() / cH
    spatial_coords = torch.stack([xcoords,ycoords],dim=0)
    spatial_coords = spatial_coords.unsqueeze(dim=0)
    spatial_coords = spatial_coords.repeat(N,1,1,1)
    x = torch.cat([x,spatial_coords],dim=1)
    x = x.permute(0,2,3,1)
    x = x.flatten(1,2)

    K = rearrange(self.k_proj(x), "b n (head d) -> b head n d",
        head=self.n_heads)
    K = self.k_norm(K)

    Q = rearrange(self.q_proj(x), "b n (head d) -> b head n d",
        head=self.n_heads)
    Q = self.q_norm(Q)

    V = rearrange(self.v_proj(x), "b n (head d) -> b head n d",
        head=self.n_heads)
    V = self.v_norm(V)
    A = torch.nn.functional.elu(self.q_lin(Q) + self.k_lin(K))
    A = self.a_lin(A)
    A = torch.nn.functional.softmax(A,dim=3)
    with torch.no_grad():
        self.att_map = A.clone()
    E = torch.einsum('bhfc,bhcd->bhfd',A,V)    ◁──
    E = rearrange(E, 'b head n d -> b n (head d)')    ◁──
    E = self.linear1(E)
    E = torch.relu(E)
    E = self.norm1(E)
    E = E.max(dim=1)[0]
    y = self.linear2(E)
    y = torch.nn.functional.elu(y)
    return y
```

Additive attention (label pointing to `A = torch.nn.functional.elu(self.q_lin(Q) + self.k_lin(K))`)

Saves a copy of the attention weights for later visualization (label pointing to `self.att_map = A.clone()`)

Batch-matrix multiplies the attention weight matrix with the node matrix to get an updated node matrix. (label pointing to `E = torch.einsum('bhfc,bhcd->bhfd',A,V)`)

Collapses the head dimension with the feature d dimension (label pointing to `E = rearrange(E, 'b head n d -> b n (head d)')`)

10.5 Double Q-learning

Now let's get to training it. Because this Gridworld environment has sparse rewards, we need to make our training process as smooth as possible, especially since we're not using curiosity-based learning.

Remember back in chapter 3 when we introduced Q-learning and a target network to stabilize training? If not, the idea was that in ordinary Q-learning we compute the target Q value with this equation:

$$Q_{new} = r_t + \gamma \cdot \max(Q(s_{t+1}))$$

The problem with this is that every time we update our DQN according to this equation so that its predictions get closer to this target, the $Q(s_{t+1})$ is changed, which means the next time we go to update our Q function, the target Q_{new} is going to be different even for the same state. This is problematic because as we train the DQN, its predictions are chasing a moving target, leading to very unstable training and poor performance. To stabilize training, we create a duplicate Q function called the *target function* that we can denote Q', and we use the value $Q'(s_{t+1})$ to plug into the equation and update the main Q function.

$$Q_{new} = r_t + \gamma \cdot \max(Q'(s_{t+1}))$$

We only train (and hence backpropagate into) the main Q function, but we copy the parameters from the main Q function to the target Q function, Q', every 100 (or some other arbitrary number of) epochs. This greatly stabilizes training because the main Q function is no longer chasing a constantly moving target, but a relatively fixed target.

But that's not all that's wrong with that simple update equation. Because it involves the max function, i.e., we select the maximum predicted Q value for the next state, it leads our agent to overestimate Q values for actions, which can impact training especially early on. If the DQN takes action 1 and learns an erroneously high Q value for action 1, that means action 1 is going to get selected more often in subsequent epochs, further causing it to be overestimated, which again leads to training instability and poor performance.

To mitigate this problem and get more accurate estimates for Q values, we will implement double Q-learning, which solves the problem by disentangling action-value estimation from action selection, as you will see. A *double deep Q-network* (DDQN) involves a simple modification to normal Q-learning with a target network. As usual, we use the main Q-network to select actions using an epsilon-greedy policy. But when it comes time to compute Q_{new}, we will first find the argmax of Q (the main Q-network). Let's say $\text{argmax}(Q(s_{t+1})) = 2$, so action 2 is associated with the highest action value in the next state given the main Q function. We then use this to index into the target network, Q', to get the action value we will use in the update equation.

$$a = \text{argmax}(Q(s_{t+1}))$$

$$x = Q'(s_{t+1})[a]$$

$$Q_{new} = r_t + \gamma \cdot x$$

We're still using the Q value from the target network, Q', but we don't choose the highest Q value from Q'; we choose the Q value in Q' based on the action associated with the highest Q value in the main Q function. In code:

```
>>> state_batch, action_batch, reward_batch, state2_batch, done_batch =
    get_minibatch(replay, batch_size)
>>> q_pred = GWagent(state_batch)
```

```
>>> astar = torch.argmax(q_pred,dim=1)
>>> qs = Tnet(state2_batch).gather(dim=1,index=astar.unsqueeze(dim=1)).squeeze()
>>> targets =
        get_qtarget_ddqn(qs.detach(),reward_batch.detach(),gamma,done_batch)
```

The get_qtarget_ddqn function just computes $Q_{new} = r_t + \gamma \cdot x$:

```
>>> def get_qtarget_ddqn(qvals,r,df,done):
>>>     targets = r + (1-done) * df * qvals
>>>     return targets
```

We provide done, which is a Boolean, because if the episode of the game is done, there is no next state on which to compute $Q(s_{t+1})$, so we just train on r_t and set the rest of the equation to 0.

That's all there is to double Q-learning; just another simple way to improve training stability and performance.

10.6 Training and attention visualization

We have most of the pieces now, but we need a few other helper functions before training.

> **Listing 10.8 Preprocessing functions**

```
import gym
from gym_minigrid.minigrid import *
from gym_minigrid.wrappers import FullyObsWrapper, ImgObsWrapper
from skimage.transform import resize

def prepare_state(x):                                    ← Normalizes the state tensor
    ns = torch.from_numpy(x).float().permute(2,0,1).unsqueeze(dim=0) #  and converts to PyTorch tensor
    maxv = ns.flatten().max()
    ns = ns / maxv                                       Gets a random mini-batch
    return ns                                            from the experience replay
                                                         memory
def get_minibatch(replay,size):                          ←
    batch_ids = np.random.randint(0,len(replay),size)
    batch = [replay[x] for x in batch_ids] #list of tuples
    state_batch = torch.cat([s for (s,a,r,s2,d) in batch],)
    action_batch = torch.Tensor([a for (s,a,r,s2,d) in batch]).long()
    reward_batch = torch.Tensor([r for (s,a,r,s2,d) in batch])
    state2_batch = torch.cat([s2 for (s,a,r,s2,d) in batch],dim=0)
    done_batch = torch.Tensor([d for (s,a,r,s2,d) in batch])
    return state_batch,action_batch,reward_batch,state2_batch, done_batch

def get_qtarget_ddqn(qvals,r,df,done):                   ← Calculates the
    targets = r + (1-done) * df * qvals                    target Q value
    return targets
```

These functions just prepare the state observation tensor, produce a mini-batch and calculate the target Q value as we discussed earlier.

In listing 10.9 we define the loss function we will use and also a function to update the experience replay.

Listing 10.9   Loss function and updating the replay

```
def lossfn(pred,targets,actions):          ◁── Loss function
    loss = torch.mean(torch.pow(\
                           targets.detach() -\

    pred.gather(dim=1,index=actions.unsqueeze(dim=1)).squeeze()\
                           ,2),dim=0)
    return loss

def update_replay(replay,exp,replay_size):     ◁─┐ Adds new experiences
    r = exp[2]                                     │ to the experience replay
    N = 1                                          │ memory; if the reward
    if r > 0:                                      │ is positive, we add 50
        N = 50                                     │ copies of the memory.
    for i in range(N):
        replay.append(exp)
    return replay

action_map = {       ◁─┐ Maps the action
    0:0,                │ outputs of the
    1:1,                │ DQN to a subset
    2:2,                │ of actions in the
    3:3,                │ environment
    4:5,
}
```

The update_replay function adds new memories to the experience replay if it is not yet full; if it is full, it will replace random memories with new ones. If the memory resulted in a positive reward, we add 50 copies of that memory, since positive reward memories are rare and we want to enrich the experience replay with these more important memories.

All the MiniGrid environments have seven actions, but in the environment we will use in this chapter, we only need to use five of the seven actions, so we use a dictionary to translate from the output of DQN, which will produce actions 0–4, to the appropriate actions in the environment, which are {0,1,2,3,5}.

The MiniGrid's action names and corresponding action numbers are listed here:

```
[<Actions.left: 0>,
<Actions.right: 1>,
<Actions.forward: 2>,
<Actions.pickup: 3>,
<Actions.drop: 4>,
<Actions.toggle: 5>,
<Actions.done: 6>]
```

In listing 10.10 we jump into the main training loop of the algorithm.

Listing 10.10 The main training loop

```
from collections import deque
env = ImgObsWrapper(gym.make('MiniGrid-DoorKey-5x5-v0'))          ◁─┐ Sets up
state = prepare_state(env.reset())                                  │ environment
GWagent = MultiHeadRelationalModule()        ◁─┐ Creates main
Tnet = MultiHeadRelationalModule()           ◁─┘ relational DQN
maxsteps = 400                        ◁─┐
env.max_steps = maxsteps                │ Creates target DQN
env.env.max_steps = maxsteps            │
                                   Sets the maximum
epochs = 50000                     steps before game
replay_size = 9000                 will end
batch_size = 50
lr = 0.0005                                        Creates the experience
gamma = 0.99                                       replay memory
replay = deque(maxlen=replay_size)           ◁─┘
opt = torch.optim.Adam(params=GWagent.parameters(),lr=lr)
eps = 0.5
update_freq = 100
for i in range(epochs):                                      Uses an epsilon-
    pred = GWagent(state)                                    greedy policy for
    action = int(torch.argmax(pred).detach().numpy())        action selection
    if np.random.rand() < eps:                          ◁─┘
        action = int(torch.randint(0,5,size=(1,)).squeeze())
    action_d = action_map[action]
    state2, reward, done, info = env.step(action_d)
    reward = -0.01 if reward == 0 else reward        ◁─┐ Rescales the reward to
    state2 = prepare_state(state2)                     │ be slightly negative on
    exp = (state,action,reward,state2,done)            │ nonterminal states

    replay = update_replay(replay,exp,replay_size)
    if done:
        state = prepare_state(env.reset())
    else:
        state = state2
    if len(replay) > batch_size:

        opt.zero_grad()

        state_batch,action_batch,reward_batch,state2_batch,done_batch =
    get_minibatch(replay,batch_size)

        q_pred = GWagent(state_batch).cpu()
        astar = torch.argmax(q_pred,dim=1)
        qs =
    Tnet(state2_batch).gather(dim=1,index=astar.unsqueeze(dim=1)).squeeze()

        targets =
    get_qtarget_ddqn(qs.detach(),reward_batch.detach(),gamma,done_batch)

        loss = lossfn(q_pred,targets.detach(),action_batch)
        loss.backward()
        torch.nn.utils.clip_grad_norm_(GWagent.parameters(), max_norm=1.0)
        opt.step()
```

Clips the
gradients to
prevent overly
large gradients

```
if i % update_freq == 0:
    Tnet.load_state_dict(GWagent.state_dict())
```

Synchronizes the main DQN with the target DQN every 100 steps

Our self-attention double DQN reinforcement learning algorithm will learn how to play fairly well after about 10,000 epochs, but it may take up to 50,000 epochs before it reaches maximum accuracy.

Figure 10.22 shows the log-loss plot we get, and we also plotted the average episode length. As the agent learns to play, it should be able to solve the games in fewer and fewer steps.

If you test the trained algorithm, it should be able to solve $\geq 94\%$ of the episodes within the maximum step limit. We even recorded video frames during training, and the agent clearly knows what it is doing when you watch it in real time. We have omitted a lot of this accessory code to keep the text clear; please see the GitHub repository for the complete code.

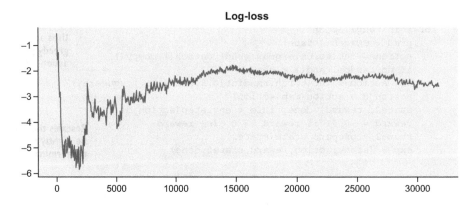

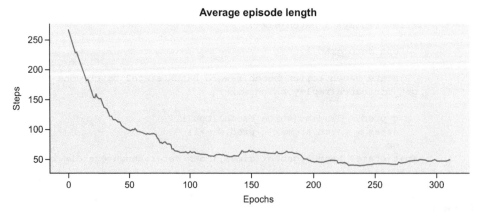

Figure 10.22   **Top: Log-loss plot during training. The loss drops quickly in the beginning, increases a bit, and then very slowly begins decreasing again. Bottom: Average episode length. This gives us a better idea of the performance of the agent since we can clearly see it is solving the episodes in a shorter number of steps during training.**

10.6.1 *Maximum entropy learning*

We are using an epsilon-greedy policy with epsilon set to 0.5, so the agent is taking random actions 50% of the time. We tested using a number of different epsilon levels but found 0.5 to be about the best. If you train the agent with epsilon values ranging from a low of 0.01, to 0.1, to 0.2, all the way to a high of say 0.95, you will notice the training performance follows an inverted-U curve, where too low a value for epsilon leads to poor learning due to lack of exploration, and too high a value for epsilon leads to poor learning due to lack of exploitation.

How can the agent perform so well even though it is acting randomly half the time? By setting the epsilon to be as high as possible until it degrades performance, we are utilizing an approximation to the principle of maximum entropy, or *maximum entropy learning*.

We can think of the entropy of an agent's policy as the amount of randomness it exhibits, and it turns out that maximizing entropy up until it starts to be counterproductive actually leads to better performance and generalization. If an agent can successfully achieve a goal even in the face of taking a high proportion of random actions, it must have a very robust policy that is insensitive to random transformations, so it will be able to handle more difficult environments.

10.6.2 *Curriculum learning*

We trained this agent only on the 5 × 5 version of this Gridworld environment so that it would have a small chance of randomly achieving the goal and receiving a reward. There are also bigger environments, including a 16 × 16 environment, which would make randomly winning extremely unlikely. An alternative to (or addition to) curiosity learning is to use a process called *curriculum learning*, which is when we train an agent on an easy variant of a problem, then retrain on a slightly harder variant, and keep retraining on harder and harder versions of the problem until the agent can successfully achieve a task that would have been too hard to start with. We could attempt to solve the 16 × 16 grid without curiosity by first training to maximum accuracy on the 5 × 5 grid, then retraining on the 6 × 6 grid, then the 8 × 8 grid, and finally the 16 × 16 grid.

10.6.3 *Visualizing attention weights*

We know we can successfully train a relational DQN on this somewhat difficult Gridworld task, but we could have used a much less fancy DQN to do the same thing. However, we also cared about visualizing the attention weights to see what exactly the agent has learned to focus on when playing the game. Some of the results are surprising, and some are what we would expect.

To visualize the attention weights, we had our model save a copy of the attention weights each time it was run forward, and we can access it by calling `GWagent.att_map`, which returns a *batch* × *head* × *height* × *width* tensor. All we need to do is run the model forward on some state, select an attention head, and select a node to visualize, and then reshape the tensor into a 7×7 grid and plot it using `plt.imshow`.

```
>>> state_ = env.reset()
>>> state = prepare_state(state_)
>>> GWagent(state)
>>> plt.imshow(env.render('rgb_array'))
>>> plt.imshow(state[0].permute(1,2,0).detach().numpy())
>>> head, node = 2, 26
>>> plt.imshow(GWagent.att_map[0][head][node].view(7,7))
```

We decided to look at the attention weights for the key node, the door node, and the agent node to see which objects are related to each other. We found the node in the attention weights that corresponds to the node in the grid by counting the grid cells, since both the attention weights and the original state are a 7×7 grid. We intentionally designed the relational module such that the original state and attention weight matrices are the same dimensionality; otherwise it becomes difficult to map the attention weights onto the state. Figure 10.23 shows the original full view of the grid in a random initial state and the corresponding prepared state.

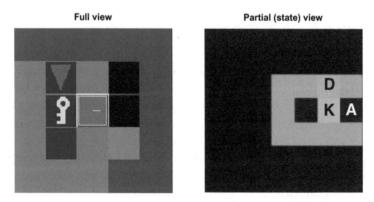

Figure 10.23   Left: The full observation of the environment. Right: The corresponding partial state view that the agent has access to.

The partial view is a little confusing at first because it is an egocentric view, so we annotated it with the positions of the agent (A), key (K), and the door (D). Because the agent's partial view is always 7×7 and the size of the full grid is only 5×5, the partial view always includes some empty space. Now let's visualize the corresponding attention weights for this state.

In figure 10.24, each column is labeled as a particular node's attention weights (i.e., the nodes to which it is paying attention), restricting ourselves to just the agent, key, and door nodes out of a total of $7 \times 7 = 49$ nodes. Each row is an attention head, from head 1 to head 3, top to bottom. Curiously, attention head 1 does not appear to

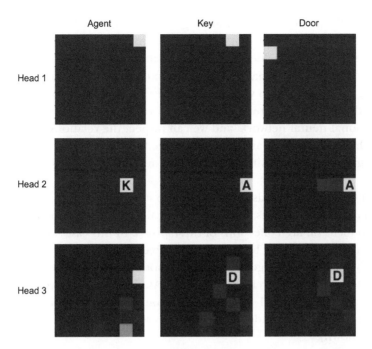

Figure 10.24 Each row corresponds to an attention head (e.g., row 1 corresponds to attention head 1). Left column: The self-attention weights for the agent, which shows the objects to which the agent is paying most attention. Middle column: The self-attention weights for the key, which shows the objects to which the key is paying most attention. Right column: The self-attention weights for the door.

be focusing on anything obviously interesting; in fact, it is focusing on grid cells in empty space. Note that while we're only looking at 3 of the 49 nodes, even after looking at all of the nodes, the attention weights are quite sparse; only a few grid cells at most are assigned any significant attention. But perhaps this isn't surprising, as the attention heads appear to be specializing.

Attention head 1 may be focusing on a small subset of landmarks in the environment to get an understanding of location and orientation. The fact that it can do this with just a few grid cells is impressive.

Attention heads 2 and 3 (rows 2 and 3 in figure 10.24) are more interesting and are doing close to what we expect. Look at attention head 2 for the agent node: it is strongly attending to the key (and essentially nothing else), which is exactly what we would hope, given that at this initial state its first job is to pick up the key. Reciprocally, the key is attending to the agent, suggesting there is a bidirectional relation from agent to key and key to agent. The door is also attending to the agent most strongly, but there's also a small amount of attention given to the key and the space directly in front of the door.

Attention head 3 for the agent is attending to a few landmark grid cells, again, probably to establish a sense of position and orientation. Attention head 3 for the key is attending to the door and the door is reciprocally attending to the key.

Putting it all together, we get that the agent is related to the key which is related to the door. If the goal square was in view, we might see that the door is also related to the goal. While this is a simple environment, it has relational structure that we can learn with a relational neural network, and we can inspect the relations that it learns. It is interesting how sparsely the attention is assigned. Each node prefers to attend strongly to a single other node, with sometimes a couple other nodes that it weakly attends to.

Since this is a Gridworld, it is easy to partition the state into discrete objects, but in many cases such as the Atari games, the state is a big RGB pixel array, and the objects we would want to focus on are collections of these pixels. In this case it becomes difficult to map the attention weights back to specific objects in the video frame, but we can still see which parts of the image the relational module as a whole is using to make its decisions. We tested a similar architecture on the Atari game Alien (we just used 4×4 kernel convolutions instead of 1×1 and added some maxpooling layers), and we can see (in figure 10.25) that it indeed learns to focus on salient objects in the video frame (code not shown).

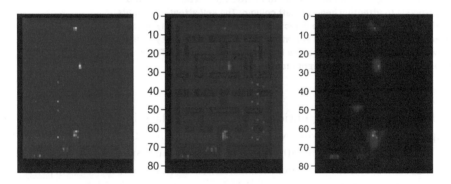

Figure 10.25   Left: Preprocessed state given to the DQN. Middle: Raw video frame. Right: Attention map over state. We can see that the attention map is focused on the alien in the bottom center of the screen, the player in the center, and the bonus at the top, which are the most salient objects in the game.

Relational modules using the self-attention mechanism are powerful tools in the machine learning toolkit, and they can be very useful for training RL agents when we want some idea of how they're making decisions. Self-attention is one mechanism for performing message passing on a graph, as we discussed, and it's part of the broader field of graph neural networks, which we encourage you to explore further. There are many implementations of graph neural networks (GNNs) but particularly relevant for us after this chapter is the *graph attention network*, which uses the same self-attention mechanism we just implemented but with the added ability to operate on more general graph-structured data.

Summary

- Graph neural networks are machine learning models that operate on graph-structured data. Graphs are data structures composed of a set of objects (called nodes) and relations between objects (called edges). A natural graph type is a social network in which the nodes are individuals and the edges between nodes represent friendships.

- An adjacency matrix is a matrix with dimensions $A:N \times N$ where N is the number of nodes in a graph that encodes the connectivity between each pair of nodes.

- Message passing is an algorithm for computing updates to node features by iteratively aggregating information from a node's neighbors.

- Inductive biases are the prior information we have about some set of data; we use them to constrain our model toward learning certain kinds of patterns. In this chapter we employed a relational inductive bias, for example.

- We say a function, f is invariant to some transformation, g, when the function's output remains unchanged when the input is first transformed by g: $f(g(x)) = f(x)$.

- We say a function, f, is equivariant to some transformation, g, when applying the transformation to the input is the same as applying the transformation to the output: $f(g(x)) = g(f(x))$.

- Attention models are designed to increase the interpretability and performance of machine learning models by forcing the model to only "look at" (attend to) a subset of the input data. By examining what the model learns to attend to, we can have a better idea of how it is making decisions.

- Self-attention models model attention between objects (or nodes) in an input rather than just the model attending to different parts of the input. This naturally leads to a form of graph neural network, since the attention weights can be interpreted as edges between nodes.

- Multi-head self-attention allows the model to have independent attention mechanisms that can each attend to a different subset of the input data. This allows us to still get interpretable attention weights but increases the bandwidth of information that can flow through the model.

- Relational reasoning is a form of reasoning based on objects and relationships between objects, rather than using absolute frames of reference. For example, "a book is on the top" relates the book to the table, rather than saying the book is at position 10 and the table is at position 8 (an absolute reference frame).

- Inner (dot) product is a product between two vectors that results in a single scalar value.

- Outer product is a product between two vectors that results in a matrix.
- Einstein notation or Einsum lets us describe generalized tensor-tensor products called tensor contractions using a simple syntax based on labeling the indices of a tensor.
- Double Q-learning stabilizes training by separating action-selection and action-value updating.

11

In conclusion:
A review and roadmap

In this final chapter we'll first take a moment to briefly review what we've learned, highlighting and distilling what we think are the most important skills and concepts to take away. We have covered the fundamentals of *reinforcement learning* and if you have made it this far and have engaged with the projects, you're well-positioned to implement many other algorithms and techniques.

This book is a *course* on the fundamentals of *deep reinforcement learning*, not a textbook or reference. That means we could not possibly have introduced all there is to know about DRL, and we had to make tough choices about what to leave out. There are a number of exciting topics in DRL we wished we could have included, and there are some topics that, despite being "industry standards," were inappropriate to include in a project-focused introductory book like this one. However, we wanted to leave you with a roadmap for where to go from here with your new skills.

In the second part of this chapter, we'll introduce at a high-level some topics, techniques, and algorithms in DRL that are worth knowing if you're serious about continuing in the DRL field. We didn't cover these areas because most of them involve advanced mathematics that we do not expect readers of this book to be familiar with, and we did not have the space to teach more mathematics.

11.1 *What did we learn?*

Deep reinforcement learning is the combination of deep learning and reinforcement learning. Reinforcement learning is a framework for solving *control tasks*, which are problems in which an *agent* can take actions that lead to positive or negative rewards, given some *environment*. The environment is the universe in which the agent acts. The agent can either have full access to the state of the environment, or it may only have partial access to the state of the environment, which is called *partial observability.* The environment evolves in discrete time steps according to some dynamical rules, and at each time step the agent takes an action that may influence the next state. After taking each action, the agent receives feedback in the form of a reward signal. We described a mathematical formalization of this called the *Markov decision process* (MDP).

An MDP is a mathematical structure that includes a set of states, S, that the environment can be in, and a set of actions, A, that the agent can take, which may depend on the particular state of the environment. There is a *reward function*, $R(s_t, a_t, s_{t+1})$, that produces the *reward signal*, given the transition from the current state to the next state and the agent's action. The environment may evolve deterministically or stochastically, but in either case, the agent initially does not know the dynamical rules of the environment, so all state transitions must be described probabilistically from the perspective of the agent.

We therefore have a conditional probability distribution over next states, s_{t+1}, given the current state and the action taken by the agent at the current time step, denoted $\Pr(S_{t+1} \mid s_t, a_t)$. The agent follows some policy, π, which is a function that maps a probability distribution over actions given the current state s_t: $\pi{:}S \to \Pr(A)$. The objective of the agent is to take actions that maximize the time-discounted cumulative rewards over some time horizon. The time-discounted cumulative reward is termed the *return* (often denoted with the character G or R), and is equal to

$$G_t = \sum_t \gamma^t r_t$$

The return, G_t at time t, is equal to the sum of discounted rewards for each time step until the end of the episode (for episodic environments) or until the sequence converges for non-episodic environments. The γ factor is a parameter in the interval $(0,1)$ and is the discount rate that determines how quickly the sequence will converge, and thus how much the future is discounted. A discount rate close to 1 will mean that future rewards are given similar weight to immediate rewards (optimizing over the long term), whereas a low discount rate leads to preferring only short-term time horizons.

A derived concept from this basic MDP framework is that of a *value function.* A value function assigns a value to either states or state-action pairs (i.e., a value for taking an action in a given state), with the former being called a *state-value function* (or often just the value function) and the latter being the *action value* or *Q function.* The value of a state is simply the expected return given that the agent starts in that state and follows some policy π, so value functions implicitly depend on the policy. Similarly, the action value or *Q value* of a state-action pair is the expected return given that the agent takes the action in that state and follows the policy π until the end. A state that puts the agent in close position to win a game, for example, would be assigned a high state value assuming the underlying policy was reasonable. We denote the value function as $V_\pi(s)$, with the subscript π indicating the dependence of the value on the underlying policy, and the Q function as $Q_\pi(s,a)$, although we often drop the π subscript for convenience.

Right now we understand the function $Q_\pi(s,a)$ as being some sort of black box that tells us the exact expected rewards for state action a in state s, but, of course, we do not have access to such an all-knowing function; we have to estimate it. In this book we used *neural networks* to estimate value functions and policy functions, although any suitable function could work. In the case of a neural-based $Q_\pi(s,a)$, we trained neural networks to predict the expected rewards. The value functions are defined and approximated recursively, such that $Q_\pi(s,a)$ is updated as

$$V_\pi(s) = r_t + \gamma V_\pi(s')$$

where s' refers to the next state, or s_{t+1}. For example, in Gridworld, landing on the goal tile results in +10, landing on the pit results in –10, and losing the game, and all other non-terminal moves, are penalized at –1. If the agent is two steps away from the winning goal tile, the final state reduces to $V_\pi(s_3) = 10$. Then, if $\gamma = 0.9$, the previous state is valued at $V_\pi(s_2) = r_2 + 0.9V_\pi(s_3) = -1 + 9 = 8$. The move before that must be $V_\pi(s_1) = r_1 + 0.9V_\pi(s_2) = -1 + 0.8 \cdot 8 = 5.4$. As you can see, states farther from the winning state are valued less.

Training a reinforcement learning agent, then, just amounts to successfully training a neural network to either approximate the value function (so the agent will choose actions that lead to high-value states) or to directly approximate the policy function by observing rewards after actions and reinforcing actions based on the rewards received. Both approaches have their pros and cons, but often we combine learning both a policy and a value function together, which is called an *actor-critic algorithm*, where the actor refers to the policy and the critic refers to the value function.

11.2 The uncharted topics in deep reinforcement learning

The Markov decision process framework and value and policy functions we just reviewed were detailed in chapters 2–5. We then spent the rest of the book implementing more sophisticated techniques for successfully training value and policy functions in difficult environments (e.g., environments with sparse rewards) and environments with multiple interacting agents. Unfortunately, there were many exciting things we didn't have the space to cover, so we'll end the book with a brief tour of some other areas in deep reinforcement learning you might want to explore. We'll only give a taste of a few topics we think are worth exploring more and hope you will look into these areas more deeply on your own.

11.2.1 Prioritized experience replay

We briefly mentioned the idea of *prioritized replay* earlier in the book when we decided to add multiple copies of the same experience to the replay memory if the experience led to a winning state. Since winning states are rare, and we want our agent to learn from these informative events, we thought that adding multiple copies would ensure that each training epoch would include a few of these winning events. This was a very unsophisticated means of prioritizing experiences in the replay based on how informative they are in training the agent.

The term *prioritized experience replay* generally refers to a specific implementation introduced in an academic paper titled "Prioritized Experience Replay" by Tom Schaul et al. (2015), and it uses a much more sophisticated mechanism to prioritize experiences. In their implementation, all experiences are recorded just once, unlike our approach, but rather than selecting a mini-batch from the replay completely randomly (i.e., uniformly), they preferentially select experiences that are more informative. They defined informative experiences as not merely those that led to a winning state like we did, but rather those where the DQN had a high error in predicting the reward. In essence, the model preferentially trains on the most surprising experiences. As the model trains, however, the once surprising experiences become less surprising, and the preferences get continually reweighted. This leads to substantially improved training performance. This kind of prioritized experience replay is standard practice for value-based reinforcement learning, whereas policy-based reinforcement learning still tends to rely on using multiple parallelized agents and environments.

11.2.2 *Proximal policy optimization (PPO)*

We mostly implemented *deep Q-networks* (DQN) in this book rather than policy functions, and this is for good reason. The (deep) policy functions we implemented in chapters 4 and 5 were rather unsophisticated and would not work very well for more complex environments. The problem is not with the policy networks themselves but with the training algorithm. The simple REINFORCE algorithm we used is fairly unstable. When the rewards vary significantly from action to action, the REINFORCE algorithm does not lead to stable results. We need a training algorithm that enforces smoother, more constrained updates to the policy network.

Proximal policy optimization (PPO) is a more advanced training algorithm for policy methods that allows for far more stable training. It was introduced in the paper "Proximal Policy Optimization Algorithms" by John Schulman et al. (2017) at OpenAI. We did not cover PPO in this book because, while the algorithm itself is relatively simple, understanding it requires mathematical machinery that is outside the scope of this introductory book. Making deep Q-learning more stable required only a few intuitive upgrades like adding a target network and implementing double Q-learning, so that is why we preferred to use value learning over policy methods in this book. However, in many cases, directly learning a policy function is more advantageous than a value function, such as for environments with a continuous action space, since we cannot create a DQN that returns an infinite number of Q values for each action.

11.2.3 *Hierarchical reinforcement learning and the options framework*

When a child learns to walk, they aren't thinking about which individual muscle fibers to activate and for how long, or when a businessperson is debating a business decision with colleagues, they aren't thinking about the individual sequences of sounds they need to make for the other people to understand their business strategy. Our actions exist at various levels of abstraction, from moving individual muscles up to grand schemes. This is just like noticing that a story is made up of individual letters, but those letters are composed into words that are composed into sentences and paragraphs and so on. The writer may be thinking of a general next scene in the story, and only once that's decided will they actually get to typing individual characters.

All the agents we've implemented in this book operate at the level of typing individual characters so to speak; they are incapable of thinking at a higher level. *Hierarchical reinforcement learning* is an approach to solving this problem, allowing agents to build up higher-level actions from lower ones. Rather than our Gridworld agent deciding one step at a time what to do, it might survey the board and decide on a higher-level sequence of actions. It might learn reusable sequences such as "move all the way up" or "move around obstacle" that can be implemented in a variety of game states.

The success of deep learning in reinforcement learning is due to its ability to represent complex high-dimensional states in a hierarchy of higher-level state representations. In hierarchical reinforcement learning, the goal is to extend this to representing states *and* actions hierarchically. One popular approach to this is called the *options framework*.

Consider Gridworld, which has four primitive actions of up, right, left, and down, and each action lasts one time step. In the options framework, there are options rather than just primitive actions. An option is the combination of an *option policy* (which like a regular policy takes a state and returns a probability distribution over actions), a *termination condition*, and an *input set* (which is a subset of states). The idea is that a particular option gets triggered when the agent encounters a state in the option's input set, and that particular option's policy is run until the termination condition is met, at which point a different option may be selected. These option policies might be simpler policies than a single, big, deep neural network policy that we have implemented in this book. But by intelligently selecting these higher-level options, efficiencies can be gained by not having to use a more computationally intensive policy for taking each primitive step.

11.2.4 *Model-based planning*

We already discussed the idea of *models* in reinforcement learning in two contexts. In the first, a model is simply another term for an approximating function like a neural network. We sometimes just refer to our neural network as a model, since it approximates or models the value function or the policy function.

The other context is when we refer to *model-based* versus *model-free learning*. In both cases we are using a neural network as a model of the value function or a policy, but in this case model-based means the agent is making decisions based on an explicitly constructed model of the dynamics of the environment itself rather than just its value function. In model-free learning, all we care about is learning to accurately predict rewards, which may or may not require a deep understanding of how the environment actually works. In model-based learning, we actually want to learn how the environment works. Metaphorically, in model-free learning we are satisfied knowing that there is something called gravity that makes things fall, and we make use of this phenomenon, but in model-based learning we want to actually approximate the laws of gravity.

Our model-free DQN worked surprisingly well, especially when combined with other advances like curiosity, so what is the advantage of explicitly learning a model of the environment? With an explicit and accurate *environment model*, the agent can learn to make long-term plans rather than just deciding which next action to take. By using its environment model to predict the future several time steps ahead, it can evaluate the long-term consequences of its immediate actions, and this can lead to faster learning (due to increased sample efficiency). This is related to, but not necessarily the same as, the hierarchical reinforcement learning we discussed, since hierarchical reinforcement learning does not necessarily depend on an environment model. But with an environment model, the agent can plan out a sequence of primitive actions to accomplish some higher-level goal.

The simplest way to train an environment model is to just have a separate deep learning module that predicts future states. In fact, we did just that in chapter 8 on *curiosity-based learning*, but we did not use the environment model to plan or look into the future; we only used it to explore surprising states. But with a model, $M(s_t)$, that takes a state and returns a predicted next state, s_{t+1}, we could then take that predicted next state and feed it back into the model to get the predicted state s_{t+2}, and so on. The distance into the future we could predict depends on the inherent randomness in the environment and the accuracy of the model, but even if we could only accurately predict out to a few time steps into the future, this would be immensely useful.

11.2.5 Monte Carlo tree search (MCTS)

Many games have a finite set of actions and a finite length, such as chess, Go, and Tic-Tac-Toe. The Deep Blue algorithm that IBM developed to play chess didn't use machine learning at all; it was a brute force algorithm that used a form of tree search. Consider the game of Tic-Tac-Toe. It is a two-player game typically played on a square 3×3 grid where player 1 places an X-shaped token and player 2 places an O-shaped token. The goal of the game is to be the first to get three of your tokens lined up in a row, column, or diagonal.

The game is so simple that the human strategy also generally involves limited tree search. If you're player 2 and there's already one opposing token on the grid, you can consider all possible responses to all possible open spaces you have, and you can keep doing this until the end of the game. Of course, even for a 3 × 3 board, the first move has nine possible actions, and there are eight possible actions for player 2, and then seven possible actions for player 1 again, so the number of possible trajectories (the game tree) becomes quite large, but a brute force exhaustive search like this could be guaranteed win at Tic-Tac-Toe assuming the opponent isn't using the same approach.

For a game like chess, the game tree is far too large to use a completely brute force search of the game tree; one must necessarily limit the number of potential moves to consider. Deep Blue used a tree-search algorithm that is more efficient than exhaustive search but still involved no learning. It still amounted to searching possible trajectories and just computing which ones led to winning states.

Another approach is the *Monte Carlo tree search*, in which you use some mechanism of randomly sampling a set of potential actions and expanding the tree from there, rather than considering *all* possible actions. The AlphaGo algorithm developed by DeepMind to play the game Go used a deep neural network to evaluate which actions were worth doing a tree search on and also to decide the value of selected moves. Therefore, AlphaGo combined brute force search with deep neural networks to get the best of both. These types of combination algorithms are currently state-of-the-art for games in the class of chess and Go.

11.3 The end

Thank you for reading our book! We really hope you have learned a satisfying amount about deep reinforcement learning. Please reach out to us in the forums at Manning.com with any questions or comments. We look forward to hearing from you.

appendix
Mathematics,
deep learning, PyTorch

This appendix offers a rapid review of deep learning, the relevant mathematics we use in this book, and how to implement deep learning models in PyTorch. We'll cover these topics by demonstrating how to implement a deep learning model in PyTorch to classify images of handwritten digits from the famous MNIST dataset.

Deep learning algorithms, which are also called *artificial neural networks*, are relatively simple mathematical functions and mostly just require an understanding of vectors and matrices. Training a neural network, however, requires an understanding of the basics of calculus, namely the derivative. The fundamentals of applied deep learning therefore require only knowing how to multiply vectors and matrices and take the derivative of multivariable functions, which we'll review here. *Theoretical machine learning* refers to the field that rigorously studies the properties and behavior of machine learning algorithms and yields new approaches and algorithms. Theoretical machine learning involves advanced graduate-level mathematics that covers a wide variety of mathematical disciplines that are outside the scope of this book. In this book we only utilize informal mathematics in order to achieve our practical aims, not rigorous proof-based mathematics.

A.1   *Linear algebra*

Linear algebra is the study of linear transformations. A *linear transformation* is a transformation (e.g., a function) in which the sum of the transformation of two inputs separately, such as $T(a)$ and $T(b)$, is the same as summing the two inputs and transforming them together, i.e., $T(a + b) = T(a) + T(b)$. A linear transformation also has the property that $T(a \cdot b) = a \cdot T(b)$. Linear transformations are said to preserve the operations of addition and multiplication since you can apply these operations either before or after the linear transformation and the result is the same.

One informal way to think of this is that linear transformations do not have "economies of scale." For example, think of a linear transformation as converting money as the input into some other resource, like gold, so that $T(\$100) = 1$ *unit of gold*. The unit price of gold will be constant no matter how much money you put in. In contrast, nonlinear transformations might give you a "bulk discount," so that if you buy 1,000 units of gold or more, the price would be less on a per unit basis than if you bought less than 1,000 units.

Another way to think of linear transformations is to make a connection to calculus (which we'll review in more detail shortly). A function or transformation takes some input value, x, and maps it to some output value, y. A particular output y may be a larger or smaller value than the input x, or more generally a *neighborhood* around an input x will be mapped to a larger or smaller neighborhood around the output y. Here a *neighborhood* refers to the set of points arbitrarily close to x or y. For a single-variable function like $f(x) = 2x + 1$, a neighborhood is actually an interval. For example, the neighborhood around an input point $x = 2$ would be all the points arbitrarily close to 2, such as 2.000001 and 1.99999999.

One way to think of the derivative of a function at a point is as the ratio of the size of the output interval around that point to the size of the input interval around the input point. Linear transformations will always have some constant ratio of output to input intervals for all points, whereas nonlinear transformations will have a varying ratio.

Linear transformations are often represented as *matrices*, which are rectangular grids of numbers. Matrices encode the coefficients for multivariable linear functions, such as

$$f_x(x,y) = Ax + By$$

$$f_y(x,y) = Cx + Dy$$

While this appears to be two functions, this is really a single function that maps a 2-dimensional point (x,y) to a new 2-dimensional point (x',y') using the coefficients A,B,C,D. To find x, you use the f_x function, and to find y' you use the f_y function. We could have written this as a single line:

$$f(x,y) = (Ax + By,\ Cx + Dy)$$

This makes it more clear that the output is a 2-tuple or 2-dimensional vector. In any case, it is useful to think of this function in two separate pieces since the computations for the x and y components are independent.

While the mathematical notion of a vector is very general and abstract, for machine learning a vector is just a 1-dimensional array of numbers. This linear transformation takes a 2-vector (one that has 2 elements) and turns it into another 2-vector, and to do this it requires four separate pieces of data, the four coefficients. There is a difference between a linear transformation like $Ax + By$ and something like $Ax + By + C$ which adds a constant; the latter is called an *affine* transformation. In practice, we use affine transformations in machine learning, but for this discussion we will stick with just linear transformations.

Matrices are a convenient way to store these coefficients. We can package the data into a 2 by 2 matrix:

$$F = \begin{bmatrix} A & B \\ C & D \end{bmatrix}$$

The linear transformation is now represented completely by this matrix, assuming you understand how to use it, which we shall cover. We can apply this linear transformation by juxtaposing the matrix with a vector, e.g., *Fx*.

$$F = \begin{bmatrix} A & B \\ C & D \end{bmatrix} \begin{bmatrix} x \\ y \end{bmatrix}$$

We compute the result of this transformation by multiplying each row in *F* with each column (only one here) of *x*. If you do this, you get the same result as the explicit function definition above. Matrices do not need to be square, they can be any rectangular shape.

We can graphically represent matrices as boxes with two strings coming out on each end with labeled indices:

We call this a string diagram. The *n* represents the dimensionality of the input vector and the *m* is the dimensionality of the output vector. You can imagine a vector flowing into the linear transformation from the left, and a new vector is produced on the right side. For the practical deep learning we use in this book, you only need to understand this much linear algebra, i.e., the principles of multiplying vectors by matrices. Any additional math will be introduced in the respective chapters.

A.2 *Calculus*

Calculus is essentially the study of differentiation and integration. In deep learning, we only really need to use differentiation. *Differentiation* is the process of getting a derivative of a function.

We already introduced one notion of derivative: the ratio of an output interval to the input interval. It tells you how much the output space is stretched or squished. Importantly, these intervals are oriented intervals so they can be negative or positive, and thus the ratio can be negative or positive.

For example, consider the function $f(x) = x^2$. Take a point x and its neighborhood $(x - \varepsilon, x + \varepsilon)$, where ε is some arbitrarily small value, and we get an interval around x. To be concrete, let $x = 3$, $\varepsilon = 0.1$; the interval around $x = 3$ is $(2.9, 3.1)$. The size (and orientation) of this interval is $3.1 - 2.9 = +0.2$, and this interval gets mapped to $f(2.9) = 8.41$ and $f(3.1) = 9.61$. This output interval is $(8.41, 9.61)$ and its size is $9.61 - 8.41 = 1.2$. As you can see, the output interval is still positive, so the ratio $\frac{df}{dx} = \frac{1.2}{0.2} = 6$, which is the derivative of the function f at $x = 3$.

We denote the derivative of a function, f, with respect to an input variable, x, as df/dx, but this is not to be thought of as a literal fraction; it's just a notation. We don't need to take an interval on both sides of the point; an interval on one side will do as long as it's small, i.e., we can define an interval as $(x, x + \varepsilon)$ and the size of the interval is just ε, whereas the size of the output interval is $f(x + \varepsilon) - f(x)$.

Using concrete values like we did only yields approximations in general; to get absolutes we'd need to use infinitely small intervals. We can do this symbolically by imagining that ε is an infinitely small number such that it is bigger than 0 but smaller than any other number in our number system. Now differentiation becomes an algebra problem.

$$f(x) = x^2 \tag{1}$$

$$\frac{df}{dx} = \frac{f(x + \varepsilon) - f(x)}{\varepsilon} \tag{2}$$

$$= \frac{(x + \varepsilon)^2 - x^2}{\varepsilon} \tag{3}$$

$$= \frac{x^2 + 2x\varepsilon + \varepsilon^2 - x^2}{\varepsilon} \tag{4}$$

$$= \frac{\varepsilon(2x + \varepsilon)}{\varepsilon} \tag{5}$$

$$= 2x + \varepsilon \tag{6}$$

$$2x \approx 2x + \varepsilon \tag{7}$$

Here we simply take the ratio of the output interval to the input interval, both of which are infinitely small because ε is an infinitesimal number. We can algebraically reduce the expression to $2x + \varepsilon$, and since ε is infinitesimal, $2x + \varepsilon$ is infinitely close to $2x$, which we take as the true derivative of the original function $f(x) = x^2$. Remember, we're taking ratios of oriented intervals that can be positive or negative. We not only want to know how much a function stretches (or squeezes) the input, but whether it changes the direction of the interval. There is a lot of advanced mathematics justifying all of this (see nonstandard analysis or smooth infinitesimal analysis) but this process works just fine for practical purposes.

Why is differentiation a useful concept in deep learning? Well, in machine learning we are trying to *optimize* a function, which means finding the input points to the function such that the output of the function is a maximum or minimum over all possible inputs. That is, given some function, $f(x)$, we want to find an x such that $f(x)$ is smaller than any other choice of x; we generally denote this as $argmin(f(x))$. Usually we have a loss function (or cost or error function) that takes some input vector, a target vector, and a parameter vector and returns the degree of error between the predicted output and the true output, and our goal is to find the set of parameters that minimizes this error function. There are many possible ways to minimize this function, not all of which depend on using derivatives, but in most cases the most effective and efficient way to optimize loss functions in machine learning is to use derivative information.

Since deep learning models are nonlinear (i.e., they do not preserve addition and scalar multiplication), the derivatives are not constant like in linear transformations. The amount and direction of squishing or stretching that happens from input to output points varies from point to point. In another sense, it tells us which direction the function is curving, so we can follow the curve downward to the lowest point. Multivariable functions like deep learning models don't just have a single derivative but a set of partial derivatives that describe the curvature of the function with respect to each individual input component. This way we can figure out which sets of parameters for a deep neural network lead to the smallest error.

The simplest example of using derivative information to minimize a function is to see how it works for a simple compositional function. The function we will try to find the minimum of is:

$$f(x) = \log(x^4 + x^3 + 2)$$

The graph is shown in figure A.1. You can see that the minimum of this function appears to be around –1. This is a compositional function because it contains a polynomial expression "wrapped" in a logarithm, so we need to use the chain rule from calculus to compute the derivative. We want the derivative of this function with respect to x. This function only has one "valley," so it will only have one minimum; however, deep learning models are high-dimensional and highly compositional and tend to have many minima. Ideally, we'd like to find the global minimum that is the lowest point in the function. Global or local minima are points on the function where the slope (i.e., the derivative) at those points is 0. For some functions, like this simple example, we can compute the minimum analytically, using algebra. Deep learning models are generally too complex for algebraic calculations, and we must use iterative techniques.

The chain rule in calculus gives us a way of computing derivatives of compositional functions by decomposing them into pieces. If you've heard of *backpropagation*, it's

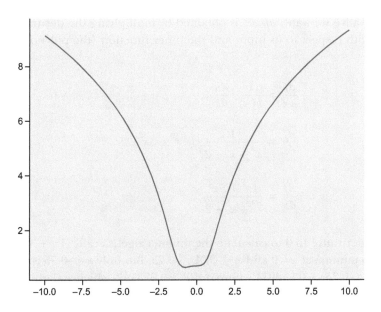

Figure A.1 The output of a simple compositional function,
$f(x) = \log(x^4 + x^3 + 2)$

basically just the chain rule applied to neural networks with some tricks to make it more efficient. For our example case, let's rewrite the previous function as two functions:

$$h(x) = x^4 + x^3 + 2$$

$$f(x) = \log(h(x))$$

We first compute the derivative of the "outer" function, which is $f(x) = \log(h(x))$, but this just gives us df/dh and what we really want is df/dx. You may have learned that the derivative of natural-log is

$$\frac{d}{dh}\log h(x) = \frac{1}{h(x)}$$

And the derivative of the inner function $h(x)$ is

$$\frac{d}{dx}(x^4 + x^3 + 2) = 4x^3 + 3x^2$$

To get the full derivative of the compositional function, we notice that

$$\frac{df}{dx} = \frac{df}{dh} \cdot \frac{dh}{dx}$$

That is, the derivative we want, df/dx, is obtained by multiplying the derivative of the outer function with respect to its input and the inner function (the polynomial) with respect to x.

$$\frac{df}{dx} = \frac{1}{h(x)} \cdot \frac{dh}{dx}$$

$$\frac{df}{dx} = \frac{1}{x^4 + x^3 + 2} \cdot (4x^3 + 3x^2)$$

$$\frac{df}{dx} = \frac{4x^3 + 3x^2}{x^4 + x^3 + 2}$$

You can set this derivative to 0 to calculate the minima algebraically: $4x^2 + 3x = 0$. This function has two minima at $x = 0$ and $x = -3/4 = -0.75$. But only $x = -0.75$ is the global minimum since $f(-0.75) = 0.638971$ whereas $f(0) = 0.693147$, which is slightly larger.

Let's see how we can solve this using *gradient descent*, which is an iterative algorithm to find the minima of a function. The idea is we start with a random x as a starting point. We then compute the derivative of the function at this point, which tells us the magnitude and direction of curvature at this point. We then choose a new x point based on the old x point, its derivative, and a step-size parameter to control how fast we move. That is,

$$x_{new} = x_{old} - \alpha \frac{df}{dx}$$

Let's see how to do this in code.

Listing A.1 Gradient descent

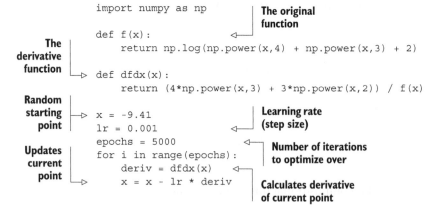

```
import numpy as np

def f(x):
    return np.log(np.power(x,4) + np.power(x,3) + 2)

def dfdx(x):
    return (4*np.power(x,3) + 3*np.power(x,2)) / f(x)

x = -9.41
lr = 0.001
epochs = 5000
for i in range(epochs):
    deriv = dfdx(x)
    x = x - lr * deriv
```

The original function

The derivative function

Random starting point

Learning rate (step size)

Number of iterations to optimize over

Updates current point

Calculates derivative of current point

If you run this gradient descent algorithm, you should get $x = -0.750000000882165$, which is (if rounded) exactly what you get when calculated algebraically. This simple process is the same one we use when training deep neural networks, except that deep neural networks are multivariable compositional functions, so we use partial derivatives. A partial derivative is no more complex than a normal derivative.

Consider the multivariable function $f(x,y) = x^4 + y^2$. There is no longer a single derivative of this function since it has two input variables. We can take the derivative with respect to x or y or both. When we take the derivative of a multivariable function with respect to all of its inputs and package this into a vector, we call it the *gradient*, which is denoted by the nabla symbol ∇, i.e., $\nabla f(x) = [df/dx, df/dy]$. To compute the partial derivative of f with respect to x, i.e., df/dx, we simply set the other variable y to be a constant and differentiate as usual. In this case, $df/dx = 4x^3$ and $df/dy = 2y$. So the gradient $\nabla f(x) = [4x^3, 2y]$, which is the vector of partial derivatives. Then we can run gradient descent as usual, except now we find the vector associated with the lowest point in an error function of the deep neural network.

A.3 *Deep learning*

A deep neural network is simply a composition of multiple layers of simpler functions called *layers*. Each layer function consists of a matrix multiplication followed by a nonlinear *activation function*. The most common activation function is $f(x) = \max(0,x)$, which returns 0 if x is negative or returns x otherwise.

A simple neural network might be

Read this diagram from left to right as if data flows in from the left into the L1 function then the L2 function and becomes the output on the right. The symbols k, m, and n refer to the dimensionality of the vectors. A k-length vector is input to function L1, which produces an m-length vector that then gets passed to L2, which finally produces an n-dimensional vector.

Now let's look at what each of these L functions are doing.

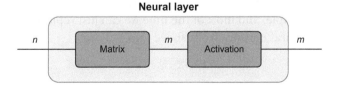

A neural network layer, generically, consists of two parts: a matrix multiplication and an activation function. An n-length vector comes in from the left and gets multiplied by a matrix (often called a parameter or weight matrix), which may change the dimensionality of the resulting output vector. The output vector, now of length m, gets passed through a nonlinear activation function, which does not change the dimensionality of the vector.

A deep neural network just stacks these layers together, and we train it by applying gradient descent on the weight matrices, which are the parameters of the neural network. Here's a simple 2-layer neural network in Numpy.

Listing A.2   A simple neural network

```
def nn(x,w1,w2):
    l1 = x @ w1                      ◄──┐  Matrix multiplication
    l1 = np.maximum(0,l1)            ◄──┐
    l2 = l1 @ w2                        │  Nonlinear
    l2 = np.maximum(0,l2)              │  activation function
    return l2

                                          Weight (parameter) matrix,
w1 = np.random.randn(784,200)      ◄──┘  initialized randomly
w2 = np.random.randn(200,10)
x = np.random.randn(784)           ◄──┐  Random input vector
nn(x,w1,w2)

array([326.24915523,    0.         ,    0.         , 301.0265272 ,
        188.47784869,    0.         ,    0.         ,    0.         ,
          0.        ,    0.         ])
```

In the next section you'll learn how to use the PyTorch library to automatically compute gradients to easily train neural networks.

A.4   *PyTorch*

In the previous sections you learned how to use gradient descent to find the minimum of a function, but to do that we needed the gradient. For our simple example, we could compute the gradient with paper and pencil. For deep learning models, that is impractical, so we rely on libraries like PyTorch that provide *automatic differentiation* capabilities that make it much easier.

The basic idea is that in PyTorch we create a *computational graph,* similar to the diagrams we used in the previous section, where relations between inputs, outputs, and connections between different functions are made explicit and kept track of so we can easily apply the chain rule automatically to compute gradients. Fortunately, switching from numpy to PyTorch is simple, and most of the time we can just replace numpy with torch. Let's translate our neural network from above into PyTorch.

Listing A.3   PyTorch neural network

```
import torch                        ◄──┐  Matrix multiplication

def nn(x,w1,w2):
    l1 = x @ w1                      ◄──┘
    l1 = torch.relu(l1)             ◄──┐  Nonlinear
    l2 = l1 @ w2                        │  activation function
    return l2
```

```
w1 = torch.randn(784,200,requires_grad=True)
w2 = torch.randn(200,10,requires_grad=True)
```
◁─┐ **Weight (parameter) matrix, with gradients tracked**

This looks almost identical to the numpy version except that we use `torch.relu` instead of `np.maximum`, but they are the same function. We also added a `requires_grad=True` parameter to the weight matrix setup. This tells PyTorch that these are trainable parameters that we want to track gradients for, whereas x is an input, not a trainable parameter. We also got rid of the last activation function for reasons that will become clear. For this example, we will use the famous MNIST data set that contains images of handwritten digits from 0 to 9, such as the one in figure A.2.

Figure A.2 An example image from the MNIST dataset of hand-drawn digits.

We want to train our neural network to recognize these images and classify them as digits 0 through 9. PyTorch has a related library that lets us easily download this data set.

Listing A.4 Classifying MNIST using a neural network

```
mnist_data = TV.datasets.MNIST("MNIST", train=True, download=False)   ◁── Downloads and loads the MNIST dataset

lr = 0.001
epochs = 2000
batch_size = 100
lossfn = torch.nn.CrossEntropyLoss()   ◁── Sets up a loss function
for i in range(epochs):
    rid = np.random.randint(0,mnist_data.train_data.shape[0],size=batch_size)   ◁── Gets a set of random index values
    x = mnist_data.train_data[rid].float().flatten(start_dim=1)   ◁── Subsets the data and flattens the 28 x 28 images into 784 vectors
    x /= x.max()   ◁── Normalizes the vector to be between 0 and 1
    pred = nn(x,w1,w2)   ◁── Makes a prediction using the neural network
    target = mnist_data.train_labels[rid]   ◁── Gets the ground-truth image labels
    loss = lossfn(pred,target)   ◁── Computes the loss
    loss.backward()   ◁── Backpropagates
    with torch.no_grad():   ◁── Does not compute gradients in this block
        w1 -= lr * w1.grad   ◁── Gradient descent over the parameter matrices
        w2 -= lr * w2.grad
```

You can tell that the neural network is successfully training by observing the loss function fairly steadily decreasing over training time (figure A.3). This short code snippet trains a complete neural network to successfully classify MNIST digits at around 70% accuracy. We just implemented gradient descent exactly the same way we did with our simple logarithmic function $f(x) = \log(x^4 + x^3 + 2)$, but PyTorch handled the gradients for us. Since the gradient of the neural network's parameters depends on the input data, each time we run the neural network "forward" with a new random sample of

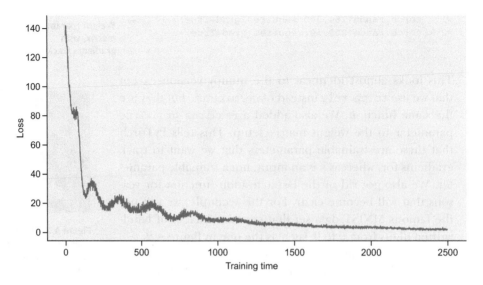

Figure A.3   The loss function for our neural network trained on the MNIST dataset.

images, the gradients will be different. So we run the neural network forward with a random sample of data, PyTorch keeps track of the computations that occur, and when we're done, we call the backward() method on the last output; in this case it is generally the loss. The backward() method uses automatic differentiation to compute all gradients for all PyTorch variables that have requires_grad=True set. Then we can update the model parameters using gradient descent. We wrap the actual gradient descent part in the torch.no_grad() context because we don't want it to keep track of these computations.

We can easily achieve greater than 95% accuracy by improving the training algorithm with a more sophisticated version of gradient descent. In listing A.4 we implemented our own version of *stochastic gradient descent*, the *stochastic* part because we are randomly taking subsets from the dataset and computing gradients based on that, which gives us noisy estimates of the true gradient given the full set of data.

PyTorch includes built-in optimizers, of which stochastic gradient descent (SGD) is one. The most popular alternative is called Adam, which is a more sophisticated version of SGD. We just need to instantiate the optimizer with the model parameters.

> **Listing A.5   Using the Adam optimizer**

```
mnist_data = TV.datasets.MNIST("MNIST", train=True, download=False)

lr = 0.001
epochs = 5000
batch_size = 500
lossfn = torch.nn.CrossEntropyLoss()
optim = torch.optim.Adam(params=[w1,w2],lr=lr)
```

Sets up the loss function ⟶

⟵ Sets up the ADAM optimizer

```
for i in range(epochs):
    rid = np.random.randint(0,mnist_data.train_data.shape[0],size=batch_size)
    x = mnist_data.train_data[rid].float().flatten(start_dim=1)
    x /= x.max()
    pred = nn(x,w1,w2)
    target = mnist_data.train_labels[rid]
    loss = lossfn(pred,target)                    Backpropagates
    loss.backward()                          ←────────────┐
    optim.step()          ←──┐          Updates the
    optim.zero_grad()    └─▷      parameters
```

Resets the gradients

Updates the parameters

You can see that the loss function in figure A.4 is much smoother now with the Adam optimizer, and it dramatically increases the accuracy of our neural network classifier.

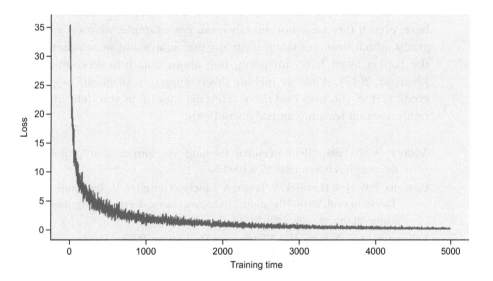

Figure A.4 The loss plot of our neural network trained on MNIST with the built-in PyTorch optimizer Adam.

Reference list

We did our best to cite the projects and papers we used in the individual chapters, but a lot of the approaches and ideas we used were inspired by the sources listed here, even if they were not directly used. For example, we used a lot of string diagrams, which were not taken from any one source but were inspired by several of the papers listed here, including one about quantum mechanics (Coecke and Kissinger, 2017). While we include this bibliography primarily to give credit where credit is due, you may find these references useful as you delve deeper into deep reinforcement learning and adjacent fields.

Andrew, A.M. 1998. "Reinforcement learning: An introduction." *Kybernetes* 27. https://doi.org/10.1108/k.1998.27.9.1093.3.

Battaglia, P.W., J.B. Hamrick, V. Bapst, A. Sanchez-Gonzalez, V. Zambaldi, M. Malinowski, A. Tacchetti et al. 2018. "Relational inductive biases, deep learning, and graph networks." http://arxiv.org/abs/1806.01261.

Bellemare, M.G., Y. Naddaf, J. Veness, and M. Bowling. 2013. "The arcade learning environment: An evaluation platform for general agents." *Journal of Artificial Intelligence Research* 47:253–279. https://doi.org/10.1613/jair.3912.

Bonchi, F., J. Holland, R. Piedeleu, P. Sobociński, and F. Zanasi. 2019. "Diagrammatic algebra: From linear to concurrent systems." *Proceedings of the ACM on Programming Languages* 3:1–28. https://doi.org/10.1145/3290338.

Bonchi, F., R. Piedeleu, P. Sobocinski, and F. Zanasi. 2019. "Graphical affine algebra." *2019 34th Annual ACM/IEEE Symposium on Logic in Computer Science.* https://doi.org/10.1109/LICS.2019.8785877.

Brockman, G., V. Cheung, L. Pettersson, J. Schneider, J. Schulman, J. Tang, and W. Zaremba. 2016. "OpenAI Gym." http://arxiv.org/abs/1606.01540.

Coecke, B., and A. Kissinger. 2017. *Picturing Quantum Processes: A First Course in Quantum Theory and Diagrammatic Reasoning.* Cambridge University Press.

Hessel, M., J. Modayil, H. Van Hasselt, T. Schaul, G. Ostrovski, W. Dabney, D. Horgan, et al. 2018. "Rainbow: Combining improvements in deep reinforcement learning." *32nd AAAI Conference on Artificial Intelligence, AAAI 2018,* 3215–3222.

Kaiser, L., M. Babaeizadeh, P. Milos, B. Osinski, R.H. Campbell, K. Czechowski, D. Erhan, et al. 2019. "Model-based reinforcement learning for Atari." http://arxiv.org/abs/1903.00374.

Kulkarni, T.D., K.R. Narasimhan, A. Saeedi, and J.B. Tenenbaum. 2016. "Hierarchical deep reinforcement learning: Integrating temporal abstraction and intrinsic motivation." *Advances in Neural Information Processing Systems* 29 (NIPS 2016): 3682–3690.

Kumar, N.M. 2018. "Empowerment-driven exploration using mutual information estimation." http://arxiv.org/abs/1810.05533.

Mnih, V., A.P. Badia, L. Mirza, A. Graves, T. Harley, T.P. Lillicrap, D. Silver, et al. 2016. "Asynchronous methods for deep reinforcement learning." *33rd International Conference on Machine Learning* (ICML 2016) 4:2850–2869.

Mnih, V., K. Kavukcuoglu, D. Silver, A.A. Rusu, J. Veness, M.G. Bellemare, A. Graves, et al. (2015). "Human-level control through deep reinforcement learning." *Nature* 518:529–533. https://doi.org/10.1038/nature14236.

Mott, A., D. Zoran, M. Chrzanowski, D. Wierstra, and D.J. Rezende. 2019. "Towards interpretable reinforcement learning using attention augmented agents." http://arxiv.org/abs/1906.02500.

Mousavi, S.S., M. Schukat, and E. Howley. 2018. "Deep reinforcement learning: An overview." *Lecture Notes in Networks and Systems* 16:426–440. https://doi.org/10.1007/978-3-319-56991-8_32.

Nardelli, N., P. Kohli, G. Synnaeve, P.H.S. Torr, Z. Lin, and N. Usunier. 2019. "Value propagation networks." *7th International Conference on Learning Representations, ICLR 2019.* http://arxiv.org/abs/1805.11199.

Oh, J., S. Singh, and H. Lee. 2017. "Value prediction network." In I. Guyon, U.V. Luxburg, S. Bengio, H. Wallach, R. Fergus, S. Vishwanathan, and R. Garnett (eds.), *Advances in Neural Information Processing Systems 30* (NIPS 2017): 6119–6129. http://papers.nips.cc/paper/7192-value-prediction-network.pdf.

Pathak, D., P. Agrawal, A.A. Efros, and T. Darrell. 2017. "Curiosity-driven exploration by self-supervised prediction." *2017 IEEE Conference on Computer Vision and Pattern Recognition Workshops (CVPRW)*, 488–489. https://doi.org/10.1109/CVPRW.2017.70.

Salimans, T., J. Ho, X. Chen, S. Sidor, and I. Sutskever. 2017. "Evolution strategies as a scalable alternative to reinforcement learning." http://arxiv.org/abs/1703.03864.

Schaul, T., J. Quan, I. Antonoglou, and D. Silver. 2016. "Prioritized experience replay." *4th International Conference on Learning Representations, ICLR 2016—Conference Track Proceedings.* http://arxiv.org/abs/1511.05952.

Schulman, J., F. Wolski, P. Dhariwal, A. Radford, and O. Klimov. 2017. "Proximal policy optimization algorithms." http://arxiv.org/abs/1707.06347.

Silver, D. 2015. "Lecture 1: Introduction to Reinforcement Learning Outline." http://www0.cs.ucl.ac.uk/staff/d.silver/web/Teaching_files/intro_RL.pdf.

Spivak, D., and R. Kent. 2011. "Ologs: a categorical framework for knowledge representation." https://arxiv.org/abs/1102.1889.

Stolle, M., and D. Precup. 2002. "Learning options in reinforcement learning." *Lecture Notes in Computer Science (Including Subseries Lecture Notes in Artificial Intelligence and Lecture Notes in Bioinformatics)* 2371:212–223. https://doi.org/10.1007/3-540-45622-8_16.

Vaswani, A., N. Shazeer, N. Parmar, J. Uszkoreit, L. Jones, A.N. Gomez, L. Kaiser, et al. 2017. "Attention is all you need." *31st Conference on Neural Information Processing Systems* (NIPS 2017). http://papers.nips.cc/paper/7181-attention-is-all-you-need.pdf.

Weng, L. 2018. "Attention? Attention!" *Lil' Log* (June 24, 2018). https://lilianweng.github.io/lil-log/2018/06/24/attention-attention.html.

Wu, Z., S. Pan, F. Chen, G. Long, C. Zhang, and P.S. Yu. 2019. "A comprehensive survey on graph neural networks." http://arxiv.org/abs/1901.00596.

Yang, Y., R. Luo, M. Li, M. Zhou, W. Zhang, and J. Wang. 2018. "Mean field multi-agent reinforcement learning." *35th International Conference on Machine Learning (ICML 2018)* 12:8869–8886.

Zambaldi, V., D. Raposo, A. Santoro, V. Bapst, Y. Li, I. Babuschkin, K. Tuyls, et al. 2018. "Relational deep reinforcement learning." http://arxiv.org/abs/1806.01830.

Zambaldi, V., D. Raposo, A. Santoro, V. Bapst, Y. Li, I. Babuschkin, K. Tuyls, et al. 2019. "Deep reinforcement learning with relational inductive biases." *7th International Conference on Learning Representations, ICLR 2019.*

Zhang, Z., P. Cui, and W. Zhu. 2018. "Deep learning on graphs: A survey." http://arxiv.org/abs/1812.04202.

Zhou, M., Y. Chen, Y. Wen, Y. Yang, Y. Su, W. Zhang, D Zhang, et al. 2019. "Factorized Q-learning for large-scale multi-agent systems." https://doi.org/10.1145/3356464.3357707.

Ziegel, E.R. 2003. "The elements of statistical learning." *Technometrics* 45. https://doi.org/10.1198/tech.2003.s770.

index

RELATED MANNING TITLES

Deep Learning with Python
by François Chollet

ISBN 9781617294433
384 pages, $49.99
November 2017

Grokking Deep Learning
Andrew W. Trask

ISBN 9781617293702
336 pages, $49.99
January 2019

GANs in Action
by Jakub Langr and Vladimir Bok

ISBN 9781617295560
240 pages, $49.99
September 2019

Deep Learning for Vision Systems
by Mohamed Elgendy

ISBN 9781617296192
475 pages, $49.99
April 2020

For ordering information go to www.manning.com